Micronesia
a travel survival kit

Glenda Bendure
Ned Friary

Micronesia – a travel survival kit

2nd edition

Published by
Lonely Planet Publications
Head Office: PO Box 617, Hawthorn, Vic 3122, Australia
Branches: PO Box 2001A, Berkeley, CA 94702, USA and London, UK

Printed by
Colorcraft Ltd, Hong Kong

Photographs by
Glenda Bendure & Ned Friary

Front cover: Carp Island – Palau
Back cover: Balabat men's house – Yap

First Published
April 1988

This Edition
January 1992

Although the authors and publisher have tried to make the information as accurate as possible, they accept no responsibility for any loss, injury or inconvenience sustained by any person using this book.

National Library of Australia Cataloguing in Publication Data

Bendure, Glenda
   Micronesia – a travel survival kit.

   2nd ed.
   Includes index.
   ISBN 0 86442 115 X.

   1. Micronesia – Description and travel – Guide-books.
   I. Friary, Ned. II. Title.

919.6504

text, maps & illustrations © Lonely Planet Publications 1992

photos © photographers as indicated 1992

Glenda Bendure

Glenda grew up in California's Mojave Desert. Her first trip overseas was as a high school AFS exchange student to India. A few years later a Chuukese exchange student lived with her family, introducing her to Micronesia.

Ned Friary

Ned grew up near Boston and has travelled extensively throughout the US and Central America. He studied Social Thought & Political Economy at the University of Massachusetts in Amherst and upon graduating headed west.

They met in Santa Cruz, California, where Glenda was attending university and Ned was living on a small organic farm. In 1978, with Lonely Planet's first book *Across Asia on the Cheap* in hand, they flew to London and hit the overland trail across southern Europe, through Iran and Afghanistan, on to trains in India and treks in Nepal. The next six years were spent exploring Asia and the Pacific, teaching English in Japan in between jaunts. They now live on Cape Cod in Massachusetts where Ned is the director of a shelter for the homeless and Glenda writes a travel column for the *Cape Cod Times*.

Ned and Glenda are also the authors of Lonely Planet's *Hawaii – a travel survival kit*.

From the Authors

A special thanks to Ariel Ablao, Maria Andriano, Beverly Battaglia, Reg Brown, Lee Boblitt, B M Bourke, Sean Cahill, Alfred Capelle, M D Carey, Dr Anthony Chan, Peter Cromer, Laura DeGroote, Randy Dyer, John Engbring, Don Evans, Margie Falunruw, Joel Fentin, Mike Flaherty, Kevin Foster, Robert & Margaret Glover, Fr Francis X Hezel, Teddy John, Diane Kelly, Jim & Barbara Kershner, Lothar Kirsch, Gerald Knight, Ray Kruger, Richard Macaranas, Deirdre Marshall, Samuel McPhetres, Daniel Moriarty, Allan Murphy, Madison Nena, Ellen Opie, Barbara & Harvey Pace, Lisa Parker, Judah Rekemesik, Michael

Reynolds, T & J Rohler, Koichy Sana, Ben Santos, Harvey Segal, Hal Smith, Susan Anne Snow, William Stewart, Joe Suka, Joyleen Temengil, Nancy Vander Velde, Bernardette Wehrly, Emily Wen, Brother Terry...and all the others who helped us along the way.

Thanks also to tourist bureaus in the Marshalls, Kosrae, Pohnpei, Chuuk, Yap, Guam, Saipan and Palau; to the Peace Corps volunteers who shared their insights with us; and to those at the Alele Museum (Majuro), Micronesian Seminar (Chuuk), Micronesian Area Research Center (Guam) and Belau National Museum (Koror) who helped us with research.

From the Publisher

This second edition of *Micronesia – a travel survival kit* was edited in Melbourne, Australia, by Debbie Rossdale; Tom Smallman saw it through production. Chris Lee Ack was responsible for map drawing and cover design. Jane Hart was responsible for the title page, illustrations and layout. Vicki Beale helped with design and layout and Sharon Wertheim did the indexing.

Thanks also to those travellers who wrote in with information:

Beverley Battaglia (USA), B M Bourke (Aus), M D Carey, Dr Anthony Chan (HK), Jim Crater (USA), Stefano Di Gaspero (It), Randy Dyer (USA), Michael Edgley, Joel Fentin (USA), Brian Harrison (UK), Gary Heathcote (G), Jeff Herrin (USA), Lothar M Kirsch (D), Valerie Layton (USA), D Marshall (Aus), Allan Murphy (J), Lori O'Connell (USA), Ed Rampell (USA), Lynette Regan (Aus), T & J Roklen (USA), John Schneidhorst, Hal Smith (USA), W Tapanila (C), Will Werley (USA), Tom Witt (USA)

Aus – Australia, C – Canada, D – Germany, G – Guam, HK – Hong Kong, It – Italy, J – Japan, UK – United Kingdom, USA – United States of America

Warning & Request

Despite clocks running on Micronesian time, not everything moves slowly in the islands. Things change – prices go up, schedules alter, good places go bad, and bad places go bankrupt. So if you find things better or worse, recently opened or long since closed, please write and tell us so we can make the next edition better!

Your letters will be used to help update future editions, and where possible, important changes will also be included as a Stop Press section in reprints.

All information is greatly appreciated, with the best letters receiving a free copy of the next edition, or any other Lonely Planet book of your choice.

Contents

INTRODUCTION...9

FACTS ABOUT THE REGION 12

History 12   Government 26   Religion...........................28
Geography 21   Economy 26   Language.........................28
Climate 23   Population 27
Flora & Fauna.........23   Culture 27

FACTS FOR THE VISITOR 29

Visas.......................29   Electricity 32   Activities 44
Customs...................29   Weights & Measures 32   Highlights........................44
Money......................29   Books & Maps 33   Accommodation................45
What to Bring 30   Media 35   Food 46
Tourist Offices 30   Film & Photography 36   Drinks.............................47
Business Hours & Holidays .....31 Health 36   Other Highs.....................47
Post & Telecommunications...31   Women Travellers 42   Things to Buy...................47
Time.......................32   Dangers & Annoyances 43

GETTING THERE & AWAY 49

Air..........................49   Tours 52   Leaving Micronesia 53
Sea 52

GETTING AROUND...54

Air..........................54   Land 54   Sea................................55

REPUBLIC OF THE MARSHALL ISLANDS 57

History 58   Laura 68   Mili Atoll.........................76
Geography 62   Places to Stay 69   Maloelap Atoll 77
Climate 62   Places to Eat..................69   Arno Atoll.......................78
Government 62   Entertainment 70   Likiep Atoll 78
Economy.................62   Things to Buy 70   Wotje Atoll......................79
Health Problems 63   Getting There & Away 71   Mejit Island 79
People 64   Getting Around 71   Aluit Atoll.......................80
Religion...................64   **Kwajalein Atoll ....72**   Kili Island.......................80
Language.................64   Kwajalein Island 72   Aur Atoll 80
Holidays..................64   Ebeye Island 72   Ailinglaplap Atoll 81
Majuro.................64   Roi-Namur & Sando Islands 74   Other Atolls.....................81
Information...............65   Mejato Island 74   Getting There & Away 81
Holidays & Festivals ....66 **Outer Islands.................75**   Getting Around 82
Activities..................66   Accommodation 75
D-U-D Municipality......66   Food & Drink..................75

FEDERATED STATES OF MICRONESIA (FSM)..83

Political Beginnings ....83 People & Culture 88   Places to Stay 97
Geography 84   Language 89   Places to Eat..................98
Government 84   Holidays 89   Entertainment 98
Economy.................85   Orientation 89   Things to Buy.................98
Kosrae.................86   Activities........................89   Getting There & Away 98
History 86   Tofol 91   Getting Around 99
Geography 88   Lelu Island 92   **Pohnpei....................... 99**
Climate 88   South of Tofol 94   History 100
Economy.................88   Tafunsak.........................95   Geography.......................102

Climate 102	Getting There & Away............120	Chuuk's Outer Islands.............138
Economy.....................103	Getting Around 120	**Yap.....................................140**
People 103	**Chuuk (Truk) 121**	History.....................................140
Culture 103	History 121	Geography.............................143
Language 104	Geography 122	Climate....................................144
Holidays.....................104	Climate....................................123	Government 144
Activities...................104	Economy..................................123	Economy 144
Kolonia 105	People 123	People 145
Sokehs Island..............108	Culture 123	Culture.....................................145
Palikir 109	Language..................................124	Language..................................146
Nett Municipality 110	Holidays 125	Holidays & Festivals...............146
Around the Island 110	Activities.................................125	Activities..................................147
South-west Pohnpei...............111	Moen (Weno) Island 126	Yap Proper...............................147
Nan Madol.....................112	Places to Stay 130	Places to Stay 154
Islands In Pohnpei Lagoon......114	Places to Eat...........................130	Places to Eat...........................155
Outer Atolls 115	Entertainment.........................132	Entertainment.........................156
Places to Stay.................117	Things to Buy 132	Things to Buy 156
Places to Eat 118	Getting There & Away............132	Getting There & Away 157
Entertainment...................119	Getting Around 133	Getting Around 157
Things to Buy 120	Islands in Chuuk Lagoon........133	Outer Islands 157

REPUBLIC OF PALAU..161

History 161	Getting There & Away............175	Klouklubed.................................184
Geography...................165	Getting Around 175	Orange Beach.............................184
Climate 166	**The Rock Islands 176**	South Beaches...........................184
Government 166	Diving & Snorkelling 176	Places to Stay & Eat.................185
Economy......................166	Organised Tours 178	Getting There & Away 185
People 167	Marine Lakes 178	Getting Around 185
Religion 167	70 Islands (Ngerukuid) 178	**Angaur 186**
Language 167	Places to Stay 178	Orientation 187
Holidays......................167	**Babeldaob 179**	Diving 187
Koror 167	Organised Tours 179	Places to Stay & Eat.................188
Orientation..................169	Airai State 180	Getting There & Away 189
Information..................169	Ngaraard State 181	Getting Around 189
Snorkelling..................169	Places to Stay 181	**Kayangel 189**
Malakal Island 170	Getting There & Away............181	Places to Stay 189
Arakabesang Island 171	Getting Around 181	Getting There & Away 189
Places to Stay.................171	**Peleliu 181**	**South-West Islands 190**
Places to Eat 173	History 181	Getting There & Away 190
Entertainment 174	Orientation..............................183	
Things to Buy 174	Diving & Snorkelling 183	

GUAM 191

History 192	Orientation..............................197	Places to Stay 211
Geography...................194	Information..............................198	Places to Eat...........................214
Climate 194	Activities.................................199	Entertainment.........................215
Government 195	Agana 201	Things to Buy 216
Economy......................195	Tumon Bay & Points North....203	Getting There & Away 216
People 196	Southern Guam 206	Getting Around 216
Language 196	Cocos Island 211	
Holidays & Festivals 197	Offshore Islands......................211	

COMMONWEALTH OF THE NORTHERN MARIANAS...............................218

History 218	People 222	Activities..................................225
Geography...................221	Language..................................222	Garapan.....................................226
Climate 221	**Saipan............................... 223**	North of Garapan 228
Government..................221	Information 223	Cross-Island Rd.......................232
Economy......................221	Holidays & Festivals 225	South Of Garapan 233

Managaha Island 233
Places to Stay......................234
Places to Eat 236
Entertainment 237
Things to Buy 237
Getting There & Away 237
Getting Around 238
Tinian **238**
Festivals 240
Activities 240

San Jose 241
South of San Jose....................241
North of San Jose....................243
Aguijan Island.........................244
Places to Stay.........................245
Places to Eat...........................245
Getting There & Away............245
Getting Around 245
Rota....................................**246**
Festivals 246

Activities 246
Songsong Village 248
Central & Northern Rota 249
East of Songsong 252
Places to Stay 252
Places to Eat...........................253
Entertainment.........................254
Getting There & Away............254
Getting Around 254

GLOSSARY **256**

INDEX **258**

Maps 258   Text 258

Map Legend

BOUNDARIES

.... International Boundary
.... Internal Boundary
.... National Park or Reserve
.... The Equator
.... The Tropics

SYMBOLS

⊙ NEW DELHI .... National Capital
● BOMBAY .... Provincial or State Capital
● Pune .... Major Town
● Borsi .... Minor Town
■ .... Places to Stay
▼ .... Places to Eat
≙ .... Post Office
✈ .... Airport
i .... Tourist Information
◉ .... Bus Station or Terminal
66 .... Highway Route Number
☪ ✝ ✝ ...... Mosque, Church, Cathedral
∴ .... Temple or Ruin
✚ .... Hospital
✳ .... Lookout
Å .... Camping Area
⊓ .... Picnic Area
⌂ .... Hut or Chalet
▲ .... Mountain or Hill
.... Railway Station
.... Road Bridge
.... Railway Bridge
.... Road Tunnel
.... Railway Tunnel
.... Escarpment or Cliff
.... Pass
.... Ancient or Historic Wall

ROUTES

.... Major Road or Highway
.... Unsealed Major Road
.... Sealed Road
..... Unsealed Road or Track
.... City Street
.... Railway
.... Subway
.... Walking Track
.... Ferry Route
.... Cable Car or Chair Lift

HYDROGRAPHIC FEATURES

.... River or Creek
.... Intermittent Stream
.... Lake, Intermittent Lake
.... Coast Line
.... Spring
.... Waterfall
.... Swamp

.... Salt Lake or Reef

.... Glacier

OTHER FEATURES

Park, Garden or National Park

.... Built Up Area

... Market or Pedestrian Mall

.... Plaza or Town Square

.... Cemetery

Note: not all symbols displayed above appear in this book

Introduction

Micronesia is entirely in the North Pacific, a term that doesn't exactly conjure up exotic images the way 'South Pacific' does. Yet all the idyllic island clichés fit perfectly: Micronesia has warm aqua waters lapping at pristine bleached sands, swaying coconut palms, lush tropical jungles, tumbling waterfalls and traditional thatched huts.

Micronesia's 2100 islands lie scattered between Hawaii and the Philippines. Though they cover an ocean expanse the size of the continental United States of America, their total land mass is less than Rhode Island, the smallest US state. Many world maps don't even bother dotting them in.

Four colonial powers have used these tiny specks of land as stepping stones between continents, first as provision ports on trade routes and later as military bastions. The island groups have recently emerged as 'island nations', each with some sort of political identity of its own, yet all still firmly locked into a future with the USA.

Not only are they spread out over a great distance but each of the island groups has its own culture and character. The inhabited areas vary from idyllic villages with no cars or electricity to the high-rise resort developments of Guam and Saipan.

Steeped in a rich yet largely unknown history, the ruins of the great stone cities of Pohnpei's Nan Madol and Kosrae's Lelu are on an archaeological par with the stone statues of Easter Island and the Mayan ruins of Central America. You can still get a glimpse of these abandoned worlds by navigating the Venice-like canals of Nan Madol or walking Lelu's coral rock pathways.

Unfrequented Yap has giant stone money, grass skirts, men's houses and Micronesia's most traditional lifestyle. With only a few small hotels and no developed tourist sights Yap offers the sort of unspoiled earthy attractions that independent travellers yearn for.

Now that jets fly into Kosrae, all the major district centres are linked by air. Kosrae itself is a beautiful mountainous island and a friendly backwater that still seldom sees

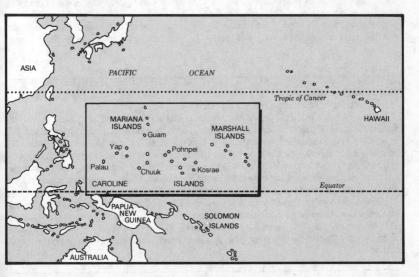

more than a handful of visitors at any one time.

With more ocean than land, some of Micronesia's best sights are underwater. Around Palau, three ocean currents converge to bring in some of the most varied and dazzling marine life in the world – and it's all accessible from your own private beach on one of Palau's Rock Islands. Micronesia's clear 80°F (27°C) waters with coral gardens and zillions of tropical fish offer unsurpassed snorkelling and diving.

In Chuuk (formerly Truk), the lagoon bed holds an entire Japanese fleet, frozen in time where it sank in February 1944. Complete with saké cups and skeletons, jeeps and tanks tied on board and fighter planes still waiting in the holds, the wrecks have been declared an underwater museum.

Some of the bloodiest battles of WW II were fought in Micronesia. On Peleliu, Saipan and Tinian, Japanese and Americans killed each other by the thousands. These days the battle scars and WW II ruins have been turned into sightseeing attractions and both US and Japanese war veterans and relatives of war dead make up a sizable (though dwindling) portion of Micronesia's visitors. Not a lot of people live on these islands, the saying goes, but a lot of people died here.

Micronesia is caught between past tradi-tions and present realities. Many islanders who still make their homes of coconut fronds and sail outrigger canoes now also have electric generators and VCRs; visiting neighbours to watch the latest video has become a popular pastime.

The Marshall Islands include more than a thousand flat coral islands with white sand beaches and turquoise lagoons. To some it's a tropical paradise but many Marshallese are struggling with the 20th century. Some have been victimised by nuclear testing while another 8500 live in overcrowded conditions on the doorstep of a US military base.

Throughout Micronesia young men, many with US college degrees and a craving for Western lifestyles, are moving away from subsistence farming and fishing only to find high unemployment in the district centres. Alcoholism, discontent and high suicide rates are a real part of some islanders' lives.

Still, outside the larger towns, many of Micronesia's islands remain distant from the pollution and problems of the modern world.

Micronesia can be explored in depth or taken in small chunks; there is plenty of variety. You can take small prop planes or two-week ship journeys to some of the most remote and unspoiled islands on earth where you can stay in traditional huts and become a beachcomber; or you can island hop

---

Micronesia Defined

The boundaries of Micronesia are not cut and dried.

No one disputes the inclusion of the Mariana, Marshall and Caroline island chains and most definitions of the 'new Pacific' stop there. Those islands (with the exception of the US territory of Guam) became known after WW II as the Trust Territory of the Pacific Islands – officially a United Nations territory, but for all practical purposes an American colony.

The Gilbert Islands have historically been considered part of Micronesia, though the new nation of Kiribati includes not only the Gilberts but also the Phoenix and Line island chains which are part of Polynesia, and Kiribati is not included in this book.

The independent nation of Nauru, a small single island of phosphate which is being mined into oblivion to provide its inhabitants with one of the world's highest per capita incomes, is also by some definitions considered Micronesian. Nauru, just south of the equator and politically set apart from the other islands, doesn't encourage visitors and is not included here. ■

through the district centres, rent cars to drive around in and spend sunset hours on a beach lounge chair with a tropical drink in hand.

Much of Micronesia remains virtually untouched by mass tourism. For the traveller looking to get off the beaten track, it's a rare find.

Facts about the Region

HISTORY

In the most commonly accepted theory of Micronesian origins, the first settlers of this region canoed across the Pacific from the Philippines and Indonesia to settle on the high western islands of the Marianas, Yap and Palau.

Although some historians speculate that western Micronesia was populated as early as 2000 to 4000 BC, the earliest carbon dating in the region thus far dates artefacts found on Saipan back only to 1500 BC.

Much later, so the theory goes, voyagers from Melanesia settled the eastern islands of the Marshalls and then worked their way west to Kosrae, Pohnpei and Chuuk. In time they continued still further west, settling the outer atolls of Yap and Palau. Although spread over an enormous expanse of ocean, the islands settled by these Melanesian

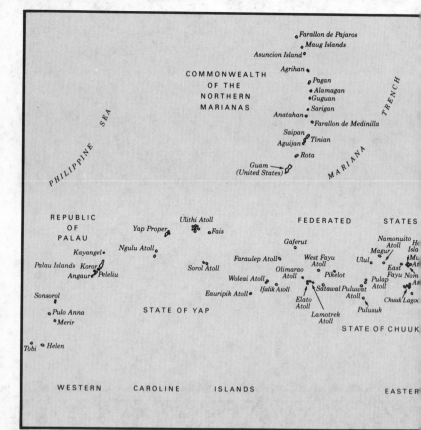

descendants still share related cultures and languages. Micronesians themselves have no legends of a life outside Micronesia.

In 1986 an American archaeologist investigating the effect of ongoing radiation experiments on Bikini Atoll in the Marshall Islands discovered bone fragments and the remains of a village. These artefacts have been carbon dated to 1960 BC, making Bikini the site of the earliest human settlement yet discovered in all of Micronesia.

Pre-European Contact

Micronesia's inhabited island groups had thriving cultures and well-established societies long before the arrival of the Europeans.

As the islands had no metals they were in a 'Stone Age' and the most impressive archaeological remains are achievements in stone. While Europe was lost in the Dark Ages, Micronesia was flourishing with civilisations that built the great stone cities of Nan Madol in Pohnpei and Leluh in Kosrae.

Hundreds of years before the birth of Christ, the Chamorro people of the Marianas were quarrying large *latte* stones to use as foundation pillars for their buildings.

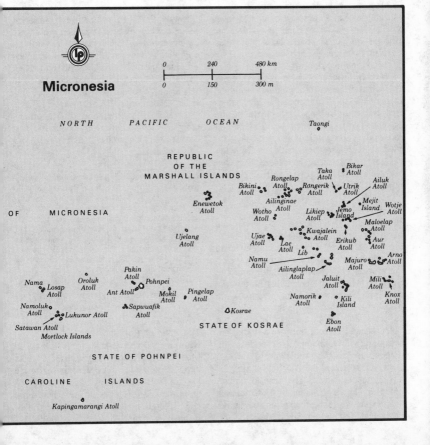

The Yapese, who quarried immense circles out of the limestone found on Palau to use as money, carried the stones back to Yap on barges behind their canoes. They were superb ocean navigators and built an empire that stretched across hundreds of miles of ocean. In Palau, on the northernmost point of the main island of Babeldaob, there are two rows of large basalt monoliths. Their original use remains a mystery but their size and layout suggests they may have been part of a structure that held thousands of people. There are elaborately terraced hillsides nearby that date back to 100 AD though no one knows who built them or why.

Most of what is known today about ancient Micronesian societies comes from village remains or archaeological digs as, prior to European contact, the islanders had no written languages and passed down all information through oral histories.

Western influences, such as the diseases that killed off most of the population and the missionaries that converted the rest, shredded the traditional social fabric of the islands. The missionaries, by discouraging talk of the early religions and gods, contributed to the loss of oral traditions. In many places the old stories have been forgotten completely, resulting in a sort of cultural amnesia.

The First Europeans

In the late 1400s Portuguese explorers, in a quest for spices, established a trade route around Africa and across the Indian Ocean to the Spice Islands, or the Moluccas, which are now part of present-day Indonesia. The Spanish, who were denied this Portuguese trade route by a decree from the pope, were forced to sail west to get to the east.

The search for an alternate route to the Spice Islands led to a flurry of exploration, beginning with Christopher Columbus who discovered parts of the Americas while floundering around the Atlantic looking for a route to the Pacific. The Americas were, however, just a pain in the arse for Columbus and the next few explorers, posing a massive obstacle en route to the Spice Islands.

The first Europeans to actually set foot in Micronesia were with the Spanish expedition of Portuguese explorer Ferdinand Magellan in 1521. It had taken 30 years to successfully find a way around the Americas. Magellan became the first navigator to lead his ships around the tip of South America into the Pacific and the expedition was the first to circumnavigate the globe.

It is an indication of the vastness of the Pacific and the smallness of its islands that Magellan managed to sail across the entire ocean from South America's Cape Horn to the Mariana Islands, close to the Asian mainland, without encountering any of the scattering of islands along the way.

By the time they arrived in the Marianas, Magellan and his scurvy-ridden crew were eating rats and boiled leather to ward off complete starvation. Although the islanders provided the starving crew with food, drink and shelter, they also helped themselves to whatever they could carry off the ships. This led to retaliation by the Spanish.

Antonio Pigafette, one of Magellan's crew, wrote the following about the first encounter between Europeans and Micronesians.

...the people of these islands boarded the ships and robbed us, in such a way that it was impossible to preserve oneself from them. Whilst we were lowering the sails to go ashore, they stole away with much address and diligence the small boat called the skiff, which was made fast to the poop of the captain's ship, at which he was much irritated, and went on shore with forty armed men, burned forty or fifty houses, with several small boats, and killed seven men of the island; they recovered their skiff.

This was just the first of many confrontations between explorers and Micronesians.

The Spanish Period

Numerous explorers soon followed in Magellan's path, beginning with the Spanish expedition under Juan Garcia Jofre de Loaysa in 1526. The tiny islands of Micronesia, devoid of cloves or gold, held little interest for the explorers other than as a quick stopover to replenish water and food. Certainly no one ever set out to 'discover' Micronesia and it took more than 300 years for all of the islands to get added to the charts.

In 1565 Spanish trade ships started making annual trips between Mexico and the Philippines. These 'Manila Galleons' picked up silk, spices and tea from Chinese traders in Manila and took them to Acapulco, where they loaded newly mined silver and carried it back to the Philippines.

The 'new' transpacific shipping corridors, established by the European traders to take advantage of favourable trade winds, actually followed routes the ocean-going Micronesians had been sailing for centuries. Because the ships attempted to stick to these precise routes very few Micronesian islands outside these corridors were discovered during the 16th and 17th centuries.

In one notable exception, after a mutiny in 1565, the Spanish ship *San Lucas* dropped a few degrees from the usual route to avoid other Spanish ships. In doing so it was the first European vessel to come upon Chuuk Lagoon and a number of Marshallese atolls.

Spain's interest in Micronesia at this time was centred almost entirely on the Marianas, where the galleons made regular stops to replenish supplies. Spanish missionaries arrived in the Marianas in 1668, accompanied by the military and government authorities sent to establish colonial rule. Spanish culture, language and Catholicism were forced upon the Chamorros.

The Caroline Islands got their first Spanish missionaries in the early 1700s, but they had only a nominal presence. Outside the Marianas there were no significant European influences in Micronesia until the late 1700s when British, American and European traders began plying the waters for commercial purposes.

Whalers, Traders & Missionaries

Beginning in 1817 with Otto Kotzebue, French and Russian explorers began carefully exploring and mapping Micronesia's islands. They also wrote and sketched some colourful accounts of the island people and their lifestyles.

The first British whalers began to arrive in the early 1800s and American whaleships, out of New England, arrived a couple of decades later though in much greater numbers. During the whaling boom, which peaked in the 1840s, there were as many as 500 ships hunting whales in the Pacific.

Whaling was not a romantic business; it was back-breaking work. The whaleships were virtually factories which could stay at sea for years on end, boiling down blubber into oil and storing it in tanks on board. The islands were used to replenish food, water and wood. Desertion was common.

Traders were also infiltrating Micronesia at this time, setting up posts to deal in copra and beches-de-mer (sea cucumbers).

Whalers and traders were not usually the cream of civilised society. The sailors picked fights, taunted the islanders and spurred massacres, although quite often it was the islanders who would do away with the crews. Kosrae had so much trouble with the 'degenerate Whites' that jumped ship that the chief initiated a policy of putting deserters back out to sea on the next ship that pulled into port.

When the sailors came into port, usually after many months at sea, they were ready to party and they wanted women. In the process they brought venereal and other contagious diseases to which the islanders, with no inbuilt immunities, were particularly susceptible.

Foreign diseases such as syphilis, smallpox, measles and influenza had devastating effects and caused a rapid depopulation of the islands. A single smallpox epidemic in 1854 killed approximately 50% of Pohnpei's population.

Prior to the arrival of the whaling ships, Kosrae's population was estimated to be about 6000. By the time the whalers had left the population had dropped to 300 and the Kosraeans were ripe for the prudish morality the Congregationalists were about to lay on them.

The American Board of Commissioners for Foreign Missions began sending missionaries to eastern Micronesia in 1870, after two decades of Protestant work had proven fairly successful in Hawaii.

The Protestant missionaries in the east, like the Catholic priests in the west, brought more than religion. They brought Western clothing for the scantily clad islanders, as well as Western laws and values. They were the first to put the native languages into a written form, primarily so the Bible could be translated, and they set up schools to teach the people to read and write.

The 1800s was a time of major change in Micronesia and the introduction of alcohol, firearms, new animals, new tools and new ideas all had a dramatic effect upon the islands.

German Period

The start of the German period in Micronesia was more of a commercial venture than a fully fledged attempt to colonise. Disregarding Spanish claims in the region, the Germans arrived in Micronesia in the 19th century to develop the copra trade.

The first German company to set up operations in Micronesia was Godeffroy & Sons who, from their headquarters in New Guinea, opened an office in Yap in 1869.

Meanwhile, 2200 miles to the east, the Germans were negotiating a treaty with the chiefs of Jaluit Atoll in the Marshall Islands. In 1878 Germany established a protectorate over the Marshalls.

Spain grumbled about German activity in the Carolines but did little else until 1885 when the dispute was taken to Pope Leo XIII for arbitration. The pope ruled that Spain owned the land and had administrative rights, but that Germany had a right to establish plantations and commerce. For Spain, it was largely a face-saving decision and her days as a major colonial power were numbered.

In 1898 the United States, looking to get in on the action, abruptly declared war on a reluctant Spain. As an outcome of the Spanish-American War the US was ceded Spain's Pacific possessions of Guam, the Philippines and Wake Island (as well as Puerto Rico and Cuba). As part of the deal, the US paid US$20 million to Spain.

Not particularly keen on selling her remaining Micronesian possessions to gunboat diplomats, Spain went into secret negotiations with Germany for the sale of the Carolines and the remaining Marianas. In 1899 the Germans, now eager to become established as a colonial power, agreed on a purchase price of 25 million pesetas, or about US$4¼ million.

The period of German administration therefore began with a simple real estate transaction. It was to last a mere 15 years. Commercial development was mainly in terms of copra production, though there were also some phosphate mining operations. German interests, led by the Jaluit Company, controlled the copra trade in the Marshalls and eastern Carolines and they governed the islands through local chiefs. In Yap and Palau the copra market was largely in the hands of Japanese traders.

The Micronesians were encouraged to grow coconuts and were given seeds, tools and long-term contracts. To increase labour for German mines and plantations outer islanders were sometimes removed from their atolls. Communally held land, often seemingly idle, was redistributed to the new arrivals or leased by the government to private businesses. Germany's main legacy in Micronesia rests in the social disruptions caused by forced relocations and altered land use policies.

Germany's presence, however, was limited to a small group of government officials, businessmen and missionaries. The total population of Germans in all Micronesia numbered well under 1000. Some of the businesses, such as the German South Seas Phosphate Company in Angaur and the Jaluit Company, made money but in the overall picture German government subsidies to faltering businesses outweighed the total profits taken in Micronesia.

With the onset of WW I German forces fled Micronesia, allowing the Japanese fleet to sail in without resistance.

Japanese Period

Japan had control of the whole of Micronesia, with the exception of Guam, between the two world wars, a period of about 30 years.

Throughout Germany's occupation, Japan had been tightening its economic ties with Micronesia and just prior to WW I maintained more than 80% of all trade with 'German Micronesia'. The Japanese imported turtle shell, mother of pearl, beche-de-mer and other products from the islands.

With the outbreak of hostilities in Europe, Japan made her move to bring Micronesia closer to home and in October 1914 the Japanese Navy seized possession of the German colonies under the pretext of alliance obligations with Britain. The Japanese then proceeded to occupy the islands, starting in the east with the Marshalls and moving westward.

Japan wasted no time developing the infrastructure and administration necessary for the complete annexation of Micronesia. The League of Nations formally mandated control of Micronesia to Japan in 1920.

By this time Saipan, the nearest island to Japan, was already home to a growing number of Japanese colonists and entrepreneurs who had sugar cane production underway. A Japanese conglomerate, the South Seas Development Company, bought them out in 1921 and rapidly became the dominant force in Micronesia's development and exploitation.

The Japanese left no doubt they were there to stay. Micronesia was an extension of the empire's boundaries, an expansion of its horizons. Their intent was to make Micronesia as Japanese as possible. They built Buddhist temples and Shinto shrines, geisha houses and public baths. Each administrative centre became a little Tokyo.

The building of roads, harbours, hospitals and water systems were followed by seaplane ramps, airfields and other fortifications; the latter in violation of the League of Nations mandate. The Japanese withdrew from the League of Nations in 1935 but remained firmly in control of Micronesia.

Administrative buildings were constructed of heavy concrete capable of withstanding not only typhoons but also direct aerial bombings. Many of these buildings, with their 20-inch thick walls and steel reinforcements, were to weather both.

Although the mandate called for the economic and social development of Micronesia, the Japanese geared this development not toward benefiting the local population but rather toward supporting and fortifying their own settlements. Expatriates came to outnumber the Micronesians. By 1940 the Japanese population in the Marianas, Carolines and Marshalls was more than 70,000, compared to about 50,000 Micronesians.

In the Marianas, railroads were built to carry the sugar from the plantations to the harbourside refineries and from there the sugar and alcohol was shipped to the Japanese homeland. Throughout Micronesia, fisheries projects, copra and tapioca production, phosphate and bauxite mining and trochus shell production were developed and began to thrive.

The Japanese, drawing from their own experiences of life on their resource-scarce home islands, created an astonishing level of agricultural activity in Micronesia. With exports greater than imports it was an economic viability that would never be remotely approached under the Americans. In terms of production it was Micronesia's heyday.

Not that all that necessarily made it the most pleasant of times for the Micronesians themselves, whose place in this profitable system was clearly at the bottom. There was a two-tier system of education which saw Japanese children attending excellent schools, while the three years of compulsory education for Micronesians was primarily geared to teaching them a servant's form of the Japanese language. This subordination prevailed in wage scales and social treatment as well.

Although the economy was an impressive one, for the Micronesians it was a trickle-down economy and during wartime, when the trickle stopped, it was the local islanders who were the first to feel hard times and hunger.

The Japanese not only made the islands more productive than they had ever been before, they also set Micronesia on a shifting course from a traditional subsistence life-style to a moneyed economy with a penchant for imported goods.

In boom towns like Garapan and Koror, the sudden development awed many locals and they acquired a taste for the goods in the store windows. Many wanted a piece of the pie, or more precisely, they wanted the rice, canned food and sugar candies that only money could buy.

WW II

The war in the Pacific was launched with the Japanese air attacks on Honolulu's Pearl Harbor on 7 December 1941, and against the US territory of Guam on the same day, 8 December across the International Date Line.

Undefended, Guam surrendered two days later, just hours after Japanese forces came ashore. With its capture, the Japanese possessed all of Micronesia and it was two years before any serious counteroffensive was launched by the US.

On 1 February 1944, US Admiral Chester Nimitz, Commander in Chief of the Pacific Fleet, started his drive across the Pacific with an attack on Kwajalein Atoll in the Marshall Islands, a major Japanese air and naval base.

By 4 February the US had captured Kwajalein and the undefended Majuro Atoll to the south and from these two outposts the Americans began air raids on Japanese bases in the western Carolines.

On 17 February the US made a surprise attack on a fleet of Japanese warships and commercial vessels harboured in Chuuk Lagoon (called Truk Lagoon at the time). This supposedly impenetrable fortress was the Imperial Japanese Fleet's most important base in the central Pacific. The US hit more than 200 planes on the ground and sent nearly 60 ships to watery graves. The 200,000 tons of equipment sunk in the two days of fighting was to be a record for WW

II. After the raid the few surviving Japanese ships evacuated Chuuk, leaving behind 30,000 Japanese troops who had little to do but wait out the war.

With the Chuuk base neutralised and no longer able to provide support to other Pacific bases, the US continued moving west from Majuro, capturing Enewetok and other smaller atolls and islands in the Marshalls.

In June 1944, US forces moved west from the Marshalls with their Fifth Fleet, the largest armada ever assembled. Nearly 600 battleships, carriers, cruisers and destroyers carried a quarter of a million American troops across the Pacific.

The fight for the Marianas began with the US invasion of Saipan on 15 June. Tinian and Guam were invaded in July and all three islands were 'liberated' by the beginning of August. These battles were some of the war's most brutal and costly. They marked a major turning point in the war as the US finally had air bases within striking distance of Japan.

With the Marianas secured, only Palau was left, and in retrospect it would have been better off left alone. Though it was earlier feared that air raids from Palau would threaten a planned US invasion of the Philippines, Japanese air power in the western Pacific had nearly collapsed and the Palau bases had little significance in the declining days of the war.

Despite that, however, the US attacked the Palauan island of Peleliu on 15 September. It was secured after a month of even bloodier battles than those witnessed in the Marianas.

With planes taking off from Micronesian airstrips, the air bombing of Japan began in force in November 1944. In August 1945 two planes, leaving from Tinian, dropped the first atomic bombs used in warfare on the industrial ports of Hiroshima and Nagasaki. The devastation of those cities and the awesome death toll was followed days later by the unconditional surrender of the Japanese.

The Micronesians had watched the impressive Japanese construction of fortified command posts, communications buildings, hospitals, airports and harbours. Caught in the crossfire, they watched as the US turned it all into crumbling rubble. Whole towns such as Koror, Garapan and Sapou were levelled, some of them never to be rebuilt. For Micronesia, the Rising Sun had set.

In the months following the end of the war, thousands of Japanese were shipped home, most of them civilians or soldiers from uninvaded islands. The US took few military prisoners since most Japanese soldiers chose to fight to the death or commit suicide rather than surrender. Many Japanese civilians killed themselves as well, rather than risk the torturing which they had been told the Americans would inflict upon them.

Thousands of Americans and tens of thousands of Japanese died fighting in Micronesia. Thousands of Micronesians died too, though no one paid much attention to Micronesian body counts. In all the volumes written about WW II they are scarcely mentioned. Their islands were the stage but the islanders were not the players, merely the victims.

The Americans Move In

Even though Micronesians played no role in the Pacific conflict, the US government immediately began to treat Micronesia as its 'spoils of war'. The occupying forces were suddenly American instead of Japanese and when the war ended, the occupation continued.

The US Navy took command of the islands in 1945 and effectively sealed Micronesia off to visitors. Some areas remained closed until 1962.

The remoteness of the islands and the fact that the Micronesians were so few in number, left them unseen, unheard and isolated to all beyond their shores. It was an isolation that the US military took measures to maintain.

The Nuclear Age

Throughout Micronesia, islanders had been rocked by two military superpowers battling on their shores. Yet for the Marshallese, the destruction did not cease with the end of the Pacific conflict; for them the most fearsome display of firepower still lay ahead.

Soon after the end of the war, the US took over sections of the Marshalls to test nuclear weapons and the little-understood effects of radiation.

On 1 July 1946 the first nuclear device was exploded over Bikini Atoll. Experiments began at Enewetok Atoll in 1948. There would be 66 nuclear tests altogether that would leave some atolls uninhabitable and hundreds of islanders victims of radiation.

The most powerful bomb ever tested by the US was detonated over Bikini's lagoon in 'Operation Bravo' on 1 March 1954. The 15-megaton hydrogen bomb had a tonnage of TNT greater than the total tonnage of explosives used during the entire course of WW II. Operation Bravo's H-bomb was a thousand times more powerful than the bomb dropped on Hiroshima.

Pulverised coral from Bikini's reef was scattered, along with radioactive fallout, over an area of about 50,000 sq miles. It filtered down upon the Marshallese on the islands of Rongelap and Utrik, upon US weather station personnel on Rongerik and upon the unlucky crew of the Japanese fishing vessel *Lucky Dragon*. More than 300 people and their offspring were affected. The US evacuated the islanders 48 hours later, but by that time many had already suffered severe radiation burns from 'Bikini snow'.

Nuclear experiments ended in 1958 with an international test-ban treaty, just prior to US plans to blast nuclear warheads into space from Bikini Atoll. The warheads were instead launched from Johnston Island in 1961.

Trust Territory

In 1947 the United Nations established a trusteeship in Micronesia. Called the Trust Territory of the Pacific Islands, it had six districts: the Northern Marianas, Pohnpei (including Kosrae), Chuuk, Yap, the Marshalls and Palau. The United States was given exclusive rights for administering the islands.

The UN designated the area a 'strategic trust', allowing the US to establish and maintain military bases in Micronesia and prevent other nations from doing the same.

In 1951 the US Department of the Interior took over from the navy, moving the Trust Territory headquarters from Honolulu to Guam. The Northern Marianas was the only district not to come under Interior Department jurisdiction; it remained under military control until 1962.

Under UN guidelines, the US was obliged to foster the development of political and economic institutions with the goal of helping the Micronesians achieve self-government and self-sufficiency. Instead, 20 years of neglect were followed by 20 years of promoting welfare dependency.

Instead of developing an economic infrastructure and promoting industry, the US pumped in money for government-operated services. Instead of encouraging farming and fishing, they passed out USDA food commodities. They built airports, schools, old age centres and other projects, creating an abundance of government jobs with no internal base capable of bankrolling it all. It was an economy reliant on imported greenbacks.

With anticolonial sentiment high in the '60s, the US found itself, with its Micronesian possessions, coming under mounting criticism.

Yielding to Micronesian aspirations, steps were taken for the islanders to assume a degree of self-government. In 1965 the US agreed to the formation of the Congress of Micronesia as a forum for islanders to deliberate their future political status. The congress was a two-house legislature made up of elected representatives from all island groups.

Executive authority in the Trust Territory, however, remained under the control of the American High Commissioner. On top of that, just to make sure nothing got out of hand, the CIA kept tabs on island legislators by bugging the offices of the Congress of Micronesia.

Peace Corps

With the arrival of the Peace Corps in 1966 a new breed of Americans appeared on the scene. They were more concerned with the interests of the people of Micronesia than they were in the strategic interests of the United States. For the first time, Americans slept, ate and lived with the Micronesians, and a fair number stayed on to marry into Micronesian life.

For awhile there was one volunteer for every 100 Micronesians and the US government saw the Peace Corps as a way of spreading American influence. By putting a volunteer on every inhabited island, they brought English as a unifying language to the distant corners of Micronesia. What they hadn't calculated on was the idealism and the critical outlook on American policies that the volunteers would also bring.

Volunteers worked in community development projects and as legal advisors. Peace Corps lawyers taught the Micronesians that they had certain legal rights, including the right to challenge US government policies. The US Defense Department became particularly concerned with challenges to land policies. In response to the volunteers' activities in Micronesia, the Nixon administration phased out the Peace Corps' legal services programme.

Emerging States

When negotiations for self-government were first started, the US had initially expected that the six Trust Territory districts would join together as one Micronesian nation, but this was not to be.

In January 1978 the people of the Northern Marianas opted to become American citizens with US Commonwealth status.

In July 1978 the remaining six districts (Kosrae had become a separate district in 1977) voted on a common constitution. It failed to pass in the Marshalls and Palau.

The four central districts which had voted in favour – Pohnpei, Kosrae, Chuuk and Yap – became the Federated States of Micronesia (FSM). Their constitution went into effect in May 1979.

The Marshalls became a separate political entity, the Republic of the Marshall Islands.

Their constitution also became effective in May 1979.

The Palauans renamed their islands the Republic of Palau and voted for a constitution that went into effect in January 1981. It included a provision which totally banned the use, testing and storage of nuclear weapons and materials on its land and in its surrounding waters.

The internal governments of each of these emerging nations are based on the US system of executive, legislative and judicial branches, with the exception of the Marshallese government which also incorporates elements of the British parliamentary system. In all three nations, traditional village councils and high-ranking chiefs retain some powers through advisory boards.

In 1982 each of the new nations signed separate Compacts of Free Association with the USA, all getting different economic deals. In theory the compacts allow the new nations to manage their internal affairs, although their relationships with other nations are subject to US restrictions. In return for millions of dollars paid to the fledgling governments, the compacts allow the USA to maintain sweeping military rights throughout Micronesia.

As part of the process for dissolving the Trust Territory, each compact had to be approved by four separate groups in turn: by the peoples of each new nation in a general election, by the legislatures of those nations, by the US Congress and by the UN Security Council.

The compacts of the FSM and the Marshalls were approved in plebiscites in 1983, and then ratified by their respective congresses. Finally the US Congress approved the two compacts, with the provisions going into effect in November 1986.

However, over the next few years, unresolved issues in Palau stalled not only Palau's own political process, but the dissolution of the Trust Territory as well.

The compact between the US and Palau permits the US to transfer and store nuclear materials in the area, a clear violation of Palau's constitution. In vote after vote, Palauans have consistently approved the compact by the majority vote required, but with fewer than the 75% required to overturn the anti-nuclear provision in their constitution. The compact and the constitution, both legally approved by Palauans, are in legal conflict with one another. In what many people see as a strongarm tactic, the US refuses to renegotiate the compact and remains steadfast on requiring nukes.

Throughout the 1980s the UN Security Council maintained that it would make only one vote to dissolve the trusteeship, rather than disband it a portion at a time. That position was sustained with the certainty of a veto by the USSR who was not keen on seeing the entire region remain in US hands and who called the compacts 'virtual slavery' for Micronesians.

With the warming of the Cold War, the USSR dropped its objection to the Trust Territory's piecemeal disbandment and in December 1990 the United Nations Security Council voted (with only Cuba dissenting) to terminate the trusteeship for the Commonwealth of the Northern Mariana Islands, the Federated States of Micronesia and the Republic of the Marshall Islands. The council allowed Palau to be dealt with separately.

After WW II the UN established 11 trusteeships of former colonial possessions. One by one they attained self-governing status and with the independence of Papua New Guinea in 1975, Micronesia had the dubious distinction of being the only remaining Trust Territory. That distinction now belongs to Palau alone.

The USA has since rolled back much of Palau's autonomy and has declared that the orders of the US Department of the Interior, which administers the Trust Territory, supercede Palau's own constitutional laws.

GEOGRAPHY

It's no easy task counting the islands of Micronesia – there are more than 2100 of them. Some are just small flat specks that disappear and reappear with the tides; some are still growing, through coral build-up or volcanic flows; and most are uninhabited. With the vast majority of these islands covering less than one sq mile each, they are aptly named Micronesia – 'small islands'.

Micronesia's islands are scattered over three million sq miles of the western Pacific between Hawaii and the Philippines. They are divided geographically into three archipelagoes – the Marshalls, Carolines and Marianas.

All are in the tropics, except two of the Marianas which poke up just north of the Tropic of Cancer. The southernmost island is Kapingamarangi, one degree north of the equator.

Together the islands have a total land mass of 919 sq miles. In comparison Hawaii totals 6450 sq miles, Bali is 2147 and Tahiti is 402.

The islands of Micronesia are classified as 'high' or 'low'. The main islands in western Micronesia are high types and are actually the exposed peaks of a volcanic mountain ridge that runs from Japan through the Northern Marianas, Guam and Palau and on down to New Guinea. While basically of volcanic formation, some of the islands are partly or wholly capped with a layer of limestone. The Northern Marianas have Micronesia's only active volcanoes; Pohnpei, Kosrae and Chuuk, in the eastern Carolines, are also high volcanic islands; while Yap is a raised part of the Asian continental shelf.

High islands, which make up the vast majority of Micronesia's land area, usually have good soil, abundant water and lush vegetation. Guam is the largest island, followed by Babeldaob in the Republic of Palau.

The highest point in Micronesia is 3166 feet above sea level, on Agrihan Island in the Northern Marianas. A canyon, known as the Mariana Trench, runs for 1835 miles alongside the Mariana Islands and has the world's greatest known ocean depth. The canyon is more than seven miles deep so, if measured from the bottom of the canyon, the Mariana Islands would be the highest mountains in the world!

All of the more than 1100 islands that comprise the Marshall Islands, as well as the small islands of the central Carolines between Yap and Chuuk's high islands, and the outer islands of Pohnpei and Palau, are low coral islands.

Some are like the archetypal cartoon island – just a patch of white sand with a single coconut tree – while other islands are grouped together on the rims of atolls. Micronesia has the world's first, second and fourth largest atolls: Kwajalein in the Marshalls, Namonuito in Chuuk, and Ulithi in Yap, respectively.

Low islands have practically no topsoil and the sand has a high salt content, so vegetation is limited. Though the islands have no springs or rivers, many sit atop freshwater lenses that can be tapped by wells.

Coral Atolls

Charles Darwin was the first to recognise that atolls are made from coral growth which has built up around the edges of a submerged volcanic mountain peak.

In a scenario played out over hundreds of thousands of years, coral first builds up around the shores of a high island producing a fringing reef. Then, when the island begins to slowly sink under its own weight, the coral continues to grow upwards at about the same rate. This forms a barrier reef which is separated from the shore by a lagoon. By the time the island has completely submerged, the coral growth has become a base for an atoll, circling the place where the mountain top used to be.

The classic atoll shape is roughly oval, with islands of coral rubble and sand built up on the higher points of the reef. There are usually breaks in the reef rim large enough for boats to enter the sheltered lagoon.

The coral is made up of millions of tiny rock-like limestone skeletons. These are created by tentacled coral polyps which draw calcium from the water and then excrete it to form hardened shells to protect their soft bodies. Only the outer layer of coral is alive. As polyps reproduce and die, the new polyps attach themselves in successive layers to the empty skeletons already in place.

CLIMATE

Micronesia has a tropical oceanic climate that is consistently warm and humid, with some of the most uniform year-round temperatures in the world. Temperatures range between 70°F and 90°F (21°C to 32°C), with the average daily temperature for all of Micronesia about 81°F (27°C). Humidity percentages average in the high 70's.

Generally the most comfortable months are January through March or, stretching the seasons, November through April. These months usually see less rainfall, somewhat lower humidity and slightly cooler weather. Refreshing north-easterly trade winds blow across much of Micronesia from December to March.

The average annual rainfall is about 85 to 150 inches, but this varies from place to place. Some of the northern Marshalls get only 20 inches a year, while Pohnpei's rainforest interior gets over 400 inches per year. Rainfall decreases in the Carolines from east to west.

Typhoons

A typhoon is a tropical storm in the western Pacific with winds over 75 miles per hour. (The same storm, if found in the Atlantic or eastern Pacific, would be called a hurricane.)

Typhoons can occur in any month, though are most frequent between August and December. Guam and the Northern Marianas are particularly susceptible, being directly in the storm track. For travellers staying in modern hotels, it mostly means heavy winds and rains, damp rooms and the loss of a day outdoors. Most of the serious damage occurs from downed trees and to thatched huts or tin-roofed shanties that get blown apart.

Typhoons which sweep across low coral islands have been known to destroy every home and wipe out most of the trees and vegetation.

Supertyphoons are those with winds in excess of 150 miles per hour. At the other end of the scale are 'banana typhoons', those with winds that do little more than knock down banana trees.

FLORA & FAUNA
Flora

The coconut palm tree is Micronesia's most important plant. Copra, the dried meat of the nut from which coconut oil is made, is its most important export. The nut also provides food and drinking liquid, while the flowers provide sap for making a wine called tuba. Rope is made from the green coconut husks and fuel and charcoal are made from mature husks. The wood is used for lumber and carving, the fronds for thatch and baskets.

Breadfruit trees provide timber and their large green globular fruits are a major food source. Timber also comes from mahogany and other trees including the betel nut tree (Areca palm), although the latter is more treasured for its nuts. Pandanus is eaten and the leaves are used for making mats, baskets and fans.

Other traditional food plants include taro, yams, tapioca and bananas. The lush heart-shaped leaves of the taro plant, which is cultivated in mud flats, are big enough to use as umbrellas. Tapioca looks a bit like tall marijuana plants.

Mangrove swamps are common along the shores of many of the high islands. The most unique thing about mangrove trees are their looping prop roots that arch above the water before reaching down into the mud. Mangrove trees help to expand the shoreline as their roots extend away from shore and sediments collect around them.

Colourful tropical plants and flowers are abundant in Micronesia, especially on the high islands. Common varieties include hibiscus, bougainvillea, purple-flowered beach morning glories, plumeria, lilies, lantana and crotons. The Marianas are especially noted for their flame trees (royal poinciana) which have scarlet blossoms.

Plants such as coleus, caladium and philodendron, which in colder climates are painstakingly nurtured indoors in pots, grow in wild abandon in Micronesia, reaching gigantic proportions. Two of the more peculiar plants found in Micronesia are the low-growing insectivorous pitcher plant and the 'sensitive plant', a small green ground cover with thin compound leaves that close up when touched.

Fauna

The closer an island group is to the Asian land masses, the more numerous its birds and animals. High islands have a greater variety and support larger populations than coral atolls. The Marshalls therefore, have few creatures other than seabirds and shorebirds while Palau, predictably, has the greatest variety.

The only land mammals native to Micronesia are bats. Fruit bats, with wingspans of up to three feet, are found on all island groups except the Marshalls. They are common at dusk in Palau's Rock Islands and on Chuuk, Pohnpei and Yap. Due to a Chamorro penchant for eating the furry flying beasts, they are now on the endangered list in Guam and rare in the Northern Marianas. Despite being a protected species, poaching continues to threaten remaining fruit bat populations and imported fruit bats sell for a premium on Guam.

Animals that have been introduced into the islands include dogs, cats, mice, rats, pigs, cattle, horses and goats. Angaur in Palau has monkeys; and sambar deer are found on Pohnpei, Rota, Guam and Saipan, though they are seldom seen.

Guam has carabao (water buffalo), which were probably brought in by Jesuit missionaries in the 1600s. Carabao are most often seen in the southern part of Guam where they are used on small farms as beasts of burden. They are large clumsy animals and not always good-tempered with strangers.

Palau has estuarine crocodiles (and a few New Guinea crocodiles) that frequent both saltwater and freshwater areas, favouring muddy mangrove swamps. They are primarily nocturnal, but sometimes bask in the sun during the day. Adult crocodiles average 12 feet in length and can be dangerous. After a spearfisherman (who was hunting fish, not crocs) was eaten in the late 1960s, Australian hunters were brought in to pick off the larger reptiles. The crocodile that killed the fisherman was captured and part of the man's arm and flashlight were found in its stomach. Palauans occasionally hunt crocodiles with guns or spears, eating the meat and selling the skins, though officially they are now endangered and protected.

You might come across monitor lizards sunning themselves on the roads or hanging out in caves or muddy swamps. They can reach up to six feet in length but are more commonly half that size.

Sea turtles, including hawksbills, green turtles and leatherbacks, which are all endangered species, lay eggs on uninhabited sandy beaches. They've been an important food source in Micronesia for centuries.

Micronesia has a variety of crabs, including coconut crabs and mangrove crabs which both make good eating. Coconut crabs are sometimes caught by islanders and kept in cages while they grow to a meatier size, which can be up to three feet long. They are strong enough to tear open a metal rubbish bin and pry apart the bars of a steel barbecue

Green Turtle

grill. And yes, they can also rip through coconut husks and shells! (For more details on marine life see the Highlights section in the Facts for the Visitor chapter.)

Other than venomous but non-aggressive sea snakes and worm-sized blind snakes, Micronesia's only legless reptiles are on Guam and Palau. Palau has the Pacific Island boa in its forests; the Palau tree snake in its small trees and shrubs; and the dog-faced water snake in its mangrove swamps. None pose a threat to people.

The brown tree snake, which is native to the Solomon Islands and was accidentally introduced to Guam via military cargo in the late 1940s, has wiped out virtually all of Guam's forest birds. In the 1960s it was noted that the number of Guam's birds was declining and by the late 1970s many species survived only in a small forested area in the north. While pesticides and avian disease were suspected, it wasn't until the 1980s that the snake was identified as the culprit. For most birds it was too late. Nine endemic species, including the Guam flycatcher and the Guam broadbill, are now extinct, and several others survive only in precariously low numbers.

Meanwhile there are millions of brown tree snakes living without predators on Guam, roaming the forest trees at night and polishing off birds and eggs, or at least what's left of them. With so few birds left to eat, the snakes are resorting to chicken eggs, rodents and lizards.

Adult snakes can reach up to eight feet in length and though they'll take a threatening stance when cornered, they pose little danger to humans (other than babies), as their toxin is mild and is injected through chewing rather than a strike.

In addition to the devastation of the native ecology, the snakes commonly climb around electrical lines, causing power outages (blackouts) on Guam. So far little has been done to address the problem, though other Pacific islands are very worried that the snake may slink onto their islands via cargo from Guam; it's already been sighted on Saipan, Wake and Oahu.

Micronesia has a number of native skinks including a green variety, which can grow up to one foot in length, and others with iridescent blue tails. The endearing gecko, a small common house lizard that scampers along walls and ceilings by means of suction-cup-like feet, has a loud call. It prefers to live indoors with people, paying its way by eating mosquitoes and other pesky insects.

Micronesia has about 7000 varieties of insects. Mosquitoes, beach gnats and cockroaches are the most common annoyances. Great numbers of butterflies are particularly noticeable on Guam, largely because the birds and skinks that once preyed on the caterpillars are now prey themselves for the brown tree snake.

Birds The cardinal honeyeater, a small bright red and black bird, is endangered in Guam but easily seen elsewhere. It's found in gardens and forests, poking its curved bill into the centres of hibiscus and other flowers. The Northern Marianas has a beautifully plumed golden honeyeater.

The white or grey Pacific reef heron is common on reefs and in shallow water where it uses its long beak to hunt for fish and small crabs. Cattle egrets are sometimes seen in open grassy areas.

Kingfishers in Micronesia seldom fish. These pretty blue and white birds, with cinnamon-coloured touches, are found on Pohnpei, Palau and in the Marianas and their diet consists mainly of insects and lizards.

Micronesian starlings are common and widespread. Starlings like to eat papayas and some islanders like to eat starlings.

The best place to see the endangered Micronesian megapode is in Palau's Rock Islands, where some of these ground-living birds have built their nests on the picnic beaches. The megapode does not incubate its eggs, but lays them in the ground, warming them with dirt and decaying matter. Endemic to Micronesia, this species is now extinct on Guam and Rota, though there is a small group near Saipan's Suicide Cliff.

The Guam rail, a flightless bird indige-

Kingfisher

nous to Guam but wiped out on that island by the brown tree snake, has been introduced on Rota after a successful captive breeding programme saved the bird from total extinction. Palau has a banded rail.

Some of the more commonly seen shorebirds, especially during spring and autumn migrations, include: the lesser goldenplover, wandering tattler, whimbrel and ruddy turnstone. Common seabirds include the brown noddy, black noddy and white tern.

White-tailed tropicbirds, distinguishable by two long white tail feathers, are often seen riding the air currents around the cliffs where they build their nests.

More than 200 species of birds have been recorded in Micronesia and about 85 species breed in the area. Serious birdwatchers should get hold of the 12-page *Checklist of the Birds of Micronesia*, by Peter Pyle and John Engbring. It's available for $2 from the Hawaii Audubon Society, Box 22832, Honolulu, Hawaii 96822.

A Field Guide to the Birds of Hawaii & the Tropical Pacific Princeton University Press, New Jersey, 1987, hardcover by H D Pratt, P L Bruner & D G Berrett is the best general bird guide to the area.

GOVERNMENT

Guam is an incorporated US territory. The Commonwealth of the Northern Marianas is a commonwealth of the USA. The Republic of the Marshall Islands and the Federated States of Micronesia are now independent nations. The Republic of Palau has not yet achieved independence but is still a Trust Territory under US administration.

ECONOMY

The economy of Micronesia is heavily dependent upon US appropriations, which makes it possible for island governments to employ roughly 60% of the total work force. Their payrolls form the backbone of the entire economy.

However, hundreds of graduates return each year from overseas colleges to find the already bloated government departments are unable to absorb them. The jobs just aren't there. Along with their degrees, many have acquired a taste for Western lifestyles and are no longer satisfied with a subsistence life of farming and fishing. They've become a new group of young, dislodged and disillusioned unemployed.

Actually, with the exception of those in the subsistence economy, Micronesians produce very little. Many of the private sector jobs that do exist deal largely in imported goods. Few, if any, of the products found in the department stores, markets, bars, office suppliers, gas stations or Toyota dealers are produced in Micronesia.

By and large the whole moneyed economy is an artificial one bankrolled by the US. It has no local base and no way of sustaining itself. Exports have generally been limited to copra, handicrafts and a few marine products. The total value of all exports doesn't generate enough income to even pay Micronesia's fuel bills.

With the end of the trusteeship, the US is completing a vast capital improvement plan in Micronesia, including new airports, docks, water and sewerage systems, paved roads and hospitals. However, with their multi-million dollar annual repair and operation costs, these capital improvements represent yet another economic liability. In addition, although they have created a fair amount of hustle and bustle, the vast majority of the projects have been contracted out to foreign firms, providing minimal benefits to the local economy.

The nature of US expenditures in Micronesia has created a dependency, rather than fostering self-sufficiency. Micronesians still have little to barter except their water and their land, the latter for US military bases and Japanese resorts, the former to tuna fleets who want fishing rights within their 200-mile economic zones.

POPULATION

Micronesia's population is about 330,000, with 127,000 of those living on Guam.

For information on the people see the individual chapters later.

CULTURE

Traditional Micronesian societies can be divided into two groups: those on the high islands and those on the low islands.

On the high islands, people developed a land-based subsistence livelihood and tended to be homebodies. Food sources were reliable and it was a fairly easy lifestyle that supported relatively large populations. Because life wasn't a constant struggle for survival, the high islanders were able to develop stable and elaborate societies, some of which became highly stratified with caste hierarchies, chiefs, royalty and the like.

Low atoll islanders had a more challenging lifestyle, eking their living out of the sea rather than the land. They became expert navigators, sailors and fishers. They travelled great distances and though their next door neighbours were sometimes hundreds of miles away, visits were not infrequent.

Canoe journeys between islands brought trade, warfare and new ideas. Islanders near each other share things in common and can often understand each other's languages, whereas islanders at opposite ends of Micronesia are quite different and their languages mutually unintelligible. It is among the low islanders that the commonalities of culture and language are spread over the greatest distances.

Micronesian societies are made up of clan groupings descended matrilineally (except Yap, which is patrilineal) from a common ancestor. The head clan on each island can trace its lineage back to the original settlers of the island and members of that clan usually retain certain privileges.

Extended families are the norm and it's not uncommon for grandparents, cousins, children and adopted clan members to live under the same roof. If one family member gets a good job other relatives may well move in and live off the income. In general, when people visit other islands they simply look up a member of their clan to stay with.

Canoes & Navigation

Some of the greatest navigators in the Pacific have come from the resource-scarce low islands of Micronesia. With their sandy soil offering limited food supplies they took to the oceans. In general, the smaller the islands, the more ocean-going the islanders.

Without compasses or maps, Micronesians used a combination of natural aids to direct themselves around the Pacific.

The long Marshallese atolls, fairly close together in north-south lines, interrupt the large swells that move across the Pacific from east to west. Marshallese navigation depended largely on learning to feel and interpret the patterns of the currents and waves that were deflected around the islands.

The Carolinians' main navigational focus was on the sky. Because most travel was in an east-west line, they could keep on course by watching the sun and by identifying individual stars that would rise or set over particular islands. They sang ancient chants which contained information on star patterns and other navigational directions.

In addition to swell interpretations and celestial compasses, the Micronesians also keyed into other natural phenomena. For instance, to see if land was near they would watch for birds returning home to their island nests in the evening. A single stationary cloud off in the distance was often moist ocean air hovering over a high island; and although coral atolls are too flat to be seen from far away, their shallow aqua-coloured lagoons reflect a pale green light onto the underside of clouds.

Micronesian canoes have a single outrigger. In protected areas islanders used simple dugout canoes, made from a single tree trunk. On the open ocean they used huge canoes, up to 100 feet long, constructed of planks tied together with cord made from coconut husk fibres. These ocean-going vessels were often larger and faster than the ships of the early European explorers and could hold 100 passengers or more.

What to Wear

Outside Guam, Saipan or the beaches of resort hotels, skimpy swimsuits are apt to get you more attention than you'll want.

In most parts of the FSM short skirts and even shorts are deemed inappropriate for women. In Yap, Kosrae and some of the outer islands it's considered offensive for women to expose their upper thighs. In those places, although it's OK to wear a swimsuit in the water, women are expected to put on a skirt when they get out.

Though skimpy clothing is not appropriate anywhere in Micronesia, things are a bit looser on Majuro, the more developed parts of Palau and in the Marianas, where longer shorts don't pose a problem for women. Follow local custom.

For the most part it's acceptable for men to wear shorts throughout Micronesia, even on islands like Pohnpei and Moen where just about all the local men seem to be sweating it out in long pants.

RELIGION

Micronesia has been almost completely Christianised. Spanish Catholics got to the Marianas and the western islands first and New England Protestants converted the Marshalls and the eastern islands. They met somewhere in the middle, with Chuuk and Pohnpei turning out about half Catholic and half Protestant.

LANGUAGE

Micronesian languages are in the Austronesian language group. The major native languages are: Marshallese; Palauan; Chamorro, in Guam and the Northern Marianas; Yapese, Ulithian and Woleaian in Yap; Pohnpeian and Kapingamarangi-Nukuoro in Pohnpei; Chuukese and Mortlockese in Chuuk; and Kosraean. There are several more dialects spoken on the outer islands.

English is widely spoken throughout Micronesia and elderly people often speak Japanese.

Facts for the Visitor

VISAS

US citizens don't need a passport to visit Micronesia, though it makes things simpler to carry one. Without a passport, some other proof of US citizenship, such as a birth certificate, is required.

All other nationalities must carry a valid passport.

Visas are not required to visit the Northern Marianas, Marshalls, FSM or Palau for stays of up to 30 days in each. Each FSM state has its own immigration process so you automatically get a new entry permit, good for up to 30 days, each time you fly into a new district centre.

Immigration officials in Micronesia commonly ask how long you're planning to stay and then stamp that number of days into your passport. It's a good idea to go for the maximum or at least give yourself a buffer, so you won't have to bother about getting (or paying for) an extension if you decide to stay on a bit longer.

Officially, the Marshalls, the FSM and Palau require visitors to have return or onward tickets, though on our last trip no one asked to see them. The Northern Marianas and Guam require non-US citizens to have onward tickets and a visa to the next destination.

Until recently all non-US citizens, except Canadians, needed a US visa to visit Guam. There are now some exceptions.

Under Guam's visa waiver programme, citizens of the following countries may enter Guam for up to 15 days without obtaining a US visa: Australia, New Zealand, Japan, the UK, Nauru, Papua New Guinea, Western Samoa, the Solomon Islands, Vanuatu, Indonesia, Malaysia, Singapore, Hong Kong, Burma, Brunei and Taiwan.

In addition, citizens of the UK, Japan, Sweden, France, Italy, Switzerland, Germany and the Netherlands may enter the USA (and Guam) without obtaining a US visa under a new reciprocal visa waiver pro-gramme. Under this programme your stay is limited to 90 days and you must have a return ticket that is nonrefundable in the USA.

One disadvantage of both of these two visa waiver programmes is that it's not possible to extend your stay.

CUSTOMS

Sometimes Micronesian customs officers carry out baggage checks. These are usually brief and cursory, except in Palau where they're commonly quite thorough and where consequently the queues move slowly.

As elsewhere, Micronesian nations prohibit the entry of drugs, weapons, large quantities of alcohol, and fruits and plants that might contain insects or diseases harmful to local crops.

MONEY

US dollars are the only accepted currency in Micronesia. Except in the outer islands, US dollar travellers' cheques are accepted everywhere and you'll rarely have to wait in a bank queue to change them since most hotels, restaurants and larger stores will accept them as cash.

There are commercial banks on Majuro, Ebeye, Kosrae, Pohnpei, Moen, Yap, Koror, Saipan, Rota, Tinian and Guam. On the outer islands you should always bring enough cash to get you through your stay.

Plastic addicts will be pleased to know that major credit cards (particularly MasterCard and Visa) are accepted all over Guam; at most hotels and large restaurants on Saipan and Palau; at most hotels and a few restaurants on Pohnpei; at most car rentals on these islands; and by Air Micronesia agents everywhere. Credit cards are beginning to catch on at a few places on Majuro, Kosrae, Chuuk and Yap.

Tipping

Tipping of 10% to 15% is expected on Guam and in the Northern Marianas. Tipping is beginning to catch on in Palau and Pohnpei, but is generally not the custom elsewhere in Micronesia.

WHAT TO BRING

Travelling light, a good policy anywhere, is easier in the tropics as sleeping bags, heavy jackets and bulky clothing are totally unnecessary.

Dress is definitely casual. For men, dressing up means wearing a Hawaiian-print shirt; and for women, a cotton dress is as formal as it gets.

Ideal clothes are those made of cotton, which breathes best in hot humid weather; are loose fitting and don't need to be tucked in; and can be hand washed in a sink and hung up to dry without wrinkling.

One long-sleeved shirt, lightweight cotton jacket or windbreaker might be useful against indoor air-con and outside insects. There are mosquitoes in Micronesia so if you use insect repellent, bring some.

Most islanders walk in the warm rain unprotected, but if that bothers you bring an umbrella or rain jacket.

Footwear in Micronesia is predominately rubber thongs, which are sold everywhere, or other casual sandals. Sneakers can be useful for hiking off the beaten path and for walking along rough coral reefs.

A flashlight is good to have on hand for the occasional power blackout and is essential if you want to fully explore caves. A Swiss Army knife, as every traveller knows, is worth its weight in gold. If you plan to do a lot of snorkelling, it's a good idea to bring your own gear.

You might want to consider a passport pouch or money belt to wear around your neck or waist.

Zip-lock plastic sandwich bags in a couple of sizes are indispensable for keeping things dry. You can use them to protect your film and camera equipment, to seal up airline tickets and passports, and to keep wet bathing suits away from the rest of your luggage.

A one-cup immersion heater, usually available for a few dollars from hardware or

department stores, and a durable lightweight cup can come in handy. Not only can you sterilise your own water and make coffee and tea in your room but you can use it to make up a quick meal if you carry a few packets of instant oatmeal, ramen, soup or the like.

Medical supplies and toiletries are available in most places, though outside Guam and Saipan the selection may be limited. Contact lens cleaning solutions and supplies can be found in Guam, but may be unavailable elsewhere. Bring sunscreen.

You may well be able to travel lightly enough to take carry-on luggage only. In addition to one piece of luggage, you're also allowed to carry on a purse (handbag), camera bag or daypack. However, because Air Mike (Continental Air Micronesia) planes are specially designed to carry more cargo than most, some of their planes have no overhead compartments and on these all carry-on luggage has to fit under the seat in front of you. So, the trade off for not having to check your bag is often giving up your foot space.

TOURIST OFFICES

All the island groups give out brochures, maps or other standard tourist information. You can pick them up once you're there or, if you write in advance, they will mail the information to you.

Micronesian Tourist Offices

Marshalls
Tourism Office, Box 1727, Majuro, Marshall Islands 96960
Kosrae
Tourism Office, Box R&D, Kosrae, FSM 96944
Pohnpei
Tourist Commission, Box 66, Kolonia, Pohnpei, FSM 96941
Chuuk
Truk Visitors Bureau, Box FQ, Chuuk, FSM 96942
Yap
Division of Tourism, Box 36, Colonia, Yap, FSM 96943
Palau
Palau Visitors Authority, Box 256, Koror, Republic of Palau 96940

Northern Marianas
    Marianas Visitors Bureau, Box 861, Saipan, MP 96950
Guam
    Guam Visitors Bureau, Box 3520, Agana, Guam 96910

Overseas Reps
USA
    Republic of the Marshall Islands, 2433 Massachusetts Ave NW, Washington DC 20008 (☎ 202-234-5414)
    Guam Visitors Bureau, 516 Fifth Ave, New York, NY 10036 (☎ 800-228-GUAM)
Fiji
    Republic of the Marshall Islands, Box 2088, 8th Floor Ratu Sukuna House, Suva, Fiji (☎ 302-291)
Japan
    Guam Visitors Bureau, Kokusai Building 2F, 3-1-1 Marunouchi, Chiyoda-ku, Tokyo 100 (☎ 03-212-3630)
Korea
    Guam Visitors Bureau, 3rd Floor Wonchang Building, 26-3 Yoido-dong, Youngdeungpo-gu, Seoul 150 (☎ 02-783-5332)
Taiwan
    Guam Visitors Bureau, 68 Chung Shan North Rd, Sec 2, Taipei (☎ 02-541-6466)

BUSINESS HOURS & HOLIDAYS
Business hours vary throughout the islands, but 8 am to 4.30 pm Monday to Friday is fairly common. Banking hours also vary, though 10 am to 3 pm Monday to Thursday and 10 am to 5 pm on Fridays is average.

The last weeks of the year are very difficult for doing business. Not only do Christmas and New Year holidays and parties interfere, but many government employees have leftover annual leave that must be taken by the end of the year or lost, so lots of people scoot off for a quick vacation.

POST & TELECOMMUNICATIONS
Postal Rates
All of Micronesia is under the umbrella of the US Postal Service, which handles Micronesia's international mail. Micronesia has US zip codes and US postage rates apply.

Airmail rates from Micronesia are 29 cents for a one-ounce letter and 19 cents for a postcard to the USA or within Micronesia;

40 cents for a one-ounce letter and 30 cents for a postcard to Canada; 35 cents for a half-ounce letter and 30 cents for a postcard to Mexico; and 50 cents for a half-ounce letter and 40 cents for a postcard to any other foreign country. Micronesia is in US Postal Zone 8 (the same as Hawaii) for calculating parcel rates to US destinations.

Sending Mail
Service is reasonably efficient between major islands and the outside world. Mail delivery to and from the outer islands depends on the frequency of field trip ships and/or commuter flights and can be very slow.

If you're writing to someone on an outer island, you need to include their island's name, in addition to the district centre's address and zip code.

The following are the zip codes for the main postal areas in Micronesia, excluding Guam.

Koror
    Republic of Palau 96940
Kolonia, Pohnpei
    Federated States of Micronesia 96941
Chuuk
    Federated States of Micronesia 96942
Colonia, Yap
    Federated States of Micronesia 96943
Kosrae
    Federated States of Micronesia 96944

Saipan
    Commonwealth of the Northern Marianas 96950
Rota
    Commonwealth of the Northern Marianas 96951
Tinian
    Commonwealth of the Northern Marianas 96952
Majuro
    Republic of the Marshall Islands 96960

Receiving Mail

You can have mail sent to you c/o General Delivery at any of these post offices. Guam has more than a dozen post offices, but all general delivery mail should be addressed: General Delivery GMF, Barrigada, Guam 96921.

Guam and the Northern Marianas use US stamps, but the Marshalls, FSM and Palau print their own stamps which can only be used from those particular island groups.

Stamp Collecting

The Micronesian islands issue some colourful commemorative stamps. Collectors can order FSM stamps direct from the FSM Philatelic Bureau, Kolonia, Pohnpei, FSM 96941. Marshallese stamps can be ordered from the Philatelic Center of the Republic of the Marshall Islands, One Unicover Center, Cheyenne, Wyoming 82008-0021.

Telephone

Local phone services are of variable quality and outside Guam and Saipan the telephone system does not always reach all parts of even the district centres. Outer islands can be reached by radio, which are sometimes solar-powered.

Guam and Saipan have pay phones, but on most islands it's common practice to just ask to use the phone at stores or hotel front desks.

The FSM doesn't have coin-operated pay phones but has debit card phones in which you purchase a plastic card for $10 (or $25) to insert whenever you make a phone call. When $10 worth of calls have been made, the phone service is cut off and you have to insert another card to keep talking. Though some people find this system useful for making long-distance phone calls, it's a real irritant if you just want to call for a taxi from the airport.

Long-distance telephone services (as well as telex, telegraph and fax) are available in the major district centres. Rates are generally $2.50 to $5 per minute to most places outside Micronesia, usually with a three-minute minimum. Calls from one FSM state to another cost $3 for every three minutes during the day, half that at night. Calls from Guam to the USA are about $1 a minute during off-peak hours.

When making international calls to Micronesia, use the area code 670 for the Northern Marianas, 671 for Guam, 680 for Palau, 691 for the FSM and 692 for the Marshalls.

TIME

The International Date Line runs between Hawaii and the Marshalls. Going from the USA to Micronesia you lose a day, while on the return you gain a day.

Micronesia has four time zones. Guam is 10 hours ahead of Greenwich Mean Time.

So when it's 12 noon in Guam, the Northern Marianas, Yap and Chuuk it is: 1 pm in Pohnpei and Kosrae; 2 pm in Majuro; and 11 am in Palau. It is also 12 noon in Port Moresby, Sydney and Melbourne; 11 am in Tokyo; 10 am in Manila and Hong Kong; 2 am in London; 4 pm the day before in Honolulu; 6 pm the day before in San Francisco; and 9 pm the day before in Boston.

ELECTRICITY

Electricity is 110/120 volts, 60 cycles, and a flat two-pronged plug is used, the same as in the USA.

WEIGHTS & MEASURES

Micronesia, like the USA, uses the imperial system of measurement. Distances are in inches, feet, yards and miles; weights are in ounces, pounds and tons. For those accustomed to the metric system of measurement, there is a conversion table at the back of this book.

Top Left: Pandanus - Majuro
Top Right: Orchid
Bottom Left: Bougainvillea
Bottom Right: Carnivorous pitcher plant - Yap

Top: Outrigger canoe - Saipan
Left: Pinatang Park - Rota
Right: Carp Island - Palau

BOOKS & MAPS

The only real bookshops in Micronesia are the Faith Book Stores in Guam and Saipan and the PMA Bookstore in Pohnpei. Some grocery stores sell paperback novels and duty-free shops often have souvenir-style picture books about the islands.

A small but select collection of books about Micronesia is available from the Alele Museum (Box 629, Majuro, Marshall Islands 96960). You can either get them while you're in Majuro or write for a book list and order by mail.

Theses, short papers and reprinted articles on current issues are available from the Micronesian Seminar (Box 250, Chuuk, FSM 96942), which offers such titles as *The Role of the Beachcombers in the Caroline Islands, Education For What?* and *Suicide Epidemic Among Micronesian Youth*, and from the Micronesian Area Research Center (University of Guam, Mangilao, Guam 96913). Both places charge a modest fee for photocopying and will send a list of available publications upon request.

Hawaii's East-West Center publishes, or has access to, a lot of obscure titles like *Pohnpei: Household Income, Expenditure, & the Role of Electricity* and *Nuclear Activities & the Pacific Islanders*. Their selection ranges from free, reprinted articles to expensive books. You can get a listing from the Distribution Office, East-West Center, 1777 East-West Rd, Honolulu, Hawaii 96848.

The Bishop Museum (Box 19000-A, Honolulu, Hawaii 96817) and the University of Hawaii Press (2840 Kolowalu St, Honolulu, Hawaii 96822) each has its own catalogue of books about the Pacific, including Micronesia, which they will send you upon request.

History

The First Taint of Civilization (University of Hawaii Press, Honolulu, 1983, hardcover) by Francis X Hezel SJ, is an excellent anecdotal history of the Caroline and Marshall Islands during the pre-colonial era from 1521 to 1885. Hezel, a long-time resident in Micronesia and head of the Micronesian

Seminar, presents some poignant insights into the culture and history of the islands.

Micronesia: Winds of Change (Government of the Trust Territory of the Pacific Islands, 1980), edited by Francis X Hezel SJ & M L Berg, is a colourful history taken from the accounts of early explorers, missionaries and others involved in Micronesia between 1521 and 1951. It has terrific old etchings and photos.

Lee Boo of Belau (University of Hawaii Press, Honolulu, 1987, hardcover) by Daniel J Peacock, covers the events surrounding Captain Wilson's voyage to Palau in 1783, his return to Britain with the young Prince Lee Boo of Palau, and Lee Boo's adventures in London before succumbing to smallpox in 1784.

Nan'yo: The Rise & Fall of the Japanese in Micronesia, 1885-1945 (University of Hawaii Press, Honolulu, 1988, hardcover) by Mark R Peattie, is one of the best books about the Japanese colonial empire in Micronesia.

Politics

Micronesia: A Trust Betrayed (Carnegie Endowment for International Peace, New York, 1975) by Donald McHenry, is an insightful history of the Trust Territory and the events leading up to the Compacts of Free Association.

Micronesia at the Crossroads (University of Hawaii Press, Honolulu, 1974, paperback) by Carl Heine, is an appraisal of Micronesia's political dilemma in its relationship with the US government. This is one of the few books on the situation from the viewpoint of a Micronesian.

The American Touch in Micronesia (W W Norton & Co, New York, 1977) by David Nevin, looks at fumbling American colonialism and the effects of power, money and corruption in Micronesia.

Culture

There are a good number of scholarly anthropological works about Micronesia, many written by individuals who have lived on remote islands and studied a single group of people in depth. The following books are the ones geared more to the general reader.

An Introduction to the Peoples & Cultures of Micronesia (Addison-Wesley Publishing Co, Redding, Massachusetts, 1972) by G Alkire, is a comprehensive study resulting from Alkire's 3½ years of field work in the islands. Alkire is an authority on Micronesian societies and this book is a sort of bible of Micronesian cultural anthropology.

Prehistoric Architecture in Micronesia (University of Texas Press, Austin, 1988, hardcover) by William N Morgan, is a study of the unique traditional architecture found on Kosrae, Pohnpei, Yap, Palau and the Marianas, including the stone cities of Lelu and Nan Madol.

Man This Reef (Micronitor News & Printing Co, Majuro, 1983) by Gerald Knight, is a translated collection of tales and legends as told by an elderly Marshallese storyteller. Knight is the former curator of the Alele Museum in Majuro.

Book of Luelen (University of Hawaii Press, Honolulu, 1977) is an accounting of Pohnpei's history and traditions by an elderly Pohnpeian man who wanted Pohnpei's stories to remain alive. It was translated and edited by John L Fischer, Saul H Riesenberg and Marjorie G Whiting.

Islands Islands: A Special Good (Caulderwood-McCandless Publishing, Newport Beach, California, 1986, paperback) by Bernadette V Wehrly, is a collection of poems, songs, stories and legends from the FSM, with a separate section by poet Petrus Martin of the Mortlock Islands.

Diving & Marine Life

The *Diver's Guide to Guam & Micronesia* (Guam Publications, Agana, 1989, paperback)by Guam journalist Tim Rock, describes in detail 47 dive and snorkelling locations in Guam; 22 in Palau; 15 in Chuuk; and a half dozen dives each in Yap, Saipan and Rota. This book is a must for serious divers. It can be ordered from Marine Images, Box 24666, GMF, Guam 96921 for $14, postage included.

Ghost Fleet of the Truk Lagoon (Pictorial Histories Publishing Co, Missoula, Montana) by William H Stewart, is an account of the American attack on the Japanese naval base in Chuuk Lagoon during WW II. Stewart includes maps and photographs showing how and where the more than 60 ships were sunk.

Micronesian Reef Fishes (Coral Graphics, Guam, 1989, hardcover or paperback), by Robert F Myers, is a comprehensive, 452-page book with 975 colour photos. It identifies more than 1250 of the most common reef fishes found in Micronesian waters, as well as 150 pelagic fish.

General

A Reporter in Micronesia, (W W Norton & Co, New York 1966) by E J Kahn,is a very readable log of Kahn's travels around the islands. His journeys were mostly by field ship, as Micronesia then had no jet traffic, no tourist hotels and very few visitors.

Micronesia: The Breadfruit Revolution, (East-West Center Press, Honolulu, 1971, hardcover), by Byron Baker, features black-and-white photographs by Robert Wenkam offering glimpses of Micronesian life two decades past.

Micronesia: Island Wilderness by Kenneth Brower, also features photography by Robert Wenkam. This is a handsome coffee-table book with some stunning colour plates.

Micronesia: The Land, the People & the Sea (Mobil Oil, Micronesia, 1981) by Kenneth Brower, covers the relationship between the Micronesians and the sea. There are good sections on navigation, canoes and ruins.

Kosrae: The Sleeping Lady Awakens (Kosrae Tourist Division, Kosrae, 1989, paperback) by Harvey Gordon Segal, is an insightful and comprehensive book on the human and natural history of Kosrae. It also covers sights and general information of interest to visitors.

A Guide to Pohnpei – An Island Argosy (Rainy Day Press, Box 574, Pohnpei 96941; 1987, paperback) by Gene Ashby, covers

Pohnpei's history, government, culture, flora, fauna and island sights.

Micronesian Customs & Beliefs and *Never &Always: Micronesian Legends, Fables & Folklore* (Rainy Day Press, 1989, paperback) compiled by Gene Ashby, are collections of legends and stories written by the students at the Community College of Micronesia.

This Living Reef (Quadrangle/The New York Times Co, New York, 1974, hardcover) by environmentalist Douglas Faulkner, is a beautiful book, heavy on colour photographs of coral, fish and underwater life.

Eyes of Fire: The Last Voyage of the Rainbow Warrior (Lindon Publishing, Auckland, New Zealand, 1987) by David Robie gives the account of the *Rainbow Warrior*'s 1985 evacuation of the Rongelapese from their radioactivity-contaminated atoll in the Marshall Islands. This was the last voyage the Greenpeace ship made before being blown up in New Zealand by French agents.

MEDIA
Newspapers

Micronesia's only daily newspaper is Guam's *Pacific Daily News* (Box DN, Agana, Guam 96910), which is flown to capital towns all around Micronesia. PDN, as the paper is commonly called, is a member of the Gannett group of newspapers and provides a good mix of regional and international news.

Also in Guam is the *Guam Tribune* (Tribune Box EG, Agana, Guam 96911), which comes out four times a week. The Marshalls has a weekly newspaper, the *Marshall Islands Journal* (Box 14, Majuro, Marshall Islands 96960). In the Northern Marianas the *Saipan Tribune* (Caller Box AAA-34, Saipan, MP 96950) and the *Marianas Variety* (Box 231, Saipan, MP 96950) come out a couple of times a week.

If you're contemplating an extended stay in any of these places, sending for copies of the newspaper in advance will help you get a feel for island happenings and politics.

Magazines

Guam & Micronesia Glimpses (Box 8066, Tamuning, Guam 96931) is a full-colour magazine with features and photographs emphasising destinations, historical events, community projects and the arts throughout Micronesia. A one-year subscription (six issues) costs $12 to the USA, $16 to Canada and $28 to other countries.

Hafa (130 E Marine Drive, Suite 210, Agana, Guam 96910) is a monthly general interest magazine that focuses on Guam's people and places and on Chamorro interests.

Guam Business News (Box 3191, Agana, Guam 96910) is a substantial monthly magazine geared for the business community in Guam and the Northern Marianas.

Air Micronesia's glossy inflight magazine, titled *Continental's Islands*, is published quarterly. It usually has a couple of feature articles in English, but most of the magazine is in Japanese.

Pacific Magazine (Box 25488, Honolulu, Hawaii 96825) and *Pacific Islands Monthly* (GPO Box 1167, Suva, Fiji) cover the entire Pacific region with an emphasis on politics, business and development. Of the two, *Pacific Magazine* has the most coverage of Micronesia.

Newsletters

Charles Scheiner researches and writes *Belau Update* (Box 1182, White Plains, New York 10602), a newsletter detailing the latest on Palau's struggle for self-government. It's mailed out two to three times a year to peace activists worldwide. There's no set subscription rate, but the project is supported by donations.

The Micronesia Institute (☎ 202-842-1140), 1275 K St NW, Suite 360, Washington DC 20005, was founded to provide an independent link between Micronesian countries and funding resources in the USA. The institute helps formulate educational, cultural, health, social and small business development programmes, with the primary focus on self-help and self-sustaining projects. It periodically prints a newsletter about its activities in the islands.

Radio & TV

All the islands, with the exception of Kosrae and Chuuk, have at least one TV station. Guam has three local TV stations and the standard US cable connections including HBO, live news from the US mainland and the Disney and Playboy stations. Saipan and Rota also have an extensive selection of channels on cable TV.

Outside Guam and the Northern Marianas, TV stations are more temperamental. Sometimes they're on, sometimes they're off, sometimes they're just down for long periods of time. When they're running they usually show videotaped US programmes that are several days or weeks old, complete with commercials from Honolulu or Los Angeles.

All the main district centres have radio stations, usually with both local and American music.

FILM & PHOTOGRAPHY

The high temperatures in the tropics, coupled with high humidity, greatly accelerate the deterioration of film. The sooner you have exposed film developed, the better the results. Sending off your film in pre-paid mailers is a good way to avoid carting it around. Print film and some slide films can be professionally processed on Pohnpei and Guam.

Don't leave your camera in direct sunshine any longer than necessary. A locked car can heat up like an oven in just a few minutes.

Another problem that often arises is moisture condensing on film and lenses that have been taken from air-con rooms into the warm, moist outside air. One way to avoid this is to keep your camera in an area of the room less affected by the air-con, such as a closet or the bathroom. Or try keeping it wrapped inside a camera case or carry-bag for an hour or so after leaving a place with air-con.

Sand and water are intense reflectors and in bright light they'll often leave foreground subjects shadowy. You can try compensating by adjusting your f-stop or attaching a polarising filter, or both, but the most effective technique is to take photos in the gentler light of early morning and late afternoon.

Print film is available on the main islands, though it takes a bit more searching to find slide film. Film is a bit more expensive in Micronesia than in the USA and you should check the expiry dates.

HEALTH

In general, Micronesia is a healthy place to visit. Still, infections, sunburn, diarrhoea and intestinal parasites all warrant precautions.

If you're new to the heat and humidity you may find yourself easily fatigued and more susceptible to minor ailments. Acclimatise yourself by slowing down your pace. The climate is one of the reasons Micronesia is so laid-back, so learn to go with the flow.

Pre-Departure Preparations

Health Insurance A travel insurance policy to cover theft, loss and medical problems may be a wise idea. There are a wide variety of policies and your travel agent will have recommendations. Check the small print. For instance, some policies specifically exclude 'dangerous activities' which can even include scuba diving. Check if the policy covers an emergency flight home. If you have to stretch out you will need two seats and somebody has to pay for them!

Medical Kit A small, straightforward medical kit is a wise thing to carry. A possible kit list includes:

• Aspirin or Panadol – for pain or fever.
• Antihistamine (such as Benadryl) – useful as a decongestant for colds, allergies, to ease the itch from insect bites or stings or to help prevent motion sickness.
• Antibiotics – useful if you're travelling well off the beaten track, but they must be prescribed and you should carry the prescription with you.
• Kaolin preparation (Pepto-Bismol), Imodium or Lomotil – for stomach upsets.

- Rehydration mixture – for treatment of severe diarrhoea, this is particularly important if travelling with children.
- Antiseptic, mercurochrome and antibiotic powder or similar 'dry' spray – for cuts and grazes.
- Calamine lotion – to ease irritation from bites or stings.
- Bandages and Band-aids – for minor injuries.
- Scissors, tweezers and a thermometer (note that mercury thermometers are prohibited by airlines).
- Insect repellent, sunscreen, suntan lotion, chap stick and water purification tablets.

Health Preparations Make sure you're healthy before you start travelling. If you're intending to be in Micronesia a long time make sure your teeth are OK; many outer islands have no dentists and outside of Saipan and Guam dental care varies.

If you wear glasses take a spare pair and your prescription. If you require a particular medication take an adequate supply, as it may not be available on many islands. Take the prescription, with the generic rather than the brand name, as it will make getting replacements easier. It's a wise idea to have the prescription with you to show you legally use the medication – it's surprising how often over-the-counter drugs from one place are illegal without a prescription or even banned in another.

Immunisations Vaccinations provide protection against diseases you might meet along the way. The only immunisations required to enter Micronesia are for cholera and yellow fever, but that's only if you're coming from an infected area. Although not required, tetanus shots are recommended and if you're going to the Marshalls or Chuuk a typhoid shot is a good idea.

Tetanus boosters are necessary every 10 years. Typhoid protection lasts for three years. With typhoid shots, you may get some side effects such as pain at the injection site, fever, headache and a general unwell feeling. All vaccinations should be recorded on an International Health Certificate, which is available from your physician or government health department.

Basic Rules
Care in what you eat and drink is the most important health rule; stomach upsets are the most likely travel health problem but the majority of these upsets will be relatively minor. Don't become paranoid, as trying the local food is part of the experience of travel after all.

Food Food in Micronesia is usually sanitarily prepared and requires no unusual precautions. Just the same, places that look clean and well run are a safer bet than those that look run down. In general, restaurants busy with customers will be fine, while empty restaurants are more questionable.

Make sure your diet is well balanced and you get enough protein. Rice and fish are plentiful in Micronesia, so this shouldn't be much of a problem. Fruit is a good source of vitamins.

Poisonous Fish Ciguatera fish poisoning is a problem throughout the Pacific and is most common in areas, such as the Marshalls, where coral reefs are well developed. (The Majuro hospital averages six cases a month.)

More than 300 species of fish can be toxic when eaten. Sometimes the same species can be safe in some areas and poisonous in others, so get local advice before eating your catch. Cooking the fish doesn't destroy the toxin.

Reef fish served in restaurants pose little risk as restaurateurs know which species to avoid; and tuna, which is the most common fish served in Micronesia, is an unaffected deep-water fish.

The symptoms, if you do eat the wrong fish, can include nausea, stomach cramps, diarrhoea, paralysis, tingling and numbness of the face, fingers and toes, and a reversal of temperature feelings so that hot things feel cold and vice versa. Extreme cases can result in unconsciousness and even death. Vomit

until your stomach is empty and get immediate medical help.

Water Tap water is not always safe to drink. There are a lot of parasites in Micronesia, including giardia and amoeba, and unclean water is a great way to discover them.

Often the problem derives not so much from impure water as from poor water distribution. In some places ageing sewer and water pipes are laid alongside each other, and when the water is turned off for more than a few hours for rationing purposes, cross-seepage can occur.

When in doubt stick with readily available canned beverages or bottled water. Tea or coffee should also be OK, since the water should have been boiled.

To avoid dehydration, you should make a conscious effort to drink an ample supply of liquids to replace the body fluids you quickly lose in the heat and humidity of the day. Always carry a water bottle with you on long trips. Drinking coconuts, which are readily available most places, are not only a good source of uncontaminated water but they're also an excellent rehydration drink, full of vitamins and minerals.

Water Purification The simplest way of purifying water is to boil it thoroughly. Technically this means boiling for 10 minutes, something which happens very rarely!

Simple filtering will not remove all dangerous organisms, so if you cannot boil water it should be treated chemically. Chlorine tablets (Puritabs, Steritabs or other brand names) will kill many but not all pathogens. Iodine is very effective in purifying water and is available in tablet form (such as Potable Aqua), but follow the directions carefully and remember that too much iodine can be harmful.

If you can't find tablets, tincture of iodine (2%) can be used. Two drops of tincture of iodine per quart or litre of clear water is the recommended dosage; the treated water should be left to stand for 30 minutes before drinking. Flavoured powder will disguise the taste of treated water and is a good idea if you are travelling with children.

Everyday Health A normal body temperature is 98.6°F or 37°C; more than 2°C higher is a 'high' fever. A normal adult pulse rate is 60 to 80 per minute (children 80 to 100, babies 100 to 140). As a general rule the pulse increases about 20 beats per minute for each °C rise in fever.

Respiration (breathing) rate is also an indicator of illness. Count the number of breaths per minute: between 12 and 20 is normal for adults and older children (up to 30 for younger children, 40 for babies). People with a high fever or serious respiratory illness (like pneumonia) breathe quickly than normal. More than 40 shallow breaths a minute usually means pneumonia.

The common cold is alive and well in tropical Micronesia and many travellers seem to get persistent coughs. Probably the most effective way to avoid susceptibility is to be in prime condition before you travel. Over-zealous air-conditioning can be a particular problem. In a restaurant you may have to position yourself in a corner away from the blast; and at night you should adjust the air-con vent so it's not aimed directly at your bed and keep a blanket within reach.

Many health problems can be avoided by taking care of yourself. Clean your teeth with purified water rather than straight from the tap. Keep out of the sun when it's hot. Seek local advice: if you're told the water is unsafe due to jellyfish or crocodiles, don't go in. In situations where there is no information, discretion is the better part of valour.

Medical Problems & Treatment

Sunburn Sunburn is a definite possibility in this region because the islands are so close to the equator, where fewer of the sun's rays are blocked by the atmosphere. Don't be fooled by what appears to be a hazy overcast day, as the rays still get through.

Fair-skinned people can get first and second degree burns in the hot Micronesian sun and wearing a hat for added protection is a good idea. The most severe sun is between 10 am and 2 pm.

Sunscreen with a SPF (sun protection factor) of 10 to 15 is recommended if you're not already tanned and if you're going into the water, use one that's water-resistant. You may want to wear a T-shirt (or even light cotton pants) while snorkelling, especially if you plan to be out in the water for a long time. You'll not only be protecting against sunburn but potential skin cancer and premature ageing of the skin. Calamine lotion is good for mild sunburn.

Prickly Heat Prickly heat is an itchy rash caused by excessive perspiration trapped under the skin. It usually strikes people who have just arrived in a hot climate and whose pores have not yet opened sufficiently to cope with greater sweating. Keeping cool by bathing often or even resorting to air-con may help until you acclimatise.

Heat Exhaustion Dehydration or salt deficiency can cause heat exhaustion. Take time to acclimatise to high temperatures and make sure you get sufficient liquids. Salt deficiency is characterised by fatigue, lethargy, headaches, giddiness and muscle cramps and in this case salt tablets may help. Vomiting or diarrhoea can deplete your liquid and salt levels.

Heat Stroke This serious, sometimes fatal, condition can occur if the body's heat-regulating mechanism breaks down and the body temperature rises to dangerous levels. Long, continuous periods of exposure to high temperatures can leave you vulnerable to heat stroke. You should avoid excessive alcohol or strenuous activity when you first arrive in a hot climate.

The symptoms are feeling unwell, not sweating very much or at all and a high body temperature (39°C to 41°C). Where sweating has ceased the skin becomes flushed and red. Severe, throbbing headaches and lack of coordination will also occur, and the sufferer may be confused or aggressive. Eventually the victim will become delirious or convulse. Hospitalisation is essential, but meanwhile get patients out of the sun, remove their clothing, cover them with a wet sheet or towel and then fan continually.

Fungal Infections The same climate that produces lush tropical forests also promotes a prolific growth of skin fungi and bacteria. Hot weather fungal infections are most likely to occur on the scalp, between the toes or fingers (athlete's foot) or in the groin (jock itch or crotch rot).

Keeping your skin cool and allowing air to circulate is essential. Choose cotton clothing rather than synthetics and sandals over shoes.

If you do get an infection, wash the infected area daily with a disinfectant or medicated soap and water, and rinse and dry well. Apply an antifungal powder like the widely available Tinaderm. Try to expose the infected area to air or sunlight as much as possible and wash all towels and underwear in hot water as well as changing them often.

Motion Sickness Eating lightly before and during a trip will reduce the chances of motion sickness. If you are prone to motion sickness try to find a place that minimises disturbance – near the wing on an aircraft or close to midships on boats. Fresh air usually helps; reading or cigarette smoke doesn't. Commercial antimotion-sickness preparations, which can cause drowsiness, have to be taken before the trip commences; when you're feeling sick it's too late. Ginger is a natural preventative and is available in capsule form.

Diseases of Insanitation

Diarrhoea A change of water, food or climate can all cause the runs; diarrhoea caused by contaminated food or water is more serious. Despite all your precautions you may still have a bout of mild travellers' diarrhoea but a few rushed toilet trips with no other symptoms is not indicative of a serious problem.

Dehydration is the main danger with any diarrhoea, particularly for children, so fluid replenishment is the number one treatment. Weak black tea, bottled water or coconut liquid are all good. With severe diarrhoea a rehydrating solution is necessary to replace minerals and salts. You should stick to a bland diet as you recover.

Lomotil or Imodium can be used to bring relief from the symptoms, although they do not actually cure the problem. Only use these drugs if absolutely necessary – eg, if you *must* travel. For children Imodium is preferable, but do not use these drugs if the patient has a high fever or is severely dehydrated.

Giardia This intestinal parasite is present in contaminated water. The symptoms are stomach cramps, nausea, a bloated stomach, watery, foul-smelling diarrhoea and frequent gas. The disease can appear several weeks after you have been exposed to the parasite. The symptoms may disappear for a few days and then return; this can go on for several weeks. Metronidazole known as Flagyl is the recommended drug, but it should only be taken under medical supervision. Antibiotics are of no use.

Dysentery This serious illness is caused by contaminated food or water and is characterised by severe diarrhoea, often with blood or mucus in the stool. There are two kinds of dysentery. Bacillary dysentery is characterised by a high fever and rapid development; headache, vomiting and stomach pains are also symptoms. It generally does not last longer than a week, but it is highly contagious.

Amoebic dysentery is more gradual in developing, has no fever or vomiting but is a more serious illness. It is not a self-limiting disease: it will persist until treated and can recur and cause long term damage.

A stool test is necessary to diagnose which kind of dysentery you have, so you should seek medical help urgently. In case of an emergency, note that tetracycline is the prescribed treatment for bacillary dysentery, metronidazole for amoebic dysentery.

Cholera Cholera is spread through poor sanitation conditions. The minimum precautions where cholera is suspected include drinking only bottled liquids and not eating raw fish. Also avoid swimming in polluted lagoons, especially near populated areas.

Cholera vaccination is not very effective. However, outbreaks of cholera are generally widely reported, so you can avoid problem areas. The disease is characterised by a sudden onset of acute diarrhoea with 'rice water' stools, vomiting, muscular cramps, and extreme weakness. Seek immediate medical help and treat for dehydration, which can be extreme.

In Micronesia, only Chuuk has had sporadic outbreaks of cholera in the recent past. In the last epidemic, in 1982 to '83, there were 2254 reported cases and 17 deaths. After years of neglecting the region's public utilities, the negative publicity from this last epidemic finally spurred the US to install extensive public water and sanitation systems on Chuuk's main islands of Moen and Dublon.

During that epidemic, all passengers flying from Chuuk to any other FSM state needed proof they had been treated in Chuuk with tetracycline for three days prior to departure.

In February 1984 the last two cases of cholera in Chuuk were diagnosed and the World Health Organisation has since declared Chuuk cholera free.

Cuts, Bites & Stings

Cuts & Scratches Skin punctures can easily become infected in hot climates and may be difficult to heal. Treat cuts with an antiseptic solution or mercurochrome. Where possible avoid bandages and Band-aids, which can keep wounds wet.

Insect Bites & Stings Other than mosquitoes and sand gnats, there are very few pesky insects in Micronesia that bite. Calamine lotion will give relief for those that do.

There is no malaria at all in Micronesia.

Lice All lice cause itching and discomfort. They make themselves at home in your hair (head lice), your clothing (body lice) or in your pubic hair (crabs). You catch lice through direct contact with infected people or by sharing combs, clothing and the like. Powder or shampoo treatment will kill the lice and infected clothing should then be washed in very hot water.

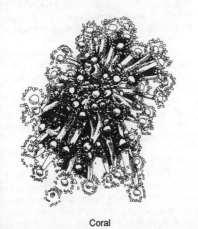

Coral

Coral Cuts Coral cuts are notoriously slow to heal, as the coral injects a weak venom into the wound.

Most coral cuts occur when swimmers are pushed onto the coral by rough waves and surges. It's a good idea to wear diving gloves when snorkelling over shallow reefs and suitable footwear when walking on coral. Clean any cut thoroughly.

Learn to identify fire coral, which is usually in the form of vertical sheets of brown coral rimmed in a light green color. Touching the rim can give you a stabbing pain as severe as a jellyfish sting.

Fish Stings Incidences with venomous sea creatures in Micronesian waters are pretty rare. You should, however, learn to recognise such venomous varieties as the turkey fish, lionfish, scorpion fish and stonefish. The latter two are sometimes seen in quite shallow water and all can inject venom through their dorsal spines.

The sting causes a sharp burning pain, followed by numbness around the area, nausea and headaches. Immediately stick the affected area in water as hot as bearable (be sure not to unintentionally scald the area due to numbness) and go for medical treatment.

Cone Shells Cone shells should be left alone unless you're sure they're empty. There is no safe way of picking up a live cone shell, as the animal inside has a long stinging tail that can dart out and reach anyplace on its shell to deliver a puncture wound. Stings can result in numbness at the wound site, breathing distress and sight and speech disturbances. A few species, such as the textile cone, have a venom so toxic that the sting could prove fatal. If you should get stung by such a shell, seek immediate medical attention.

Sea Urchins & Starfish Sea urchins and crown of thorns starfish have long spines that can puncture the skin and break off, causing burning and possible numbness. You can try to remove the spines with tweezers or by soaking the area in warm water and epsom

Cone Shell

salts, though more serious cases may require surgical removal.

Jellyfish Take a peek into the water before you plunge in, to make sure it's not jellyfish territory. These gelatinous creatures with stinging tentacles are fairly common around Guam, for example, where even the dangerous sea wasps and Portuguese man-of-war have occasionally been sighted.

The Portuguese man-of-war is not technically a jellyfish but is a colonial hydrozoan, or a colony of coelenterates, rather than a solitary coelenterate like the true jellyfish.

The sting of a jellyfish varies from mild to severe, depending on the variety. A man-of-war sting is very painful, similar to a bad bee sting except that you're likely to get stung more than once from clusters of long tentacles. Even touching a man-of-war a few hours after it's washed up on shore can result in a burning sting.

You can at least partly neutralise the venom of a sting by dousing the skin with vinegar, or even urine. Calamine lotion, antihistamines and analgesics may reduce the reaction and relieve the pain. For serious stings, which are usually followed by swelling, bleeding, stomach spasms, difficulty in breathing, chest pains or the like, seek immediate medical attention.

Women's Health
Poor diet, lowered resistance due to the use of antibiotics and even contraceptive pills can lead to vaginal infections when travelling in hot climates. Keeping the genital area clean, and wearing skirts or loose-fitting trousers and cotton underwear will help to prevent infections.

Yeast infections, characterised by a rash, itch and discharge, can be treated with a vinegar or even lemon-juice douche or with yoghurt. Nystatin suppositories are the usual medical prescription.

Medical Care
Each main population centre in Micronesia has a hospital or clinic and treatment is usually at reasonable rates. Most of the clinics have been built in the last 10 years with American aid, and are quite modern and competently staffed. Still, the best medical treatment is generally found on Guam and Saipan, though costs are high there, on par with the rest of the USA.

Many outer islands have no health services available so if you're going to someplace remote, it's a good idea to take along a first aid kit with some of the more common medical supplies.

WOMEN TRAVELLERS
Although most places in Micronesia shouldn't be a hassle, women travelling alone may occasionally get some unwanted attention.

Duly earned or not, Chuuk seems to have the worst reputation. Although it's largely their demeanor, some young Chuukese males may seem to have surly macho stares. Women travelling alone are particularly likely to hear a few come-ons and under-the-breath innuendos. Foreign women aren't exactly singled out but neither are they left out. Chuukese women have their own defence, which largely consists of maintaining an aloofness and pretending they don't hear. Although this little macho game doesn't make a very favourable impression, women are not necessarily any more likely to be in physical danger here than elsewhere.

DANGERS & ANNOYANCES
Marine Dangers
Most underwater experiences in Micronesia are safe, and while you shouldn't miss out for fear of monsters lurking in the depths, it's important to be aware of potential dangers.

There are a few venomous varieties of fish in Micronesian waters, including scorpion fish and stonefish which inhabit shallow waters and can inject venom through their dorsal spines. Refer to Cuts, Bites & Stings in the Health section earlier for more details on these and other marine dangers.

Sharks The probability of shark attacks on humans has been greatly exaggerated. Still, they *are* out there in the deeper waters and it doesn't hurt to have a healthy respect for them.

The few attacks that do occur in Micronesia are usually during spearfishing. When the shark tries to chomp down on a bloody, just-speared fish, the spearer sometimes gets in the way. Still, even these incidents are rare. And just for the record, the Yap Institute of Natural Science notes that people eat sharks 600,000 times more often than sharks eat people!

Sharks are attracted by shiny things and by anything bright red or yellow, which might influence your choice of swimsuit colour. Those popular day-glo orange life jackets are said to be known as 'yummy orange' in shark circles.

Strong Currents & Riptides
Be careful of water funnelling off the reefs into channels when the tide's going out as it can have a very strong pull.

You can quickly use up all your energy and lose ground if you try to fight a strong current. It's easier to swim across a current than against it. If you do find yourself being carried out through a reef passage, once outside the reef you should be able to move down along the reef and cross back over it to a calmer area.

Property
In Micronesia, most things are shared and individual property in the Western sense is a rather foreign concept. If you don't want visitors, particularly when you're out, be careful to leave your doors locked. The more remote the place you're staying, the more likely you'll have the village kids just walking in.

Don't tempt anyone. If you have anything that looks appealing, lock it up in your bags. The old adage 'out of sight, out of mind' holds true in Micronesia. Two-way zippers on soft luggage and backpacks allow for use of a small lock, which might be enough to deter the overly curious.

The simplest way to feel at ease is not to bring anything you don't mind parting with. Keep your passport and air tickets on you and if you have a camera you might want to bring a day pack to carry it around with you.

Privacy
The concept of privacy is also a different affair in Micronesia compared to most Western societies. You can often tell which house in a village has a VCR by the crowds standing outside looking in the windows; it's an acceptable way to watch a movie. If you stay with a local family and are given your own room it won't be uncommon for groups of the extended family to come by and join you for impromptu visits. You should see this not as an intrusion, but as an indication that you're being honoured and accepted as part of the family.

Payday Weekends
Throughout most of Micronesia every other Friday is payday. From payday until Sunday a number of Micronesian males go on a drinking binge and, for the most part, they don't make happy-go-lucky drunks. Many islanders have a low tolerance for alcohol and it often acts as a key that unleashes suppressed feelings. Domestic violence, suicide and the desire to settle up pent-up accounts all tend to come to a head on this weekend. A few places have responded by enacting prohibition, though most of Micronesia just sits it all out. The problem tends to be worse in district centres.

ACTIVITIES
Diving & Snorkelling
What Micronesia lacks in land, it makes up for in water. Some of the region's most spectacular scenery is underwater and the traveller who never looks below the surface is missing out on some incredible sights.

Micronesia's water temperature is about 80°F (27°C). Wet suits are not required for warmth, although some divers wear them as protection against coral cuts.

Divers the world over know about Chuuk's underwater wreck museum and Palau's great drop-offs. These are, without doubt, the finest diving spots in Micronesia and among the very best locales in the world.

There are many other superb, though less famous, diving opportunities in Micronesia, including unspoiled reefs, forests of towering sea fans, coral gardens, underwater caves and the scattered wrecks of whaleboats and WW II ships and planes.

There are dive shops in Majuro, Kosrae, Pohnpei, Chuuk, Yap, Palau, Guam, Saipan, Rota and Tinian. Details on diving facilities are given in each island section.

It's recommended that you bring your own buoyancy compensator and other personalised equipment with you. A dive computer can be very useful, as can some advance training in decompression diving, especially if you plan to dive Chuuk's wrecks.

If you've never been scuba diving before, here's your chance to learn. Some dive shops offer non-divers an introductory dive down to about 30 feet, which costs anywhere from $45 to $95. You can also take an intensive three or four-day course to become fully certified at several places in Micronesia.

On the other hand you could just pack a mask and snorkel and enjoy it all for free. It's nice to have your own flippers too, though they are a bit heavier to carry around. If you really want to travel light, snorkelling gear can be rented from many places for $5 to $10 a day.

For information on diving holiday packages to various parts of Micronesia, refer to the Tours section in the Getting There & Away chapter.

HIGHLIGHTS
Marine Life
Micronesia has an incredible abundance and variety of fish in every imaginable, and some quite unimaginable, colour and shape. There are hundreds of types of hard and soft corals, anemones, colourful sponges and many varieties of shellfish, including giant tridacna clams.

Sea cucumbers, particularly common in the Marianas, dot the bottom of shallow waters near shore. Their entrails squish underfoot if you happen to step on one, but they're harmless. One variety of these creatures are the beche-de-mer that traders were after in the 1800s. When boiled, dried and smoked they are considered delicacies and aphrodisiacs in China and South-East Asia.

Micronesia has hawksbill and other sea turtles, sperm whales, beaked whales and porpoises. Palau has the rare dugong, or sea

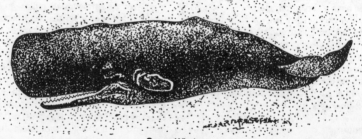

Sperm Whale

cow, which is an herbivorous, seal-like mammal, about nine feet in length.

Two quality colour posters depicting 95 of the most commonly eaten fish found in the FSM, along with the names of the fish in the four main FSM languages and English, can be ordered for $12 (including postage) from Micronesian Islands Conservation, Box 159, Kolonia, Pohnpei, FSM 96941. This non-profit organisation also sells a detailed map of the islands of Micronesia, including locations of bird and sea turtle nesting areas, for the same price.

ACCOMMODATION

Camping

Throughout Micronesia most of the land, including the beaches, is privately owned and uninvited campers are about as welcome as they would be if they walked into your backyard at home and started pitching a tent. So if you want to camp, get permission from the landowners first.

In any case, camping is very uncommon in most places, especially throughout the FSM, and you're likely to collect a crowd of curious onlookers.

Some of the best, and locally accepted, camping in Micronesia is on the Rock Islands, Angaur and Peleliu in Palau; and on Tinian and Rota in the Northern Marianas. For more details refer to those sections.

If you decide it's worth your while to carry camping gear, you won't need a sleeping bag but you'll sleep more comfortably with some sort of covering that is gnat and mosquito-proof.

Hotels

All islands where Air Micronesia lands have Western-style hotels. In the overall picture Micronesian hotels tend to be a bit pricey for what you get and there aren't a lot of real cheapies.

Depending on the island, hotel rates usually start between $20 and $40, though on Rota you'll have to plunk down at least $50. What you get for the lowest rates varies quite a bit from island to island. A few are rock-bottom places where the mattresses sag, the walls are dirty and the bathroom is down the hall, though many others are clean and comfortable, with private bathrooms, air-con and a friendly atmosphere. Rooms which cost $25 in Palau are pleasant and good value, for instance, while $35 rooms in Majuro are quite basic and not very enticing.

Hotels with Micronesian influences are far too few in number, though there are some wonderful exceptions. The new Pathways Hotel in Yap has traditionally designed thatched cottages that could well be used as a model to show other hoteliers what kind of accommodation visitors are really hoping to find. In Pohnpei, the Village Hotel and the Hotel Pohnpei are two others which attempt to balance traditional aesthetics with modern conveniences.

Outside the district centres, you can experience Micronesian hospitality in some nice island-style accommodations for $7 to $20 a night. These include the men's house in the traditional village of Bechiyal on Yap, family guest houses on the Palauan islands of Angaur and Peleliu, beach huts on Pohnpei's lagoon islands and thatched cottages on a couple of the outer islands of the Marshalls.

All the main islands, except Kosrae, have modern, comfortable hotels that are at least a bit upscale, with rates in the $60 to $90 range.

Guam, Saipan and Palau all have luxurious beachside resort hotels, though rates are $100-plus. A couple of these are tastefully laid out while others resemble bustling inner-city highrises that process package tourists in one end and out the other.

Some hotels offer discounts to government employees, Peace Corps volunteers, the military and businesspeople. It never hurts to ask if a hotel has business or corporate rates. You can call yourself a travelling salesperson, researcher or whatever you fancy yourself to be and if you have a business card, all the better.

Outer Islands

Few of the outer islands have hotels or guest houses for visitors. It's generally best to make some sort of arrangement for accommodation in advance through the island's mayor or chief magistrate. Although you could try doing it by mail before you go, it's often less confusing to just radio ahead through the governor's office or tourist office in the district centre.

If you do just fly out to one of the islands or get off a boat somewhere, the local school principal might allow you to stay in the schoolhouse, especially if school's not in session. You could also approach the local mayor or chief or perhaps a Peace Corps volunteer.

Usually people are warm and friendly and will help you out. However, because islanders feel obligated to provide for visitors, foreigners can sometimes impose without realising it. Be careful not to take advantage of Micronesian hospitality. While islanders readily welcome each other into their homes, it's a long-established system founded on reciprocity and kinship obligations and the casual visitor should not expect the same rights.

If you stay with a family you should offer them something, but unless money is requested, giving coffee, rice or other gifts is probably a more appropriate way to pay for your stay.

FOOD

Considering the geographic spread, it is surprising how similar the food is throughout Micronesia.

Fish is plentiful, fresh and delicious. Grilled tuna is often one of the best and cheapest meals available, while another good choice is reef fish, which is usually grilled and served whole.

Main Dishes

Western foods like hamburgers, sandwiches, fried chicken and steak are found on most menus. Almost equally as common is Japanese food, such as sashimi, teriyaki and ramen. Breakfasts are typically Western style, with toast, coffee, eggs, bacon (or Spam!) and French toast.

Fish, shellfish, coconuts, breadfruit, taro, tapioca and bananas are Micronesian staples.

Traditional local dishes are not often served in restaurants however, although mangrove crab and fried breadfruit find their way onto a few menus.

Breadfruit is prepared much like potatoes – either boiled, fried, mashed, roasted or baked. Preserved (fermented) breadfruit, which was traditionally a provision food for long canoe journeys, is definitely an acquired taste. Taro root is baked or boiled, rather than smashed up into a Hawaiian-style poi.

Turkey tails are a really hot item, particularly in Chuuk and the Marshalls. You'll often see them amidst the hot dogs and reef fish on picnic barbecue grills.

Micronesians developed a taste for rice during the Japanese era, and it remains the single largest imported food. Canned fish and high-salt, high-fat canned meats are other popular imported foods, as are chocolate chip cookies and candy bars. In grocery stores, banana cake mix may be easier to find than bananas. When buying groceries, watch out for wormy food and check the expiry dates.

Dog is a popular food in Pohnpei, but you don't have to worry much about having it thrust upon you by surprise. It's regarded as a speciality food, served primarily at occasions such as funeral feasts.

Some of Micronesia's more exotic dishes include crocodile (Palau), fruit bat (Guam), sea turtle, mangrove crab and coconut crab.

There's more food variety in Guam than in the rest of Micronesia. On Guam it's easy to find spicy Chamorro food, good salad bars, Mexican food and Korean, Chinese, Thai and other Asian cuisines.

Fruit & Vegetables

If you've imagined a wild abundance of exotic tropical fruits, you'll probably be disappointed. You can buy bananas, papayas and coconuts in local markets and on a lucky day you might find citrus, passion fruit, soursop or mangoes. But despite year-round sun, many fruits in Micronesia are seasonal and unfortunately, fresh fruit is rarely served in restaurants. Families often grow just enough for their own use and feed the surplus to their pigs, so those sweet papayas you were hoping to see on the breakfast menu might well be going to the family porker instead.

Fresh vegetables, especially crisp salad types, are scarce, as they're not part of the typical Micronesian diet. Most vegetables are imported so the more remote the island, the scarcer they are. What you do find often looks ready for composting.

In Micronesia 'green salad' usually refers to a small clump of shredded cabbage and occasionally some cucumber slices, with a dribble of Thousand Island salad dressing.

DRINKS
Nonalcoholic Drinks
Tap water is safe in Guam and the Northern Marianas, but it's more risky elsewhere in Micronesia and it's a good idea to boil it when you're unsure, or avoid it altogether.

Bottled water is usually available in grocery stores throughout the islands. Soft drinks, coffee and tea are easy to get almost everywhere.

Although coconuts are plentiful, not many travellers carry a machete with them so they can whack one open any time they find one! If you buy a coconut from a fruit stall the vendor will open it for you. Otherwise, if you've got a coconut that's already husked, look for the three dots that resemble a face with two eyes and a mouth. It's easy to poke a hole through the 'mouth' with a pointed object to get to the juice inside.

Alcohol
Alcohol is available almost everywhere in Micronesia, the major exception being a few dry islands in Chuuk and the Marshalls. Budweiser is truly the king of beers in Micronesia, so whoever has the Bud concession must be making a killing!

Among island drinks, *tuba*, which is labouriously made from coconut sap, is the most common.

Then there's *yeast*, which is coconut water or fruit juice, mixed with sugar and bakers yeast. The fermenting takes place in the stomach and the high continues until the fermenting stops – up to 24 hours later. It's a cheap way to get drunk, though apparently not always a pleasant one.

OTHER HIGHS
Sakau, extracted from the roots of a pepper plant, is a mild narcotic that can give the drinker a pretty good buzz. For the most part the mind stays clear and the body numbs up. These days in Micronesia it's only available in Pohnpei where sakau bars still outnumber alcohol bars two to one.

Betel nut is readily available in Yap and Palau and anywhere else there are Yapese and Palauans. Unlike places in Asia where it's chewed dry and brown, Micronesians like it green, mixed with a little lime and wrapped in a pepper leaf. It produces a very mild short-lived high.

There's still debate as to whether Peace Corps volunteers introduced marijuana to Micronesia or whether Micronesian students returning home from school in the States brought the first seeds. One way or the other its cultivation is now widespread in the islands. Attitudes and procurement procedures vary from place to place. For the most part people are reasonably tolerant, although in Guam things can get a little more heavy-handed, and the possession of marijuana is illegal everywhere.

THINGS TO BUY
Micronesia has less of a variety of handicrafts than you'd probably expect, although there's some fine basketwork and weaving to be found on many of the islands.

Yap has some of the most interesting traditional crafts, including hibiscus fibre skirts and other functional items still used by the Yapese. The Marshall Islands have stick charts and high-quality baskets; Palau has carved wooden storyboards; and Chuuk has carved love sticks and masks. The Northern Marianas and Guam are devoid of any real native handicrafts.

The best wood carvings in Micronesia are those of marine animals made by the Kapingamarangi islanders on Pohnpei.

Gourmet pepper and island-made coconut soaps and oils are other Pohnpeian specialties. The Marshalls, FSM and Palau sell their own colourful postage stamps which make fine, lightweight souvenirs.

Sea turtle shells make beautiful jewellery – too beautiful, in fact, for the welfare of the turtles. Although the islanders have taken turtles for subsistence purposes for centuries, a combination of driftnetting and worldwide demand for the ornamental shells has thrown sea turtles onto the endangered species list. Tortoise shell jewellery, as well as the whole shells, are prohibited entry into the USA, Canada, Australia and most other countries.

The importation of black coral is likewise banned in more than 100 countries. The purchase of other corals, which are often dynamited from their fragile reef ecosystem and sold in chunks or made into jewellery, should also give pause to the environmentally conscious.

Getting There & Away

AIR

For the vast majority of travellers, getting to Micronesia means flying. Air gateways to Micronesia include Honolulu, Sydney, Brisbane, Port Moresby, Manila, Seoul, Taipei, Bali, Fiji, Tuvalu, Kiribati and several cities in Japan. Travellers coming from elsewhere need to first find their way to one of these connections.

Micronesian-Based Airlines

The USA and Pacific addresses and phone numbers for the international airlines based in Micronesia are:

Continental Air Micronesia (Air Mike)
 Australia – 13th Floor, 83 Clarence St, Sydney, NSW (☎ 232-8222)
 Indonesia – Hotel Bali Beach, Sanur, Denpasar (☎ 87774)
 Japan – Suite 242, Kokusai Building, 3-1-1 Marunouchi, Chiyoda- ku, Tokyo (☎ 03-592-1631; toll free 0120-24-2414)
 Korea – The Westin Chosun Hotel, Room 206, 87 Sokong-Dong, Seoul (☎ 773-0100)

Micronesia – Box 8778, Tamuning, Guam 96911 (☎ 646-0220/1/2)
 Philippines – 6760 Ayala Ave, SGV Building, Makati, Metro Manila (☎ 818-8701)
 USA – 1001 Bishop St, Suite 110, Honolulu, Hawaii 96814
 Air Mike's toll-free number within Hawaii, the US mainland and Canada is ☎ 800-231-0856

Airline of the Marshall Islands (AMI)
 Micronesia – Box 959, Majuro, Marshall Islands 96960 (☎ 3373)
 USA – 1441 Kapiolani Blvd, Honolulu, Hawaii 96814 (☎ 949-5522)
 AMI's toll-free number from within the USA is ☎ 800-543-3898
 Fiji – Nadi (☎ 679-7252)

To/From the USA

Island Hopping Continental Air Micronesia (known throughout the islands as Air Mike) is the only airline that island hops between Honolulu and Guam. The route is: Honolulu, Johnston, Majuro, Kwajalein, Kosrae, Pohnpei, Chuuk, Guam.

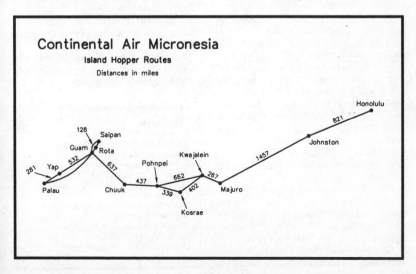

Continental Air Micronesia
Island Hopper Routes
Distances in miles

The island hopper flights leave Honolulu for Guam on Monday, Wednesday, Friday and Saturday mornings, crossing the International Date Line before arriving at Majuro, the first destination where civilians can disembark. You lose a day, arriving one day later than you leave.

The plane refuels on Johnston but no stopovers are permitted on this small, flat coral island which is shaped like an aircraft carrier. Nuclear testing was carried out on Johnston Island after WW II and it now serves as a disposal site for chemical munitions and remains a field command of the US defence nuclear agency.

Kwajalein is another military base and home to the airfield you use if you're going to Ebeye Island. If you want to visit Ebeye you need to get military clearance from Majuro first.

The one-way island hopper fare allowing all stopovers between Honolulu and Guam costs $630. Air Mike's family plan allows an accompanying spouse to pay $476.

The same ticket between Los Angeles or San Francisco and Guam costs $773. Spouses can travel for $580. Stopovers are allowed in Honolulu and it's a one-year open ticket.

It costs $30 more to have Rota and Saipan added on to these tickets.

If you're going the full distance you'll definitely save money by buying the island hopper as opposed to point-to-point tickets. For example, Honolulu to Majuro costs $555, just $75 less than the whole island hopper route to Guam. Majuro to Kosrae flights cost $272 and Kosrae to Pohnpei is $130. The only discount fares on these one-way tickets are through the family plan, which allows a 25% discount for an accompanying spouse and a 33% discount for children.

Note that the island hopper stops on Kosrae only on Tuesdays and Thursdays going west from Majuro and on Mondays and Wednesdays going east from Guam, bypassing Kosrae on the other flights.

On Sunday, Wednesday and Friday evenings there's a special flight that goes from Guam to Chuuk to Pohnpei, and back again, with cut-rate fares. On this flight one-way fares are $92 between Pohnpei and Chuuk, versus the regular fare of $179; $177 between Pohnpei and Guam, versus the regular fare of $367; and $120 between Chuuk and Guam, versus the regular fare of $242. Air Mike doesn't really promote these evening flights outside the islands, but they've been going on for years.

If you're booking in the USA you can use Continental's toll-free international number: ☎ 800-231-0856.

Many of Continental's agents aren't all that familiar with Air Mike's various fares and may tell you there is no family plan on the island hopper, no special night fares, etc so you need to be persistent. If you're not satisfied with the answers you get, call back and get another agent.

Once you're finally flying with Air Mike you'll find a certain down-home quality quite in touch with Micronesian flavour. If you island hop you'll see the same faces over and over again, and half the people on the flights always seem to know each other.

Honolulu to Majuro In addition to Air Mike flights, Airline of the Marshall Islands (AMI) flies between Honolulu and Majuro four times a week, usually stopping in Kwajalein on the way.

The Honolulu-Majuro fare is $555 one way, or $577 return for a one-year ticket with a seven-day advance purchase.

Flight Times
Honolulu-Johnston – two hours, five minutes
Johnston-Majuro – three hours, 10 minutes
Majuro-Kwajalein – 50 minutes
Kwajalein-Kosrae – one hour, 10 minutes
Kosrae-Pohnpei – one hour
Pohnpei-Chuuk – one hour, 10 minutes
Chuuk-Guam – 1½ hours
Guam-Yap – one hour, 25 minutes
Yap-Koror – 50 minutes
Guam-Koror – one hour, 55 minutes
Guam-Saipan – 35 minutes
Guam-Honolulu – 7½ hours

Direct to Guam Continental flies direct daily from Honolulu to Guam. One-way tickets cost $401. Through the family plan, the head of household pays $345 and accompanying spouse and children each pay $230.

Direct flights from Los Angeles to Guam cost $612 one way. With the family plan, the head of household pays $525, while the spouse pays $350 and children pay $341.

Northwest Orient flies from Honolulu to Guam via Tokyo for $507 one way and from Los Angeles or San Francisco for $676 one way.

Both Continental and Northwest offer round-trip excursion tickets to Guam, for stays of less than 60 days. They cost $686 from Honolulu and $910 from the US West Coast between January and May and from September to mid-December; and $748 from Honolulu and $1133 from the US West Coast during the rest of the year.

These excursion tickets don't allow island hopping. If you want to island hop one way and return on a direct flight, you need to piece together two one-way tickets.

If you're considering a round-the-world ticket, Guam can be added on to some of them.

To/From Guam, Yap & Palau

You can continue from Guam to Yap and Palau (Koror) via Air Mike.

The regular economy fare on a return ticket from Guam to Palau, with a stopover in Yap, is $592, while the full one-way fare from Guam to Palau, with a stopover in Yap, is $320. These prices are easy to beat however.

Discounted direct flights between Guam and Palau (either way) cost $166 on Sunday, Monday and Thursday evenings.

And though the full one-way fare between Guam and Yap is $208, on Sundays seats are only $120.

Also, the Sunday flight from Palau to Yap and the Wednesday flight from Yap to Palau cost $80, though all other flights between the two islands cost $141.

So, one of the cheapest ways to get to both Yap and Palau is to fly from Guam to Yap on Sunday, Yap to Palau on Wednesday and then back to Guam on one of the evening flights, for a total of $366.

Be aware that every now and then Air Mike changes the days of its discounted flights, so check before making up your itinerary.

It's also possible to have Palau as the starting or ending point of a longer routed ticket, such as one starting from Los Angeles or Honolulu. Sometimes the price works out favourably and sometimes it doesn't, but it's worth checking out and such a ticket would allow you to fly any day you wanted.

To/From Guam to Saipan

Air Mike is currently the only island carrier flying between Guam, Rota and Saipan. For more details refer to the Getting Around chapter or the relevant island section later in the book.

To/From Indonesia

Continental Airlines flies from Bali to Guam on Tuesdays, Wednesdays and Fridays for $451 one way. An excursion ticket which requires a stay of at least six days and no more than 90 days costs $697.

To/From Hong Kong

Northwest Orient flies from Hong Kong to Guam via Tokyo for $454 one way, or $632 with a 45-day excursion ticket.

To/From the Philippines

Philippine Airlines flies once a week between Manila and Guam for $419 one way. A 45-day excursion ticket is $591.

Continental Airlines flies daily from Manila to Guam. The one-way fare is $416 and allows a stopover in Palau. An excursion ticket, valid for seven to 45 days, costs $487, but doesn't allow stopovers. Once a week the Manila-Guam flight stops in Saipan.

Between Manila and Palau, Continental charges $173 one way, $346 return.

To/From Japan

There are multiple daily flights from Japan to Saipan and Guam.

Continental Airlines flies direct to Saipan and Guam from Fukuoka, Nagoya, Okinawa, Sapporo, Sendai and Tokyo; Japan Air Lines from Nagoya, Osaka and Tokyo; All Nippon Airways from several cities in Japan; and Northwest Orient from Tokyo.

The one-way fare from Osaka or Tokyo to Saipan is Y70,500 (US$538); to Guam, Y72,900 (US$556). An excursion ticket from Osaka or Tokyo to Saipan is Y81,000 (US$618); to Guam, Y84,000 (US$641).

The one-way fares are roughly double what the fares are for the reverse routes, going from Saipan or Guam to Japan! If you're travelling around Asia and want to stop in Japan on your way to Guam (or elsewhere in Micronesia), try to get a through ticket before you arrive in Japan so you don't get stuck having to buy an inflated ticket in yen.

Reservations are almost impossible to make around the time of Japan's New Year's vacation (Christmas through the first week of January), the Golden Week period (the last week of April and the first week of May) and during Obon (August), as almost all the seats are pre-booked for package tours during these holiday times.

If you're heading back to the States from Japan, or vice versa, island hopping through Micronesia is a great alternative to a nonstop transpacific flight!

To/From Korea
Continental Airlines flies return trips between Seoul and Guam on Sundays, Mondays, Wednesday and Fridays. The fare is $356 one way, or $640 for a 45-day excursion ticket.

Continental also flies from Seoul to Saipan for $329 one way, or $592 for a 45-day excursion ticket.

Korean Air Lines flies from Seoul to Saipan on Mondays, Wednesdays, Fridays and Sundays and from there goes on to Guam. The fare is $430 one way, $750 return.

To/From Taiwan
Continental Airlines flies between Taipei and

Guam on Mondays, Wednesdays, Fridays and Saturdays. The one-way fare is $263, while a 45-day excursion ticket costs $502.

To/From the South Pacific
The Airline of the Marshall Islands flies to Majuro from Nandi in Fiji, via Tarawa in Kiribati and Funafuti in Tuvalu. Flights leave Majuro on Tuesdays and Fridays and return from Fiji on Wednesdays and Saturdays.

The fare between Tarawa and Majuro is $177 one way, or $297 return with an excursion ticket. The one-way fare between Funafuti and Majuro is $454. The fare between Nandi and Majuro is $602 one way, or $832 with an excursion ticket. Excursion tickets require a seven-day advance purchase and allow a maximum stay of 23 days.

Continental flies from Port Moresby in Papua New Guinea to Guam on Sundays for $403 one way, or $745 return with an excursion ticket valid for seven to 45 days.

To/From Australia & New Zealand
Continental Airlines flies direct to Guam from Sydney and Brisbane. The fare from Sydney is A$750 in the low season, A$820 in the high season. Continental also flies to Majuro via Fiji: the full economy fare is A$1383 one way, A$2055 return.

From New Zealand Air Nauru flies to Guam via Naura every two weeks. The economy fare from Auckland to Nauru is NZ$563 one way, NZ$1126 return. From Nauru to Guam the fare is US$168 one way, US$336 return.

SEA
Though there are inter-island boats within Micronesia, it's rare to find any sort of passenger vessel going to Micronesia from other countries, save for the occasional private yacht.

TOURS
Conventional sightseeing package tours in Micronesia are pretty much limited to tours from Japan geared for Japanese tourists. There are a number of diving plans or

'adventure' tours available however, many of which are tailored for individual travellers. If diving is your main focus, some of the dive holiday packages can work out cheaper than if you were to piece together the dives and hotels by yourself, especially if you want to stay in the more upscale hotels. The dive trip rates do not include airfare and prices are based on double occupancy.

Tropical Adventures (☎ 206-441-3483, 800-247-3483), 111 2nd Ave North, Seattle, WA 98109, arranges dive vacations in Chuuk, Palau, Pohnpei and Yap. For $845 you can have eight days in Palau, staying at the Palau Marina Hotel and going out on 12 dives with Fish 'N Fins, or eight days in Chuuk, staying at the Truk Continental Hotel and going out on 12 dives with Micronesia Aquatics. For $1399 there's a 13-day trip to both islands.

Trip-N-Tour (☎ 619-724-0788, 800-348-0842 in the USA, 800-527-5228 in Canada), 846 Williamston St, Suite 202, Vista, CA 92084, specialises in customising individual trips to Micronesia, including Chuuk, Guam, Palau, Yap, Pohnpei, the Northern Marianas and Arno Atoll in the Marshalls. As an example, they charge $553 for five days of diving with Yap Divers and six days at the ESA Hotel, or $717 for divers who want to stay at the more upscale Manta Ray Bay Hotel.

Aqua-Trek, with offices in the United States (☎ 415-398-8990, 800-541-4334), 110 Sutter St, Suite 811, San Francisco, CA 94104 and Australia (☎ 61-02 358-4433), 156 McElhone St, Woolloomooloo NSW 2011 can arrange dive holidays for individuals in Yap, Palau, Chuuk, Pohnpei and Rota. Typical rates are $325 for four nights at the Village Hotel in Pohnpei and two days of diving, or $795 for a week at the Palau Marina Hotel in Koror and five days of diving with Fish 'N Fins.

Sea Safaris (☎ 213-546-2464, 800-262-6670), 3770 Highland Ave, Suite 102, Manhattan Beach, CA 90266, puts together dive packages for Guam, Palau, Pohnpei, Chuuk, Yap, Kosrae, Rota and Saipan.

Oceanic Society Expeditions (☎ 415-441-1106, 800-326-7491) Fort Mason Center, Building E, San Francisco, CA 94123, the travel arm of the environmental group Friends of the Earth, leads two-week tours to Pohnpei, Palau and Yap, with an emphasis on Micronesian culture and snorkelling. The cost is $3490, including airfare from Los Angeles and some meals.

Steve Currey Expeditions (☎ 801-224-6797, 800-937-7238), Box 1574, Provo, Utah 84603, has nine-day trips throughout the year to an uninhabited island in Arno Atoll in the Marshall Islands. Accommodation is in beachside tents. Activities include kayaking, fishing, snorkelling, lobster hunts and the like. The cost is $2685 including all meals and return airfare from Honolulu ($1980 for children 12 and under), plus $200 more for scuba divers.

Valor Tours (☎ 415-332-7850), Box 1617, Schoonmaker Building, Sausalito, CA 94965, plans guided tours for WW II veterans who want to revisit sites where they fought during the war.

Live-Aboard Dive Boats

The SS *Thorfinn* and the *Truk Aggressor*, based in Chuuk Lagoon, and the *Sun Tamarin*, based in Palau, are live-aboard dive boats that include all diving, accommodation and meals. They can be booked through Tropical Adventures, Sea Safaris and other travel agents. See the Chuuk and Palau chapters for more information.

LEAVING MICRONESIA

Unfortunately, airport departure taxes are gaining in popularity in Micronesia. Currently you have to dish out $5 in Kosrae and Pohnpei and $10 in Majuro, Chuuk and Palau.

Getting Around

AIR

Air Mike links Micronesia's eight major district centres of Majuro, Kosrae, Pohnpei, Chuuk, Guam, Saipan, Yap and Palau, and also flies to Rota.

Some island groups have domestic airlines connecting the district centres with their outer islands. The government-supported Airline of the Marshall Islands (AMI) is by far the most extensive, linking every inhabited Marshallese atoll. One-way fares range from $21 to $154.

Pacific Missionary Aviation (PMA) links Pohnpei with the outer islands of Pingelap, Mokil and Nukuoro. On Yap, PMA flies between Yap Proper and the outer islands of Ulithi, Fais and Woleai. One-way fares range from $50 to $140. In addition to these flights, PMA does some impressive rescue and medical evacuations on the outer islands.

On Palau, Paradise Air flies a six-seater Cessna from Koror to the outer islands of Peleliu and Angaur. Their fares are very reasonable ($20 and $26 respectively) and they provide one of the best views in Micronesia, as they overfly the Rock Islands on the way.

In the Marianas, Air Mike links Guam, Rota and Saipan, with numerous flights a day. A return excursion ticket from Guam to Rota and Saipan, or vice versa, costs about $100.

From Saipan, Freedom Air has daily shuttle flights to Tinian for $50 return.

More information on these flights are provided in the respective island sections.

Island Airlines

Continental Air Micronesia (Air Mike)
  Majuro – ☎ 3209
  Kosrae – ☎ 370-3024
  Pohnpei – ☎ 320-2424
  Chuuk – ☎ 330-2424
  Yap – ☎ 350-2127
  Palau – ☎ 488-2448
  Guam – ☎ 646-0220/1/2
  Saipan – ☎ 234-6492
  Rota – ☎ 532-3893

Airline of the Marshall Islands (AMI)
  Majuro – ☎ 3373
  Kwajalein – ☎ 2416
Pacific Missionary Aviation (PMA)
  Pohnpei – ☎ 320-2796
  Yap – ☎ 350-2360
Paradise Air
  Koror, Palau – ☎ 488-2348

LAND

Most of the major islands have fairly extensive road systems. Usually the main drag around town and the road out to the airport are paved but beyond that it varies, and unpaved roads are as common as not.

In some places you can just cruise along, while other roads are little more than pitted washed-out obstacle courses, challenging you to get through without bottoming out. To challenge you even further, the car agencies often rent low-riding compact cars.

On some of these dirt roads you'll pass heavy machinery running up and down smoothing over the ruts. They keep particularly busy between the washouts caused by heavy rain storms.

Bus

Fledgling public bus systems operate on Guam and Saipan. The next closest thing to a bus system in Micronesia is on Yap, where the school buses will take visitors between Colonia and outlying villages on a space-available basis.

Taxi

Majuro gets the prize for its inexpensive system of shared taxis that cruise up and down the main road, making it one of the easiest places in Micronesia to visit without having to rent a car. As long as the taxi is not full, it can be waved down and another passenger taken on. Rates are charged for each person according to their own destination, and are as low as 30 cents.

Moen Island (Chuuk) also has a shared taxi system, with rides usually given in the back of pick-up trucks. You can go anywhere around the island on the main roads for a dollar or less.

Pohnpei has a taxi system of minivans, though fares are not a bargain. It costs $1 for in-town rides and up to $30 for rides to out-of-the-way places.

Yap, Koror (Palau), Saipan and Guam have private taxis. Rates are quite reasonable in Yap and a bit more expensive in Palau, while those in Saipan and Guam are comparable to Western fares.

Car

Rental cars are available on the major islands, though they occasionally book out completely during busy times.

The minimum rates range from $20 to $40 per day and there's usually no mileage charge. The cars are seldom more than three years old but then again, between the salt air and the rough roads, that's about their average life expectancy.

Because most cars are rented on a 24-hour basis, you can get two days usage by renting at midday and driving around all afternoon, then heading out in a different direction the next morning before the car is due back.

Major car rental chains operate in Guam and Saipan and cars can easily be booked in advance from their overseas offices. This is a good idea as otherwise you may find the cheaper cars already rented out when you arrive. Unless you have a pre-paid deal, there are no cancellation penalties.

Upon renting a car you should check it over carefully and note on the contract any major scratches, dents or other damage before you drive away, to avoid hassles when you return the car.

On some islands it's hard to find cars with insurance. It's a mixed bag – you save a few bucks, but as the person at one rental booth told us: 'you hit it, you buy it'.

Hitching

The usual hitchhiking safety precautions apply, especially for women, but with the exception of Guam, getting lifts in Micronesia should not be too difficult.

Kosrae, for example, has no taxis but drivers nearly always offer rides to people walking along the road, a courtesy which is pretty common throughout the region.

Be careful of getting dropped off in remote locations that see little traffic, unless you're prepared to walk back.

SEA
Field Trip Ships

Field trip ships link several of Micronesia's district centres with the outer islands, carrying both supplies and passengers and loading copra for the return journeys.

Ships leave from Majuro in the Marshalls and from the FSM islands of Moen (Chuuk), Pohnpei, Kosrae and Yap Proper.

Some of the routes have the ships out for weeks, while the shorter routes, such as Pohnpei to Pingelap, take only a few days. You can get lists of departure dates in advance, but they shouldn't be taken too seriously as the ships often run behind schedule.

Don't expect much in the way of comfort – these are definitely not cruise ships, though all vessels have both deck and cabin class. Deck class is cheap, but the cabins aren't terribly expensive either.

The meals usually consist of monotonous dishes of rice, canned fish and canned meat so you'll probably want to bring at least some of your own food.

For more details, see the respective island sections.

Public Boats

Chuuk is unique for its extensive weekday system of commuter boats which bring people to Moen from the other islands in Chuuk Lagoon in the morning and return them to their home islands in the late afternoon.

Chuuk also has fishing boats that double as passenger carriers, running sporadically between Moen and some of the islands outside Chuuk Lagoon. These fishing boats don't really run on any schedule, so you have to catch them when they're in port.

Palau has government boats that take passengers from Koror to Peleliu and Angaur once or twice a week and to Kayangel and various points on the island of Babeldaob less frequently.

The fares for all these boats are quite reasonable, generally just a few dollars.

There are also a few small cargo boats which take passengers between nearby islands, such as Saipan and Tinian. Just go down to the docks and ask around.

Speedboats

There are lots of private speedboats in Micronesia which commute back and forth between islands within the same lagoon. Depending on how rough the seas are, traffic sometimes crosses open ocean to neighbouring islands as well.

Hitching a ride on one of these boats is not all that difficult if you're friendly and offer a few dollars to help pay for the petrol.

Republic of the Marshall Islands

The Marshalls consist of more than a thousand small coral islands. They are particularly narrow and they are all, without exception, flat. Most can be walked across in a couple of minutes.

The Marshall Islands have little fertile topsoil and are devoid of rivers. Aside from coconuts, pandanus and breadfruit, few crops grow in the salty sand of most atolls so the Marshallese long ago turned to the sea for their resources. They became, by absolute necessity, expert fishers and navigators.

The Marshalls had little to tempt conquerors or settlers and because they hadn't much food, water or wood to offer, even whalers and explorers seldom stayed long.

As a gentle people in an isolated part of the Pacific, the Marshallese and their islands were easy prey as nuclear testing subjects after WW II. Though the bomb tests have stopped, the Marshallese are still grappling with the lingering effects of radiation as well as ongoing US missile tests. No other Micronesians have suffered under US colonialism to the extent that the Marshallese have.

Majuro, the capital of the Marshall Islands, is quite Westernised, rather overcrowded and by no means a resort area. Although Majuro has some nice sandy beaches, much of the shoreline, particularly around the population centre of D-U-D, is strewn with trash.

Most of the outer islands, however, still retain the more pristine nature you'd expect to find in the tropical Pacific.

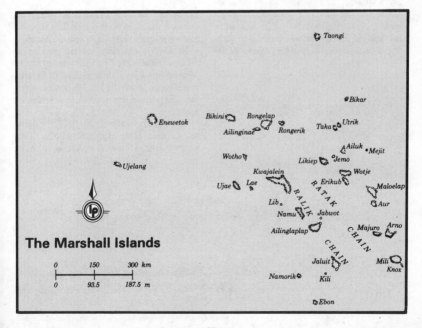

The Marshall Islands

History

The Marshalls were never unified under a single leader, though one chief often controlled several atolls and at times the entire Ralik chain was under a single chief. Chiefs had absolute authority though their wealth and power depended upon the loyalty and tribute payments made by the commoners.

Living on such narrow stretches of sand, land control has always been an extremely important issue for the Marshallese. Islanders married for land, went to war for land and when all else failed, they employed magic to get land.

Pandanus was an important food in the northern islands, breadfruit equally so in the south, while coconut production and fishing were important everywhere.

Because their islands are so widely scattered, the Marshallese developed some of the best canoe-building and navigational skills in the Pacific.

Stick Charts The low elevation of the Marshalls and the distances between the atolls make them particularly difficult to sight from the sea. In travels between islands, early inhabitants learned to read the patterns of the waves by watching for swells which would show that land was ahead.

Stick charts were used to teach the secrets of navigation. They were made by tying flat strips of wood together in designs which imitated the wave patterns. Shells were then attached to these sticks to represent the islands.

Three kinds of charts were used. The *mattang* showed wave patterns around a single island or atoll and was used first to teach the basic techniques. The *medo* showed patterns around a small group of atolls and the *rebillit* mapped an entire chain, showing the relationships between the islands and the major ocean swells.

All the information contained on the stick charts was memorised and the charts themselves were not actually taken on journeys. Not many present-day Marshallese understand how to read stick charts, though due to their popularity as souvenirs many islanders can still make them.

European Contact Because the Marshalls were off the main trade routes they received few visits from early European explorers.

In 1525 a Spaniard named Alonso de Salazar became the first European to sight a Marshallese island. Although other Spanish expeditions landed in the Marshalls during the 1500s Spain did nothing to colonise the area.

The islands were named after the English sea captain John Marshall who in 1788 sighted Arno, Majuro, Aur, Maloelap, Wotje

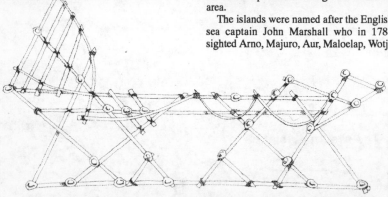

Stick Chart

and Ailuk and docked at Mili. His visit was probably the first made by Europeans in the Marshalls in 200 years and the exchange between the British and the 'Marshallese' was friendly.

The Russian explorer Otto von Kotzebue made a more thorough expedition in the early 1800s and drew up the first good maps of the islands.

Whalers, Traders & Missionaries Traders and whalers first showed up in the region in the early 1800s but they avoided the Marshalls once the islanders' reputation for violence spread. A 30-year period from the mid-1820s was a time of especially brutal attacks on European and American traders. The kind-hearted Marshallese had suddenly become, for Westerners, the most feared people in Micronesia.

In case after case, ship officers putting into port at various atolls in the Marshalls recorded the death of a captain or crew members in the ship's log. Sometimes the scouting parties that went ashore just completely disappeared and in the early 1850s the entire crews of three trading ships were massacred at Namorik, Ebon and Jaluit.

Some of the fighting was prompted by the stealing of island women. The high chief of the southern Ralik chain was partly responsible for attacks in his area in revenge for the death of his brother during an earlier encounter.

Violence was on the decline when the first Protestant missionaries to the Marshalls arrived on Ebon in 1857. The missionaries were at first welcomed, or at least tolerated, by the chiefs. Schools and churches were opened side by side and conversions came quickly. By the time the chiefs realised their traditional authority was being usurped by Western values and the Christian god, it was too late. Getting rid of the missionaries would not solve the problem. By 1872 Marshallese graduates of the mission schools were running most of the churches themselves.

German Period Germany annexed the Mar-

shalls in 1885, but didn't move government officials in until 1906. Instead, island affairs were left to the Jaluit Gesellschaft, a group of powerful German trading companies.

Coconut plantations and copra facilities had been set up as far back as the 1860s, including a coconut oil factory on Ebon in 1861 and trading stations on Mili, Ebon, Jaluit, Namorik, Majuro and Aur atolls.

Japanese Period The Japanese took control from 1914 and colonised the Marshalls extensively, developing and fortifying large bases.

They also took over the copra business, but unlike the Germans the Japanese sold copra directly to traders instead of going through local chiefs. This policy undermined, even further, the traditional authority of the chiefs in the islands.

WW II The first Micronesian islands captured by the Americans in WW II were at Kwajalein Atoll in February 1944. Roi-Namur, the main Japanese air base in the Marshalls, fell first, followed by Kwajalein Island with its almost-completed airstrip.

Majuro Atoll, which had been left undefended, was taken next and quickly developed into a base for fast carriers. From Majuro and the air base at Kwajalein, the USA then staged attacks on the Caroline Islands.

The USA bypassed four Marshallese atolls still in Japanese hands, but within weeks had captured Enewetok Atoll and about 30 more Marshallese islands before heading west.

Americans & Atomic Bombs After the war, the Americans immediately moved in and started atomic bomb experiments on Bikini and Enewetok atolls. Kwajalein Atoll was later established as a missile testing site.

Some of the islanders who breathed radioactive air or lived on contaminated land have died from radiation-related ailments while others have lingering health problems. Many wonder if they were deliberately used as test

First Day Cover - Marshall Islands

subjects for monitoring radiation's long-term effects on humans.

Bikini Atoll Bikini, site of the earliest known habitation in Micronesia, was the first atoll to be nuked back to the Stone Age.

Early in 1946 a US Navy spokesman met with the religiously fervent Bikini islanders, following church services, to inform them that their islands were needed for 'a greater good'. After deliberations, Bikini's Chief Juda responded that if the USA wanted to use Bikini for the 'benefit of all mankind' his people would go elsewhere. Still awed by the American firepower which had recently defeated the Japanese Imperial Navy, the Bikinians may not have felt in a position to baulk. Undoubtedly the Americans also knew that protesting is not a Marshallese custom.

The 161 Bikinians were relocated on the assurance they could move back once the tests were over. A few months later a nuclear device was exploded 500 feet over Bikini's lagoon, the first of 23 nuclear tests that would leave the islands uninhabitable, the Bikinians displaced and their society disrupted.

The Bikinians were first moved to Rongerik Atoll, a place of bad reputation in Marshallese legend. They got sick from eating poisonous fish in the lagoon and nearly starved from inadequate food supplies. Two years later they were moved to Kwajalein Atoll and then later to Kili Island.

In the 1970s the Bikinians were told it was safe to move back home and a resettlement programme began. The Bikinians, who had been awaiting the day they could return, were shocked to find two entire islands blown away and most of the others treeless, blasted apart and covered with wreckage and debris. Nevertheless, they remained on Bikini and tried to get their lives back in order.

In 1978 US tests showed that by eating food grown in the caesium-contaminated soil the Bikinians had collected high levels of radioactivity in their bodies, so they were moved off again.

Scientists from the Lawrence Livermore Laboratory in California are using Bikini to study ways to clean up radiation. Researchers are focusing on three alternatives: scraping up all the island's topsoil, irrigating the island with sea water to leach out the caesium, and applying large amounts of potassium to the soil to block the uptake of caesium in plants. By their estimates Bikini's

24 islands could be made habitable within a decade at a cost of about $100 million.

Enewetok Atoll Enewetok islanders were evacuated to Ujelang Atoll before atomic bomb tests began in 1948. Over a 10-year period 43 atomic bombs were detonated from Enewetok.

In 1980, after a $120 million clean-up programme, the islanders were allowed to return to Enewetok Island, in the southern part of the atoll.

The more highly contaminated island of Engebi in the northern part of the atoll has a ban on visits lasting more than a couple of hours.

Between the two is Runit Island, where contaminated items from the atoll were stashed under a huge 18-inch-thick concrete dome nicknamed Cactus Crater. The radiated debris and soil will supposedly be safe in 50,000 years. The concrete may last 300!

A 9.8-megaton hydrogen bomb which exploded in 1958 on Enewetok was the focus of a recent multimillion dollar geological study which showed the bomb had blasted a mile-wide, 200-foot-deep crater in the lagoon and fractured the rock to a depth of 1400 feet beneath the crater's surface. The geological impact of such massive bending and breaking of the earth's bed remains unknown.

Rongelap Atoll The immensely powerful hydrogen bomb 'Bravo' that exploded on Bikini in March 1954 sent clouds of deadly radioactivity toward inhabited Rongelap Atoll, 100 miles to the east. The fallout came down as powdered ash six hours after the blast.

Immediate signs of radiation sickness included nausea, hair loss and severe radiation burns. It wasn't until three days after the blast that the US military evacuated the Rongelapese to Kwajalein for decontamination. The Rongelapese were returned to their atoll in 1957.

The Rongelapese have health problems that include high rates of mental retardation, leukemia, stillbirths and miscarriages. Almost 75% of the people who were under the age of 10 on the day of the blast have had surgery for thyroid tumors.

Despite an aerial survey showing that some of the islands of Rongelap were as 'hot' as islands in Bikini, and a ban placed on eating shellfish because of accumulated radiation, the US continued to insist that Rongelap was safe and refused to help resettle the approximately 350 islanders.

In 1985 the Greenpeace ship *Rainbow Warrior* moved the Rongelapese to a new home on Mejato Island in Kwajalein Atoll, 110 miles to the south. The boat was later sunk in New Zealand by French agents who hoped to stop *Rainbow Warrior*'s activities aimed at ending nuclear testing in the South Pacific.

Half Life, a film by Australian director Dennis O'Rourke, tells the plight of the islanders and convincingly presents a picture of the Rongelapese being used as nuclear guinea pigs.

Utrik Atoll Though their plight is not as well known, the islanders of Utrik Atoll also received fallout from the Bravo test and have similar radiation related medical problems.

Bikini

According to legend Bikini was the favourite island of Loa, creator of the Marshalls. Loa used the words *lia kwel*, 'You are a rainbow', to describe Bikini. Eventually the term grew to describe anything lovely and is said to be the source of the current greeting *yokwe*.

In case you're wondering, the bikini swimsuit was originally named *atome* by its French designer, a year after the first atomic bomb tests at Bikini. ∎

Geography

There are 1225 islands and islets in the Marshalls. Only five are single islands. The rest are grouped into 29 coral atolls.

The atolls run roughly north-south in two nearly parallel chains about 150 miles apart and 800 miles long. The eastern chain is called *Ratak* which means 'toward dawn' and the western chain is *Ralik*, 'toward sunset'.

With a total land area of only 70 sq miles, the Marshall Islands are scattered across 750,000 sq miles of ocean. True to classic atoll form the islands are narrow and low and encircle central lagoons. The widest island, Wotje, is less than a mile across and the highest elevation, just 34 feet, is on Likiep.

The southern islands have more vegetation than those in the north. Virtually all of them have gorgeous white sand beaches.

Climate

In Majuro, the average daily temperature is 81°F (27°C). As the lowest temperatures occur during heavy rains, and most heavy rains fall during the day, night-time temperatures actually average a couple of degrees higher than daytime temperatures.

The northern Marshalls are quite dry, averaging just 20 inches of rain each year. Rainfall increases as you head south, with some islands getting up to 160 inches a year.

On Majuro, the wettest months are September through November (about 14 inches) and the driest period is January through March (with about eight inches a month).

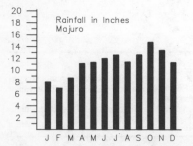

Full-blown tropical storms or typhoons are rare, but can be devastating when they whip across the low unprotected islands.

Government

Desiring to be politically independent of other Micronesian islands, the Marshallese began pulling out of the Congress of Micronesia as early as 1973. Their constitution became effective on 1 May 1979 and the nation is now known as the Republic of the Marshall Islands.

As with the other Trust Territory districts, the Marshallese signed a Compact of Free Association with the United States. The compact with the USA was not overwhelmingly popular. Almost 90% of the Bikinians voted against it, for instance, afraid the USA would use conditions of the compact to limit compensation and deny further responsibility for cleaning up Bikini. The compact, passed in September 1983 with the approval of 58% of Marshallese voters, went into effect in 1986.

The Marshallese government is modelled after a combination of both the British and US systems. The unicameral 33-member parliament, called Nitijela, meets in Majuro in January and August, for a total of about 50 days each year. The Nitijela elects one of its members as president of the Marshall Islands; the current president is Amata Kabua. There is also a national Council of Iroij (chiefs), which is basically an advisory board.

The Marshall Islands are divided into 24 municipalities, each of which has its own mayor and is represented by at least one senator in the Nitijela. The major district centres are Majuro, Ebeye, Wotje and Jaluit.

Economy

The Marshallese economy is largely reliant on US aid. In addition to $40 million annually in compact monies, the USA is paying $170 million rent for Kwajalein bases and $80 million for development projects on Kwajalein Atoll over a 30-year period.

What industry does exist is small scale. Some locally generated income comes from

Marshall Islands Flag

copra production, tourism and handicrafts, though with little land available, the Marshallese are turning to the sea for a source of income.

Aquaculture projects are now underway on several islands. Giant clams obtained from Palau are being cultivated on Majuro and Likiep atolls and on Wau Island on Mili. Oyster and sea cucumber cultivation, black pearl culture and seaweed farming are also being developed.

The Japanese fishing industry harvests about 42 million pounds of tuna and billfish in Marshallese waters each year and it's thought that these rich fishing grounds could support three times the current catch. Until recently, the only monies the Marshallese collected from all the fishing in their waters was through licensing fees, but the government is now trying to develop its own fishing fleet and currently has two purse seiners fishing for tuna.

With US compact monies beginning to decrease, the Marshallese are trying to generate income in a variety of creative ways. One plan is to collect licensing fees through a new international ship registry programme. Some foreign ships formerly registered in war-torn Liberia, as well as US oil tankers and ships from Panama and Hong Kong, are now flying the flag of the Marshall Islands.

The Marshallese government has also initiated a new programme offering to sell Marshallese citizenship to overseas aliens. After having no takers at $200,000 the Foreign Ministry recently cut the fee in half.

In what's been dubbed the 'Trash for Cash' scheme, the Marshall Islands has been showing a great deal of interest in serving as a waste disposal site. In exchange for accepting 10% of the US West Coast's household garbage – about seven million tons annually – the Marshallese have been offered $56 million per year, enough to cover the nation's annual budget.

The garbage entrepreneurs are also touting the trash as a easy source of landfill. One plan calls for the first shipments to be used to create a six-mile-long causeway connecting some of Kwajalein's coral islands. Engineers question the plan's feasibility and environmentalists are horrified, as even common household garbage is loaded with toxic waste that would leach into the lagoon. For now the plan has been shelved, not because of protests in the Marshalls, but due to a lack of support in the US cities that were to supply the garbage.

Health Problems

Much of Micronesian society has been traumatised by its inability to rapidly absorb massive doses of Westernisation. Dietary health problems in the Marshalls are among the most blatant examples.

Although the Marshallese eagerly took to a new diet heavy in processed sugars, genetically they have been unable to assimilate it. The sugar-laced cereals, soft drinks, and the extensive variety of packaged junk food that crams supermarket shelves have left 30% of the population potentially diabetic. At Majuro's new hospital, 75% of inpatients are diabetic.

Malnutrition is also severe. There have been cases of blindness from vitamin A deficiency, even though vitamin A-rich pandanus, papaya and pumpkins are locally grown. Surprisingly, a high percentage of deaths related to malnutrition are amongst the people of the agriculturally productive Laura Village on Majuro. Rather than eating the produce, some families cart it off to the market and sell it to get money to buy more tantalising junk food.

People

The population of the Marshall Islands is 46,000, with the majority of islanders living on the Majuro and Kwajalein atolls. Population growth is a major problem, as the number of Marshallese has more than doubled over the past 20 years and about half of the population is now less than 15 years old.

The Marshallese are a soft-spoken, good-natured people with a rich oral tradition of chants, songs and legends. Most women wear bright, floral print muu-muu dresses.

Religion

The Protestant 'Boston Mission' that started converting the Marshallese in the mid-1800s effectively wiped out the ancient religion of the islanders.

Nowadays a number of denominations are still vying for the souls of the Marshallese. There are many Protestant sects, including Congregationalist, Assembly of God, Baptist, Seventh Day Adventist and Jehovah's Witnesses. There's also a large Catholic church, a Bahai centre, a Salvation Army mission and a rapidly growing Mormon presence.

Language

Marshallese is the official language, but English is taught in schools and is widely understood. The islanders' gentleness is reflected in their traditional greeting *Yokwe yuk*, which means 'Love to you'. 'Thank you' is *Kommol tata*.

Holidays

The Marshallese celebrate New Year's Day, Nuclear Victims Day on 1 March, Constitution Day on 1 May, Labor Day on 5 September, Independence Day on 21 October, Thanksgiving on the last Thursday in November and Christmas Day.

Majuro

Most travellers to the Marshalls get only as far as Majuro Atoll, the nation's political and economic centre.

The atoll has 57 small islets curving 63 miles in an elongated oval shape. The larger

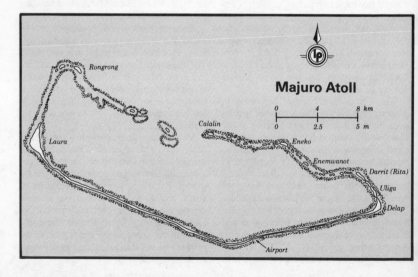

Majuro Atoll

Top: Coconut seller - Moen
Left: Storyboard maker - Palau
Right: Making a thatched roof - Kosrae

Top: Reef Island - Chuuk Lagoon
Bottom: Pingelap Atoll - Pohnpei

islets have been connected by a single 35-mile stretch of paved road, making it appear that most of Majuro is one long narrow island. The highest elevation is 20 feet.

When author Robert Louis Stevenson visited Majuro in 1889 he called the atoll the 'Pearl of the Pacific', but it's a far less pristine Majuro that one sees today.

One of the problems with 20,000 people living on such a narrow sandbar is that there's just no place to dispose of the packaging of Western culture. Tin cans, junked cars and disposable diapers (nappies) pile up by roadside dumping stations and spill into the lagoon.

Though Majuro is the most populated and the most Westernised of the Marshall Islands, there's still a simple island flavour to it all. Even in the main municipality of D-U-D you might wake to crowing roosters, and it's a common sight to see pigs rooting through fallen coconuts.

There's a lot you can learn about life in the Marshalls just from visiting Majuro. You can grasp what it's like to live on a ribbon of land so thin that as often as not you can see the ocean on both sides, and by visiting Laura Village you can see a rural lifestyle somewhat similar to the outer islands.

The name Majuro means 'many eyes' and it has always been one of the more heavily settled Marshallese atolls.

Information

The public library, next door to Alele Museum, has a Pacific room with a good selection of books, magazines and journals on Micronesia. It's open from 10 am to 5 pm Monday, Thursday and Friday; 10 am to 6.30 pm Tuesday and Wednesday; and 9 am to noon and 1 to 5 pm Saturday.

The *Marshall Islands Journal*, published on Fridays, costs 50 cents and is easy to find in stores around town. Guam's *Pacific Daily News* is available at the RRE Hotel, Quik Stop Coffee Stop and at larger stores. Majuro has two radio stations and a TV station.

Located in the section of D-U-D known as Small Island, the Airline of the Marshall Islands (☎ 3733) is open from 8 am to 5 pm

Monday to Friday. Air Mike (☎ 3209) is in the RRE Hotel building.

The locally produced *Marshall Islands Guidebook* (printed by Micronitor News & Printing Co, with most articles written by *Marshall Islands Journal* editor Giff Johnson) is available at RRE Hotel and major stores for $7. It has colourful information about the Marshalls, a short English/Marshallese dictionary and the island's telephone directory.

There's a laundromat at the side of Ajidrik Hotel and another on Small Island.

Money The Bank of Guam is on the 1st floor of the RRE Hotel building, the Bank of the Marshall Islands is next to the main post office and the Bank of Hawaii is at the side of Gibson's. Banking hours are from 10 am to 3 pm Monday to Thursday and from 10 am to 5 pm on Fridays, except for the Bank of Hawaii which stays open until 6 pm on Fridays.

Post & Telecommunications Majuro's main post office, next door to Robert Reimers Enterprises in Uliga, is open from 8.30 am to noon and 1 to 4 pm on weekdays and from 8 to 10 am on Saturdays. The Delap sub-station post office next to Gibson's department store is open from 8.30 to 11 am and 2 to 3.30 pm Monday, Tuesday and Thursday and from 8 am to noon and 1 to 3 pm Wednesday and Friday.

All mail to the Marshalls goes through Majuro and uses the zip code 96960, except for mail to Ebeye which uses 96970 and mail to Jaluit which uses 96961.

Long-distance calls can be made 24 hours a day from the little concrete building next to the National Telecommunications Authority satellite dish in Delap. Calls cost $2.50 per minute to the USA. It costs $4 per minute to Australia and $5 per minute to Europe, with a three-minute minimum. Hotel guests can make overseas calls from the larger hotels, though there's usually a service charge.

When calling the Marshalls from overseas, add 692-9 to Marshallese phone numbers, all of which are four digits when dialled within the Marshalls.

Emergency Majuro's modern 80-bed hospital (☎ 3399) is in Delap. Dial ☎ 3666 for police emergencies.

Holidays & Festivals

Majuro school children celebrate Constitution Day, 1 May, by participating in numerous sporting events.

Majuro has a lot of fishing tournaments, mostly coinciding with public holidays, including those on the weekend closest to the 4th of July, Labor Day in early September and Compact Day in late October. For more information, write to the Marshalls Billfish Club, Box 1139, Majuro, Marshall Islands 96960.

The Alele Museum sponsors a Folk Art Festival with traditional crafts, food, song and dance during the latter part of August. On Christmas Day people gather at the churches for singing, dancing and skits that last all day long.

Activities

Diving & Snorkelling Majuro is a good place to find rare varieties of tropical fish. If you're looking for sharks you can find them too, especially white-tipped and grey reef sharks.

Diving is possible all year-round, though the best months are May to October when the water is calmest. There's good diving in Majuro's channels and good diving and snorkelling along the islands north-west of Rita on the lagoon side. The farther from Rita you go, the clearer the water gets. Enemwanot has good snorkelling and Calalin, the last island before the main channel, is excellent, though beware of currents.

If you want to snorkel without having to find boat transportation, there's a shallow coral reef at Laura Beach, at the west end of Majuro. On the ocean side of the Majuro Bridge there are some aqua-coloured shoreline pools that were quarried out of the coral rock. Though the sea life in the pools is

limited, it's re-establishing itself with small tropical fish, spiny black sea urchins and moray eels.

Matthew Holly (☎ 3669) Box 319, of Marshall Island Aquatics Majuro, Marshall Islands 96960 offers Majuro's only dive services. He charges $25 to $30 per person, per dive; $200 per day for six people with two dives each; or you can negotiate something in between. Snorkellers who go out with divers pay $20 per day.

Matt can arrange boat tours and diving at Mili, Maloelap, Kwajalein and Arno atolls. He rents filled tanks for $5 each, a full set of diving gear for $15 and snorkelling gear for $6. To find the dive shop, look for the sign 'Pier 7 Marina' in Uliga and go around the back.

You can buy snorkelling equipment at Ace Hardware in the RRE Hotel building, Gibson's or Marshall Islands Aquatics.

Tennis There are two public tennis courts, lighted for night use, in Uliga.

D-U-D MUNICIPALITY

Three of Majuro's islands – Delap, Uliga and Darrit (Rita) – are joined into one municipality with the unappealing moniker 'D-U-D'. (Pronounce each letter separately, rather than spitting out the single syllable 'dud'.)

D-U-D is the nation's capital and the majority of Majuro's residents are concentrated there. The lagoon around D-U-D is polluted and not good for swimming. Poor sanitation conditions are compounded by causeways and bridges that close up the lagoon and result in poor water circulation.

Delap

The community of Delap begins as you cross over the Majuro Bridge. The pink house with the spiffy tennis courts just past the bridge is the home of President Amata Kabua.

The Marshall Islands government offices are spread around Delap, with the centre of it all being the new $9 million capitol complex which is under construction at the elbow of D-U-D, where the land curves

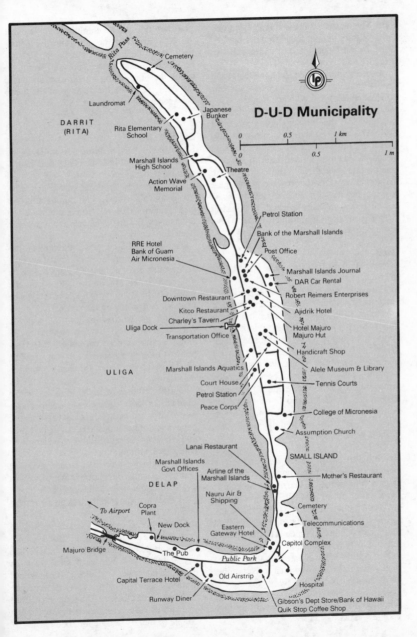

D-U-D Municipality

DARRIT
(RITA)

Rita Pass

Cemetery

Laundromat

Japanese Bunker

Rita Elementary School

Marshall Islands High School

Action Wave Memorial

Theatre

Petrol Station

Bank of the Marshall Islands

Post Office

RRE Hotel
Bank of Guam
Air Micronesia

Marshall Islands Journal

DAR Car Rental

Downtown Restaurant

Robert Reimers Enterprises

Kitco Restaurant

Ajidrik Hotel

Charley's Tavern

Uliga Dock

Transportation Office

Hotel Majuro
Majuro Hut

Handicraft Shop

ULIGA

Marshall Islands Aquatics

Alele Museum & Library

Court House

Tennis Courts

Petrol Station

Peace Corps

College of Micronesia

Assumption Church

Lanai Restaurant

SMALL ISLAND

Marshall Islands Govt Offices

Airline of the Marshall Islands

Mother's Restaurant

DELAP

Nauru Air & Shipping

To Airport

Copra Plant

New Dock

Cemetery

Telecommunications

Eastern Gateway Hotel

Majuro Bridge

The Pub

Public Park

Capitol Complex

Capital Terrace Hotel

Old Airstrip

Hospital

Runway Diner

Gibson's Dept Store/Bank of Hawaii
Quik Stop Coffee Shop

0   0.5   1 km
0   0.5   1 m

north. The new complex will have a circular parliamentary hall for the Nitijela, a meeting room for the House of Iroij and a 200-seat spectator gallery.

Majuro's airstrip used to be in Delap, and opposite the old runway there's now a grassy beachside park lined with coconut trees.

Next to the new dock where the field trip ship pulls in is the Tobolar Copra Processing Plant. The field trip ship, which carries supplies to the outer islands, returns loaded with the copra that's then piled high in the processing plant warehouse. Believe it or not, that mountain of gritty brown coconut meat is what gets transformed into pure transparent oil! If you're interested in looking around, someone will probably offer to give you a little tour.

Uliga

Most of Majuro's businesses and services are in Uliga.

The Alele Museum and the public library are housed together in a modern building next to the courthouse. The museum is small but has quality exhibits of early Marshallese culture, including stick charts, shell fishhooks and model canoes. One particularly interesting highlight is the collection of photographs of the Marshalls taken at the turn of the century by Joachim deBrum, the son of a Portuguese whaler who lived on Likiep Atoll. The museum is open from 10 am to noon and 3 to 5 pm Monday to Friday. There's no entrance fee.

Darrit (Rita)

US forces stationed on Majuro during WW II gave the island of Darrit the nickname 'Rita', after pin-up girl Rita Hayworth, and the name has stuck. They also named Laura.

Die-hard sightseers may want to seek out the Japanese bunker, which is Majuro's only remaining WW II fortification, or the overgrown Action Wave Memorial raised after a tidal wave destroyed the area in November 1979. Neither is particularly interesting nor easy to find. The bunker is beyond the high school and is reached by tramping through people's yards.

At low tide people commonly wade over the reef to and from the islands north of Rita. If you catch the lowest tide the water should be less than a foot deep, but be careful to watch the tides if you intend to come back the same way. The inside page of the local newspaper has a tide chart.

LAURA

Laura, a quiet green refuge 30 miles away from the bustle of D-U-D, is the atoll's agricultural centre.

Laura has a pretty white sand beach at its tip, Majuro's finest. Though during the week, visitors may well have Laura Beach to themselves, on the weekends it's a popular place for family picnics.

The road to Laura passes the airport, the runway of which is sloped to allow it to serve as Majuro's main water catchment source. A dirt path to the left, immediately past the runway, goes straight out to the beach where there's a shipwreck on the shore.

Further up the road on the right is Peace Park Majuro built by the Japanese. Its amphitheatre, cement monument and flagpole all look rather lonely and out of place on the beach but there are shady spots for picnicking.

On the left side of the road as you enter Laura there's a Taiwanese experimental farm where corn, cabbage, soybeans, cucumbers, papaya and other crops are grown, and pigs and chickens are raised. You're welcome to take a look around.

The Japanese erected a stone memorial marker for a major typhoon that hit Laura in 1918. To find it, drive to the end of the paved road, continue about 400 yards on a dirt road and turn left.

On Sundays, roadside stands spring up near Laura, selling coconut frond picnic baskets to people headed to the beach. The baskets are filled with such local treats as drinking coconuts, breadfruit, IQ (coconut pudding) and pumpkin, as well as reef fish and barbecued chicken. The price varies, but you can usually get a basket that will fill a couple of hungry people for about $10.

PLACES TO STAY

Majuro hotels tend to be rather high priced for what you get, and those at the lower price range are plain and rather cheerless. The RRE Hotel and the Royal Garden Hotel take credit cards, but the others do not. There's a hotel tax of 3% plus $2 per room per night.

Places to Stay – bottom end

The *Ajidrik Hotel* (☎ 3171), Box E, Majuro, Marshall Islands 96960, tucked behind the Downtown Restaurant in Uliga, has 15 air-con rooms with mini-refrigerators, TV and private baths. Singles/doubles cost $35/38. The staff is friendly and provides airport transportation.

The *Capital Terrace Hotel* (☎ 3527), Box 107, Majuro, Marshall Islands 96960, is a small family-run hotel above a little grocery store in Delap. Rooms, which are on the small side, have air-con, TV, mini-refrigerators, telephones (50 cents for local calls) and private baths and cost $40.

The dingy *Majuro Hotel* (☎ 3324), Box 185, Majuro, Marshall Islands 96960, above the Majuro Hut restaurant in Uliga, has 11 rooms which might be considered as a last resort. Singles/doubles cost $37/40.

For long-term stays, you might try the *Airport Motel*, Box 786, Majuro, Marshall Islands 96960, about a mile east of the airport. One-bedroom units with kitchens, bathrooms and washing machines cost $550 monthly. In between tenants, they occasionally have rooms that they rent by the night for $60.

Places to Stay – top end

RRE Hotel (Hotel Robert Reimers) (☎ 3250), Box 1, Majuro, Marshall Islands 96960, is a comfortable, modern 18-room hotel in the centre of town, popular with business travellers. Rooms have refrigerators, TV and rattan furnishings, including tables, chairs and settees. There's purified water and free local phone calls. Rooms on the inside corridor are larger, have bathtubs and cost $60/65 for singles/doubles, while rooms with lanais and views of the lagoon cost $75/80 for singles/doubles. There are also 12 ground-level trailer units between the hotel and the lagoon which cost as much as the view rooms but are not as appealing.

The new *Royal Garden Hotel* (☎ 3701), Box 735, Majuro, Marshall Islands 96960, is on a little white sand beach two miles west of D-U-D, has big rooms with all amenities, including TV, bathtubs, phones, carpeting and refrigerators. It's almost luxurious, the staff is friendly and the rooms have ocean views. Though the Royal Garden is not the cheapest, it's the best value of Majuro's hotels. Single rooms have queen beds and cost $60 for either a single person or a couple. Double rooms have two queen beds and cost $75. Transportation is one drawback here; if you don't have a car it can be a long wait between taxis.

The multistorey *Eastern Gateway Hotel* (☎ 3337), Box 106, Majuro, Marshall Islands 96960, a project financed by the Republic of Nauru, has been under construction for years. When it's finally done it will supposedly be Majuro's first luxury hotel. Plans call for 65 rooms, tennis courts and a top-floor restaurant. In the meantime there are older bungalows on the lagoon side that get cool breezes and construction noise. Singles/doubles cost $50/55, though you get the feeling that hotel guests are rather in the way. There's a small restaurant patronised by the construction crew.

PLACES TO EAT

Food in Majuro is reasonably priced and fresh fish is found in most restaurants. Water is not safe to drink from the tap.

Places to Eat – bottom end

From the outside, the *Kitco Restaurant*, in the centre of D-U-D, looks like nothing more than a windowless cinder-block garage, but in fact it's a good place for inexpensive food and the most popular eatery in town. They have French toast for $1, breakfast combos for $2, inexpensive sandwiches and a full chalkboard of dishes from ramen to teriyaki steak for $2 to $4. It's open from 6 am to 9 pm.

The nearby *Downtown Restaurant* is disappointing. Their prices are higher than Kitco's, but the food isn't as good.

Majuro Hut is a bit spiffier looking than the other inexpensive restaurants in D-U-D, with decor left over from the Chinese restaurant that was there before. They have ramen for $1.50 and fried fish or teriyaki chicken plates for $3.50.

Quik Stop Coffee Shop, a little diner next to Gibson's, has sandwiches for $1 to $3 and greasy onion rings or fries for $1.25. You can try beru (pumpkin pudding) here for 60 cents or jakaro (a coconut drink) for 90 cents. It's open from 7 am to 9 pm daily.

The *Runway Diner*, out on what used to be the old airport runway, has inexpensive Oriental, Marshallese and American food. For breakfast, you can get a cheese omelette, toast and coffee for $2. At dinner, fresh fish with IQ (coconut pudding) and salad costs $3.50. *Ni* (coconut juice) is 50 cents. This old-style diner has booths, lots of orange formica and a friendly crowd.

Mother's Restaurant, next to Momotaro's store at Small Island, has half a dozen small tables in a non-smoking environment. They have good chicken teriyaki, as well as some vegetarian dishes.

Charley's Tavern (☎ 3341), next to Kitco Restaurant, has take-out pizza.

There's a deli attached to RRE store but it's uninspiring.

Places to Eat – top end

Tide Table Restaurant, upstairs at the RRE Hotel, has good food and fine views of the lagoon. At lunch they have dishes such as yakisoba or fish & chips, and specials such as lobster in black bean sauce, for $4 to $6. At dinner, complete seafood or steak meals cost $8 to $15. Hours are from 7 am to 2 pm and from 5 to 9.30 pm. Sunday brunch, served from 11 am to 2 pm, is good and includes lots of fresh fruit, pastries and a fair variety of main dishes; it costs $9 for adults, $3.50 for children.

Royal Garden Restaurant, in the Royal Garden Hotel, has sandwiches for about $3 and pasta, seafood, Filipino dishes and Japanese food in the $6 to $9 range. It's a pleasant setting with a good ocean view and it's not uncommon to find President Kabua dining here in the evening.

The *Lanai Restaurant*, at Small Island next to the Airline of the Marshall Islands office, has good seafood at moderate prices.

ENTERTAINMENT

A small movie theatre in Rita shows current Hollywood films and kung-fu movies.

The Pub (☎ 3625), tucked in behind Ace International Agencies in Delap, is Majuro's most popular night-time spot, with both a bar and disco. In Majuro, it's not uncommon for women to ask men to dance, and it can be considered rude to refuse. The Pub is open from 8 pm to 2 am Tuesday to Saturday.

The *Tide Table Restaurant* has a bar that's open from 4 pm daily, with happy hour from 4 to 6 pm. There's an excellent sunset view, as the restaurant faces west across the lagoon.

Royal Garden Hotel has a popular happy hour on Fridays.

Though it's not as cheery, *Charley's Tavern* in Uliga is another place to knock back a few beers in the evening. They have happy hour drinks with free pupus (hors d'oeuvres) from 5 to 7 pm.

Another option is to go along with the novel suggestion in a brochure put out by the tourist office:

Sometimes it would be very wonderful to purchase a case of beer and go to a beach, sit, watch and enjoy the moon comes over the ocean while consuming the beer.

THINGS TO BUY

The best known Marshallese handicrafts are stick charts, carved models of outrigger canoes and intricately woven items such as baskets, wall hangings and purses made from pandanus leaves, coconut fronds and cowrie shells. Marshallese handicrafts are among the best in Micronesia both in quality and price.

There's a handicraft cooperative behind the museum, open daily except Sundays, and another shop on the road near the Assumption Church. You can sometimes watch women working on handicrafts at either place. There are also two handicraft booths at the airport, but even during flight times you can't count on them being open.

You can get colourful commemorative postage stamps at the post office and first day covers at the Alele Museum. The Alele Museum sells books on Micronesia, T-shirts and cassette tapes of Marshallese chants and stories.

Majuro is *the* place to buy 'Nuclear Free Pacific' or 'Bikini – Paradise Lost' T-shirts, as well as more standard designs. Men's Hawaiian-style shirts are about the same price here as in Hawaii.

Majuro stores are more modern than those in the FSM, so if you're continuing on in that direction buy anything you might need before you leave.

GETTING THERE & AWAY
Air
Majuro is a free stopover on Air Mike's island hopper route between Honolulu and Guam. Otherwise, the Honolulu-Majuro ticket costs $555 one way, or $577 return, on either Air Mike or Airline of the Marshall Islands (AMI).

AMI also flies twice a week from Nandi, in Fiji, to Majuro for $602 one way, or $832 return with an excursion ticket. The same flight can bring you from Tarawa in Kiribati to Majuro for $177 one way, or $297 with an excursion ticket, or from Funafuti in Tuvalu for $454 one way. Excursion tickets require a seven-day advance purchase and allow a maximum stay of 23 days.

Majuro has a $10 departure tax.

GETTING AROUND
To/From the Airport
Most hotels provide a free minivan service to and from the airport. A few of them meet the flights whether they have guests or not, while others show up only to meet guests with reservations. Taxis from the airport to D-U-D cost $2.

Taxi & Minivan
Majuro has a fine, inexpensive shared taxi system. Taxis are sedans, clearly marked with taxi signs. You stand at the side of the road and wave at the taxis and as long as they're not full they'll stop and pick you up. It costs just 30 cents to go anywhere within D-U-D.

A couple of private companies offer a similar service using minivans. Whereas taxi routes are determined by wherever the passengers want to go, including side roads and residential areas, the vans generally stick to the main road, some of them making a straight run between the RRE Hotel and Laura. The cost is 25 cents within D-U-D, $1.50 from D-U-D to Laura, and varying amounts for points in between.

If you're outside D-U-D you may have to wait well over an hour before a minivan or taxi comes by, but in town they're quite frequent.

Car
Domnick Auto Rental, or DAR, charges $37 per day for an air-con sedan, plus $3 for insurance. Their main office (☎ 3680 or 3174), Box 153, Majuro, Marshall Islands 96960, is inside a video shop on the ocean-side road in Uliga. They also have a rental booth at the airport (☎ 3547), but they don't always have cars available there.

The RRE Hotel and the Royal Garden Hotel also charge $40, including insurance, though both rent primarily to their hotel guests.

Visitors are allowed to drive in Majuro as long as they have a valid driver's licence from their home country.

Boat
Hotels can arrange boat rentals or you can try to save money by cutting out the intermediaries and making arrangements yourself with someone who has a speedboat. Bargain the price. Marshallese are generally very fair and won't cheat you but if you throw money around they'll take it.

Kwajalein Atoll

Nowhere in Micronesia is the US military presence so ominous as on Kwajalein Atoll, a missile testing range operated by the US Department of Defense.

Kwajalein is the world's largest coral atoll. Its 97 islands have a total land mass of just 6½ sq miles but they surround an immense 1100-sq-mile lagoon.

The lagoon, sometimes called 'the world's largest catcher's mitt', is the target and splash-down point for intercontinental ballistic missiles (ICBMs) fired from the Vandenberg Air Force Base in California, 4200 miles away.

The missile tests, which generally occur at night, often light up the sky with a brilliant display of explosions, burning debris and sonic booms.

Kwajalein's $2 billion facility is currently a test range for anti-ballistic missiles and Strategic Defense Initiative (SDI) systems, on the cutting edge of the 'Star Wars' programme. In 1990 a Minuteman missile launched from California on a 30-minute journey to Kwajalein was tracked for the first time using airborne SDI sensors.

The Kwajalein Missile Range (officially called US Army Kwajalein Atoll, or USAKA) includes Kwajalein Island in the southern part of the atoll, Roi-Namur Island in the north and some smaller islands between the two. It's a world of radiation shields, radar systems, microwave dishes and sophisticated computers and tracking equipment.

Although Kwajalein is on the same side of the International Date Line as the rest of Micronesia, it uses the same date as the USA to avoid potential goof-ups between missile launchers in California and missile retrievers in Kwajalein. When it's noon Sunday in Majuro, it's noon Saturday in Kwajalein.

The Americans stationed on Kwajalein Island include an active group of divers who probably know quite a bit about the more than 30 WW II-era Japanese ships at the bottom of the lagoon, but their main function is diving for missile pieces after a splashdown.

None of the islands in Kwajalein Atoll apart from Ebeye and Kwajalein have accommodation for visitors.

KWAJALEIN ISLAND

About 3000 American civilian contract workers and their families live on Kwajalein Island.

Recreational facilities include a golf course, two swimming pools, three baseball diamonds, tennis courts, movie theatres, handball and basketball courts, a bowling alley and a dart league. Everything is free to residents, including taxi vans to get around.

There's also a dinner club, restaurants and snack bars, a chapel, schools from kindergarten through to high school, a supermarket and a modern department store. As much as possible, it is American suburbia transplanted.

Places to Stay

If you have permission from the military commander to stay on Kwajalein Island there are dormitory rooms with two to three beds, hot water and bath for about $12. You may need a sponsor on the base to use these facilities however.

EBEYE ISLAND

About 1000 Marshallese labourers work on Kwajalein Island and live on 78-acre Ebeye Island, three miles to the north. They support an additional 7500 relatives and friends in inadequate, overcrowded conditions.

The contrasts between the two islands are startling. Workers are shuttled by boat between their meagre homes and their affluent work sites. Marshallese are not allowed to shop at Kwajalein's fancy subsidised stores, make use of its modern 25-bed hospital or swim in its 'public' pools. They can look at the good life but they can't touch.

In 1935 Ebeye had 13 people in three households. With the development of the Kwajalein Missile Range in the early 1960s, Kwajalein Island residents were evacuated to Ebeye. Other Kwajalein Atoll islanders joined them as the 'mid-corridor' islands were also evacuated to free up most of the lagoon for catching missiles.

The US Army constructed apartment units, a saltwater sewerage system, a power plant and a freshwater system on Ebeye – but allotted no money for maintenance. The systems soon fell into disrepair.

As if concentrating all the atoll's people on tiny Ebeye wasn't problem enough, the menial jobs that opened up on the base attracted Marshallese from other atolls, particularly those who had relatives on Ebeye. With traditional Marshallese custom dictating that members of each extended family take in relatives in need, the neat little apartments built by the military were on their way to becoming Micronesia's most overcrowded ghetto.

In 1968 Marshallese workers began receiving the US minimum wage, which was much higher than the average salary elsewhere in the Marshalls. By 1970 Ebeye had 4000 people and by 1978 the population had swelled to 8000 – on an island just one mile long and less than 200 yards wide. One-room shacks and lean-tos of plywood, tin, cinder block and plastic sheeting were jammed side by side. The island came to be known as the 'Slum of the Pacific'.

A new sewerage system built in 1979 broke down soon after its completion, electrical power was out more often than not, running water was restricted to as little as 15 minutes a day and sanitation conditions were appalling. Pollution levels in the lagoon were hundreds of times higher than those considered safe by World Health Organisation standards, yet those same waters were the children's only playground. Typhoid, diabetes, malnutrition and dysentery were all in epidemic proportions. It wasn't until the early 1980s, after islanders had disrupted military tests by staging a series of 'sail-ins' to restricted parts of the atoll, that the US government really began taking Ebeye's problems seriously. The lease agreement granting the USA continued use of Kwajalein Atoll was renegotiated, with the rent increasing from a couple of hundred thousand dollars to $9 million a year.

About half of that money was allotted for development and the Kwajalein Atoll Development Authority (KADA) was established to coordinate projects.

As part of lease negotiations, the USA also provided a new power plant, which came on line in 1987. It is combined with an Israeli-designed water desalination plant that innovatively uses waste heat from the power plant to produce as many as 300,000 gallons of fresh water daily, enough to meet Ebeye's needs.

As part of KADA's projects, Ebeye's dusty potholed roads are being paved, sidewalks are going in, the sewerage system has been rebuilt and a new multimillion dock is under construction.

Long-range development plans call for the construction of a causeway that will stretch six miles northward from Ebeye and join half a dozen other islands, using them to relieve Ebeye's overcrowding.

Gugeegue, the island at the far end of the proposed causeway, is currently under development in what is being promoted as the Marshalls' first planned urban community. With 59 acres, Gugeegue is the largest of these islands and is expected to eventually house up to 3000 people. Until the causeway is built, boats will ferry islanders between Gugeegue and Ebeye.

Though some things are obviously getting better, Ebeye is still saddled with enormous problems. Infant mortality and suicide rates are high and alcoholism is rampant. And though new buildings are replacing the old, the island still has little greenery and scarcely a tree – there simply isn't room.

Needless to say, Ebeye is not a big tourist spot, but it is a real eye-opener. The people are generally very friendly, especially the children.

Places to Stay

The *Anrohasa Hotel* (☎ 3161), Ebeye, Marshall Islands 96970, is a seven-room hotel run by Fountain and Ann Inok. Rooms are small but have carpeting, TV, a refrigerator and a desk and chair. There are plans to add a 20-room addition and there's a small restaurant downstairs.

The *KADA Hotel* (☎ 3049), Ebeye, Marshall Islands 96970, gives priority to government guests and businesspeople. There are just two rooms, both dormitory style, one with three beds, the other with five. Each has air-con, a bathroom with hot water and a shower. Beds cost $20.

Ebeye is a busy place and with all the new development going on it's difficult to get a room, though there are a couple of other small hotels under construction. Because of the extreme overcrowding, families on Ebeye have no room to spare for visitors.

Places to Eat
LaBobby's Kitchenette, a clean, modern restaurant with air-con and formica tables, is one of Ebeye's busiest restaurants. It has an extensive menu, take-out service and good hamburgers.

RRE Store on Ebeye sells take-out barbecued chicken and ribs, pizza, sandwiches and other deli foods.

Getting Around
Taxi From Ebeye's dock you can get a taxi to anywhere on the island for 30 cents, though it only takes 20 minutes to walk from one end of the island to the other. Most taxis are extended cab pick-up trucks and you ride in the cab or hop in the back, wherever there's room.

Boat It's possible to rent boats on Ebeye to visit islands around the atoll, but you'll have to bargain the price. Ask around and be sure to talk directly to the boat owner. Before setting off to any of the other islands you need to get permission from the landowner on Ebeye first, but this shouldn't be hard to do. Avoid military installations around the lagoon as you'll be arrested for trespassing.

ROI-NAMUR & SANDO ISLANDS
Fifty miles north of Ebeye, Roi-Namur houses radar and other tracking equipment. Like Kwajalein, it's a restricted military

facility and another 'little America' with modern amenities once again available to Americans only.

Sando is the home of Marshallese workers commuting to Roi-Namur, much like Ebeye is to Kwajalein. The Japanese had communications facilities on Sando and large bomb shelters still stand, though they were damaged by heavy bombing during WW II. Live shells are still occasionally found on Roi-Namur and Sando.

The USA built a modern bomb shelter for the 400 people of Sando for use during missile tests. The islanders, who once dutifully practiced drills, no longer bother to go to the shelter when US missiles are shot their way.

MEJATO ISLAND
Mejato, in the north-west part of the atoll, is home to 350 Rongelapese, many of whom were irradiated in US nuclear testing.

After years of US failure to respond to the islanders' concerns with contamination on Rongelap, Greenpeace helped the Rongelapese relocate to Mejato in 1985. During their first few years on Mejato, the Rongelapese suffered food shortages as a result of problems in bringing in enough supplies from Ebeye, 70 miles to the south. One of the obstacles was the waters around Mejato, which are too shallow for most cargo boats to land.

Greenpeace came to the rescue again in 1988, providing the islanders with $50,000 to build a 40-foot catamaran to transport food and supplies.

GETTING THERE & AWAY
Although Kwajalein Island is a closed military base, it is the transit point if you're entering Ebeye by air.

If you want to visit Ebeye you have to apply for a permit at the Marshall Islands government complex in Delap (Majuro). It shouldn't be difficult to get, as even a fellow traveller on a writing assignment for Greenpeace was granted a permit without any hassle.

Air Mike stops on Kwajalein Island as part

of the island hopper flight. Airline of the Marshall Islands flies between Majuro and Kwajalein daily, except Sundays, for $94 one way.

Once you're on Kwajalein, you'll be escorted to Dock Security Checkpoint where you will be asked again to show your permit to enter Ebeye. The ferry to Ebeye, aboard a new US Army catamaran, is free and takes just 15 minutes.

Field trip ships stop at Ebeye. The one-way deck fare is $14.10.

Outer Islands

Something of Marshallese traditional island life still remains in the quiet village communities away from Majuro and Kwajalein. The pace on the outer islands is relaxed and very s-l-o-w.

Usually a few people on each island speak English and nearly everyone is friendly. Because of the language barrier some people may appear shy while others will strike up a conversation just to practise their English.

If you're visiting somebody special you might even rate a real Marshallese welcome. On these occasions a group of women singing in harmony and bearing baskets piled with food will surround the visitors. The women give the guests flower headbands and leis and then everybody stands around exchanging compliments.

One Peace Corps volunteer, describing a visit by her brother, told how some of the older village women welcomed him by rubbing baked breadfruit on his stomach and chanting about how good-looking he was. For better or worse, this isn't something the average traveller will encounter!

Although some outer islanders still use the *korkor*, a dug-out fishing canoe made from a breadfruit log, 'boom-booms', or motorboats, are steadily gaining in popularity. Both kinds of boats are used for frequent *jambos*, trips or picnics, to uninhabited atoll islands.

Accommodation
The Marshallese in the islands and atolls away from Majuro and Kwajalein are used to weekly flights dropping off the occasional visitor now and again. Although most atolls do not have arrangements for visitors, the Marshallese are warm, hospitable people and you should be able to find a family to stay with or at least a place to camp. You need to get permission before setting up a tent though, as all land belongs to someone.

If you're already in Majuro, the best thing to do is to radio ahead to the mayor of the atoll you wish to visit. It's not an absolute necessity but it is common courtesy to let them know you're coming.

If you have a lot of time before your arrival to the Marshalls, you could trying writing in advance. Just direct the letter to, for example: Mayor of Wotje, Wotje Atoll, Marshall Islands 96960.

If there's a Peace Corps volunteer on the island (you can find out from their Majuro office), they might welcome the company or at least be able to help you find a place to stay.

Sugar, coffee, cigarettes and candy (no health problems here!) are gifts that will win you friends and encourage someone to let you stay on their property or in their home. Don't expect this to be a freebie. Many islanders are quite fond of money and you should be prepared to pay.

Trade items can often be more useful than cash, especially if they are things not readily available from the field trip ships. Printed T-shirts, jeans, baseball caps, lighters, flashlights, D-size batteries, pocket knives and cassette tapes of Western music are popular items.

Most outer islands do not have electricity, running water or flush toilets. Some houses are of concrete and others are made of thatch with coral rock floors. Instead of beds, pandanus mats are piled on the floor.

The Marshallese take excellent care of guests and will share what they have.

Food & Drink
Restaurants don't exist outside the major

atolls. You can make do with local store provisions, eat with the family you stay with or bring food with you from Majuro which you can then either eat or trade for local fresh foods.

Usually there are a couple of small stores with a very limited inventory of staples, such as rice, flour, tea and canned meats. Island meals usually consist of a combination of those items and local foods like breadfruit, pandanus, pumpkin, taro and fish.

Most of the outer islands are dry, though alcohol is often illegally made and consumed. Visitors who drink are not usually appreciated.

To be safe, all water should be boiled, even if it's from catchments – and without fail if it's not.

MILI ATOLL

Mili is a good choice for travellers who want to visit one of the outer atolls, as it has friendly people and beautiful beaches, it's not far from Majuro and it's cheap to get to. Best of all, there's a place to stay.

After Kwajalein, Mili has the most land area of the Marshallese atolls – just over six sq miles. The population is about 850.

Mili played a part in one of the bloodier and most famous mutinies of the whaling years. In 1824 the captain and officers of the Nantucket whaleship *Globe* were murdered and the mutineers, led by Samuel Comstock, chose Mili as their hideout. Other crewmen, however, stole the ship and abandoned the mutineers on the island. A US naval ship that came ashore two years later learned that Comstock and all but two of his crew had been killed by the islanders, apparently in retaliation for their cruelty.

In 1937 famed US aviator Amelia Earhart disappeared in this part of the Pacific in the midst of a flight around the world. Though the mysterious circumstances surrounding her death remain unknown, she was reportedly seen in Mili under Japanese custody long after her disappearance.

Mili was a main WW II Japanese base and there are many abandoned weapons, Japanese and US war planes and bombed-out

buildings still scattered around. Where the plane lands, you'll see an old rusted WW II gun adorned with lush green vines.

It's a pleasant quarter mile walk to the hotel from the airstrip. Along the way you'll see large bomb craters now covered with vines and coconut trees. Mili has a mosquito problem as these bomb craters make perfect spawning grounds. Bring mosquito repellent or coils or both with you. (Mosquito coils and coffee also make nice gifts for people on Mili.)

There's a good beach across from the hotel and the little shacks behind are used to make copra. The whole lagoon side of the island is trimmed with sandy white beaches, while shell collecting is good on the ocean side. At low tide you can easily walk along the reef to the neighbouring islands, some of which have only a single house upon them.

Places to Stay & Eat

The *Mili Hotel* has three little thatched-roof bungalows nestled back from the lagoon amid a cluster of coconut trees. Each has one big room with a bed and a tiny bathroom with plumbing, although there's no hot water. One of the cottages is occupied by a Peace Corps volunteer. There are plans to build a few more cottages right on the beach.

Make your reservations while you're still on Majuro through the Gushi wholesale office (☎ 3688). The hotel rate is $20 per night.

Meals are available for a reasonable price, but unfortunately there are almost no vegetables on the island and people on Mili don't fish much, so you might get stuck eating a lot of canned corned beef and rice. The best idea is to bring your own food from Majuro, which can be cooked at the hotel. It's also a good idea to take bottled water.

Getting There & Away

AMI flies between Majuro and Mili on Mondays, Wednesdays and Fridays for $42 one way.

There's also a 50-foot schooner that makes the four-hour ride from Majuro's Uliga Dock to Mili about once a week. The cost is $5 one way. To make arrangements, call Kejjo Bien (☎ 3145).

MALOELAP ATOLL

Taroa (Tarawa) Island, in Maloelap Atoll, was the main Japanese airbase in the eastern Marshalls during WW II and most visitors these days come to see war relics. There are numerous twisted wreckages of Zeros and Betty bombers, pillboxes, guns and the remains of an airfield, narrow-gauge railroad and a radio station. The southern tip of the island has coastal defence guns, including a 127 mm anti-aircraft gun and a Howitzer on wheels.

You can stumble across some of the stuff on your own, but a lot of it is hidden under thick jungle foliage and is difficult to find. A few islanders are willing to trek with visitors and show them the sites, so if you're interested just ask around.

Off Taroa's lagoon beach the Japanese freighter *Toroshima Maru* lies half submerged where it was sunk by B52s. Periscopes and the mast can still be seen, but it's pretty well stripped, except for some live depth charges. If you swim out around it, watch for the grouper (a type of sea bass) that is said to be as large as a human. The lagoon also has its share of sharks, so watch out for them too! After the war ended, Taroa was not settled again by Marshallese until the 1970s. Now it's the centre of atoll activity because of its airport, stores and copra cooperative.

Legend has it that Taroa used to be in the centre of the lagoon in a spot where it was easy for all canoes to sail to. But the legendary figure *L'etao*, who demanded food from each of the atoll islands, got irritated with the puny offerings given by the Taroa islanders and kicked Taroa to where it is now.

Taro used to be widely grown on Taroa until the crops were destroyed by an aggressive breed of imported New Zealand pigs

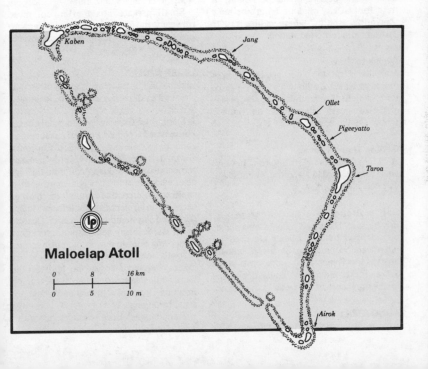

which apparently also had a reputation for chasing women and children up coconut trees. Fear not though, as it seems successive generations have mellowed out!

Maloelap Atoll, with a total population of 800 people, has four other inhabited islands. Airok is 16 miles south of Taroa; and Ollet, Jang and Kaben are respectively six, 18 and 32 miles to the north-west. Not many Japanese were stationed on the other islands so they don't have the same amount of war junk as Taroa.

Maloelap has two chiefs. One is head of Taroa, Ollet, Jang and Kaben, as well as the northern atolls of Wotje, Utrik and Ailuk, while the other presides over Maloelap's Airok Island and parts of Aur Atoll.

To Airok it takes about one hour by speedboat or just over two hours by diesel inboard. The cost is about $15 one way.

Just a few miles from both Taroa and Ollet is uninhabited Pigeeyatto, which is sometimes called 'Papaya Island' because of its fresh fruit. It has ruins of a wartime radio transmitter station where cables ran to Taroa's radio receiving station.

Places to Stay
Maloelap is used to visitors and has a thatchroofed guesthouse with two rooms on Taroa for $5 a night. You might also be able to stay at the two-room schoolhouse on Taroa if school's not in session.

Getting There & Away
AMI flies from Majuro to Taroa on Tuesdays and Saturdays and to Kaben on Wednesdays. The cost is $52 one way.

Getting Around
Private speedboats and inboard motorboats owned by individual islands are used for inter-island commuting. A diesel inboard boat ride to Kaben from Taroa costs about $20 and takes around 4½ hours, depending on the roughness of the water in the lagoon.

ARNO ATOLL
Arno is the closest atoll to Majuro, just nine miles away. It has 133 islands, two airstrips and nearly 1700 people.

The Longar area in Arno is famous for its 'love school' where young women were once taught how to perfect their sexual techniques.

The waters off Longar Point are known for superb deep-sea fishing where yellowfin tuna, marlin, mahi-mahi and sailfish abound.

The Japanese have funded a fishing project on Arno Island, which has included providing 20-foot outboard motorboats to local fishing communities and the construction of a cold storage facility and docks. About 10,000 pounds of tuna and reef fish from the project are sold on Majuro each month.

Getting There & Away
AMI flies from Majuro to Arno, landing at both Tinak and Ine islands, on Mondays, Wednesdays and Fridays. The one-way fare is $21 to Ine and $25 to Tinak.

Small private boats often commute between Arno and Majuro, though there's no scheduled service. It's possible to go over and back in a day.

LIKIEP ATOLL
Likiep Atoll is made up of about 60 islands around a shallow lagoon and has a population of 500.

During the German era, Jose deBrum, a Portuguese harpooner who arrived aboard an American whaleship, and Adolf Capelle, a German trader from a Honolulu-based company, bought Likiep Atoll from the high chief who owned it. They both married Marshallese women and settled in, planted coconuts and fruit trees and started profitable copra and ship-building companies. Descendants of deBrum and Capelle still own Likiep and operate it as a copra plantation.

Jose's son Joachim designed ships and homes and the mansion he built for his family still stands with some of the original furniture, Joachim's library and other personal belongings.

Joachim was also a photographer with a keen historian's perspective. More than 2300 glass plate negatives, taken between 1885 and 1930, and hundreds of documents and diaries have been recovered from the mansion and are being catalogued and reprinted for display in Majuro's Alele Museum.

Anyone interested in visiting the deBrum house should contact Leonard deBrum, the only surviving son of Joachim. This can be done in advance through the Alele Museum Box 629, Majuro, Marshall Islands 96960, which will forward the correspondence.

Places to Stay

Sato Maie has a family house on Likiep with rooms that can be rented for one or two weeks. The rate is $25 per day per person for both room and meals, or $20 per day if you want to bring your own food. From Majuro, the house can be booked via radio through the Office of Outer Island Affairs (☎ 3225).

Getting There & Away

AMI flies from Majuro to Likiep on Tuesdays. The cost is $94 one way.

WOTJE ATOLL

Wotje, the main island in Wotje Atoll, is literally covered from one end to the other with remnants of WW II. Huge Japanese-built structures loom out of the jungle, some bombed to pieces but others still habitable.

Large portions of the island were once paved in concrete, and machinery, fuel tanks and all sorts of unidentifiable war junk stick out everywhere. Right in the centre of the village is a large Japanese gun that can still be moved on its pivot. The lagoon is also full of wreckage, including a few ships which would probably make interesting diving.

The lagoon beaches of Wotje Island are quite beautiful and relatively clean. The nearby small islands are even better as they're mostly deserted and at low tide you can walk right over to them.

Wotje, known as the 'Marshallese garden centre', is a sub-district centre with about 650 people. Supposedly its abundant produce is due to topsoil the Japanese shipped over from Japan.

Places to Stay

There are many families on Wotje who have provided visitors with accommodation in the past and are quite willing to do so again. Mayor Helen Kobaia is friendly, speaks fluent English and may be able to help you find a place to stay.

Getting There & Away

AMI flies from Majuro to Wotje on Wednesdays. The cost is $73 one way.

MEJIT ISLAND

Mejit is a single coral island, about three-quarters of a sq mile, with a population of about 450 people. It's a beautiful island, with lush taro patches in the centre, and an abundance of coconut, breadfruit and pandanus trees.

As Mejit does not have a protective lagoon, fishing and the unloading of field trip ships can be quite perilous. This is especially true in November and December, months which also have pleasantly cooling winds. From May to July it's very humid and the mosquitoes are out in full force.

Mejit has a small freshwater lake, a rarity in the Marshalls, which even attracts a few wayward migrating ducks in the winter. If you can ignore the fact that it has quite a bit of algae, the lake is a nice place to swim.

California Beach, a beautiful beach on the north-west side of the island, is the best beach for swimming. Snorkelling is good north of California Beach.

Mejit has lots of tuna (in season), as well as lobster and octopus and, unlike other islands, no poisonous fish. Fishing is still very traditional on Mejit. The men go out fishing every morning, except Sundays, in dugout canoes called *korkor*. They are hesitant to take foreigners out fishing and consider it plain bad luck to have a woman on board.

The island is known for its beautiful quality mats which the women weave from pandanus leaves.

Mejit has one of the best outer island schools and quite a few islanders speak fluent English. The people of Mejit are very friendly and used to visitors. Peace Corps training sessions sometimes take place here and Mejit has even hosted an international gardening workshop sponsored by UNICEF.

Places to Stay

There's a government council house where you might be able to stay, but you should offer to pay something to the council for the privilege. Accommodation should become simpler in the future as the airport terminal presently under construction is scheduled to have a small hotel on the 2nd storey.

Getting There & Away

Presently AMI flies from Majuro to Mejit once a week, on Fridays, but once the hotel is finished, it's possible they'll add another flight. The cost is $92. The field trip ship usually takes about eight days from Majuro, though it can take twice that long on the return as it loads up with copra on the way back.

JALUIT ATOLL

Traditionally Jaluit was the home of the high chief of the southern Ralik islands. Today it's a sub-district centre with a population of 1700 people and is the only outer island with a public high school.

Jaluit's main island, Jabwor, was the headquarters of Jaluit Gesellschaft, a powerful group of German copra traders. It later became the German capital and Marshallese from other islands moved in, attracted by the schools, churches and higher standard of living.

When the Japanese took over they fortified the islands and started a fishing industry; the ruins of Japanese buildings and bunkers still remain. The USA captured the atoll during WW II but then mostly ignored it. In the 1950s Catholic and Protestant missions were set up and Jabwor began to prosper again.

In 1958 Typhoon Ophelia swept waves and wind over Jaluit, flooding the islands with water several feet deep, washing away most of the homes and coconut trees and killing 16 people. Jaluit is not a good place

to be during typhoons; one in 1904 swept away at least 60 people.

You can see the wreck of the ship *Alfred* still on the reef at Jabwor Pass where it sank in 1899.

Getting There & Away

AMI flies from Majuro to Jaluit on Mondays, Tuesdays and Fridays. The cost is $62 one way.

KILI ISLAND

In 1948, the US government resettled the displaced Bikinian people on Kili, a single isolated island which was uninhabited when they arrived.

The Bikinians soon learned that the canoes they had brought with them to Kili were useless as the island has no access to the sea; there is no lagoon, no port – not even a nice beach. Once a society of famed navigators, their seafaring skills are dying with the older Bikinian men.

Kili is now home to about 600 Bikinians. The biggest annual event on Kili is 'Bikini Day', held in March on the anniversary of the day in 1946 that the Bikinians became 'nuclear nomads'. Though there is feasting and sporting events, much of the day is taken up by wistful speeches from the elders about returning to their homeland.

Getting There & Away

AMI flies from Majuro to Kili on Mondays, Thursdays and Saturdays. The cost is $73 one way.

AUR ATOLL

Aur Atoll has a population of 450 people, who are equally divided between Tobal and Aur islands. The atoll is 75 miles north of Majuro and just a few miles south of Maloelap. The other islands in the atoll are officially uninhabited, though they're used for copra production and families sometimes live on these islands for stretches of a month or two.

Aur is a scenic atoll with a beautiful lagoon and excellent snorkelling. Not only is there a good variety of tropical fish and corals, but it's not uncommon to see turtles and small sharks.

Aur is a fairly traditional atoll and a good place to see both men and women making handicrafts. The people of Aur specialise in making model canoes and large wall hangings.

Places to Stay

The owner of a small island just north of Aur has begun to develop the island for visitors and is building Marshallese-style cottages, at least one of which is already complete. Rates are expected to be $10 to $15 per night. For information contact Lisen Candle, Box 58, Majuro, Marshall Islands 96960.

Getting There & Away

AMI flies from Majuro to Aur on Tuesdays and Saturdays, in conjunction with flights to Maloelap. The fare is $52 one way.

AILINGLAPLAP ATOLL

Ailinglaplap is the Marshall Island's third largest atoll, with the land area measuring 5.67 sq miles. It is home to about 1700 people, surpassed in population only by Majuro and Kwajalein. Ailinglaplap is also one of the biggest copra producers in the Marshalls.

Woja, one of the main islands, is about seven miles long and has approximately 600 people. Though there are few 'sights' as such, Woja is a lovely, lush island with white sand beaches. The large protected lagoon offers good snorkelling, swimming and fishing. The island has a good school with some US-educated teachers; many people speak English and are friendly to visitors. There's an abundance of local food, particularly in the summer, and a couple of stores (two even have refrigeration), though no restaurants or hotels. Four pick-up trucks act as taxis.

Getting There & Away

AMI flies to Woja on Wednesdays and to two other islands in the atoll, Jeh and Airok, on Thursdays and Fridays. The cost is $68 one way from Majuro.

Small private boats can take you across the lagoon from one island to another for about $45 one way, and sometimes there are government boats around which can do the same at nominal cost.

OTHER ATOLLS

Many Marshallese claim that **Wotho**, with a population of 90, is the most beautiful atoll in the world. It's where Amata Kabua, the president of the Marshalls, has said he intends to retire.

Although flying fish are caught throughout the Marshalls, they are especially associated with **Ailuk Atoll**, figuring in Ailuk's music, dance and legends. The fish are caught at night using lights and scoop nets and Ailuk is known for its delicious flying fish cuisine. The atoll has a population of about 500 people.

Bikar, **Taka** and **Taongi** atolls and **Jemo Island** are uninhabited by people, but are home to birds, coconut crabs and sea turtles.

Researchers from the East-West Center in Honolulu and the South Pacific Regional Environment Programme, who recently inspected atolls in the Marshalls, recommended designating Taongi and Bikar as National Preservation Areas. The team called Taongi (also known as Bokaak) 'possibly the only example of a completely natural, unaltered, semiarid atoll ecosystem remaining in the world today'. Taongi has an abundance of shearwaters, a kind of seabird which burrows into the sand to nest. Bikar has an especially large population of green sea turtles.

GETTING THERE & AWAY
Air

The government-owned Airline of the Marshall Islands (☎ 3733 in Majuro) operates services to about two dozen islands, touching down at every inhabited atoll.

From Majuro, AMI flies daily to Kwajalein and at least once a week to every other atoll. Some flights hop across a couple of islands at a time, so it's sometimes possible to visit different islands without returning to Majuro.

The flight schedule changes from time to time. You can write ahead for a schedule (Box 959, Majuro, Marshall Islands 96960) or pick one up at the Majuro office. AMI flies 48-passenger HS748s and 20-passenger Dornier 228s to the outer islands.

Boat

The field trip ship *Micro Pilot* has an irregular schedule which aims for nine runs a year to the outer islands, though once every two months is probably closer to reality. Typically two or three days is spent at each stop.

There are six different routes. The longest run is the western field trip which goes to Kwajalein, Lae, Ujae, Wotho, Enewetak and Ujelang, a round trip distance of about 1510 miles. The southern route takes two weeks, covering four atolls and 680 miles. The eastern route is 175 miles.

The fare is six cents per mile on deck. Cabins, which cost 10 cents per mile, have two beds, toilet and shower but no air-con. Meals are about $10 per day. Scheduling information is available from the Transportation Office (☎ 3469) Ministry of Transportation, Majuro, Marshall Islands 96960, at Uliga Dock in Majuro. Boats leave from the new dock near the copra processing plant.

Yachties should radio ahead from Majuro before visiting outer islands and should check in with the mayor upon arrival in the lagoon. This is more than a simple courtesy, as failure to notify the mayor is likely to make you an unwelcome guest.

GETTING AROUND

Outer islands usually have at least one motorboat and trips to other islands in the atoll can usually be arranged if visitors are willing to pay for petrol and maybe a little extra. Each situation is different, but the price to an island one hour away by motorboat might be about $20.

Sometimes the uninhabited atoll islands are used for copra production or to raise livestock. The more remote islands often have the best beaches and sometimes thatched shelters for overnight stays. It's cleaner swimming away from the village centres.

For a price, it should be fairly easy to get someone to take you fishing, lobstering, coconut-crab hunting and the like. Check with the mayor to see if there is a local fishing ordinance and fee. There often is, though it's not usually much and you may only need council approval. Mostly it's a courtesy that will make you friends.

Some islands have vehicles, but most of the time people just walk.

Federated States of Micronesia (FSM)

The Federated States of Micronesia consists of the four states of Kosrae, Pohnpei, Chuuk and Yap. All are part of the Caroline Islands, and all have similar colonial histories under Spain, Germany, Japan and the USA, yet the four states have their own distinctive cultures, traditions and identities.

The 100,000 residents of the FSM have eight major indigenous languages between them and no two states have the same native tongue. They communicate with each other in English, the language of their most recent colonial administrator.

More than anything else, what now ties them together is their new political affiliation as the FSM.

Political Beginnings

In July 1978, the Trust Territory districts of Pohnpei, Kosrae, Chuuk (then called Truk), Yap, the Marshalls and Palau voted on a common constitution. The Marshalls and Palau rejected it, along with the concept of a single unified Micronesian nation, and went on to establish separate political futures.

What was left became, by default, the FSM.

National and state governments were then elected. Tosiwo Nakayama of Chuuk became the first FSM president under the new FSM constitution which took effect on 10 May 1979.

In October 1982 the FSM signed a 15-year Compact of Free Association with the USA. The compact was approved by FSM voters in a 1983 plebiscite and officially implemented in November 1986. Because the UN Security Council didn't approve the termination of the trusteeship until December 1990, recognition of the FSM as a sovereign nation has been piecemeal. At last count the FSM had been officially recognised by only 18 nations, all but one of them (Israel) a Pacific rim or Pacific island nation.

One of the key aspects of the compact is that it gives the USA exclusive military access to the region and requires the FSM to refrain from any action that the USA determines to be incompatible with its obligations

---

Constitution of the Federated States of Micronesia

PREAMBLE

WE, the people of Micronesia, exercising our inherent sovereignty, do hereby establish the Constitution of the Federated States of Micronesia.

With this Constitution, we affirm our common wish to live together in peace and harmony, to preserve the heritage of the past, and to protect the promise of the future.

To make one nation of many islands, we respect the diversity of our cultures. Our differences enrich us. The seas bring us together, they do not separate us. Our islands sustain us, our island nation enlarges us and makes us stronger.

Our ancestors, who made their homes on these islands, displaced no other people. We, who remain, wish no other home than this. Having known war, we hope for peace. Having been divided, we wish unity. Having been ruled, we seek freedom.

Micronesia began in the days when man explored seas in rafts and canoes. The Micronesian nation is born in an age when men voyage among stars; our world itself is an island. We extend to all nations what we seek from each: peace, friendship, cooperation and love in our common humanity. With this Constitution we, who have been the wards of other nations, become the proud guardian of our own islands, now and forever. ■

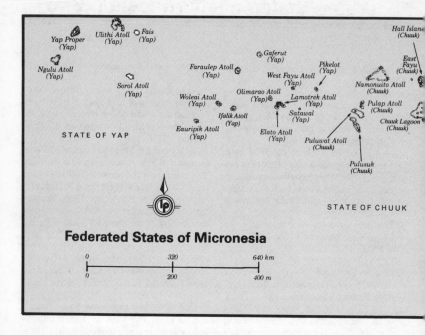

Federated States of Micronesia

to defend the area. This pretty much gives the US military carte blanche to do anything it wants in the FSM. Not all islanders were keen on this provision, but having grown dependent on US aid they needed the money that came with the compact. More than ever, the US relationship with Micronesia remains forged in greenbacks.

Geography

The FSM has 607 islands sprinkled across more than a million sq miles of the Pacific and extends 1800 miles from east to west. About 65 islands are inhabited.

The total land area is 271 sq miles. Pohnpei has nearly half the land area, with the rest almost equally divided between the other three states.

Government

The FSM has three levels of government: national, state and municipal.

The national government is divided into executive, legislative and judicial branches. The FSM Congress is unicameral, with 14 senators. Each state elects one senator at-large and the other 10 are elected based on population apportionment (five from Chuuk, three from Pohnpei, one each from Kosrae and Yap). The president and vice president, who cannot be from the same state, are elected by Congress from among its members. The national capital is in Palikir on Pohnpei.

Each state has a governor elected by popular vote for a four-year term, an elected legislature (30 legislators in Chuuk, 23 in Pohnpei, 14 in Kosrae and nine in Yap) and a state court.

On a municipal level, the traditional village leaders play an active role in government. They often select candidates for political office, and whether the village leaders approve or disapprove legislation

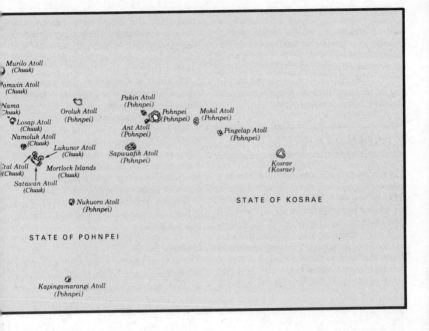

Murilo Atoll
(Chuuk)

omwin Atoll
(Chuuk)

Nama
Chuuk

Losap Atoll
(Chuuk)

Oroluk Atoll
(Pohnpei)

Pakin Atoll
(Pohnpei)

Pohnpei
(Pohnpei)

Ant Atoll
(Pohnpei)

Mokil Atoll
(Pohnpei)

Pingelap Atoll
(Pohnpei)

Namoluk Atoll
(Chuuk)

Lukunor Atoll
(Chuuk)

Sapwuafik Atoll
(Pohnpei)

tal Atoll
(Chuuk)

Mortlock Islands
(Chuuk)

Satawan Atoll
(Chuuk)

Kosrae
(Kosrae)

Nukuoro Atoll
(Pohnpei)

STATE OF KOSRAE

STATE OF POHNPEI

Kapingamarangi Atoll
(Pohnpei)

usually determines how people vote. It's common for the mayor of a municipality to be a local chief.

Economy

Over the 15 years of its compact with the USA, the FSM will receive a total of $1.33 billion in direct compact monies, as well as millions of dollars in additional grants and aid programmes.

The funding starts off top-heavy and tapers down by a third during the last years of the compact, in theory to allow the FSM to build the infrastructure needed for economic development and as seed money to stimulate private businesses. In reality, offering a bigger chunk of money right off appears to also have been a way for the USA to sweeten the deal.

Particularly in the district centres, US-funded capital improvement projects have been buzzing along constructing water and sewerage systems, hospitals, roads, docks, power plants and airfields.

Many people in the FSM still rely on subsistence farming and fishing for their livelihood. Only about 30% of the work force is employed in the money economy and the government employs well over half of those directly.

Under the Japanese the FSM was not only self-sufficient, but actually exported food. Now, however, the cost of imported food and beverages in the FSM is largely responsible for a huge trade imbalance in which imports total $60 million annually and exports less than $5 million.

The waters around the FSM are some of the world's most productive tuna fishing grounds, with a catch worth more than $200 million taken annually, mainly by Japanese and Taiwanese fleets. The $10 million the FSM collects each year as fishing fees from these foreign boats is its largest source of income following US aid. Harvesting the seas represents the FSM's single greatest potential for achieving economic independence. In an effort to get into commercial fishing more directly, the FSM is developing various fisheries projects of its own, including purchasing its first purse seiners and building fish processing plants.

Kosrae

Kosrae is a casual, unpretentious backwater, where people consistently return a smile. This is one of the least spoiled and least developed areas in Micronesia, an unhurried place that retains a certain air of innocence.

A high volcanic island whose peaks are draped in lush tropical greenery and sometimes shrouded in clouds, Kosrae is rich in natural beauty. It has an interior of uncharted rainforests, a pristine fringing reef and a coast which is a mix of sandy beaches and mangrove swamps. Flowering hibiscus, bananas and coconuts are abundant and the island is known for its citrus fruit, especially oranges, tangerines and limes.

The ruins of Kosrae's ancient stone city, Lelu, while not as well known as Pohnpei's Nan Madol ruins, are nearly as impressive and more easily accessible.

The introduction of the first jet service to Kosrae, by Air Mike in 1987, has had a surprisingly limited impact. Having more than a dozen visitors on the island at any one time is still quite unusual and, in a friendly way, people take note when someone new is in town.

Kosrae, pronounced ko-SHRYE (last syllable rhymes with 'rye'), was formerly called Kusaie.

History

Kosrae once had the most stratified society in Micronesia. By the year 1400 Kosrae was unified under one paramount chief, or

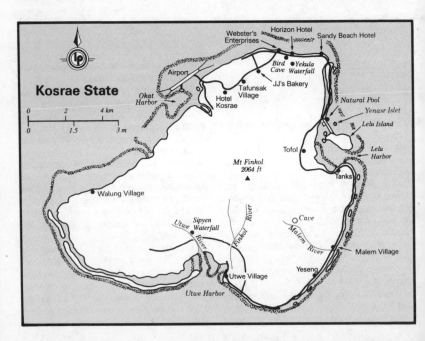

tokosra, who ruled from the island of Lelu. Essentially a handful of high chiefs owned the land, low chiefs managed it and the mass of commoners worked it. It was a feudalistic system with each group passing a percentage of their produce up the ladder.

While the commoners lived on the main island, which was then called Ualang, the royalty and their retainers lived inside more than a hundred basalt-walled compounds on Lelu and the nearby islets of Pisin, Yenyen and Yenasr. With its canal system and coral streets the fortressed island of Lelu would have rivalled its medieval counterparts in Europe.

Pohnpeian legend says that around the 14th century Kosraean warriors sailed to Pohnpei and overthrew the oppressive *saudeleur* rulers (a tyrannical royal dynasty of unclear origins) there. Chuukese legends also suggest cultural influences from Kosrae around the same time.

European Contact Kosrae was sighted by Europeans at least as early as 1801. It became known to sailors as Strong's Island, named in 1804 by the captain of the Nantucket whaler *Nancy* after the governor of Massachusetts.

It wasn't until 1824, however, that a Western ship finally pulled into harbour. It was just one of many stops in the Pacific for the sailors of the French ship *Coquille*, captained by Louis Duperrey, but for the Kosraeans it was their first contact with Westerners.

Duperrey and his crew stayed on Kosrae for 10 days and provided the outside world with an excellent account of the island. They estimated the population to be about 5000, with about 1500 living on Lelu, the ruling centre. The Kosraeans, a peace-loving people who had no weapons, were awed by the foreigners who gave them iron hatchets, a pig and other presents.

In 1827 the Russian ship *Senyavin*, captained by Fedor Lutke, docked at Kosrae and also received a hospitable welcome. Lutke noted that although the Kosraeans had dugout canoes as long as 30 feet, they had no need to go outside their own island and had no boats equipped for the open ocean.

Whalers and traders started calling at Kosrae in the early 1830s, attracted by deepwater harbours and reports of plentiful supplies of food, water, wood and women.

Not all early confrontations were peaceful ones however. In 1835 Kosraeans torched the Hawaiian ship *Waverly* and massacred the entire crew, apparently as revenge against the sailors who had boldly bedded island women without first getting permission from Kosraean men. The Boston trading ship *Honduras* was similarly attacked the same year and only two of the crew managed to escape.

In the early 1840s relations again became harmonious under the reign of chief Awane Lapalik I, who was known as 'Good King George' by visiting Westerners. From then until the decline of whaling in the Pacific in the mid-1860s, whaleships visited Kosrae by the dozens each year.

Missionaries In 1852, when the first missionaries arrived from Hawaii, the contagious diseases introduced by foreign sailors had already begun taking a disastrous toll on the islanders. The Kosraean people were in serious danger of being completely wiped out.

Ironically this made the missionaries' goal of total conversion considerably easier, not only by lessening organised resistance but by lowering the number of souls which needed saving. Around 1880, when the population hit an all-time low of about 300, virtually every remaining Kosraean was converted to Christianity.

The conversion was thorough. Traditional songs, dances, myths and other oral histories were discouraged or banned and ultimately forgotten. Tattooing went out of fashion, alcohol was forbidden and the ceremonial use of *seka*, a narcotic drink like Pohnpei's sakau, was no longer allowed.

Under church influences, Kosrae's traditional matrilineal society developed into a Western-style patrilineal system.

Traders Traders started arriving in full force in the 1870s. One of Kosrae's most famous visitors during this time was the American 'Bully' Hayes, a notorious swindler and trader who roamed the Pacific after years of involvement in the China opium trade. He was a frequent visitor to Kosrae where he traded in beche-de-mer, copra and coconut oil.

In March 1874 Hayes' 218-ton brigantine *Leonora* sank in Utwe Harbor during a sudden storm, becoming Kosrae's most famous shipwreck. Hayes was murdered at sea three years later in a brawl with his ship's cook, Dutch Pete.

Some believe that at the time of his death, Hayes was on his way back to Kosrae to recover the treasure he had rescued from the sinking *Leonora* and reputedly buried somewhere on the island. These rumours have inspired many a treasure hunt on Kosrae.

Japanese Period The Japanese, who arrived in 1914, exploited Kosrae's natural resources and took over three of the island's four coastal villages, forcing the Kosraeans to move inland.

Developments in agriculture, forestry, fishing and copra helped support the Japanese war effort during WW II, as well as provide for the 7000 Japanese living on the island. Kosrae was never invaded by Allied forces during the war.

Post WW II After the war, when the USA took over and the Trust Territory was set up, Kosrae was included in the Pohnpei district. For three decades thereafter Kosrae played only a secondary role as development was centred on Pohnpei, 350 miles to the northwest.

In 1977 Kosrae broke away from Pohnpei, becoming a separate district within the Trust Territory and later a separate FSM state. Although Kosrae gets more money this way than it would as an appendage of Pohnpei State, a desire for a bigger slice of the pie was not the only motive. Kosraeans and Pohnpeians had never before considered themselves one political unit until lumped together at the whim of the US administration.

Kosrae's current governor, who was elected in 1990 for a four-year term, is Thurston Siba.

Geography

Kosrae is roughly triangular, covering an area of 42 sq miles. It's one-third the size of Pohnpei, an island it resembles in shape and topography.

Kosrae has a rugged interior of mountain ridges and river valleys. Mt Finkol, the highest point, rises to 2064 feet. Lelu, Utwe and Okat are the main deep-water harbours and all villages are along the coast.

Kosrae is the easternmost island of both the Federated States of Micronesia and the Caroline Island chain. It is the only state in the FSM with no outer islands.

Climate

Temperatures on Kosrae average 80°F year-round. Rainfall averages 185 to 250 inches per year and is heaviest in summer, with more falling on the west coast than on the east. Trade winds come mainly from the north-east and are weakest from May to November. Kosrae is fortunate to lie outside the main typhoon tracks and even strong storms are relatively rare.

Economy

Most people still rely on subsistence farming and fishing for their livelihood. Less than 15% of the population works in the money economy and 80% of those work for the government.

Citrus is exported but on a very small scale. A small experimental agricultural farm behind the tourist office is part of a plan to help farmers increase production.

People & Culture

Kosrae's population is about 7000.

In Kosrae when you talk about the culture, you talk about religion – the most essential part of modern Kosraean society. About 90% of all Kosraeans are Congregationalists.

The religious beliefs and practices of the

late 1800s that so totally overtook the islanders have changed little over the years, though today the ministers are Kosraean.

The church has a firm grip on most aspects of Kosraean life and while it no doubt helps to make Kosrae a homogenous, law-abiding society it also tends to foster intolerance. Conversion to another faith, even another Protestant faith, is usually seen as a disgrace to the rest of the family. The convert is commonly disinherited and cut off from family land.

It is Kosraean custom to be quiet on Sunday. Not only are stores closed on Sundays, but even fishing and recreational activities are frowned upon. US Civic Action Team soldiers building roads on the island caused quite a sensation a few years back by water skiing in the harbour on Sunday.

An information board at the airport reads:

Sunday is reserved as the day of rest, so you'll find all businesses are closed. Restaurants are open in the evening. All visitors are invited to join in our church services, which begin at 10 am in each village. Come and listen to our church choirs, to witness an important aspect of our culture.

Language

English is the official language of the government and is widely spoken, though Kosraean, the native language, is more commonly used in everyday conversation.

'Good morning' or 'hello' is *lotu mwo* and 'thank you (very much)' is *kulo (na maluhlap)*.

Early whalers used the expression 'ah shit' so often that the islanders picked up on it and identified the whalers as *ahset*. This is still the common word for 'foreigner' today.

Holidays

Kosrae celebrates New Year's Day, Kosrae Constitution Day on 11 January, FSM Constitution Day on 10 May, Kosrae Liberation Day on 8 September, FSM Independence Day on 3 November, Thanksgiving on the last Thursday in November and Christmas Day.

Liberation Day, which commemorates the day the Americans liberated Kosrae from the Japanese at the end of WW II, is marked by sports competitions and canoe races between village teams.

Christmas features singing competitions between church choirs, a memorable experience as Kosraeans are outstanding singers.

Another way to experience Kosraean singing is to just head for the nearest village church on any Sunday. The hymns are sung in four-part harmony and the whole congregation joins in.

Orientation

Kosrae is divided into four districts, called municipalities, which are named after the main village in each: Lelu, Malem, Utwe and Tafunsak.

Historically Kosrae's population was disbursed around the coast in about 70 villages and many of the names of now- uninhabited villages are still used to designate sites.

The airport is on an artificial island off the north-west side of Kosrae. From the airport, the main road runs clockwise around the coast, ending in Utwe. Most of the road between the airport and Tofol is now paved, and there are plans to eventually pave the section between Tofol and Utwe.

Walung, a major village on the west coast, can only be reached by boat.

Kosrae's government centre is in Tofol, two miles south of the causeway to Lelu Island.

Activities

Hiking If you're interested in hiking, see Killin Killin at the Kosrae Community Action Program (☎ 370-3217) in Tofol. KCAP runs a youth training programme and a Micronesia Bound course, aimed mostly at high school drop-outs who are taught wilderness survival techniques during hikes into Kosrae's interior.

Killin knows the trails on Kosrae and may be able to arrange a guide for serious hikers.

One of the nicest trails is from Tofol up to a plateau that looks down on Lelu and Okat harbours, the reefs and the airport. It takes about 1½ hours one way. If you're in good physical condition you could climb from there up to the right breast of the Sleeping Lady, an additional 1½ hours.

If not, it's a moderate four-hour walk from the plateau down the other side to Okat Harbor. Part of the way the trail goes through a *ka* (terminalia) forest. The wood from these trees is used to make racing canoes. If you're descending to Okat, you'll want to arrange to arrive at the harbour at low tide as the last part of this walk is over sand bars and through mangroves.

Diving Kosrae has unspoiled coral reefs close to shore and both walk-in and boat diving. The confluence of two currents makes for prolific and varied marine life. Underwater visibility can easily be 100 feet, and in summer as much as 200 feet!

There's an American PBY search plane in about 60 feet of water at the mouth of Lelu Harbor on the right shoal side. The place where the guns used to be is visible and a

glove still stuck to the co-pilot's wheel looks eerily like a hand floating underwater.

Two Japanese boats, a 300-foot freighter and a fishing ship, which were both skip-bombed and blown apart, are popular dives. A more recent wreck, a medi-vac plane that crashed into the sea immediately after take-off, is broken in three pieces and crumpled like an accordion on the ocean floor.

Bully Hayes' ship, the *Leonora*, remained untouched in Utwe Harbor for more than 90 years. After a diving team from the Scripps Oceanographic Institute in California and a private group from Kwajalein stripped arte-facts from the wreck, the site was officially designated off-limits to sport divers. Now the wreck is protected under law and can only be visited with advance notice and when accompanied by a guide authorised by the Historic Preservation Office.

There's good diving between Utwe Harbor and Walung, where large groupers, barracuda and hump-headed parrotfish can be seen. At several places you can just step into the water at high tide, swim out 50 or 100 feet and start diving.

The most shark activity, including tiger sharks and small docile whitetips, is between Walung and Okat. Kosraeans say there hasn't been a shark attack in three genera-tions.

Three small dive operators have just recently started up businesses.

Dive Caroline (☎ 370-3239), Box DC, Kosrae, FSM 96944 is the largest operation, with a divemaster, a 25-foot 185-hp boat and Kosrae's only dive shop. The shop is across the road from Sandy Beach Hotel. Dive Caroline is a partnership between the hotel owner, Donald Jonah, and a German couple, Martin and Renate Horn.

Two-tank dives cost $65, with a minimum of three divers. The shop rents BCD, regula-tor and console for $18 to divers who go out on their tours.

Dive Caroline also rents tanks and weights for $8.50, fills tanks for $4.50 and rents snorkel sets from $4.50 per day.

Dive Kosrae (☎ 370-3062), Box 24, Kosrae, FSM 96944, is owned and operated by American Roger Emerson, a professional tropical fish collector who can take up to four divers out on his boat.

Jack Sigrah, a native Kosraean, offers unguided dive services for up to five divers through JS Dive Tours (☎ 370-2081), Box 135, Kosrae, FSM 96944. Jack has a 23-foot Yamaha skiff and can also take people snorkelling, deep-sea fishing and out for coastal cruises.

Snorkelling & Swimming The best spots for snorkelling and swimming change with the seasons and the trade winds. It's good between Malem and Utwe in the winter, though there are riptides and larger waves around Malem. The areas near Tafunsak Village, around the bridge to the airport and off Kosrae's north-east point are good in the summer, but can be rough from December to February.

The natural swimming hole formed in the reef alongside Lelu causeway is good for swimming. Snorkellers will find fish, but not much coral.

Farther out on the reef, near Yenasr Islet, there's another natural pool that's larger and deeper. This is where the early Kosraeans deposited the bones of their kings. Snorkelling is said to be good...if you dare!

Snorkellers who go out with the dive companies are often taken to Walung, which has coral gardens.

Local women go swimming in clothes that cover their knees. Swimsuits and short shorts are not acceptable in public buildings or around town.

Other Recreation Kosrae has a huge new gym, behind the high school in Tofol, that doubles as a meeting hall for special events. There's also an adjacent athletic field and an unlighted tennis court, all open to the public.

TOFOL

Tofol is the state administrative centre, though it's so small that it seems odd to think of it as the centre of anything. It's just a few buildings scattered here and there along a couple of dusty roads.

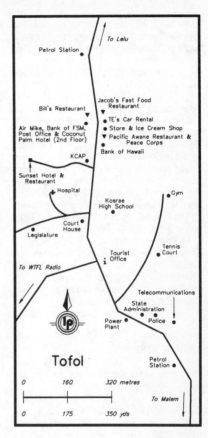

Tofol

You can get an excellent view of Tofol and Lelu Island by following the narrow dirt road up to the radio station. Though it's possible to drive up (carefully, in first gear!), it takes just 10 minutes to walk up and you'll be able to take a closer look at Kosrae's lush flora, including a stand of painted eucalyptus trees with rainbow-coloured bark.

Construction has begun on a new visitor centre in Tofol, on the main road opposite the drive to the radio station. The building resembles a traditional-style Kosraean house with a high-pitched roof and is being built of native materials including thatch and mangrove-log posts. The centre will include the tourist office and a handicraft shop. Until it is completed, the tourist office (☎ 370-2228) remains behind the legislature building, at the Department of Conservation & Development office.

Information

Kosrae's banks, Air Mike office (☎ 370-3024), hospital, high school (with the state's only library, such as it is) and sole post office are all in Tofol.

The post office is open from 8 am to 4 pm Monday to Friday. Both banks, the Bank of the FSM and the Bank of Hawaii, are open from 9.30 am to 2.30 pm Monday to Friday.

The Peace Corps office is on the 2nd floor above the Pacific Awane Restaurant.

International telephone calls can be made 24 hours a day from the FSM Telecommunications building in Tofol. The office also provides fax service until about 4 pm. When on Kosrae, you only need to dial the last four digits of Kosrae phone numbers.

Pacific Daily News is sold at Bill's restaurant.

LELU ISLAND

Lelu (also spelled Leluh) is a separate island connected to the rest of Kosrae by a causeway.

The early Kosraeans artificially extended the low part of Lelu by piling stones and packing coral upon the surrounding reef. They then used the new land to build a massive walled city for Kosraean royalty.

Lelu Hill, the island's high point, has a scattering of caves and tunnels used by the Japanese during WW II. There's a good view of the harbour from the top of the hill, which once held a Japanese observation tower and gun emplacements. A trail goes up the hill, but as it's across private land, it's best to find a local guide. You might try asking at the museum.

Museum

The state museum is housed in the oldest non-traditional building on the island – a small cement warehouse built in the 1890s.

The museum has charts and photos of archaeological work done at the ruins and a few artefacts such as ancient food pounders.

The museum is a good place to start a visit to Lelu ruins. Not only can you get a free brochure to a self-guided walk through the ruins, but if the museum staff is not busy they can provide a guide to go through the ruins with you.

The museum is open from 7.30 to 11.30 am and 12.30 to 4.30 pm Monday to Thursday. There's no admission fee for the museum or the ruins.

Lelu Ruins

The construction of Lelu dates back at least as far as 1400 AD, and probably as early as 1250 AD. In its heyday this royal city and feudal capital covered the entire lowland area of Lelu Island, and though the outskirts of this massive complex have been torn down the remaining ruins still cover a third of the island.

A ride around Lelu's perimeter road reveals only a sleepy waterfront village and a smattering of homes and businesses, with not a single stone wall in sight. But Lelu is deceptive, as the ruins are just behind these homes, beyond their backyards, almost completely hidden with thick tropical vegetation.

Once inside the complex, Lelu's walls rise up around you and your perspective changes completely. Suddenly you're in an ancient, hidden city, the kind of isolated setting you might imagine trekking hours through dense jungle to find. The ruins are vast and encompassing and the outside world feels far away.

Still extant are the dwelling compounds of some of the high chiefs, two royal burial mounds, a few sacred compounds and numerous large walls of huge hexagonal basalt logs that have been stacked log-cabin style. Pounding stones used for food preparation or making seka are identifiable by their smooth, indented surfaces.

To enter the ruins, take the driveway between the two houses directly across the road from the museum. Follow the path behind the houses, past the left side of the pigpen, and within a minute you'll be within

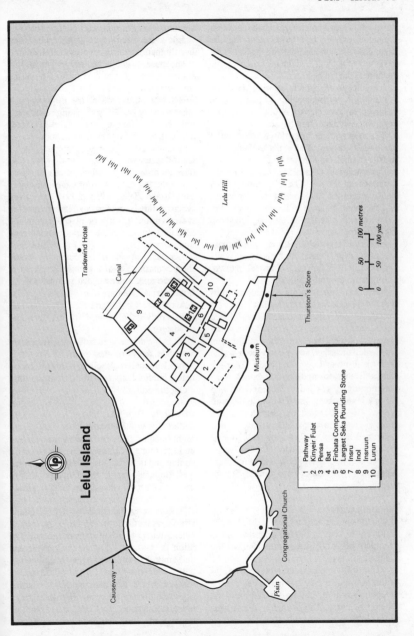

Lelu Island

Causeway →

Tradewind Hotel

Canal

Lelu Hill

Pisin

Congregational Church

Museum

Thurston's Store

1 Pathway
2 Kinyeir Fulat
3 Pensa
4 Bat
5 Finbata Compound
6 Largest Seka Pounding Stone
7 Insru
8 Inol
9 Insruun
10 Lurun

0   50   100 metres
0   50   100 yds

the ruins. Continue straight ahead through the complex and just before crossing the canal take the stone footpath on the left to get to **Kinyeir Fulat**, one of the most impressive section of the ruins.

Kinyeir Fulat, which has stacked prismatic basalt walls reaching 20 feet high, is believed to have served as both a dwelling compound and meeting house.

The compounds opposite Kinyeir Fulat are called **Pensa**. The walls at Pensa are mostly of medium-sized round basalt stones, with some brain coral added in, a later-day architectural feature. The high chief's feast house occupied the south-east compound and the adjacent areas of Pensa, which were used for food preparation, still contain about 20 pounding stones.

Bat is the large dwelling compound across the canal from Pensa. Its high basalt walls are thought to be among the newest in town, dating from around 1600 AD.

Insru and **Inol** contain mounded tombs which served as temporary resting places for deceased royalty. It was a sacred area, closed to commoners except for a group of wailing female mourners who, from the time the king was laid in the crypt, kept a continuous watch over his tomb and decaying body. After the king's flesh decomposed, the bones were ceremoniously carried to Yenasr Islet and dropped into a deep, natural hole in the reef.

In 1910 a German excavation found a male skeleton in one of the tombs. It was presumed he was the last king to be buried on Lelu and that in the whirlwind of Christian conversion his bones, and with them Kosraean traditions, were quickly abandoned.

Sleeping Lady

If you look south across Lelu Harbor toward Tofol you'll see the rugged ridgeline of the mountain range that forms the profile of the 'Sleeping Lady'.

According to legend the gods were angry with a woman so they laid her in the sea in a sleeping position and turned her into the island of Kosrae. The woman was menstruating at the time, or so the story goes, which

accounts for the rich red soil found in the jungle at the place which would be between her thighs. Kosraean men used to trek into the interior to gather the red soil from this sacred place and use it to make a paint for their canoes.

To view the profile, try to imagine a woman lying on her back facing south-east, with her hair flowing out behind her head. The pointy 'breasts' are easy to spot.

Lelu Causeway

There's a natural saltwater swimming pool off to the left at the start of the causeway to Lelu Island. The pool is full of water even when the tide is low and the flats surrounding it are exposed. It's a good place to swim and a concrete platform and stairs provide easy access.

On the west side of the causeway where there was once a tiny airstrip, the land is being dredged and reshaped to create a small boat marina. This area now holds the FSM Aquaculture Center and the Public Market with small stalls selling fish, produce and handicrafts.

At low tide the area between Lelu causeway and the north-east point of Kosrae is good for shell collecting. On full moon nights some islanders go out 'moonshelling' along the reef.

SOUTH OF TOFOL
Views & WW II Remains

The rusted remains of two Japanese midget tanks sit along the coast next to the Mobil oil storage tanks two miles south of Tofol, near the village of Sansrik. From this spot there's also a very good view of the Sleeping Lady mountain ridge across the bay.

The view to the north is of Lelu Island which, according to legend, was formed when a whale got trapped inside the reef. The hill is the humped body, the flat part the tail.

About 200 yards past the Mobil tanks, partly hidden behind a small house on the right side, are 115 concrete steps heading skyward. It's a climb to nowhere these days, but a Japanese weather station and lookout tower were once on top. Local basketball teams train by running up and down the stairs.

Malem

Malem, five miles south of Tofol, is the third largest village in Kosrae. The village sits at the mouth of the Malem River.

Behind the municipal building in Malem there's a small stone monument put up by the Kosraean-Japanese friendship society to honour the WW II dead.

The first road to the right past the municipal building goes by the Malem Congregational Church (marked Zion Hall) and up to a small dam that marks the beginning of a short, overgrown trail leading to the old Japanese command post. Nothing remains of the commander's house, but you can see the cave that served as his bunker by walking up the right side of the river for a couple of minutes. Look carefully for a cave opening on the right.

If you want to see the cave, you should ask permission at Timothy's, next to the church, as the path crosses private property.

Yeseng, the next village, has several concrete WW II bunkers scattered along the beach behind people's homes.

Utwe

Utwe (also called Utwa), five miles past Malem, is at the mouth of the Finkol River at the east side of Utwe Harbor.

This is a pleasant village to stroll around. People can often be seen sitting outside their homes weaving coconut fronds or cooking over an open fire while naked children play nearby.

If you want to hike there's a pretty walk from Utwe up the Finkol River. After about 45 minutes or so you'll come to some nice pools. You can do this first section on your own; ask anyone in Utwe how to get started.

With a guide you could continue walking upriver for about three hours to some pyramid tiers. They're overgrown with vegetation but you can still see a basalt altar built to honour the ancient Kosraean deity *Sinlaka* who was goddess of breadfruit harvests, famines and typhoons.

Inland Road

At 4½ miles beyond Malem, just before entering Utwe, there's a wide dirt road leading inland opposite a pole marked with an 'X'. This is the start of a new road along the southern part of the island that will eventually complete the island circle route. It currently goes in about six miles. Driving along this road gives you a glimpse into the interior and in places the feeling of passing through uncharted jungle.

If you're searching for sights, you might want to visit the **Sipyen Waterfall**, which is 3½ miles up the inland road. After the road climbs through a cut in the mountains it will descend steeply. Park off to the right side of the road at the bottom of the descent, where the guardrail stops. From the road you can hear (but not see) the falls. It's a five-minute walk up the river, though there's not a real trail and you must walk along the stream bed rocks, some of which are mossy. The waterfall, about 25 feet high and four to five feet wide, is pleasant enough but by no means spectacular and the shallow pool beneath the falls is not deep enough for swimming.

TAFUNSAK

The municipality of Tafunsak stretches along the entire west flank of Kosrae. It includes Walung Village, Okat Harbor and the airport, as well as Tafunsak Village and several smaller villages on the north side of the island.

Airport to Lelu

The drive between the airport and Lelu is the prettiest on the island, offering views of both the mountains and the coast, as well as close-up looks of Kosrae's luxuriant greenery.

The bridge coming from the airport crosses a channel through the reef with striking turquoise waters. Just beyond this there's a mangrove swamp where you might spot a grey Pacific reef heron *(noklap)* perched on one of the bleached white logs in the shallow water.

As you get closer to Lelu, there are picturesque white sand beaches lined with coconut palms.

Bird Cave

A large swampy cave at the west side of the rock quarry in the Wiya area is home to a colony of swiftlets *(kalkaf)* who cling to the cave walls by their claws and build nests of dried saliva and moss. When flying they look like small bats.

Islanders collect the bird droppings in the cave bottom to use as a rich fertiliser. Like lots of other places in Kosrae, this big swampy cave is thought to be haunted. In this case the belief is spurred on by rumours of Kosraean bodies left in the back of the cave by the Japanese.

Although the tourist bureau promotes the cave as an attraction, if you're not really interested in caves and swiftlets this is a good site to bypass. If you do visit, tread gently. Swiftlets are vulnerable to disruption by humans and may abandon a cave that is visited too often. The cave itself is not particularly attractive and smells of decaying matter.

Yekula Waterfall

Behind the old high school in Yekula Village there was once a good waterfall, though the stream has been diverted and the 40-foot falls are now quite thin.

If you want to take a look, find the dirt drive heading inland about 250 yards east of Horizon Hotel. Park off to the side of the main road and walk in. You'll shortly come to the old high school, which was built on private land in 1958 and closed in 1979 when the current school opened in Tofol. A family stays in one of the buildings and you should ask permission to pass. The dirt path continues on the right side of the high school and leads up to the falls, about 10 minutes in all.

Tafunsak Gorge

There's a steep gorge with 70-foot walls in Tafunsak Village which could be an interesting place to explore on a sunny day. As the gorge is extremely narrow, just eight to 10 feet wide in places, it has the potential to fill up with water quickly and could be dangerous during a downpour.

To get there, take the path behind JJ's Bakery and petrol station in Tafunsak Village. It's a 45-minute walk up the gorge, following an old steel water pipe. The pipe perspires and can be quite slippery under foot. A few minutes up the trail there's a shallow pool where neighbourhood kids swim, the first of a number of waterfalls and pools along the way.

Circle-Island Rd

The new road that will eventually circle the island leads south off the main road before the bridge to the airport. The road currently runs about three miles, passing above mangrove swamps and through jungles thick with bananas, tapioca and wild ginger. Stone ruins of living compounds and canoe platforms recently uncovered during road construction can be seen a short way down on the left side of the road.

Walung

The new circle road will eventually connect Walung on the west coast with the rest of the island. Walung is the island's most traditional village and not everyone there is happy about ending their isolation. For now it's a quiet place with few visitors.

Walung has lovely sandy beaches that stretch intermittently for a couple of miles. Just inland, craggy green peaks poke their heads up above the mist.

The village has a church and elementary school as well as the foundations of an old mission. Parts of the village which are cut by channels where the tide washes in are connected by long footbridges made of logs.

The only way of getting to Walung is by boat. The tourist office can arrange for an outrigger canoe equipped with an outboard motor to take you on a fascinating trip through the mangrove channel from Utwe to Walung. You'll pass by some of the largest and oldest mangrove trees to be found in all Micronesia. The trip takes about 45 minutes and costs $35. The boat ride within the channel can only be made at high tide, though it's also possible to make the journey outside the reef.

If you want to spend more than just a day

Top: Couple in outrigger canoe - Chuuk
Left: Yapese boys
Right: Japanese war ruins, Eten - Chuuk

Top: Chuukese kids
Left: Bathing in Wichon River - Moen
Right: Majuro High School mural

in Walung, Madison Nena at the tourist office can arrange for you to stay with a family for a reasonable fee or in exchange for goods such as canned meat and rice.

The other way to get to Walung is by private speedboat from Okat Dock. The ride takes about 15 minutes, but it's not nearly as interesting. There's no scheduled service, so you'll have to arrange this yourself.

PLACES TO STAY
Camping
Camping seems to be a fairly foreign concept in Kosrae, but people are quite accommodating. If you want to set up a tent, check with the mayor of the village you want to camp in.

Hotels
Kosrae has six hotels, all offering modest accommodation. A tax of 5% is added to the hotel bill. Coconut Palm Hotel, Sandy Beach Hotel, Horizon Hotel and Hotel Kosrae provide free airport transport. Credit cards are accepted only at Sandy Beach.

Coconut Palm Hotel (☎ 370-3181), Box 87, Kosrae, FSM 96944, in the centre of Tofol, has 11 large rooms with comfortable beds, sofa, table, chairs, refrigerator and both a ceiling fan and air-con. The management is friendly and this is the most popular hotel with businesspeople. Rates are $35 for a room with one queen bed, $45 for a room with two beds.

Sandy Beach Hotel (☎ 370-3239), Box 6, Kosrae, FSM 96944, has 10 thatched cottages right on the sand at Tafunsak Beach. The verandas face the ocean and during high tide there's snorkelling just outside the front doors. The cottages have screens so mosquitoes aren't a problem unless you let them in from the bathroom which has some open thatch. Rooms with small electric fan, but no air-con or hot water, cost $25/35 for singles/doubles. For rooms with air-con and hot water, add $5. All rooms have mini-refrigerators and free bottled water. Construction has begun on four modern concrete fourplexes, also on the beach, that are intended to be more upscale. There are plans for a restaurant.

Hotel Kosrae (☎ 370-2145), Box 231, Kosrae, FSM 96944, is a new eight-room hotel on the main road about two miles from the airport. The four downstairs rooms have electric fans, share a bathroom and a refrigerator and cost $18/20 for singles/doubles. Three upstairs rooms have air-con, mini-refrigerator, two double beds, a little sofa and a private bath and cost $40 for doubles. There's one room for singles with air-con and refrigerator for $25. The hotel provides free laundry service, coffee and fruit. This is not a terribly practical location if you're not renting a car, though the management might be able to make arrangements to take guests around.

Horizon Hotel (☎ 370-3456), Box 71, Kosrae, FSM 96944, has eight rather basic rooms in a two-storey concrete hotel at the beach in Tafunsak. Rates range from $25/32 for singles/doubles for rooms with shared bath to $30/40 for rooms with private bath and ocean view. Rooms have air-con and mini-refrigerators.

Tradewind Hotel (☎ 370-3047), Box TE, Kosrae, FSM 96944, on Lelu Island, has five free-standing units with refrigerators, private bathrooms and air-con. Check to be

---

Off the Beaten Track
A sign at the airport announces:

All lands (with the exception of the government center of Tofol) and all beaches are private. Therefore it is polite to ask the landowner if he is present to visit. The answer will undoubtedly be 'of course!'. ■

sure the ventilation is adequate and the air-con works, as there have been reports of rooms being hot and stuffy. Rates of $50/70 for singles/doubles include both a room and a rental car.

Sunset Hotel (☎ 370-3172), Box 62, Kosrae, FSM 96944 in Tofol, has four rather rundown rooms with fans and a shared bathroom. Rates are $20/30 for singles/doubles.

PLACES TO EAT

Kosrae has only a few restaurants and they all serve similar types of food, with American, Filipino and Japanese dishes dominant.

Bill's Restaurant in Tofol has good food, with fish tempura, beef teriyaki, chicken in peanut sauce and similar dishes for under $5 at lunch or dinner. They also have good sashimi with rice for $3.25, sandwiches and ramen. Breakfasts are $2 to $5. Though it's not on the menu, with a little advance notice Bill's will cook up mangrove crab, either boiled plain or steamed with garlic and butter, for about $7.

Jacob's Fast Food Restaurant in Tofol has sandwiches for $2 and grilled fish, chicken stew, curry or adobo plates for $3.25. Despite its name, Jacob's is an ordinary sit-down restaurant, open for breakfast, lunch and dinner.

Sunset Restaurant in the Sunset Hotel in Tofol has breakfasts for $3 to $4 and daily specials like curry chicken, chop steak, chicken adobo and beef stew for $3.75.

The *Horizon Restaurant*, next to Horizon Hotel in Tafunsak, has standard breakfasts for $3 to $4. At lunch and dinner, fish and chicken dishes average $5, but the food's mediocre.

The *Pacific Awane Restaurant* in Tofol was being remodelled when we were last there. It was once the most popular restaurant on the island and should be worth checking out.

There's an ice-cream shop next door to Pacific Awane.

Webster's Enterprises in Tafunsak is Kosrae's largest grocery and general store, and they also sell beer and alcohol.

The Public Market on the causeway to Lelu has far fresher produce than you'll find at Webster's or other grocery stores. You might also be able to buy local foods such as boiled breadfruit, boiled taro or baked bananas there. A real treat would be *fafa*, a sweet poi made from pounded taro with a coating of sugar caramel, a Kosraean delicacy made on special occasions.

ENTERTAINMENT

Entertainment in the conventional sense is limited on Kosrae. There are no bars, discos or staged cultural shows and even the movie theatre closed down when video rentals came in.

THINGS TO BUY

Typical Kosraean crafts include wooden taro pounders, carved wooden canoes, woven bags and purses and wall hangings of fibres and shells. One place to look for handicrafts is at the Public Market on the causeway to Lelu. There's also a handicraft stand at the airport.

Kosrae: The Sleeping Lady Awakens would make an excellent memento. Author Harvey Segal, an American educator who's been around Kosrae for a few decades, has produced a lively, comprehensive book that covers Kosrae's history, culture and flora & fauna. The book is sold at the tourist office in Tofol and at the airport visitor information centre for $8 and can also be ordered by mail for $10 (which includes postage) from the Kosrae Tourism Office, Box R&D, Kosrae, FSM 96944.

GETTING THERE & AWAY
Air

Not all of Air Mike's island hopper flights stop in Kosrae. Those that do include Kosrae are on Mondays and Wednesdays going east and on Tuesdays and Thursdays going west. On rare occasions, such as in the case of a medical evacuation, Air Mike will stop in Kosrae on one of its other island hopper flights.

Flights between Pohnpei and Kosrae cost $130 one way, or $193 return for an excursion ticket with a seven-day advance purchase. For travellers island hopping between Guam and Honolulu, Kosrae is a free stopover.

Pacific Missionary Airlines no longer flies between Kosrae and Pohnpei, except for special charters.

Kosrae has a new, open-air airport terminal with a snack bar, a car rental booth and a handicraft shop that doubles as a visitor information booth. There's a telephone across from the car rental booth available for free local calls. Kosrae has a $5 departure tax.

Sea

The state owns and operates the field trip ship MV *Mutunlik* mainly for cargo runs, though the ship can also accommodate about 20 people in five private cabins and on deck. Irregular service is provided to Pohnpei; with stops on Pingelap and Mokil atolls. Trips are also occasionally made to the Marshall Islands and Nauru. The one-way deck class fares from Kosrae are: $9 to Pingelap, $14 to Mokil, $18 to Pohnpei and $30 to Majuro. Cabin class is $31, $45, $61 and $100 respectively. The Kosrae Stevedoring & Terminal Company (☎ 370-3083) on Lelu will have updated information. If you're in Pohnpei, check at the Kosrae Liaison Office near Kolonia Town Hall for the schedule.

A private boat operated by SeAir Transportation (☎ 320-2866), Box 96, Kolonia, Pohnpei, FSM 96941 runs between Pohnpei and Kosrae about once a month. The fare is $18 deck class or $63 for a cabin. It takes about three days and stops at Mokil and Pingelap en route. Yachts sometimes dock at Lelu Harbor but the word is that yachties who don't get advance permission to enter the state are often asked to leave soon after arrival.

GETTING AROUND
To/From the Airport

Most of the hotels provide airport transfers for their guests. Even if you don't have a reservation there's a fair chance a couple of the hotels will be picking up guests at the airport and if they have rooms available you can go along.

Otherwise, getting a ride from someone going into Lelu or Tofol shouldn't be a problem, as most people go that way and few will be put out if you ask for a ride.

Car

TE's (Thurston's Enterprises) Car Rental (☎ 370-3226), Box TE, Kosrae, FSM 96944, opposite Coconut Palm Hotel in Tofol, has cars for $35. Webster George Car Rental (☎ 370-3116), Box 164, Kosrae, FSM 96944, in Tafunsak has new Mazda sedans for $32. Car rentals can also be arranged through the hotels or from Thurston's Store (☎ 370-3047) on Lelu.

Hitching

It's very easy to get rides around Kosrae and there's no need to stick out a thumb. Just start walking along the road and someone will stop and offer you a ride, often in the back of a pick-up truck.

No one thinks of charging for the lift and an offer of money would probably be considered an insult, especially for short rides. There are no taxis or public buses on Kosrae.

Pohnpei

Pohnpei, with its lush vegetation, jungle hillsides and flowering hibiscus fits the typical South Sea island image, albeit a wet one. The abundant rainfall feeds a multitude of streams, rivers and tumbling waterfalls. The damp rainforest interior, which is uninhabited and difficult to reach, has soft, spongy ground and moss-covered trees.

Pohnpei's boldest landmark is the scenic Sokehs Rock, a steep cliff face often compared to Honolulu's Diamond Head. The ancient stone city of Nan Madol, abandoned on nearly a hundred artificial islets off the south-east coast, is Micronesia's best known archaeological site.

The main town of Kolonia is relatively large by island standards, yet it retains an unhurried small-town character. Outside Kolonia it's largely unspoiled and undeveloped with small villages scattered around the island.

Kolonia is the capital of Pohnpei state while Palikir, five miles outside Kolonia, is the new capital of the Federated States of Micronesia.

Pohnpei was spelled 'Ponape' until 1984 and many schools and businesses still retain the old spelling.

History
Pre-European Contact

Though Pohnpei was inhabited at least as early as 200 AD, virtually nothing is known of Pohnpeians prior to the saudeleurs. The saudeleurs ruled from Nan Madol, an elaborate city of stone fortresses and temples that probably reached its peak of power in the 13th century.

The most common story of the demise of the saudeleurs tells of conquests from Kosrae. The Thunder God, who had been severely punished for having an affair with the wife of a saudeleur on Pohnpei, set out for Kosrae in his canoe. The canoe sank, but the Thunder God was able to continue on when a floating taro flower changed into a

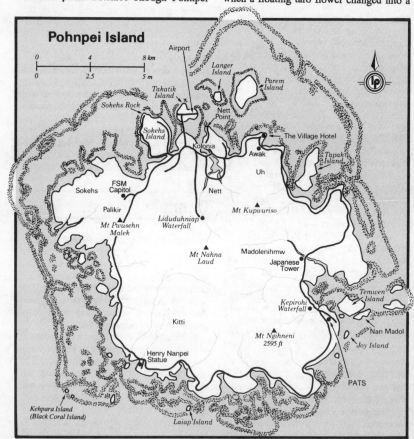

Pohnpei Island

0   4   8 km
0   2.5   5 m

Airport

Langer Island

Parem Island

Takatik Island

Sokehs Rock

Nett Point

Sokehs Island

The Village Hotel

Kolonia

Awak

Tapak Island

FSM Capitol

Uh

Sokehs

Nett

Palikir

Mt Kupwuriso

Mt Pwusehn Malek

Liduduhniap Waterfall

Mt Nahna Laud

Madolenihmw

Japanese Tower

Temwen Island

Kepirohi Waterfall

Kitti

Nan Madol

Mt Nghneni 2595 ft

Joy Island

Henry Nanpei Statue

PATS

Kehpara Island (Black Coral Island)

Laiap Island

needlefish and guided the god to the island. On Kosrae he made a woman of his own clan pregnant and the child, *Isokelekel*, was raised on the stories about the cruel saudeleur back on Pohnpei. After reaching adulthood Isokelekel gathered an army of 333 men and went to Nan Madol. He conquered the saudeleur and established a new system of royalty.

Pohnpei was divided into districts, each with two separate families of nobles. The senior man of the highest ranking family was the *nahnmwarki*, or district chief. The head of the other royal line was the *nahnken*, or secondary leader. The victorious Isokelekel became nahnmwarki of the region called Madolenihmw, the highest ranked district on Pohnpei and the one which included Nan Madol.

Sometime before the arrival of Westerners in the 1820s, Pohnpei Island was divided into the five districts of Madolenihmw, Uh, Kitti, Sokehs and Nett. These districts are the same municipalities in existence today, with the addition of the town of Kolonia, which previously was part of Nett. Each municipality still has its own nahnmwarki and nahnken and the system of ranked titles remains largely intact. The current nahnmwarki of Madolenihmw, Ilden Shelten, traces his lineage back to Isokelekel.

European Contact In 1528 a Spaniard, Alvaro de Saavedra, became the first known European to sight Pohnpei but it wasn't until 1595 that the island was actually claimed for Spain by Pedro Fernandez de Quiros. Even then, like most of the Carolines, Pohnpei was virtually ignored by the Spanish who were concentrating their efforts in the Marianas.

In 1828 Fedor Lutke, of the Russian sloop *Senyavin*, christened the island of Pohnpei and the atolls of Ant and Pakin 'the Senyavin Islands' and for quite a while the name stuck.

One of Pohnpei's more colourful early visitors was James O'Connell, probably an ex-convict from Australia, who became known as 'The Tattooed Irishman' after enduring Pohnpeian tattooing rites. O'Connell was shipwrecked on Pohnpei around 1830 and was captured by Pohnpeian islanders whom he thought were cannibals. In order to save his life he entertained the islanders by dancing an Irish jig – over and over again apparently, as the Pohnpeians were quite impressed with his antics. He not only managed to save his own life but he earned the respect of one of the chiefs and gained a 14-year-old wife as well. When the American ship *Spy* pulled into port in 1833, O'Connell escaped.

Whalers, Traders & Missionaries Whalers, traders and Protestant missionaries began arriving in Pohnpei around the mid-1800s. During each of the peak whaling years of 1855 and 1856 more than 50 whaleships dropped anchor in the island's lagoon. Pohnpei was known as Ascension Island during this period.

One bizarre event took place in 1865 during the US Civil War. The Confederate ship *Shenandoah*, on a mission to destroy the Union whaling business in the Pacific, pulled into Madolenihmw Harbor alongside four Yankee whaleships, took the officers as prisoners and set the ships on fire. The news that the Confederate South had surrendered to the Union just one week after this event did not reach the crew of the *Shenandoah*, who managed to destroy almost 40 Union whaleships throughout the Pacific before returning home.

As in other Micronesian islands, the diseases spread by visiting Westerners took their toll. The worst was the smallpox epidemic of 1854, introduced by the crew of the American whaleship *Delta*, which killed between 2000 and 3000 Pohnpeians. The indigenous population dropped from an estimated 10,000 in the early 1800s to less than 5000 by the end of the century.

In 1870 the naval cruiser USS *Jamestown* pulled into Pohnpei and forced island chiefs to sign a treaty which, among other things, allowed foreigners to buy Pohnpeian land. Kolonia was then named Jamestown.

Spanish Period The Spanish began to occupy Pohnpei in 1886, following the papal arbitration that gave Spain authority over the Caroline Islands. Just three months after his arrival, however, the island's first Spanish governor was killed in a rebellion in which Pohnpeians protested the use of forced native labour in building a fort in Kolonia. Spain's occupation of Pohnpei continued to be plagued by a series of uprisings, quite a few of which concerned the Catholic missions that the Spanish were trying to introduce into staunchly Protestant communities.

German Period The Germans arrived in 1899 after buying the Carolines from the Spanish. Their interest was in copra and other commercial products and they were rather heavy-handed in going about their development projects. They too used forced labour.

The 1910-1911 Sokehs Rebellion was sparked when a Pohnpeian working on a labour gang on Sokehs Island was given a beating by a German overseer. The Pohnpeians killed the overseer, and the revolt was on. The Germans promised revenge, though it took more than four months for ships with reinforcements to arrive from Melanesia. The Germans then blockaded Kolonia and sent troops of Melanesians charging up Sokehs Ridge. The uprising was suppressed and 17 rebel leaders were executed and thrown into a mass grave. Not wanting to see the incident repeated, the Germans exiled 426 Sokehs residents to Palau and then brought in people from other Micronesian islands to settle on Sokehs.

Japanese Period The Japanese took over in 1914. As elsewhere in Micronesia, Pohnpei became a site of intense commercial and agricultural development. The Japanese cultivated trochus shells and set up a sugar plantation to make alcohol.

At the beginning of WW II there were nearly 14,000 Japanese, Okinawans and Koreans living on Pohnpei and only about 5000 Pohnpeians.

Although Japanese military fortifications on Pohnpei were hit by US aerial bombings throughout 1944 and Kolonia was virtually levelled, Pohnpei was not invaded.

Geography

Pohnpei Island is high, volcanic and roughly circular, edged with coves and jutting peninsulas. The interior has rugged mountain ridges and deep valleys. Averaging 13 miles in diameter and with a land mass of 129 sq miles, it's the third largest island in Micronesia.

The centre of Pohnpei Island is Mt Nahna Laud but the highest peak is the 2595-foot Ngihneni. The coastline, devoid of natural sandy beaches, is mainly tidal flats and mangrove swamps. In between the island and its surrounding circular reef is a lagoon covering 70 sq miles, containing dozens of small islands.

Pohnpei State also includes eight outlying atolls, each covering less than one sq mile of land.

To the south-east, almost like stepping stones down to Kosrae, are the atolls of Mokil and Pingelap – 80 and 140 miles from Pohnpei Island. To the south-west are Sapwuafik (formerly Ngatik), 90 miles away; Nukuoro – 250 miles; and Kapingamarangi – 445 miles. Oroluk is 180 miles to the north-west and Pakin and Ant are a few miles west of Pohnpei Island.

Climate

The town of Kolonia has an average annual rainfall of 192 inches and Pohnpei's interior often gets a whopping 400 inches, making it one of the rainiest places on earth. The lowest rainfall occurs between January and March, while the wettest months are April and May. A typical Pohnpei day is cloudy with intermittent showers and the sun breaking through every now and then. Catching a good sunset is a treat to be relished.

Temperatures average 81°F (27°C) and most of the year there are north-easterly trade winds. From July to November however the winds die down, the humidity inches up and the nights especially can be oppressive.

Pohnpei is within typhoon spawning grounds, although outside the major tracks.

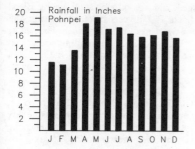

Rainfall in Inches
Pohnpei

J F M A M J J A S O N D

Economy

The majority of workers in the moneyed economy work for the government. Agriculture is important and subsistence farming is still widespread. Pohnpei is home to PATS, Micronesia's only agricultural trade school.

Pohnpei also has a sprinkling of pepper plantations. Pepper grows on climbing vines which in the wild sometimes reach to the top of full-grown trees. When cultivated, the vines are usually trained up posts six to eight feet high for easy picking. After copra, Pohnpei pepper is the leading export and a hot item in American gourmet shops.

People

The state population is 30,000. About 90% of the people live on Pohnpei Island and of those 20% are Kapingamarangis, Mortlockese, Pingelapese, Mokilese and, in smaller numbers, Kosraeans, Palauans and Americans.

The people of the remote Pohnpeian islands of Nukuoro and Kapingamarangi are the only Polynesians in Micronesia.

Culture

Sakau Many Pohnpeians spend their evenings getting turned-on by sakau, a drink made from *Piper methysticum*, the roots of a pepper shrub.

Sakau is called a mild narcotic, but it can be quite potent. It has a sedative effect, with your tongue and lips numbing out first. You then feel quite mellow and while your thinking seems clear your body doesn't always respond quite as you think it should. F W

Christian, an Englishman who did archaeological research at Nan Madol in the 1890s, perhaps described it best in his book *The Caroline Islands*: 'After four cups of sakau, one leg struggles south while the other is marching due north.'

Sakau is a bit slippery and slimy going down. Some people liken the taste to a mud milkshake, and whether it's the sakau itself or impure water sometimes used to rinse the roots, it may give the novice a case of the runs.

In Micronesia sakau is unique to Pohnpei, although the Kosraeans enjoyed it before the missionaries came along. In Polynesia it's called 'kava'.

Traditionally the pepper roots were pounded on a stone and the pulp squeezed by hand through hibiscus bark. The juices were then mixed with a little water and poured into a coconut shell which was passed around communally. Nowadays most shops use machines to do the work and serve sakau in a glass, though connoisseurs claim the hand-squeezed sakau is more potent. Sakau is perfectly legal and somewhat ceremonial.

Food Pohnpeians are big on yams and yams are big on them. Sometimes it takes 12 men just to carry one yam, as they can grow up to 10 feet in length and weigh as much as 1500 pounds!

Yams take on almost mystical qualities in Pohnpeian society and there's a lot of prestige attached to growing the biggest yam in the village. You've heard of the Eskimos having dozens of words for 'snow' – well the Pohnpeians have more than 100 words for yams.

Pohnpeians can eat yams day after day after day. Oddly (or is it?), yams are rare on restaurant menus. Breadfruit and seafood are other island staples.

Funeral feasts are important social events that can last three days and everyone brings gifts of food and sakau. Dog is a traditional feast food.

Language

Pohnpeian is the main indigenous language.

Other Micronesian languages spoken on Pohnpei are Mokilese, Pingelapese, Ngatikese and Nukuoro-Kapingamarangi, as well as Mortlockese, a Chuukese dialect. English is widely spoken and some older people speak Japanese.

The common greeting, *kaselehlia*, is a melodic word used for both 'hello' and 'good-bye' in a manner similar to the Hawaiian *aloha*.

Holidays

Pohnpei celebrates New Year's Day, Sokehs Rebellion Day on 24 February, FSM Constitution Day on 10 May, Pohnpei Liberation Day on 11 September, FSM Independence Day on 3 November, Pohnpeian Constitution Day on 8 November and Christmas Day.

In Pohnpei, each municipality has its own constitution and thus its own constitution day holiday: 27 February in Kitti, 1 May in Madolenihmw, 26 May in Uh, 25 August in Nett and 20 September in Kolonia.

Activities

Diving & Snorkelling Pohnpei has pretty coral reefs, manta rays and lots of fish. If the sea is rough divers may have to stay inside the barrier reef, which lies one to five miles offshore, and be content to explore the lagoon waters. However, visibility is much better outside the reef. Night diving is available and it's also possible to dive Nan Madol.

Snorkelling usually takes place inside the barrier reef. At Joy Island, snorkellers often see stingrays in addition to fish and coral.

Ant and Pakin atolls are considered better for diving than the main island. Ant has sheer coral drop-offs, schools of barracuda and some shark action. The one-way boat ride takes one hour to Ant and 2½ hours to Pakin. Spring, summer and autumn are the best months for diving. From December to February the waters between Pohnpei and Pakin are rough.

Dive Shops Phoenix Marine Sports (☎ 320-2362), Mapwusi Road, Kolonia, Pohnpei, FSM 96941, is a relatively new high-budget Japanese operation, with all the latest equip-

ment and a good reputation among island divers. Boat dives cost $60 for one tank, $85 for two tanks, including lunch. For Ant or Pakin, add $10. Snorkelling tours that include a visit to Nan Madol and Kepirohi Waterfall are $80. They also offer waterskiing, parasailing and trolling.

Joy Ocean Service (☎ 320-2447), Box 484, Kolonia, Pohnpei, FSM 96941, between the Joy Restaurant and the Joy Hotel, is a smaller operation than Phoenix, run by dive-master Yukio Suzuki. Joy charges $85 for two-tank dive tours by boat around Pohnpei, including lunch. Snorkellers can go out with divers for about $30. Snorkel sets rent for $4.

Seven Degrees North, Box 1267, Kolonia, Pohnpei, FSM 96941, has a 40-foot catamaran that can hold 27 passengers. Owners Brent and Raewyn Weyer are setting up Pohnpei's newest dive operation, following several years of being in the dive business in Guam. They are both PADI instructors who can certify divers. Brent is also a pilot for PMA and his plans include bringing in a seaplane to take visitors to outer atolls, such as Kapingamarangi, that don't have runways. Reservations are currently made through Village Travel (☎ 320-2777).

For other snorkelling options, see the section on Organised Tours.

Hiking Micronesia Bound (☎ 320-2365) might be able to arrange guides for serious hikers who want to hike into the interior and stay overnight, climb Sokehs Rock or undertake similar hikes. If you're interested see the director, Simeon Kihleng. Their office is in with the state administration offices down by the old Spanish wall.

Tennis There's a tennis court next to Kolonia Town Hall, a building originally constructed during the Japanese era and marked only in Japanese script.

Organised Tours Joe Henry's Water Taxi (☎ 320-2339), on the ground floor at Bernard's Restaurant, has boats for charter for snorkelling, fishing trips or whatever.

They can arrange a boat tour of Nan Madol, leaving from Kolonia and lasting about three hours, at a fee of $45 for one person, $60 for two.

Joy Hotel (☎ 320-2477) offers a boat tour of Nan Madol, leaving from Kolonia. The boat fee is $75 for one to five people, plus $18 for each additional person. In additional, there is a $3 Nan Madol sightseeing fee which is paid to the chief of Madolenihmw.

Micro-Pacific (☎ 320-2138) has a sightseeing tour of Kolonia, Pwusehn Malek, Palikir and Liduduhniap Waterfall for $35 and a tour of sunset spots for $25. Children pay half price. Their nightlife tour includes visits to a sakau bar and three alcohol bars for $35!

Iet Ehu (☎ 320-2959) is a local tour-guide service offering customised sightseeing tours, including round-the-island tours and trips to Nan Madol.

Pacific Missionary Aviation (☎ 320-2796) can provide an aerial sightseeing tour in a nine-passenger plane, at a cost of $450 per hour (about $300 for 30 to 40 minutes) per plane.

Cruises Kaselehlia Cruises (☎ 320-2151/5888) has a 40-foot trimaran called *Kaselehlia* available for day sails, sunset dinner cruises, snorkelling trips and the like. A day sail generally costs about $30 per person, including lunch at a lagoon island. The boat can hold 30 people and goes out only when there are enough people to make it worthwhile, so it's best to check ahead. Captain Snuffy Smith is a friendly, down-to-earth guy and if he's got a local group booked for a picnic out on the reef, he might well let an individual traveller tag along for $10 or so.

Fantasy Yacht Charters has a 40-foot catamaran available for sailing charters, snorkelling trips out on the reef and big-game fishing. Reservations are made through Village Travel (☎ 320-2777).

Both sailboats are moored midway off the causeway between Kolonia and Takatik Island.

Enipein Marine Park For a real Pohnpeian experience, consider a guided tour by outrigger canoe through the winding channels of a mangrove swamp. A few dozen residents of the Enipein ('Ghost Lady') area, in Kitti Municipality on the sparsely populated south side of the island, have formed a small business to provide these tours. The tours last six hours and include a trip out to a nearby reef for snorkelling, a lunch of fruit, fish and mangrove crab, plus sakau tasting for those who care to indulge. The cost is $35. Arrangements can be made by calling Louis Santos (☎ 320-2102/2693) or the tourist office.

KOLONIA

With a population of 6500, Kolonia is the largest town in the FSM.

Although it used to be likened to an American frontier town, Kolonia's appearance is rapidly changing. Modern buildings are replacing ramshackle shops and the broad main street now fills with 'rush hour' traffic.

Still, once you get into the town's back streets, an unhurried rural character surfaces. Dogs laze on the side of the roads and it seems that every other yard, no matter how small, contains a pen of squealing pigs.

Main St is the town centre. About midway down the street, beside the tourist office, there's a small Japanese tank painted in pastel camouflage splotches. A few blocks south, the state legislature buildings sit on the highest hill in Kolonia.

Along the waterfront road on the east side of town you'll find old warehouse-style businesses, a public market, new retail stores and the island's largest Protestant church, built in the early 1930s.

Information

The tourist office (☎ 320-2421), on Main St, is open from 8 am to 5 pm, Monday to Friday. They have a few brochures on Pohnpei, including a good detailed one of Nan Madol.

The Air Mike office (☎ 320-2424) is at the airport. It's officially open from 8 am to 5 pm daily, though on days with evening flights they may close earlier in the afternoon.

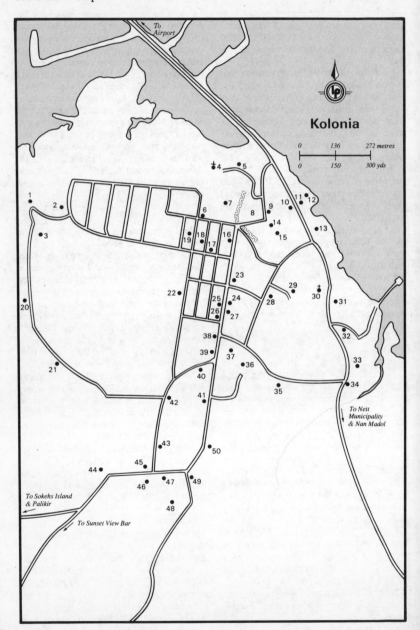

Kolonia

| 0 | 136 | 272 metres |
| 0 | 150 | 300 yds |

To Airport

To Nett
Municipality
& Nan Madol

To Sokehs Island
& Palikir

To Sunset View Bar

1	South Park Hotel	26	Ponape House
2	German Cemetery	27	Tourist Office
3	Cliff Rainbow Hotel	28	Kolonia Town Hall
4	Catholic Church	29	PMA Bookstore
5	German Bell Tower	30	Protestant Church
6	Ambros Store	31	Yoshie Enterprises
7	Spanish Fort remains	32	Hifumi Inn
8	Ball Park	33	Penny Rent-A-Car
9	Police Station	34	Yamaguchi Store
10	Australian Embassy	35	Community College of Micronesia
11	Chinese Embassy	36	State Legislature
12	Bernard's Restaurant	37	Banks/Travel Agencies
13	Public Market	38	Philippine Embassy
14	Immigration	39	Namiki Restaurant
15	Micronesia Bound	40	Town's Bakery
16	SeAir Transportation	41	Fruit Stand
17	Joy Hotel	42	Micronesian Office Supply
18	Joy Restaurant/Dive Shop	43	Laundromat
19	Peace Corps	44	PCR Restaurant/Car Rental
20	Hotel Pohnpei	45	Palm Terrace Store
21	Kapingamarangi Village/Gift Shop	46	Palm Terrace Hotel
22	Phoenix Marine Sports	47	Library
23	Telecommunications	48	Agricultural Station
24	Post Office	49	US Embassy
25	Village Travel/A-One Store	50	Kaselehlie Sakau Bar

The hospital (☎ 320-2213) is a mile southeast of Kolonia, on the road heading down the east coast.

Despite Pohnpei's heavy rainfall, parts of Kolonia still have water rationing. Tap water is not safe for drinking unless it's been treated or boiled. Bottled water is available in the stores, though it's about $2.75 a gallon.

Phoenix of Micronesia, next door to Phoenix Marine Sports, does quality film processing, with a 36-exposure roll costing $13 for prints, $8 for slides. They also sell film and make nice 50-cent postcards, each one a mounted photo.

The immigration office is down by the old Spanish fort walls.

Money The Bank of Guam and the Bank of Hawaii are together with a couple of travel agencies in a small complex at the intersection opposite the Namiki Restaurant. Both banks are open from 9.30 am to 2.30 pm Monday to Thursday and from 9.30 am to 4 pm Fridays.

Post & Telecommunications Pohnpei's main post office, on Main St, is open from 8 am to 4 pm Monday to Friday, 10 am to noon on Saturdays. Pohnpei's only other post office is in the new FSM capitol complex in Palikir.

Long-distance telephone calls can be made from the huge new FSM Telecommunications building on Main St.

Foreign Embassies As the new FSM capital, Pohnpei presently has four embassies. The USA (☎ 320-2187) and Philippine embassies are both on Main St and the Australian (☎ 320-5448) and Chinese embassies are across from each other down by the waterfront.

Bookshops PMA Bookstore, run by Pacific Missionary Aviation, is the only bookstore in Pohnpei. They sell fiction and non-fiction paperbacks and Pohnpeian and Kosraean dictionaries. It's behind the old Protestant church and is open from 8.30 am to 4.30 pm Monday to Thursday, mornings only on

Fridays. If no one's there, go to Good News Press next door for assistance.

The public library, at the side of the agricultural station, is open from 9 am to 5 pm, Monday to Friday.

The Palm Terrace Hotel sells Guam's *Pacific Daily News* and *USA Today*.

German Tower & Spanish Fort

At the north end of Main St is the tall grey German bell tower, all that's left of the Catholic mission built in 1907 by the Germans and torn down by the Japanese during WW II. A newer Catholic church is nearby.

Also in this area are the moss-covered remains of Spanish stone walls, which were built around 1887 and once enclosed Fort Alphonse and large sections of the Spanish colony. One fort wall is at the side of the ball park, while another starts across the street and runs along the road leading down to the waterfront.

Cemeteries

The cemeteries of the casualties from the Sokehs Rebellion are in the north-west part of Kolonia. The German cemetery, behind the Congregational church down the hill from the South Park Hotel, holds the remains of sailors from the German cruiser *Emden* who died fighting the Sokehs rebels. It also has the grave of Victor Berg, the German governor who died suddenly in 1907 after excavating a grave in Nan Madol.

The overgrown mass grave site for the executed Pohnpeian rebels is in a residential area to the north-east of the German cemetery.

Kapingamarangi Village

This village, on the west side of town in an area called Porakiet, is home to the Polynesians who moved to Pohnpei from Kapingamarangi and Nukuoro atolls following typhoon and famine disasters. Their breezy thatched homes with partially open-air sides are built on raised platforms a couple of feet off the ground. They live a more open and outdoor lifestyle than other Kolonia residents.

The Kapingamarangi people are easy-going and don't seem to mind visitors strolling around the village. Men make wood carvings and women do weavings which are sold in island gift shops. You might be able to purchase things directly from the craftspeople, but there's no hard sell and you'll probably have to ask if you're interested.

Agricultural Station

An agricultural station, started by the Germans and expanded by the Japanese, is in the southern part of town. While not a botanical garden, there are some nice old trees on the grounds, including a breadfruit grove near the road, tall royal palms flanking the driveway, Norfolk Island pines and a big fern-draped monkeypod tree. Many of the trees originally came from Borneo or Sumatra.

The three-storey building on the grounds once had a weather station on top. It was one of the few structures left standing in Kolonia after WW II but the building is now abandoned and condemned.

SOKEHS ISLAND

To get to Sokehs Island, take the road heading to the right at the fork past the PCR Restaurant. Once you cross the causeway onto the island the road divides, skirting the coast in both directions. Both ways finish in a dead-end as the island road doesn't connect around the northern tip.

You can walk around Sokehs Island, but it takes half a day. The northern part, where there's no driveable road, is made up of large rough rocks so you'll need sturdy shoes. This is the road the Germans ordered to be built with forced labour in 1910, prompting the labourers to resist and turning the incident into the armed Sokehs Rebellion.

After the rebellion, all Pohnpeians living on Sokehs Island were exiled and the land resettled by people from the Mortlocks in Chuuk and from Pingelap, Mokil and Sapwuafik atolls. Their descendants still live on Sokehs Island today.

Sokehs Ridge

The 900-foot Sokehs Ridge is loaded with anti-aircraft guns, naval guns, pillboxes and tunnels and there's an excellent view of Kolonia from the top. The trail up to the ridge starts behind the municipal office, the pink building just to the right after coming over the causeway. It's about a 45-minute walk up the path on a switchback trail with reinforced walls. The path isn't difficult but it starts out grassy and overgrown. If you have any problems finding the start of the trail ask someone to show you. If you come by car, you can park at the municipal office. The trail doesn't cross private property and you can do this walk on your own.

Sokehs Rock

The steep 498-foot Sokehs Rock can be climbed by those who like a challenge. After crossing the causeway, take the road to the right, which ends 1¾ miles down. The trail starts on the stone steps at the south side of the pink house which is shortly before the end of the road and a few houses before the Danpei United Church of Christ. Local kids may well offer to come along and guide you.

The trail can be fairly intense as it climbs the rock's sheer basalt face, and it can be very slippery when wet. Part way up there's a wrapped cable you can use to pull yourself along. The reward is the good view of Kolonia and the reef from the top.

PALIKIR

The new 135-acre FSM capitol complex in Palikir Valley, built on the site of a Japanese WW II airfield, is five miles south-west of Kolonia.

The complex incorporates traditional Micronesian architectural designs. The building roofs are peaked, like those of ancestral Kosraean homes. Supporting pillars cast of black concrete resemble the basalt columns of Nan Madol. The ends of the beams on the 1st storey are in the shape of Yapese stone money, whereas those on the 2nd storey look something like the bow of a Chuukese outrigger canoe.

The $13 million complex has four legisla-tive and judicial buildings grouped together, including an attractive Congressional chamber with a pyramidal roof topped by a huge skylight. A second cluster contains five buildings used for the executive branch, which administers day-to-day government operations.

The paved road to Palikir heads uphill to the left just before the causeway to Sokehs Island. This is also the start of the circle-island road. This section of the road is in excellent condition, though it has no shoulders and you'll need to watch out for children who walk along the road oblivious to cars. The entrance to Palikir is 3½ miles down.

Palikir Trail

The Palikir Trail leads from the FSM capitol complex through tropical forest and open grasslands to a hill with good views of the main island, the lagoon and the barrier reef. It's about two miles and takes about 1¼ hours round trip. One nice thing about this hike is that you don't have to worry about crossing private property. This is a hot walk and therefore good for early morning hours.

The hike begins at the back of the farthest parking lot, on the left side of the Mogethin Building, in front of the police post.

The trail starts off on a well-defined footpath and heads downhill, crosses a little stream after about five minutes, then leads up into open grassland along a path of packed red clay.

After about 15 minutes you'll come to a deeply cut stream crossing in a pretty setting with mango trees, bamboo and thick vegetation. Shortly beyond the stream the trail enters a large open field of grass and ferns.

From here you can see your destination, which is the tall hill ahead on the left. The trail passes through head-high grasses as it climbs, and the route branches off in places, so you may have to improvise a bit. The fine views from the hilltop include Sokehs Island to the north-east and a glimpse of Ant Atoll off to the south-west.

Pwusehn Malek

Legend says this high volcanic cone formation in Palikir was created during the defeat of Pohnpei's saudeleur dynasty. The ruler of Palikir changed himself into a giant rooster to fly to Nan Madol and along the way he left a huge pile of droppings.

Pohnpeians call the hill Pwusehn Malek. The English translation so stumped Pohnpei's tourist office that their brochure simply lists it as 'Mount' followed by a long blank space. The popular translation is 'Chickenshit Mountain'.

A trail up Pwusehn Malek starts by the telephone pole on the right side of the road, a little over 1½ miles south of the FSM capitol complex. It's about a 10-minute walk on a grassy and overgrown trail up to the first ridge. It's an easy trail, though when it's wet it can be muddy and slippery.

NETT MUNICIPALITY
Liduduhniap Waterfall

Liduduhniap Waterfall on the Nanpil River is a 20-minute drive from Kolonia. It's at the end of a rather rough gravel road and, depending on road conditions, you may need a 4WD vehicle to make it all the way in.

To get there, take Kolonia's waterfront road heading south and a half mile past Yamaguchi Store turn right onto the dirt road between the big mango tree and Joe's Tire. About three miles in, the road climbs a steep hill and forks at the top. Take the left fork; the falls are just a short way ahead.

The waterfall is actually twin cascades and the pools are quite good for swimming. A family up at the top charges $1 to get in.

Nahs Even if you can't get all the way up to the falls, a beautiful ceremonial *nahs* owned by the local nahnken is just 1½ miles in from the main road and well worth a look.

The nahs, which has been recently restored to showpiece condition, is made of native materials in the traditional manner. Split reeds and thatch make up the roof and sides, hand-twisted coconut sennit rope ties the beams, and all the wood pillars are set on stones so as not to touch the ground.

A black granite plaque on the grounds,

presented by the Oomoto Foundation of Japan, waxes poetic:

Into the dim reaches
Beyond cloud haze
I make my way
Toward Ponape.

Just beyond the nahs, there's a picturesque suspension bridge hung over a pool in the bend of the river. The water is deep enough for swimming.

Nett Point

Nett Point is another popular place for swimming and picnics. As in most places, it's safe if there are families around, but you might want to avoid the area if just drinkers are hanging out.

To get there, turn left onto the dirt road immediately after crossing Dausokele Bridge, a half mile past the hospital. The road leads two miles down to an old dock which offers good views of the lagoon islands and a distant glimpse of the thatched cottages of the Village Hotel to the east. From the pier, there are steps leading down into clear waters, good for swimming.

The drive itself is nice too, passing both modern and thatched homes, and providing excellent views of Sokehs Rock across the bay.

AROUND THE ISLAND

A 54-mile road circles Pohnpei, but except for about 10 paved miles around Kolonia it's a rutted dirt road and a lot of the driving can only be done at about 10 to 15 miles per hour. The less-developed west side of the island doesn't get as much traffic and the road on that side is usually in better condition. Plans call for the entire road to be paved within a few years.

For now, it takes about 1¼ hours to go the 22 miles from Kolonia to the Ponape Agriculture & Trade School (PATS) and the Madolenihmw municipal building, and about three hours to circle the entire island. Give yourself at least half a day to take in the sights.

East Pohnpei

The circle-island road, taken clockwise, leads south out of Kolonia, through small villages in Nett, Uh and Madolenihmw municipalities.

You'll see a nice cross-section of village life on this drive. Nearly every man carries a machete, and sometimes a stalk of bananas or a basket of yams as well, naked children play at the roadside and women sit in streams and do laundry.

A mile out of Kolonia the road crosses the Dausokele Bridge, which spans a wide river. The turn-off to the Village Hotel is 3½ miles beyond the bridge, on the left.

A half-mile past the Village Hotel, you'll cross a bridge and enter Awak Village in Uh Municipality. The church on the right, with a picturesque mountain backdrop, is worth a look.

Six miles past Awak Village there's a nice hillside view looking down onto lagoon islands that somewhat resemble Palau's Rock Islands.

Six miles farther, in the village of Namishi, an old Japanese lookout tower covered with vines is visible on the right side of the road.

This side of the island is Pohnpei's wetter, windward side and there's an abundance of tropical flora, including plumeria, bougainvillea, beach hibiscus, African tulip trees, breadfruit, pandanus, mangoes and bamboo.

Kepirohi Waterfall

You'll likely have seen Kepirohi Waterfall before you get there, as this is the impressive waterfall pictured in tourist brochures. The broad 70-foot falls cascade over a basalt rockface into a pool that's good for a refreshing midday dip.

The waterfall is at the far end of the village of Sapwehrek. One-third of a mile past Sapwehrek Elementary School, you'll cross a river followed by a small church on the right side of the road. Park at the church and walk back about 50 feet to the trail, which begins on the north side of the church property. It takes about 15 minutes to walk up to

the falls. The property owner usually charges visitors $1.

Ponape Agriculture & Trade School

Just a few hundred yards past the church there's a road junction. You get three choices and as usual nothing's marked.

If you're planning to visit the Ponape Agriculture & Trade School (better known as PATS) or are on your way to Nan Madol or Joy Island, then go straight ahead at this intersection rather than taking the sharp left or veering right. (If you want to continue around the island, take the road to the right.)

PATS is a private Jesuit-run high school that offers four-year courses in agriculture, construction and mechanics to boys from all over Micronesia. The school is surrounded by about 200 acres of land, some of which has been developed as an experimental farm.

Students give free tours of the school by appointment. Call a day or two in advance (☎ 320-2991) to schedule a time. The tours last about an hour and are generally held in the afternoon so as not to interfere with classes.

To get to the Madolenihmw municipal building, or to go over to Temwen Island, drive straight through the PATS complex. Across from the municipal office is Ponape Coconut Products, a small business started by PATS but now independent, which makes the coconut oil soaps and shampoos sold in gift shops around Kolonia.

SOUTH-WEST POHNPEI

Back on the circle-island drive, continuing clockwise, the road goes through a eucalyptus grove and then up and down a series of hills, the steepest of which offers a beautiful ocean view.

This back side of Pohnpei remains largely in a natural state, with only a few clusters of houses here and there, most made of thatch and bamboo. This side is also drier, with less jungle and more open vistas into the interior.

A bronze statue of Henry Nanpei (1860-1928), an influential Pohnpeian nationalist involved in the struggle against the Spanish colonists, is one of the few conventional 'sights' in the area.

The dirt road to the statue leads off to the left 12½ miles from the turn-off to PATS and a quarter mile before reaching a steel bridge that crosses the widest river on Pohnpei's south side. The statue is almost half a mile down, off to the right in a small grassy clearing. Nanpei was buried a little farther down the road, in a church cemetery.

As the cross-island road continues it edges along mangrove swamps, winds inland and back down to the coast, crosses dozens of streams and goes through a run of small villages. One very picturesque village at the north end of Kitti Municipality has houses on stilts sitting over the water and outrigger canoes floating under thatched shelters.

The distinctive conical mountain called Pwusehn Malek marks the beginning of the Palikir area and Sokehs Municipality. The FSM capitol complex is just ahead and the road continues back to Kolonia.

NAN MADOL

Nan Madol was an important political, social and religious centre built during the saudeleur dynasty. It was a place for ritual activity and the homes of royalty and their servants.

Ninety-two artificial islets, stretching out nearly a mile in length and a half-mile in width, were built on the tidal flats and reef off the south-east side of Pohnpei, near Temwen Island.

Basalt which had cooled naturally into hexagonal columns, some of them 25 feet in length and 50 tons in weight, were quarried on Pohnpei Island and hauled to the site by raft.

The columns were stacked horizontally around the edges of the islets as retaining walls and filled with coral rubble and rock. In this manner the islets were eventually raised and the twisting canals shaped into what is sometimes referred to as the 'Venice of Micronesia'. On the level surfaces were built temples, burial vaults, meeting houses,

bathing areas and pools for turtles, fish and eels.

The eastern half, Madol Powe (upper town), was the section for priests and rituals. The western half, Madol Pah (lower town), was the administration section.

The construction of Nan Madol began in force between 1100 and 1200 AD and continued for another two to three hundred years. Nan Madol was uninhabited when the first Westerners came ashore in the 1820s, but it was a recent abandonment. In 1852 missionaries recorded that elderly Pohnpeians could still remember when Nan Madol was densely populated.

The best time to visit is at high tide when small boats can easily navigate the twisting mangrove-lined channels which wind through the complex.

Though many of the ruins have collapsed it just adds to the impact, especially as you round a sharp corner in the canal and suddenly find yourself in the shadow of the massive Nan Douwas. This is the largest structure still standing and the most impressive sight.

The outer walls of the Nan Douwas compound stand 25 feet high. The inner compound contains four crypts which were burial places for the saudeleurs and later the nahnmwarkis. The largest crypt is rectangular and is in the centre of two sets of enclosing walls, covered by basalt stones about 18 feet long and weighing a ton each.

The islet of Kariahn also has high walls surrounding a tomb.

Pahn Kadira was probably the administrative centre of Nan Madol and also featured the temple of the Thunder God. A large, low platform is all that remains of the temple.

The islet of Idehd was the religious centre of Nan Madol. An annual ritual performed here by high priests culminated with the offering of cooked turtle innards fed to Nan Sanwohl, the 'holy eel' that was kept in the compound pool. The ritual was part of a two-week religious ceremony which included canoe building competitions, feasting, singing, dancing and sakau drinking.

Darong, also an important ritual area, has

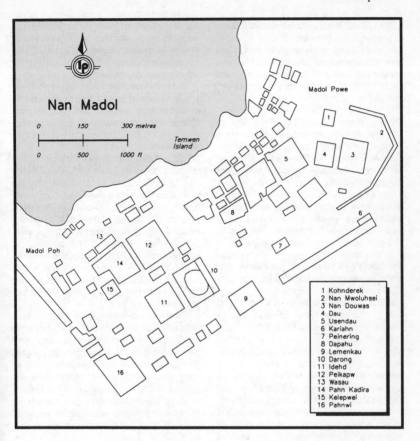

Nan Madol

0   150   300 metres

0   500   1000 ft

Temwen Island

Madol Powe

Madol Poh

1 Kohnderek
2 Nan Mwoluhsei
3 Nan Douwas
4 Dau
5 Usendau
6 Kariahn
7 Peinering
8 Dapahu
9 Lemenkau
10 Darong
11 Idehd
12 Peikapw
13 Wasau
14 Pahn Kadira
15 Kelepwei
16 Pahnwi

a natural reef pool in its centre which may have been used for raising clams. Near one wall is a large stone once used for pounding sakau.

Other major islets are Usendau, an area where priests lived; Nan Mwoluhsei ('where the voyage stopped'), the ocean entrance to Nan Madol; Pahnwi, a multi-purpose islet that included burial tombs; Kelepwel, a residential islet for servants and visitors; Wasau, an area where food was prepared; Kohnderek, a site for funeral services; Dapahu, an islet where canoes were made; Dau, a place where warriors lived; Peikapw,

an islet which had two pools for turtles; Lemenkau, the medical centre; and Peinering, a coconut processing centre.

Though Nan Madol is Pohnpei's foremost sightseeing spot for foreigners, not all Pohnpeians feel comfortable there and the local belief that people shouldn't disturb the ruins may be more than mere superstition. In 1907 the German governor died of a mysterious ailment immediately after excavating a burial tomb on Nan Madol. The German administration claimed it was heat exhaustion but a lot of older Pohnpeians still don't buy it.

Nan Madol holds its mysteries well. Some believe that the legendary lost continent of Mu, or Lemuria, may lie off its waters and Nan Madol was built as a mirror image of a sunken city that at the time of construction could still be seen lying beneath the water's surface.

Getting There & Away

The best way to visit Nan Madol is via boat through the canals. This is not only the traditional method, but also the most scenic approach and the most practical way to see the majority of the islets.

For $13 one of the caretakers on Joy Island will pick you up at the Madolenihmw municipal building, which is just beyond PATS, take you by motorboat through Nan Madol, and then return you to the municipal building. You must either drive or take a taxi to and from PATS. Tour arrangements must be made in advance at the Joy Hotel (☎ 320-2477) in Kolonia.

There are also several boat tours to Nan Madol that leave from Kolonia (see the section on Organised Tours earlier).

Another option is to wade across to Nan Madol. From the Madolenihmw municipal building, go across the causeway to Temwen Island. From the south side of Temwen you can wade over the reef to Nan Madol and explore the ruins on foot, though you'll want to coordinate this with low tide. Because Nan Madol is so spread out, you will probably be able to explore only a part of the complex this way.

ISLANDS IN POHNPEI LAGOON

The number of islands in Pohnpei's lagoon depends on the tide and how you make the count. Not including the artificial islets of Nan Madol, there are about 24 basalt islands, 30 coral islets on the barrier reef and some islands of alluvial sands.

Langer Island

The basaltic island of Langer figures in colonial history. German traders had copra operations there and the Japanese built a seaplane base on the island which survived US bombings in 1944. After WW II the seaplane ramp was used as Pohnpei's only runway, with all air travel by Grumman SA-16 amphibian, until 1970 when the current airport was built on Takatik.

Today Langer Island is a popular place for weekend family picnics and is also the site of aquaculture projects, including a giant clam hatchery built on the old seaplane ramp.

Joy Island

If you're looking to get away from it all, Joy is a quiet little island with a white sand beach and 11 unfurnished rough wood cottages with thatched roofs, back-to-basics style. Small groups sometimes come to Joy Island for picnics, but most of the time it's deserted except for the groundskeeper and boatman.

If you don't want to stay overnight, you can also visit Joy Island for sun and snorkelling. A good way to do this is to combine it with the $13 Joy tour of nearby Nan Madol, as a half-day stay on Joy Island can be had at no extra cost.

Otherwise, it costs $5 for the boat ride from PATS to Joy Island and back. Overnight lodging costs $7 per person if you bring your own bedding or $9 if they provide a futon, blanket, sheet and pillow set. You have to bring your own food, but you can use Joy's covered outdoor cooking facilities. There's an electric generator and lights in the huts. Be sure to specify a hut as far away as possible from the odoriferous toilets and pigpens.

To get to Joy Island, either drive or take a taxi to the Madolenihmw municipal building, just below PATS, where the boatman will pick you up. Everything must be pre-arranged and pre-paid at the Joy Hotel (☎ 320-2477) in Kolonia.

Black Coral Island

Black Coral Island (☎ 320-2440) is a small, tree-covered island on Pohnpei's southwestern barrier reef. The island has thatched cottages with small, simple rooms that are a little nicer than the ones at Joy Island. Snorkelling is good and it all makes for a nice quiet retreat.

Overnight rates are $7.50 per person, and futons and sheets can be rented. Day visitors pay $2.50.

Breakfast can be arranged for $3 to $4, lunch for $7 to 12, dinner for $9 to $15. Boat transportation from Seinwar School in Kitti costs $25 a round trip.

If you want to leave from Kolonia, Phoenix Marine Sports (☎ 320-2362) provides transportation to Black Coral on weekends. The cost is $140 for up to four people, $35 for each additional person.

OUTER ATOLLS

Ant Atoll

Ant, a beautiful atoll with a palm-fringed lagoon, lies a few miles south-west of Pohnpei Island. It has pristine white sand beaches and aqua waters with abundant coral and fish, and is one of Pohnpei's most popular dive destinations.

Ant has a large seabird colony, including brown noddies, great crested terns, sooty terns and great frigate birds.

The atoll is part of Kitti Municipality and belongs to descendants of Pohnpeian nationalist Henry Nanpei.

The largest of the atoll islands, Nikalap Aru, is currently being developed by the Nanpei family and Japanese investors. Ten free-standing cottages with thatched roofs have been built on the beach and another 30 are planned. Arrangements to visit Ant can be made through Fantasy Yacht Charters or Phoenix Marine Sports.

Pakin Atoll

Pakin is a small, uninhabited atoll about 25 miles off Pohnpei Island's north-west coast. It has good beaches and, like Ant, is a popular dive spot.

Oroluk Atoll

Oroluk has a sizable population of hawksbill and Pacific green turtles, as well as a dozen people. Although its 19 islands total less than quarter of a sq mile of land it has a large lagoon. The luxury cruise ship SS *Thorfinn* stops at Oroluk for snorkelling and diving.

Mokil Atoll

Mokil (also called Mwoakilloa) was once often visited by Marshallese and Gilbertese and later became a popular stop with whalers.

Mokil Atoll's three islets total about half a sq mile. Fewer than 300 people live on Kahlap, the largest and only inhabited islet. The other two, Urak and Mwandohn, are farmed.

Mokil is a tidy little place, with friendly people, a pretty lagoon and a 1000-foot airstrip served by Pacific Missionary Aviation (PMA). With advance notice, PMA can arrange through their agent on Mokil for visitors to stay in homes with island families.

Pingelap Atoll

Pingelap has three islands but all of the atoll's 750 people live on Pingelap Island. Sukoru and Deke islands are visited for gathering coconuts and crabs.

Early foreigners did not find a ready welcome in Pingelap until about the 1850s when the first whaling ships arrived. In the 1870s, Congregationalist missionaries trained two Pingelapese teachers on Pohnpei and sent them back to their home islands. In just two years they had not only converted practically the entire population, but had adults and children alike all wearing Western clothing.

Pingelap is known for *kahlek*, a kind of night fishing which uses burning torches to attract flying fish into hand-held nets. Kahlek means 'dancing' and refers to the way the men holding the torches have to sway to keep their balance when they're standing up. This sort of fishing is done from January to April.

Unfortunately, there's a lot of poverty in Pingelap, the island's not very clean and the flies and mosquitoes can be almost unbearable. Like Mokil, Pingelap has a 1000-foot airstrip serviced by Pacific Missionary Aviation.

Sapwuafik (Ngatik) Atoll

With the drawing up of its municipal constitution in 1986, Ngatik Atoll renamed itself

Sapwuafik Atoll, correcting an inaccuracy it had been carrying for 150 years. The name Ngatik now, as in pre-European times, refers solely to the largest and only populated island in the atoll.

A visit by the British ship *Lambton* in 1837 permanently changed the island society. Charles 'Bloody' Hart, the Australian captain of the ship, was after fine pieces of tortoise shell he had seen on an earlier excursion to the atoll. But the shells had religious significance to the Ngatikese and they refused to trade. In fact during the first visit, trading negotiations were halted by a group of armed islanders who attacked the crew and forced them to run for their lives back to the ship. Hart however was a swindler, accustomed to getting his own way, and although his crew had escaped unharmed they went back for revenge. The Ngatikese, armed only with clubs and slings, had little defence against the muskets of the *Lambton*'s crew, and the sailors massacred all the island men.

The 600 people of Sapwuafik are largely descended from a mix of Ngatikese women and British, American, Pohnpeian and Gilbertese men, many of them crew members of the *Lambton*.

Sapwuafik is well known for its outrigger sailing canoes, made from breadfruit logs and assembled using wooden pegs and coconut fibre twine. Unlike on other Pohnpeian atolls where islanders have switched to speedboats or attached small outboard motors to their canoes, Sapwuafik's traditional canoes are powered solely by the wind using sails lashed to bamboo poles.

The FSM government has recently allocated funds to build an airstrip on Sapwuafik.

Nukuoro & Kapingamarangi Atolls

The people of Nukuoro and Kapingamarangi atolls are physically, linguistically and culturally Polynesian. Both atolls are beautiful, with good beaches.

Nukuoro has 42 tiny islets, with a total land area of six-tenths of a sq mile, formed in a near-perfect circle around a lagoon four miles in diameter. Most of the population of about 400 live on the largest island, a third of which is covered by taro. Subsistence comes largely from taro farming and fishing.

A new airstrip being completed on Nukuoro will allow easier access. Nukuoro is a real haven, with Polynesian hospitality, and would be a fine place to spend some time just lazing around on beaches, picking up seashells and playing with island children.

Kapingamarangi Atoll is just one degree, or 65 miles south of the equator. Its 33 islets total just over half a sq mile, with a lagoon seven miles across at its widest point. The population is about 500.

Taro Patch Day, celebrated annually on 15 March in Kapingamarangi, honours the completion of a huge community taro patch in the 1940s. Feasts of roasted eel are a speciality of the day.

Both Nukuoro and Kapingamarangi are hit from time to time by severe droughts. The most recent, in 1989, dried up taro patches and stressed coconut trees, resulting in food shortages on the islands.

Getting There & Away

Until relatively recently, the only way to get to most of the outer atolls was by boat. There are now airstrips on Mokil, Pingelap and Nukuoro.

Air Pacific Missionary Aviation (☎ 320-2796) Box 517, Kolonia, Pohnpei, FSM 96941, flies to Mokil and Pingelap on Mondays and Fridays. PMA's one-way fare from Pohnpei Island is $50 to Mokil, $65 to Pingelap. Flights to Nukuoro are expected to begin soon.

Flights leave Pohnpei from a two-storey cement building on the west side of the main terminal.

Sea The government field trip ship, *Micro Glory*, aims for about 24 trips a year to the outer islands. The ship holds 125 passengers and has eight cabins. Fares are calculated on a per-mile basis.

Route 1 goes to Mokil and Pingelap, returning in about four days. The round-trip fare is $18 on deck, $62 for a cabin. Route 2 goes to Sapwuafik, Nukuoro and Kapingamarangi, and takes about seven days. The round trip costs $36 on deck, $122 for a cabin. You can take along your own food or pay $2.50 for breakfast, $3.50 for lunch and $4 for dinner.

The field trip ship leaves from the commercial dock on Takatik Island. For more information, contact the Office for Island Affairs (☎ 320-2710), Pohnpei State Goverment, Kolonia, Pohnpei, FSM 96941.

SeAir Transportation (☎ 320-2866) Box 96, Kolonia, Pohnpei, FSM 96941, a private company which operates a boat similar to the government field trip ship, runs between Pohnpei and Kosrae almost every month. The trip takes about three days one way and stops at Mokil and Pingelap. The one-way fare to Kosrae is $18 on deck, $63 for a cabin. Meal prices are $3.50 for breakfast, $4 for lunch and $4.50 for dinner, or you can bring your own food. The SeAir office is on Main St in Kolonia.

It's not uncommon for boats to the outer islands to leave days or even weeks late, or to cancel a trip altogether. Be aware, however, that we've also heard from someone who had booked reservations and arrived in Pohnpei on the day of departure only to find that the *Micro Glory* had left a day early!

PLACES TO STAY

Pohnpei has a 6% hotel tax. Palm Terrace Hotel, Joy Hotel and the Village Hotel accept MasterCard and Visa.

Hotel Pohnpei (☎ 320-2330), Box 430, Kolonia, Pohnpei, FSM 96941, near Kapingamarangi Village has 19 thatch and wood cottages, with walls of woven split bamboo, built in native Pohnpeian style. It's in a garden setting with tropical flowers and views across the water to Sokehs Rock. The cottages are screened all the way round and rooms have fans, refrigerators and bottled water. The bathroom showers are sun-lit and draped with ferns and hanging plants. Thatch doesn't block sound well however, and one reader advises to avoid rooms near the lobby

if you don't want to listen to constant radio music from the front desk. Singles/doubles cost $30/40.

Palm Terrace Hotel (☎ 320-2392), Box 310, Kolonia, Pohnpei FSM 96941, has 11 large rooms with air-con, ceiling fans, cable TV and bathrooms with tubs. The rooms are comfortable enough, but a bit run down and in need of a fresh coat of paint. Singles/doubles cost $42/49.

South Park Hotel (☎ 320-2255) Box 829, Kolonia, Pohnpei, FSM 96941, is on a hilltop overlooking the bay. If you're looking for a splurge, the new wing has the best rooms in Pohnpei, each with nice furnishings, tile floor, a mini-refrigerator and a sliding glass door opening to a large veranda with a beautiful clear-on view of Sokehs Rock. Rates are $65/75 for singles/doubles, though when the FSM legislature is in session these rooms are usually booked out. There is also a neglected wing with sparsely furnished musty rooms starting at $30/35 for singles/doubles, though these may not be around for much longer as the hotel is in the midst of renovations. All rooms have air-con and the staff is very friendly.

Joy Hotel (☎ 320-2447), Box 484, Kolonia, Pohnpei, FSM 96941, is a new in-town hotel with 10 nicely furnished rooms, each with a phone (free local calls), air-con, ceiling fan, TV, bathtub and small lanai. Rooms with one double bed are $50/58 for singles/doubles and rooms with two double beds are $55/70 for singles/doubles.

The *Cliff Rainbow Hotel* (☎ 320-2415), Box 96, Kolonia, Pohnpei, FSM 96941, has 40 air-con rooms with prices ranging from $40 to $60 for singles and $48 to $66 for doubles. The cheaper rooms are in an older section that's quite ordinary and the overall ambience is lacking.

The *Hifumi Inn* (☎ 320-2382), Box 811, Kolonia, Pohnpei, FSM 96941, down by the waterfront, has 10 very shabby rooms with shared bathroom. Rates are $13/16.50 for singles/doubles for rooms with fans, $24 for doubles for rooms with air-con.

The *Harbor View Hotel* (☎ 320-5244), Box 1328, Kolonia, Pohnpei, FSM 96941, is walking distance from the airport. Despite the name the views leave much to be desired, as the hotel is oddly situated behind a commercial dock. The 40 rooms are lacklustre and even though this is a new hotel it's already on the decline. Rates are $45/60 for singles/doubles.

The *Village Hotel* (☎ 320-2797), Box 339, Kolonia, Pohnpei, FSM 96941, has 21 thatched cottages perched on a hillside in a natural setting five miles south of Kolonia. The rooms have waterbeds and ceiling fans. This is the trendy place to stay for Kwajalein contract workers on R&R and for other tourists with American Express cards. Rates are $60 to $80 for singles and $65 to $85 for doubles, with the higher price rooms having views.

For accommodation outside the Kolonia area, see the sections on Joy Island and Black Coral Island.

PLACES TO EAT

Pohnpei has excellent fresh tuna. Sashimi is often the cheapest dish on the menu and grilled or fried fish dishes are not much more.

Joy Restaurant, a perennial favourite, has excellent Japanese food. Fresh fish is the speciality, though they also have beef and chicken dishes. The 'Joy Lunch' of fried tuna, rice, sashimi, soup and salad is recommended at $4.50. Yellowfin sashimi or fried fish burgers cost $1.25. It's open for lunch from 11 am to 3 pm Sunday to Friday, and for Sunday dinner (same menu) from 5.30 to 9 pm.

Joy Hotel Restaurant, not to be confused with Joy Restaurant, is off the lobby of the Joy Hotel. They have a variety of Japanese and Western foods and, at least by Pohnpei standards, it's almost a little elegant, with the food served in courses. The grilled tuna dinner is good and includes a big piece of fish, soup, salad and French fries for $6. Chicken teriyaki plates (with Pohnpei chicken from the island's new hatchery) are $6.50. At lunch they have sandwiches for $3 to $4. At breakfast French toast with fresh fruit, or a vegetable and cheese omelette,

costs $2.50. It's open from 7 am to 3 pm and 5.30 to 9 pm daily, except for Sundays when they close at 3 pm.

Palm Terrace Restaurant, behind the hotel of the same name, is a plain place with ordinary food but has a big local following, particularly among expatriates. Breakfasts start from about $2. At lunch or dinner you can get a fishburger with fries for $2.25. They also serve pizza, spaghetti and standard meat dishes from about $5. It's open from 6 am to 2 pm and 5 to 10 pm daily.

PCR Restaurant, up from the Palm Terrace Hotel on the way to Sokehs, offers a varied menu and the island's only sushi bar. Their Napolitan spaghetti is loaded with fish, octopus and green peppers and comes on a sizzling platter with garlic bread for $5.50. This is one of the nicer places in town to eat. It's open from 11 am to 9.30 pm Monday to Friday, from 5 to 9.30 pm on Sundays.

The *Village Hotel's* open-air thatched restaurant has an unbeatable hillside setting, with a distant view of Sokehs Rock across the lagoon. It also has Pohnpei's most expensive dinner menu with such dishes as mahi-mahi almondine for $13 and rack of lamb for two for $35. At lunch they serve moderately priced sandwiches. This is a good place to stop for breakfast if you're on your way around the island. If you have a sweet tooth, try the Pohnpei hot cakes for $3.50.

Bernard's Restaurant is a big 3rd floor waterfront restaurant with an excellent view of Pohnpei's lagoon islands. Filipino, Japanese and local food is served buffet style. You pick out what you want and pay based on your choices. Prices are moderate. It's open from 11.30 am to 5 pm Monday to Friday.

Island Buffet, on the 2nd floor of Yamaguchi Store, serves food buffet style, similar to Bernard's, with ribs, fried chicken, fried fish and the like. It's simple and reasonably priced.

Namiki Restaurant on Main St is a clean, local eatery open Monday to Saturday. Breakfast averages about $2, lunch and dinner $3 to $4.

The restaurant in the *Cliff Rainbow Hotel*

exists mainly to serve hotel guests and is not particularly good value. The best deals are at lunch, when sandwiches with fries are $2 to $3.

The restaurant in the *Harbor View Hotel* has rather average food at moderate prices.

The fruit stand near the weather station on Main St has fresh island produce, including bananas, watermelons, limes, breadfruit and yams. You can also buy produce at the public market on the waterfront road. *Town's Bakery* makes a nice banana bread for $1.

Ambros Store, Palm Terrace Store, Yoshie Enterprises and A-One Store are all fairly large grocery stores in Kolonia.

ENTERTAINMENT
Bars
The *Palm Terrace Bar*, at the side of the Palm Terrace Restaurant, is a popular watering hole favoured by American expatriates who glance up from Micronesia's longest bar to check out whoever walks through the door.

When there's a good sunset, the open-air thatched *Sunset View Bar* is the place to be. To get there head past the PCR Restaurant and where the road forks, take the left branch. After one mile turn right onto a road which is paved as far as the old telecommunications building, one third of a mile down. After another third of a mile take the far right at the three-way fork. Continue bearing right and the drive will end shortly at the cliffside bar.

The *Ocean View Bar*, on the road to Sokehs, has a good hillside view looking across Pohnpei's main harbour. They sometimes have live music and dancing in the evenings.

The *Tattooed Irishman*, the bar at the Village Hotel's open-air thatched restaurant, is a bit more genteel. For breathtaking views, order up a tropical drink and head for the gazebo.

Sakau
Sakau bars are prolific around Kolonia. Every neighbourhood has one, though most are small, casual and inconspicuous. If you see a sign hung on a shack saying *mie sakau*

pwongiet it means sakau is being served there that night.

Though not the most traditional of settings, an easy place to try sakau is at the *Kaselehlie Sakau Bar*, run by Naiten and Linda Phillip, down by the US Embassy. Unlike alcohol drinkers who tend to be boisterous and temperamental, sakau drinkers are quiet and relaxed.

If you prefer to drink sakau in your own room, bring a container and most sakau bars will fill it for you and you'll have 'sakau to go'.

Cultural Shows
Pohnpei's cultural centres offer shows of traditional dances, songs, chants and demonstrations of arts such as coconut husking and crafts. Shows usually include ritual sakau making, with samples handed around to the audience. Islanders wear traditional costumes (grass skirts for the women) and photography is permitted. The original centre, in Nett Municipality, has been joined by a couple of others, each scheduled to perform on a different day of the week. Performances are not given unless at least five people have booked, which means reservations must be made in advance through the tourist office or hotels. Each centre gives a slightly different show. The Nett Cultural Center show is at 3 pm on Fridays and charges $7.50 per person, though if you have a group you can arrange a show on a different day for $40. The centre in Uh Municipality, out by the Village Hotel, does their performance at 4 pm on Tuesdays and charges $15 per person.

THINGS TO BUY
Pohnpei has the highest quality wood carvings found in Micronesia, virtually all made by Kapingamarangi islanders who live in Kolonia. Dolphins, sharks with real shark teeth, fish, turtles and outrigger canoe models with woven sails, all carved of mangrove or ironwood, make excellent souvenirs.

Other handicrafts include grass skirts,

fans, woven fibre pocketbooks, baskets, coconut-grater benches and wall hangings.

Packages of gourmet Pohnpei pepper make good lightweight presents to carry back home. A three-ounce pack of black or white peppercorns costs about $3.50.

Pohnpei massage oils, soaps, suntan lotion and shampoos made from coconut oil are sold separately in stores for local use or gift-packaged in woven boxes at the handicraft shops.

Good places to pick up handicrafts are the gift shop at Joy Restaurant, Ponape House on Main St and the handicraft booth at the airport. The coconut oils and soaps are a bit cheaper at the Ponape Coconut Products office, down by the waterfront, south of Bernard's Restaurant; it's open 8 am to 4.30 pm Monday to Friday.

There's a small roadside handicraft shop in Kolonia's Kapingamarangi Village where wood carvings can be purchased at reasonable prices. The hours are irregular and they're closed on Sundays, but even then someone will probably get the manager to open up for you if you ask.

GETTING THERE & AWAY
Air
Air Mike flies to Pohnpei on its island hopper route, with flights coming from Honolulu three days a week and from Guam four days a week.

The regular one-way fare is $179 between Chuuk and Pohnpei and $367 between Guam and Pohnpei, though special night flights on Wednesdays, Fridays and Sundays discount seats to $92 between Chuuk and Pohnpei and $177 between Guam and Pohnpei.

The regular one-way fare from Kosrae to Pohnpei is $130, though there's an advance-purchase ticket for $193 return. From Majuro, it's $310 one way, or $548 for the round-trip excursion.

For travellers island hopping between Guam and Honolulu, Pohnpei is a free stopover. Otherwise, Honolulu to Pohnpei costs $551 one way, or $861 round trip with a seven-day advance purchase.

Airport Pohnpei's airport is on Takatik Island, connected to Kolonia by a mile-long causeway. The terminal has a snack bar, car rental booths, a handicraft shop and restrooms. Pohnpei has a departure tax of $5.

Sea
It's possible to get to Pohnpei by boat from Kosrae, either via Kosrae's field trip ship (see the Getting There & Away section in Kosrae) or via SeAir Transportation, Box 96, Kolonia, Pohnpei, FSM 96941.

GETTING AROUND
To/From Airport
Hotel Pohnpei, Palm Terrace Hotel and the Village Hotel have free airport transfers and sometimes run their minivans up to meet incoming flights to see if there are any potential customers.

Taxi
Pohnpei has a system of radio-dispatched shared taxis. You can call to have a taxi pick you up, or you can flag them down. Either way, the fare is $1 anywhere within Kolonia. It costs $5 to go from Kolonia to the Village Hotel and $30 to the Madolenihmw municipal office. These fares are per person, and taxis will stop and pick up other passengers along the way. Pohnpei has three taxi companies: Penny's (☎ 320-2940), Phillip's (☎ 320-2117) and Hervis (☎ 320-2159). The taxis are marked; some are sedans, while others are pick-up trucks or minivans.

Car
PCR Car Rental (☎ 320-2535) rents sedans with air-con for $35 and 4WD pick-up trucks for $45. Penny Rent-A-Car (☎ 320-2940) rents sedans for $35. Penny's offers no insurance, while at PCR the collision damage waiver is mandatory and costs $5. Both companies have booths at the airport, or you can rent cars from PCR's office behind PCR Restaurant and from Penny's office on the waterfront road. You can also call and have a car delivered to your hotel. Both companies charge a 6% fee if you pay by credit card.

The Palm Terrace Hotel also rents a few

cars for $35, with an $8.50 collision damage waiver fee.

There are a few other rental dealers, mostly mom-and-pop places that come and go, though they generally have just a few cars and don't offer better deals.

If you plan to drive around the entire island or explore a lot of rutted back roads, try to avoid renting a low-riding sedan, as lost oil pans are not uncommon and the rental companies will hit you for the repair costs.

Hitching

Hitching is fairly easy, although if you've got your thumb out it will often be one of the taxis that stops to pick you up – and they expect payment. On the other hand, when you're just walking along the road, people who have had some passing contact with you, such as a customs officer, will often stop and offer you a ride.

Chuuk (Truk)

Chuuk is colourful, lively and rough around the edges. Houses are commonly painted in several bright contrasting colours. On hot days village women sit bare-breasted in streams doing laundry and young children run around naked. Speedboats zip back and forth across the lagoon and from Moen you can watch the sun set behind the Faichuk Islands, often with a brilliant light show.

Chuuk's biggest draw card is its sunken wrecks and its most enthusiastic visitors are divers. A whole Japanese fleet rests on the lagoon floor – a moment in time captured in an underwater museum. Most of the wrecks lie off the islands of Dublon, Eten, Fefan and Uman and represent the largest naval loss in history.

The waters of Chuuk Lagoon are clear and calm and you don't have to be an experienced diver to take a look at its underwater attractions. Some of the shipwrecks are only a few feet under the water's surface and can be snorkelled.

With the passing of its state constitution in

1989, Truk officially renamed itself Chuuk (pronounced 'chuke'). It is a change which will take some getting used to by divers, WW II veterans, Micronesia residents and visitors alike, who have long known the island as Truk. You'll see both names in use.

History

Pre-European Contact Legend says that at a time estimated to be about the 14th century the great leader Sowukachaw came by canoe to Chuuk with his son Sowooniiras. Where they really came from is anybody's guess but most people put their money on Kosrae since in Chuuk (as in Pohnpei) there are many legends relating to Kosrae.

The arrival of these leaders represented something analogous to the end of medievalism. They are credited with introducing new varieties of breadfruit as well as a method of fermentation used to preserve breadfruit. That's important because at the time breadfruit was about all there was as a staple food crop. The arrival of Sowukachaw also represented the beginning of clan history and some sort of social ranking system. When the Chuukese trace their ancestry they go back as far as that time, but never any further.

European Contact The first Europeans to sight Chuuk Lagoon were with the Spanish ship *San Lucas*, captained by Alonso de Arellano, in 1565. The Chuukese came after them with hundreds of canoes filled with armed warriors. The Spaniards stayed only long enough to fire a few cannon shots and make their way across the lagoon and out to another passage.

When Manuel Dublon, captaining the *San Antonio*, came to Chuuk in 1814 to collect beche-de-mer he became the first European to enter the lagoon in 250 years.

The Germans took possession of Chuuk in 1899 and developed a copra trade, with their headquarters on Dublon Island.

Japanese & WW II The Japanese Navy began building bases on Dublon immediately after occupying the islands in 1914.

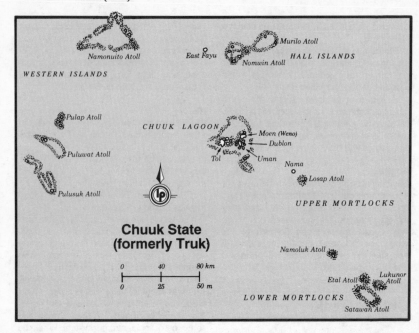

Chuuk State
(formerly Truk)

WESTERN ISLANDS

Namonuito Atoll   East Fayu   Murilo Atoll
                   Nomwin Atoll   HALL ISLANDS

Pulap Atoll

CHUUK LAGOON   Moen (Weno)
                        Dublon
Puluwat Atoll   Tol   Uman   Nama

Pulusuk Atoll   Losap Atoll

                    UPPER MORTLOCKS

0   40   80 km
0   25   50 m

                    Namoluk Atoll

                              Lukunor
                    Etal Atoll   Atoll
            LOWER MORTLOCKS
                    Satawan Atoll

During the war, Chuuk Lagoon became the Imperial Fleet's most important central Pacific base. The fortification of the islands was so great and thought to be so impenetrable that the lagoon earned the nickname 'Gibraltar of the Pacific'. As the huge sheltered lagoon had only a few passageways it could be easily defended against naval invasion, making for a perfect, calm anchorage. Unfortunately for the Japanese, these same conditions also made it easy to seal them in.

On 17 February 1944, the US Navy launched an air-bomb attack code-named 'Operation Hailstone', against the Japanese Fourth Fleet which was docked in the lagoon. Like sitting ducks, they were bombed non stop for two days and by the finish some 60 ships had sunk to the bottom. The islands of Chuuk, however, were never invaded by Allied forces.

When the US military moved in after the war, Dublon was crowded with the 30,000 Japanese soldiers who had survived the air raids but had no means of leaving the island. Since it was easiest to keep them on Dublon until they could be repatriated to Japan, the USA established its headquarters on Moen, which has been the administration centre ever since.

Geography

Chuuk State includes 192 outer islands in addition to the 15 main islands and more than 80 islets that make up Chuuk Lagoon. All in all, about 40 of Chuuk's islands are inhabited.

Chuuk Lagoon The whole lagoon area was once one large volcanic island but over the millennia most of the island has sunk. The 15 high islands in Chuuk Lagoon are the tallest peaks of that original island. The lagoon formation is similar to an atoll although, strictly defined, an atoll no longer contains high volcanic islands.

There are also numerous small low coral

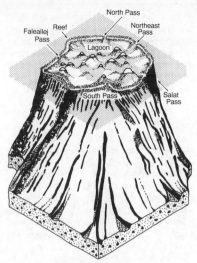

North Pass

Reef

Faleallej Pass

Northeast Pass

Lagoon

South Pass

Salat Pass

Oceanic view of Chuuk Lagoon

islands inside Chuuk's enormous lagoon, which is enclosed by 140 miles of barrier reef. At its widest point, the 822-sq-mile lagoon is almost 40 miles from one reef to another. It has five main passages.

The main populated islands in the lagoon are Moen, Dublon, Fefan, Uman, Eten, Param, Udot, Pata, Polle and Tol; most of them are mountainous and wooded. The islands in Chuuk Lagoon have a combined land area of about 46 sq miles.

Climate

The average annual temperature is a fairly constant 81°F (27°C). Annual rainfall averages 143 inches in Chuuk Lagoon. Humidity is high year-round and can get particularly uncomfortable between July and November when the north-easterly trade winds die down. The most pleasant time of year is the dry season from January to March.

Though Chuuk lies outside the main typhoon belt, it has been hit by a number of severe storms in recent years. In November 1987, Tropical Storm Nina hit Moen and other lagoon islands head on, destroying 90% of the agricultural crops and causing $6

million in damages. In November 1990, Typhoon Owen struck the Hall and Western Islands, levelling most buildings and crops, and leaving thousands of islanders homeless and without food or water.

Economy

As elsewhere in the FSM, Chuuk's moneyed economy is largely dependent on financial assistance from the USA. However subsistence farming and fishing are still widespread on Chuuk. The main subsistence crops are breadfruit, coconuts, bananas and taro. Chuuk has some small fishing fleets that provide fresh fish for the local market and its facilities are being expanded with Japanese aid. Copra production and handicrafts also provide some local income.

People

Chuuk is the most populated Micronesian island group outside Guam, with about 50,000 people. Approximately one-third live on the island of Moen.

Culture

Clans In Chuuk, each island has a predominant clan, the members of which are generally the descendants of the first people to settle that island. While the head clan no longer owns all the island's land the members still enjoy limited privileges. For instance other people on the island are often obliged to present the clan with some token of respect, such as the fruits from the first harvest.

Today the chief of the predominant clan's actual power over those outside his own clan is only nominal, though he is still called on to mediate in disputes between other island clans. He does not initiate this process, but waits until disputes are brought to him and is otherwise not in a position to tell people from other clans what to do.

Love Sticks In the days of thatched houses, love sticks were used by courting males to get a date for the evening. These slender sticks of mangrove wood were each intricately notched and carved in a design unique to its owner.

A young man would show his love stick to the object of his desire, so she would be able to recognise the carving at the appropriate time.

If all went well the suitor would wait until the young woman had gone to bed and then push the love stick in through the side of the thatched house and entangle it in her long hair. She would be woken by his gentle pulling, feel the carving to determine who was outside and, if tempted, would sneak out into the night for a secret rendezvous.

It seems like a system with a built-in potential for disaster, like poking the loved one in the eye or tangling the stick in her mother's hair, but perhaps there was more to it than is usually told. When thatched houses went out of fashion, so did love sticks. Replicas make popular souvenirs.

Magic Believers say Chuukese magic is powerful and they take it very seriously. It takes many forms – as a curse, a love potion, a way to remove evil spirits or a form of protection. Satawan Atoll is said to have the strongest magic.

Perfumed love potions, called *omung*, may contain such exotica as centipede teeth and stingray tail mixed with coconut oil. If a beautiful woman falls in love with a plain-looking man, people will joke and say he used omung. Chuukese say that nowadays money is a more effective way to win someone's heart.

Clothing Many Chuukese women wear *nikautang*, a dress with puffed sleeves, a dropped waist with lace trim and a gathered skirt that hangs below the knee. Also popular are *uros*, which are brilliantly coloured appliqued skirts.

Sometimes around Moen you see men from Chuuk's Western Islands wearing the bright cotton loincloths that are still worn on the outer islands of Chuuk and Yap.

Preserved Breadfruit One traditional Chuukese food speciality, *oppot*, is made by filling a pit with ripe cut breadfruit and alternating layers of banana leaves, then covering the top with rocks and leaving it for months, or even years. Uninitiated noses might think it rotten, but this is Chuukese preserved breadfruit, a staple on long canoe journeys or during months when fresh breadfruit is not in season.

Language
The native language is Chuukese, with several dialects. English is widely understood.

Many native words and place names have more than one spelling. This is due not only to inconsistencies among Westerners who transcribed the native language into the roman alphabet, but also because most people living in Chuuk Lagoon pronounce 'l' as 'n'.

'Good day' is *ran annim* for Chuukese from the lagoon, or *ran allim* for outer islanders. 'Thank you' is *kini so* or *kili so*. Add *chapur* for 'very much'.

To outsiders, the name change from Truk to Chuuk may be confusing, but Chuukese have always called the islands in the main lagoon 'Chuuk' when speaking in their native luuage. The pronunciation of 'Truk', a Germanic corruption of the name, was used only when speaking in English. *Chuuk* means 'mountain'. The outer islands are *fanabi – fanu* is 'island', *bi* is 'sand'.

Itang, a specialised and highly metaphorical language taught only to chiefs and people of high rank, has been in use since the 14th century. It is used to pass down secret knowledge and to call on supernatural powers.

Holidays
Chuuk celebrates New Year's Day, FSM Constitution Day on 10 May, Chuuk Constitution Day on 1 October, FSM Independence Day on 3 November and Christmas Day.

Activities
Diving Chuuk Lagoon is a wreck diver's dream. On its bottom rests about 60 Japanese ships, including oil tankers, submarines,

cruisers, tugboats and cargo ships, as well as scores of US and Japanese planes.

The ships lie just as they sank in 1944 – some upright, some intact, some in pieces strewn across the lagoon floor. Each is a separate time capsule. The holds are full of guns and trucks and fighter planes, the dining areas are littered with dishes, silverware and sake bottles and the skeletal remains of the perished crews lie 'buried' at sea.

The wrecks have become artificial reefs for hundreds of species of vividly coloured corals, sponges and anemones that have attached themselves to the metal. These shelters also attract large schools of fish. The water is warm, about 85°F, and visibility is generally 50 to 100 feet.

The largest wreck in the lagoon is the *Heian Maru*, a 535-foot passenger and cargo ship lying on its port side at 40 to 110 feet. Divers can see the ship's name and telegraph mount on the bow, large propellers, periscopes and a torpedo.

The *Fujikawa Maru*, an aircraft ferry that landed upright in 40 to 90 feet of water, is one of the most popular dives. The stern mast sticks up out of the water but it's another 60 feet down to the main deck. The hold contains four Zero fighters at 90 feet.

Underwater photographers like the *Sankisan Maru* for its excellent soft coral formations. This half-destroyed munitions freighter is upright at 50 to 100 feet and still has a cargo of trucks, machine guns and ammunition.

Although it's the wrecks that make Chuuk special, the walls on the outside of the lagoon reef also make for good diving. Visibility outside the lagoon can be up to 200 feet.

Though strictly illegal, some local fishermen tear the shipwrecks apart looking for stores of explosives, which they then use to dynamite the reefs for an easy catch of fish. Unfortunately there's a ready market for fish caught this way.

Dive Shops To keep souvenir hunters at bay, the wrecks have been declared an underwater historical park and can't be visited without an official guide. Diving permits and complete rental services are available through both dive shops.

The Blue Lagoon Dive Shop (☎ 330-2796), Box 429, Chuuk, FSM 96942, was Chuuk's first dive operation, started in 1973 by Kimiuo Aisek, and now managed by his son, Gradvin. Two tank dives cost $65. The office, in Moen centre, is open from 7 am to 5 pm daily.

Micronesia Aquatics (☎ 330-2204), Box 57, Chuuk, FSM 96942, run by former Peace Corps volunteer Clark Graham and his Chuukese wife Chineina, is just inside the gate of the Truk Continental Hotel. Graham specialises in underwater photography and insists that divers be conservation oriented.

Dive Boats Two live-aboard dive boats are based in Chuuk Lagoon.

The *Truk Aggressor* has weekly trips, from Sunday to Sunday, that include four days of wreck diving and two days of reef diving. The cost is $1895 per person, which includes everything except the airfare to and from Chuuk and alcoholic beverages. This new boat holds 20 people in 10 double cabins, each with a double and single bunk, a shower and head. Reservations are made through the Aggressor Fleet in Louisiana (☎ 504-385-2416, 800-348-2628), PO Drawer K, Morgan City, LA 70381. If you're already in Chuuk and have a couple of grand burning a hole in your pocket, you could check with the captain who docks on Sundays at the Truk Continental Hotel to see if there's space available.

The SS *Thorfinn* has a Sunday-to-Sunday package that includes six days of diving wrecks and reef walls, along with meals and accommodation, for $1550. The Thorfinn holds 26 passengers in 13 rooms, with shared showers and toilets. The ship's quite comfy and even has a hot tub on deck. Divers can also arrange to go out on a flexible schedule, with accommodation and meals for $100 a day, plus $30 a dive. Reservations are made through Seaward Holidays (☎ 330-4302), Box DX, Chuuk, FSM 96942.

Both dive boats can be booked through travel agents.

Snorkelling Boat trips for snorkellers usually include a visit to the *Dainihino Maru*, a small coral-encrusted transport ship that lies on its starboard side in 40 feet of water off Uman. It has a bow gun just three feet underwater and its deck is about eight feet down. Other wrecks visited for snorkelling are a Zero fighter in shallow waters off Eten and the *Susuki Maru*, a sub-chaser off the coast of Dublon, with its deck about 10 feet underwater.

Blue Lagoon Dive Shop charges $35 for its snorkelling tour. If three or more snorkellers are going out, they'll take a separate boat and snorkel around the shallow wrecks described above, but otherwise snorkellers go out with divers.

Yasu Mori (☎ 330-2438) charges $25 an hour per boat for snorkelling tours, with a minimum of three hours. Up to four people can go out on the boat.

Organised Tours Yasu Mori (☎ 330-2438), who operates from a desk in the lobby of the Truk Continental Hotel, runs half-day land tours of Moen for $16 per person and arranges boat tours.

The tourist office can arrange local tour guides for a modest fee.

MOEN (WENO) ISLAND

Moen is the capital and commercial centre of Chuuk. In 1989 the new state constitution officially renamed the island as Weno, though it is still most commonly referred to as Moen and even the 'Moen Municipal Office' sign has yet to change.

At just over seven sq miles, Moen is the second largest island in the lagoon. Tropical forests make up much of the interior with the highest point, the 1214-foot Mt Tonoken, nearly in the centre.

Villages circle the outer edges of Moen, with the district centre, government offices and airport on the north-west side of the island. The main road extends four-fifths of the way around Moen, with a gap between Sapuk and Neauwo on the south-east side. Though there are plans to complete the circle-island road, disputes with area prop-

erty owners who value their isolation have thus far kept the road at bay.

In response to political pressures from Chuukese women, some tired of alcohol-related domestic violence, Moen and several other islands are officially dry, though the state of Chuuk is not. As all imports are first unloaded at Moen however, alcohol has always been available on the island, at least at black market rates. Recently a handful of places on Moen have begun to sell alcohol openly and for all practical purposes the restrictions seem to be gone. Budweiser cans strewn along the roadsides and beaches are a major litter problem.

Despite ample rainfall, Moen has water rationing. Water is turned on for only two hours in the morning and two hours in the evening, though many residents and most businesses fill their own water tanks during those hours so they don't have to go without at other times.

Information

The Truk Visitors Bureau (☎ 330-4133), Box FQ, Chuuk, FSM 96942 has its main office at the Ethnographic Center, as well as a booth at the airport which is open at flight times.

Guam's *Pacific Daily News* is sold at the Seaside Restaurant, T&S Mart and Stop & Shop. Chuuk has two radio stations. There's no TV or movie theatre, but many a video shop.

Air Mike's only office (☎ 330-2425) is at the check-in counter in the airport. It's open from 8 am to 5 pm daily and until midnight on Sundays, Wednesdays and Fridays.

There's a laundromat near the Peace Corps office.

The hospital (☎ 330-244) is in Moen's centre, up from the government offices.

Money The Bank of Guam, next to the Seaside Restaurant, is open from 10 am to 3 pm Monday to Thursday, to 4 pm on Fridays. The Bank of the FSM is open from 9.30 am to 2.30 pm Monday to Thursday, to 4 pm on Fridays. On payday Fridays, expect long queues at the counters. Credit cards are not widely accepted on Moen.

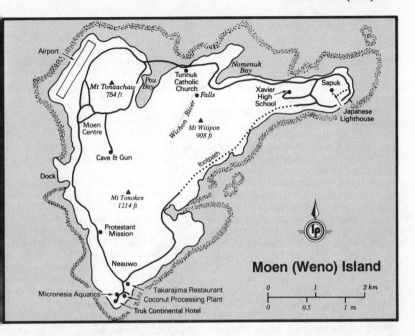

Moen (Weno) Island

Post & Telecommunications Chuuk's only post office is in Moen centre. It's open from 9 am to 3.30 pm on Mondays, 8 am to 3.30 pm Tuesday to Friday and 9 to 11 am on Saturdays.

Long-distance telephone calls can be made 24 hours a day from the FSM Telecommunications building south of the airport.

Mt Tonaachaw

When the legendary Sowukachaw arrived on Chuuk he brought a lump of basalt rock with him, stuck it on the summit of Mt Tonaachaw and built a meeting house on the mountain top from where he ruled all of Chuuk Lagoon.

The steep-sided 754-foot mountain, with its lone tree on the knobby top, is the backdrop for the airport and harbour. Though there's a trail to the top, Chuukese are wary of climbing this mountain because Neawacha, the ghost of an old woman who lives there, has the power of curses.

The US Air Force Civic Action Team (CAT) has a barracks on the side of the mountain above Moen centre, at an elevation of 250 feet. The CAT crew is made up of 13 people who do eight-month stints on the island building roads, schools and, most recently, the new dock extension.

The narrow dirt road to the CAT camp begins just east of Island Mart and ends a half mile up at the barracks, where there's a good lagoon view that's particularly nice at sunset. You can see the Faichuk Islands straight ahead past the runway and the flat island of Param to the left.

A trail that goes to the top of Mt Tonaachaw begins at the left side of the main CAT building. Follow the trail past the small house above the CAT camp and continue on up. The path starts out well defined and then becomes less so, but it's not hard to follow. It can be slippery when wet but otherwise, if you avoid the midday sun, it's not too strenuous. It takes about 30 minutes to get to the top where there's a Japanese bunker and good panoramic views.

Ethnographic Center

The Ethnographic Center at the tourist office has exhibits of wooden spears and war clubs, shell adzes, masks, fish traps, love sticks, outrigger canoe models and other interesting traditional items, such as the *ulong*, a special food bowl and stand that was used to present the season's first harvest to the high chief.

There are also artefacts from the lagoon shipwrecks, including the compass, a ship lantern and a coral-encrusted machine gun from the bridge of the *Fujikawa Maru*. A display of photos taken during the two-day US bombing assault on the Japanese fleet shows all the ships in the lagoon during the attack, the layout of Moen's South Field with its seaplane ramps and the then densely developed island of Dublon.

The tourist office is open from 7.30 to 11.30 am and 12.30 to 4.30 pm Monday to Friday. Admission to the museum is $1.50.

If you look toward the beach at the north side of the Ethnographic Center you'll see what looks like a big black marble. It's actually a Japanese memorial to war dead with the kanji character for peace, *wa*, carved into the pedestal.

Several nearshore shipwrecks can be seen along the coast in this area.

Nefo Cave & Japanese Gun

A large cave above the town holds a Japanese naval gun and offers a good view of Moen centre. To get there, head east from downtown Moen, take the paved road to the right after the hospital and follow the road up the hill to where it dead-ends at a big water tank.

Directly across the street from the driveway of the last house there's a path leading up the hill. It's a two-minute walk to the cave. Go straight through the cave to get to the gun. The reef island that can be seen on the horizon is Piis and the lagoon island to the left is Falos.

If you step out a few feet beyond the gun, you can also get a good view of Mt Tonaachaw to the right.

South Field

South Field, at the southern tip of Moen, was once a large Japanese seaplane base. The three-mile drive from Moen centre to South Field offers pretty views of both the lagoon islands and Moen's west coast, with intermittent patches of taro, mangroves, bananas and breadfruit trees.

The Truk Coconut Processing Plant is in the white metal building to the left just before the gate to the Truk Continental Hotel. If you want to see how soap is made from copra, go inside.

One of the old Japanese seaplane ramps is behind the soap factory as is a beached ferro-concrete boat, the result of a failed government-funded small industries project.

At the southernmost point of South Field is the Truk Continental Hotel, which has the only easily accessible sandy beach on Moen and a splendid lagoon view. There's another seaplane ramp here, as well as grass-covered Japanese bunkers and a few other war artefacts on the hotel grounds.

The road heading east from South Field gets rougher as it goes along, with only about a mile of it passable in a sedan

East of the Airport

From the airport heading east, the road edges along the coast and passes through small villages. After the Bethesda church comes up on the right, the road goes across Pou Bay. The bright blue church with red trim on the hill to the right is the Tunnuk Catholic Church.

Micronesian Seminar

Tunnuk Church is headquarters of the Micronesian Seminar, directed by Father Fran Hezel, one of the most respected and prolific writers on Micronesia. The seminar's library is an excellent resource centre, with an extensive collection of books, microfilms, magazines, maps, reports and theses on all parts of Micronesia. If you're doing research on Micronesia, the reading room is a pleasant place to be. It's open to the public daily, with no formal hours.

Top: Airai Bai - Palau
Left: Old age centre - Koror
Right: Breeding giant clams at MMDC - Palau

Top: Circle-Island Road - Pohnpei
Left: Village House & Golden Candles, Colonia - Yap
Right: Traditional meal of taro & pork cooked in blood - Yap

Wichon Falls

Wichon Falls are not very big, but the walk up the river is pleasant and will get you a little closer to village life. On sunny mornings the stream is the village laundromat and after school lets out kids play in the water holes.

To reach the falls go 1¼ miles past Tunnuck Church to the innermost part of Nomenuk Bay, where the Wichon River empties into the lagoon. Just before a very small bridge, you'll see a rough dirt road to the right which leads into Wichon Village.

Walk one-third of a mile up this road, turn on the first drive to the left, go behind the house and begin walking up the river. There's a crossing over rocks in the stream not far from the house and from there the falls are just a couple of minutes up. As you are crossing private property, you should ask permission to continue if you see anyone along the way.

Ancient petroglyphs in the shape of triangles, parallel lines and other geometric shapes have been carved into the smooth rock both above and near the base of the falls. Most are quite weathered, but can be made out with a determined eye.

The Wichon area figures into many Chuukese legends. One story tells of a ghost who scooped up part of nearby Mt Witipon, creating the Wichon Valley, and then flew to the Mortlocks where he dropped the land in the sea to form Losap Atoll.

Xavier High School

The Jesuit-run Xavier High School opened in 1953 as the first four-year high school in Micronesia and maintains a reputation as the region's best.

Originally the site of a German chapel, the land was taken by the Japanese in 1940 and a fortress-like wartime communications centre was constructed. The main building, with two-foot-thick reinforced concrete walls and vault-like steel doors and windows, survived two direct hits by US bombers, amazingly requiring only a patch job on the roof. The building now houses the school's classrooms.

Visitors are welcome to climb the roof for a panoramic view of Chuuk Lagoon and to walk around the grounds, providing they don't disturb classes. Cars should be parked under the big mango tree at the far right of the main building.

Go quietly through the centre doorway of the main building, past the study hall and up the stairs on the left. At the top of the stairs go through the door on the left, then turn right to get outside, where there are stairs up to the roof. You can see many of the lagoon islands from the rooftop. There's an especially attractive view of the Faichuks and in the opposite direction you can see the old Japanese lighthouse on the hill in Sapuk.

A display cabinet at the top of the stairs on the 2nd floor holds objects from sunken ships, including dishes, sake bottles and a porthole. The landing below has a collection of Chuukese seashells.

The windmill on the grounds runs the school's computers and a network of Japanese-built tunnels is burrowed into the hill, alongside the driveway leading up to the school.

Japanese Lighthouse

There's a fine view from the Japanese lighthouse in Sapuk, atop Newech Hill at an elevation of 348 feet. However it's a hit and miss affair whether you'll be able to hike up to the top without various people along the way claiming to be landowners and demanding anything from $1 to $10. The tourist office may be able to help smooth the way and perhaps even provide a guide for a small fee.

To get to the lighthouse after leaving Xavier High School, take the road going down along the water. After passing a long thin wharf the road will loop a bit inland and come to a 90° corner. Stop at the corner and look for the driveway straight ahead. The lighthouse is a 30-minute walk up that trail.

Places to Stay

The Truk Continental Hotel is the only hotel on Moen with a beachside setting. All the others are in town or in residential neighbourhoods. Chuuk has a 10% room tax.

Truk Stop (☎ 330-2798), Box 546, Chuuk, FSM 96942, a new hotel with four 2nd-storey rooms above a travel agency, is good value. The rooms have air-con, comfortable beds, full kitchens, TV with VCR and the use of free video movies. The two back rooms even have a partial lagoon view. The rate is $45 per day or $280 per week for a single or a double. Two of the rooms have both a double and a single bed, and it's $5 more for each additional person. If you don't have a reservation, look for their agent at the airport, as they usually meet incoming flights when rooms are available.

Kurassa Apartments (☎ 330-2518), Victoria Mori, Box 64, Chuuk, FSM 96942, three-quarters of a mile east of the airport, can also be recommended. There are 12 one-bedroom and studio apartments, though most are rented on a monthly basis ($400 to $500). The apartments that are rented by the day cost $40 and are nicely furnished, with air-con in the bedroom, a ceiling fan in the living room, a kitchen, tiled bathtub and daily cleaning service. Manager Vicky Mori is quite helpful and can provide free airport transfers. The little grocery store below the apartments is convenient for picking up supplies.

The *Christopher Inn* (☎ 330-2652), Box 37, Chuuk, FSM 96942, in central Moen opposite the airport, has 19 rooms that cost $40/47.50 for singles/doubles. All rooms have air-con, mini-refrigerators and private baths. It's a simple place, adequate but overpriced. With a restaurant at the side, a store below and a parking lot that serves as the local hang-out, there's quite a bit of activity and noise can be a problem. Supposedly there's a free bus to and from the airport – a two-minute walk away.

The *Truk Continental Hotel* (☎ 330-2727), Box 340, Chuuk, FSM 96942, Chuuk's only resort hotel, sits at Moen's southernmost point on the island's best beach. It has 56 rather standard Western-style rooms in several two-storey buildings, each with a balcony facing the lagoon. It's

not as fancy as the word 'resort' might imply, though it's comfortable enough and the setting is nice. There's a restaurant and a gift shop. Rooms are $89 for singles or doubles.

If you're looking for long-term rentals, the *Tradewind Hotel* (☎ 330-2277), Box 520, Chuuk, FSM 96942, has modern apartments with air-con and kitchens above the KS Store. It's in a quiet residential area on the coastal road, 1½ miles east of the airport.

See also *Falos Beach Resort* under Picnic Islands.

Places to Eat

T&S Fast-Food, next to T&S Mart, is a clean, modern, cafeteria-style snack bar serving breakfast and lunch from steamer trays. Rice is 40 cents a scoop, fish or chicken is $1.25 by the piece and beef dishes are $2.75. You can get a glass of distilled water for a quarter. It's open from 7 am to 4 pm daily.

Truk Trading Co has a snack bar with inexpensive sandwiches, fried chicken and ice cream.

Ran Annim Restaurant is an inexpensive favourite of Peace Corps volunteers. The bakery next door has good bread and tasty turnovers.

The *Seaside Restaurant*, across from Susumu's store, has Japanese and Western food at moderate prices. One of the best deals is the 'frying fish' plate which includes reef fish, rice, kimchee, shredded cabbage, miso soup and half a grapefruit for $3.

The Christopher Inn has two restaurants, both mediocre. The *Rainbow Coffee Shop*, on the 1st floor, is open from 6 am to 2.30 pm only. You can get eggs, toast and coffee for under $2 or a fish plate for $3. Upstairs, the *Roof Garden Steak House* has sandwiches from $3 to $4 and dinners from $4 to $9. The setting is white formica tables with pink plastic chairs and a 3rd-floor view of the airport through louvred windows.

Takarajima Restaurant, down near the Truk Continental Hotel, has the best Japanese food on Moen. *Oyako domburi* (sweetened chicken and egg atop rice) is good at $5 and the $6.50 lunch special is a

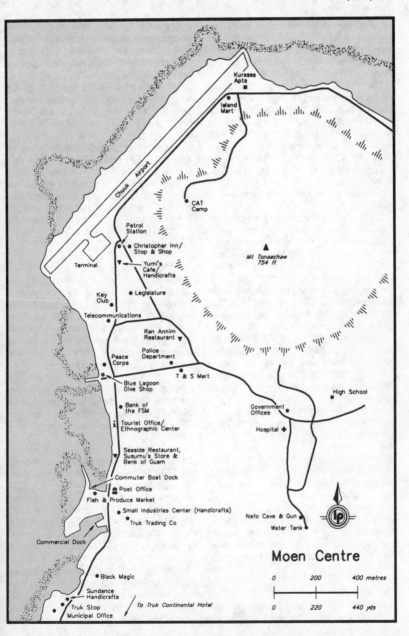

Kurassa Apts

Island Mart

Chuuk Airport

CAT Camp

Petrol Station

Christopher Inn/ Stop & Shop

Mt Tonaachaw 754 ft

Terminal

Yumi's Cafe/ Handicrafts

Key Club

Legislature

Telecommunications

Ran Annim Restaurant

Peace Corps

Police Department

T & S Mart

Blue Lagoon Dive Shop

High School

Bank of the FSM

Tourist Office/ Ethnographic Center

Government Offices

Seaside Restaurant, Susumu's Store & Bank of Guam

Hospital

Commuter Boat Dock

Post Office

Fish & Produce Market

Small Industries Center (Handicrafts)

Truk Trading Co

Nefo Cave & Gun

Water Tank

Commercial Dock

Moen Centre

Black Magic

Sundance Handicrafts

Truk Stop

Municipal Office

To Truk Continental Hotel

0	200	400 metres
0	220	440 yds

big plate of sashimi, fried fish, miso soup, rice and spaghetti. Other dishes, such as tempura, cost about $10. Saltwater aquariums spread around the restaurant add a nice touch.

The *Truk Continental* has the best setting and the highest prices although the food isn't particularly special and the service is slow. Breakfasts start around $5 and coffee is $1.25. A hamburger or fish sandwich with fries is $4.50 at lunch and the reef fish dinner costs $10. There are good views from the dining room of the Faichuks, Fefan and Dublon.

Sensitive stomachs should avoid *Yumi's Cafe*.

The fruit stalls opposite the post office sell drinking coconuts for 25 to 50 cents. Other treats include pounded taro wrapped in green taro leaves, boiled breadfruit, and limes, mangoes, cucumbers and other fresh produce, most of which comes from Fefan. You can also pick up a fragrant *mwaramwar* (head wreath) for 50 cents. Booths behind the fruit stalls sell fried reef fish and other cooked take-out foods.

Truk Trading Co and T&S Mart are Chuuk's largest grocery stores and have the freshest food. Other grocery stores are Susumu's Store and Stop & Shop. Most produce in the stores is imported, old and virtually inedible.

Stay clear of unboiled tap water. You can get a gallon of drinking water for $1.70 at T&S Mart.

Entertainment

The *Truk Continental Hotel* sometimes has traditional Chuukese folk music on weekends in the dining room.

Though Moen is officially dry, you'd never know it. The Truk Continental Hotel's beachside bar has a sign that reads 'we sell ice only' but they sell beer too, as does *Yumi's*, the *Key Club* and *Black Magic*, the latter a disco.

Things To Buy

A good place to find handicrafts is the government-run Small Industries Center which sells grass skirts, hibiscus fibre fans, storyboards, wood carvings, baskets, love sticks, masks and seashells. It's open from 8 am to 4.30 pm Monday to Saturday, though they sometimes close for lunch.

Sundance Handicrafts has high-quality wood carvings, love sticks, baskets and shell jewellery, and though the prices are slightly higher than elsewhere, it's worth the difference.

If you're short on time, you might try the handicraft shop next to Yumi's Cafe, opposite the airport, but the value's not the best.

Combs, jewellery and other items made from the shells of endangered sea turtles are sold all around Chuuk, but cannot be imported into most Western countries, including the US and Australia. Ditto for black coral products.

Getting There & Away

Air Mike is the only airline which flies to Chuuk, connecting Moen Island with Pohnpei and Guam on the island hopper route. The full one-way fare is $242 between Guam and Chuuk, $179 between Pohnpei and Chuuk. Discounted evening flights on Sundays, Wednesdays and Fridays are $125 from Guam and $92 from Pohnpei.

Airport Chuuk has a new open-air airport terminal, with a tourist information booth, car rental booths, a snack bar and restrooms. There's a $10 departure tax.

Getting Around

Car & Motorbike At Truk Stop Car Rentals (☎ 330-2701) you can rent air-conditioned Toyotas, both sedans and pick-up trucks, for $30 a day. VJ Car Rental (☎ 330-2652) at the Christopher Inn also has sedans for $30 a day. There's a 10% tax on car rentals.

Truk Continental Hotel rents mopeds for $20 a day or $10 a half-day.

Taxi Shared taxis, which are usually pick-up trucks, can be identified by signs in their front windows and will stop when flagged down. It costs 50 cents to go anywhere around the downtown area or as far as Truk

Continental Hotel, and $1 to Xavier High School. However, the farther you are from downtown Moen, the fewer the taxis. The other thing to keep in mind is that most taxis stop running around 6 pm.

ISLANDS IN CHUUK LAGOON

Outside Moen, the most easily accessible populated islands in Chuuk Lagoon are Dublon, Eten and Fefan. Uman and Param are not particularly receptive to visitors and the Tol islanders have a reputation for being a bit rough and rowdy. Many of these island-ers commute by boat to jobs on Moen while others have subsistence farms or earn money through fishing or copra.

It's a more traditional Chuukese lifestyle on the islands in the outer lagoon. On some islands people still live under thatched roofs and cook outdoors over open fires. Roads are scarce and vehicles are few.

Getting There & Away

Commuter boats leave the lagoon islands for Moen on weekday mornings and return from Moen in the early afternoons. They're obvi-ously convenient for islanders commuting to Moen to work, shop or sell their produce, but the schedules are backwards for anyone planning a day trip from Moen. The boats are often referred to as *yamma*, after their Japan-ese-made Yanmar diesel motors.

Boats from Fefan tie up at the Moen dock, on the side opposite the post office, where the Fefan women market their vegetables. Boats from Dublon, Tol and the Mortlocks are usually moored on the other side of the dock.

The *Mywei Maru*, one of the boats that goes to Tol, charges $2 one way, leaving Tol at 7.30 am and Moen at 2 pm. The *Miss Judy* leaves Dublon at 7 am and Moen at 4 pm and costs $1. Boats to Uman and Fefan also cost $1.

Many private speedboats cross the lagoon every day. If you ask around you might find someone to take you to another island in exchange for petrol money. Like the com-muter boats however, most speedboats come to Moen in the morning and return to home islands in the afternoon.

In addition, the tourist office can arrange boat rentals.

Dublon Island

Dublon is also called Tonoas, which was the island's original name until 1814 when Manuel Dublon landed there and humbly renamed it.

Dublon is a peaceful island today, with a population of only about 3000, although there are signs of its former importance under occupying powers. Both the Germans and Japanese made Dublon their administra-tive centres and the Japanese military headquarters there included submarine, sea-plane and coastal defence bases. US bombings left them in ruins.

After the war Dublon became sleepy and overgrown. It's now in line for redevelop-ment projects, but in the meantime the island still provides a good glimpse of rural Chuuk-ese life.

There are docks at Sapou, in the north-east corner of the island and in the south at the new fisheries plant. A road runs around the island and there are private pick-up trucks, but no taxis.

There are plans to start organised tours of Dublon in the near future, which will include a boat ride from Moen and a three-hour land tour by pick-up truck, at a cost of about $20. Check with the tourist office on Moen.

Sapou Overgrown vegetation in Sapou Village partly conceals the remains of what was once a good-sized city. The wooden buildings are long gone, but the cement foot-ings they were built upon are still there. Broad cement sidewalks, once covered with tin awnings to shelter the Japanese against sun and rain, are now shaded by breadfruit trees. The remains of the Japanese naval hospital can be explored on the hill above the new Youth Center.

Sapou's colourful village church, which is dark grey trimmed with bright primary colours, sports a sign in Old English lettering reading *kinamue*, which means 'peace'.

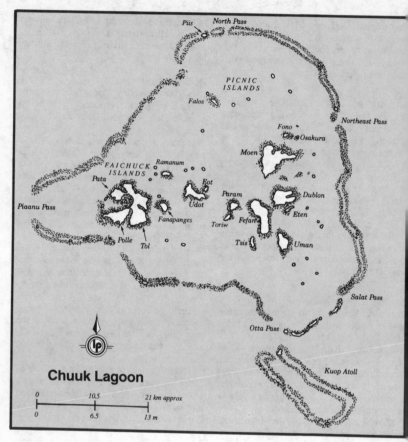

North Pass

Piis

PICNIC
ISLANDS

Falos

Northeast Pass

Fono • Osakura

Moen

FAICHUCK
ISLANDS

Ramanum

Pata

Eot

Piaanu Pass

Udot

Param

Dublon

Fanapanges

Eten

Polle

Toriw

Fefan

Tol

Tsis

Uman

Salat Pass

Otta Pass

Kuop Atoll

Chuuk Lagoon

| 0 | 10.5 | 21 km approx |
| 0 | 6.5 | 13 m |

South Dublon If you drive anticlockwise from Sapou to the south side of Dublon, you'll see a large Japanese dome-like concrete bunker on the right side of the road. An iron pipe protruding from the top served as an air vent.

Ahead, where the road splits in two, you can take the right fork which takes you to a fortified Japanese building with heavy metal doors and windows. It's now a village hangout.

A little further on is the junior high school, built on the concrete airfields of the Japanese seaplane base. There's a seaplane ramp leading down into the water. The former base for the US Air Force Civic Action Team is ahead along the shore.

Back on the main road, on the left, are the remains of a collapsed Japanese oil storage tank, now used by a local family as a garage. Ahead, up a grade to the left, a new aluminium geodesic dome covers a large freshwater reservoir. The concrete water tank was built by the Japanese who secretly placed a steel fuel tank in the centre to serve as a hidden reserve.

Turn right at the next road to get to Dublon's deepwater dock and multimillion

Dublon Island

Remains of Japanese Naval Hospital

† Village Church

Youth Centre

Sapou

School

Japanese Civil Hospital Ruins

Nukunap

Site of (former) Shinto Shrine

Catholic Mission

Bombed Oil Tanks

Fisheries Complex/Dock

Former U.S. Air Force Civic Action Base

Tunnel

Municipal Building

Saponong

Japanese Memorial

Water Reservoir

Wonpiepi

Protestant Church

General's ○ Cave

Japanese Naval Cemetery

Sapun

Junior High School (Japanese Seaplane Base)

Fortified WWII Building

Japanese Bunker

▲ Mt Tonomwan 1128 ft

Nukuno

Nechap

○ Cave

Takeshima Channel

1 m

1 km

Eten Island

Airfield

Former

▲ 202 ft

ruins

Channel

Takeshima Channel

dollar fisheries complex and freezer built with Japanese aid.

East-Central Dublon Continuing on the main road, you'll see more burned-out oil storage tanks on the right. At the crossroads, turn left and you'll pass a small Japanese memorial. Just past the municipal building turn left, then keep an eye out to the left for the entrance to a massive cement tunnel built under the mountain. The tunnel looks big enough to run a subway through and did in fact hold a fleet of military vehicles. It ran under the Japanese governor's residence and still has a rusted electric generator inside.

Further down on the left, a sign in Japanese announces a naval cemetery. Steep stairs lead up to the site but this is now private property so you should ask permission if you want to climb up, and the owner may charge you a few dollars.

Down the road on the left look closely to see the narrow overgrown entrance to the general's cave, one of five openings to an interconnecting network of tunnels. The road finishes in a dead-end a little further on at a Protestant church.

Go back the way you came and take the road diagonally opposite the municipal building. After passing a school on the left, you'll come to the ruins of the Japanese civil hospital at the crossroads. What remains of the hospital is basically just the arched concrete entrance hall, now covered in graffiti. Straight ahead are the stairs to a former Shinto shrine.

Eten Island

From a distance Eten looks like a huge aircraft carrier which, in effect, it was. The Japanese used Chuukese labour to tear down the mountain tops and carry away half the island to turn Eten into an airfield.

If you dock on Eten's north-west side, directly opposite the fisheries complex on Dublon, then it's a 10-minute walk inland to a complex of bombed-out concrete and steel buildings.

From the dock you pass a couple of houses, then walk up to the right through the village and follow the path to the right of the Catholic church. It's a well-defined trail, much of it on the pavement still left from the old airstrip.

The path leads directly to a massive two-storey concrete structure, which islanders say was hit by 15 to 20 bombs. The roof and 2nd floor are partly caved-in, with twisted steel reinforcement rods hanging down, but one room is amazingly still intact and apparently someone's living in it.

Beyond are three more similar two-storey buildings with the same style of heavy steel windows and doors as Xavier High School on Moen. There's a demolished tower and a big gun on top of the hill as well as wrecked planes in the water around the island.

Fefan Island

Fefan is known for its abundance of fresh produce and for high-quality basketry woven of banana and hibiscus fibres. Mangrove swamps line much of the shoreline, while the forested interior reaches an elevation of 984 feet. Pieces of pottery found in archaeological digs on Fefan date back 1500 years.

Mesa Wharf is on the east side of Fefan and you can take in the whole village of Mesa, such as it is, in a 10-minute stroll. The municipal office and elementary school are both visible to the left from the wharf. There's a little tea house made of corrugated iron opposite the school and a small store carrying not much of anything down past that. The village church is a few minutes walk to the right of the wharf.

On Fefan, kids come up and touch you to see if you're for real. They smile, ask your name, follow you around for a minute or two and then go back to whatever they were doing.

Most war relics are inland on the hills and difficult to reach. The hike up to some anti-aircraft guns which are spread out on top of a hill directly up from Mesa Wharf would take about 30 minutes, but there's no real trail.

A couple of pick-up trucks drive the rough circle-island road, charging $2 per person.

However, as the trip around takes about 1½ hours there's no guarantee there'll be one on your side of the island at the right time.

Faichuk Islands

The Faichuk Islands, in the western part of Chuuk Lagoon, include Tol, Polle, Pata, Udot, Eot, Ramanum and Fanapanges.

Tol, the largest and most populated of the Faichuks, is about a one-hour boat ride from Moen. Tol's Mt Tumuital, which rises 1453 feet, is the tallest mountain in Chuuk. The island's high jungle forest is the sole habitat of the Truk greater white-eye, a rare bird with one of the most restricted ranges of any in Micronesia.

The Japanese once had vehicles on Tol but the roads took a beating during the war bombing and today there are no cars.

In the 1970s, when Chuuk's political future was being debated, most Faichuk islanders wanted Chuuk to opt for commonwealth status with the USA, similar to that of the Northern Marianas. When the majority of Chuukese voted instead to become a state in the FSM, the Faichuks started statehood attempts of their own.

In the late 1970s, the FSM Congress actually approved the Faichuks as a new FSM state after 98% of Faichuk voters chose by referendum to break away from the rest of Chuuk. The movement failed with a veto by the FSM president, who was incidentally from Chuuk.

Basically the islanders are looking for their fair share of the new development which is now centred on Moen. With one-third of Chuuk's population, they feel they're entitled to one-third of the state budget. They want electricity and paved roads, and perhaps most importantly, they want a water system, as during severe droughts they sometimes run out of water completely and have to rely on drinking coconut milk.

Places to Stay There are no established accommodation on any of these islands. If you want to camp on one of the populated islands, get permission from that island's chief magistrate. The tourist office can help.

Picnic Islands

Chuukese make good use of the low coral islands scattered around the lagoon as fishing grounds and picnic or drinking spots.

Most of them are classic desert island specimens – crystal clear waters surrounding white sand beaches and small stands of coconut palms.

Snorkelling can be excellent, though in some spots dynamiting has damaged the coral. Deserted or not, all the islands are owned and you're supposed to get permission from the owners to visit. Whoever takes you out should be able to help you arrange it.

Falos Island

Falos is a tidy little island circled with soft white sand beaches and thickly shaded with coconut palms. For the casual visitor to Chuuk, this is the easiest picnic island to visit, as it's been set up for both day trips and overnight stays.

Coral close to the shore makes good snorkelling, and the deeper waters just a short way out have larger fish and even an occasional shark or two. From the beach you can see Moen, Dublon, Fefan and the Faichuks.

If you visit on weekdays you may well have the beach to yourself, while on weekends it's usually a bit livelier with people from Moen coming over to picnic. The owner's mother lives on the island all year round as caretaker, with other 'staff' coming over on the boat when there are visitors. The hosts are quite friendly and the island makes for a nice getaway.

Places to Stay *Falos Beach Resort* has 10 simple concrete, tin-roofed cottages with linoleum floors, electric lights and plywood platforms topped with futons. Ask for cottage Nos 1, 5, 6 or 7, as each one is free-standing with screened, louvred windows on all four walls to catch the breeze. Toilets and showers are outside and shared. The only drawback here is the price: $35/45 for singles/doubles, plus a 10% room tax and the boat fare. Breakfasts are $4, lunch and dinner $6 each, or you can bring your own food and they'll prepare it for free.

Getting There & Away Arrangements to visit Falos Island (☎ 330-2606), Box 494, Chuuk, FSM 96942 are made in advance at Island Mart, on the main road opposite the north-east end of the airport runway.

Day tours with lunch cost $19.50. Without lunch, the round-trip motorboat ride alone costs $12.50. The boat leaves Moen around 9 am and returns around 3 pm. The ride takes about 30 minutes one way when the lagoon waters are calm. Free pick-up service from the hotels is provided.

CHUUK'S OUTER ISLANDS

Outside Chuuk Lagoon are the Mortlocks, Hall Islands and Western Islands. Together they comprise 11 atolls and three single islands. All are flat coral formations, some just wisps of sand barely rising above the surface of the ocean.

In their isolation, the outer islands maintain a more traditional lifestyle than can be found in Chuuk central. They have footpaths but no cars or roads. A day's work might include fishing, cultivating the taro patch, preparing copra or making sleeping mats and coconut fibre ropes.

The Mortlocks

The Mortlocks stretch about 180 miles in a south-easterly direction from Chuuk Lagoon. The Upper Mortlocks include the single island of Nama, and Losap Atoll with its main islands of Losap and Piis. The Mid-Mortlocks include Etal and Namoluk atolls, as well as Kuttu and Moch, the northernmost islands in Satawan Atoll.

The Lower Mortlocks incorporate Lukunor Atoll with its islands of Lukunor and Oneop as well as the southernmost Satawan Atoll islands of Satawan and Ta.

Satawan Atoll is the largest of all Chuuk's outer island groups, though its four populated islands and 45 islets cover a total of

Dance Mask of the Mortlock Islands

only 1.8 sq miles. The main island, Satawan, is a sub-district centre with 1000 people. Satawan Island is separated from Ta by about 200 yards of shallow reef that can be walked across. Ta is just a couple of hundred yards wide, though it extends for five miles over the reef. The FSM government has allocated money to build an airstrip on Ta.

The Mortlockese are a gentle, easy-going people. They also tend to be a more religious bunch overall, perhaps because it was in the Mortlocks that Christian missionaries established Chuuk's first church, in 1875, long before they reached Chuuk Lagoon. Many religious prohibitions, such as those against building fires on Sunday, have only recently been abandoned.

The Mortlockese make traditional masks of hibiscus wood. Once worn by men during battle and to ward off evil spirits, they are now carved for Chuuk's tourist trade.

The Hall Islands

The Halls, north of Chuuk Lagoon, include the single island of East Fayu, Murilo Atoll with its islands of Murilo and Ruo, and

Nomwin Atoll with its islands of Nomwin and Fananu. Fananu Island is said to be the most attractive of all the Halls.

These islands are, in a sense, a satellite community of Chuuk Lagoon. They were once allied with Moen and with islands on the Chuuk Lagoon reef, with whom they share a common dialect.

The Western Islands

The Western Islands, Chuuk's most remote and traditional, share close ties with the outer islands of Yap. Though political distinctions divvy them up into two separate states, outer islanders in the central Carolines have more in common with each other than they do with the high islands of Yap or Chuuk Lagoon to which they belong.

On these islands the men still wear bright loincloths and the women wear only woven fibre or grass skirts. Houses are made of thatch, subsistence comes from the sea and men still sail single-hulled outrigger canoes carved from breadfruit logs, relying on centuries-old navigational methods.

Young women from the Western Islands who attend the University of Guam have been known to enter classrooms crawling on their knees if any of their male relatives are in the room. This would be expected of them in their home islands but university teachers, not too keen on the custom, eventually get them to make some concessions to Western culture.

The Western Islands include Namonuito, Pulap, Pulusuk and Puluwat atolls. As a group, the latter three are also called Pattiw. Namonuito is a huge triangular atoll, the people of Pulap are said to be Chuuk's best navigators and Pulusuk has Chuuk's only freshwater pond.

Puluwat's five islands almost surround its small lagoon, leaving just one passageway and an excellent anchorage with a safe refuge from storms. The Japanese had an airstrip and lighthouse on one of the now uninhabited islets.

Outer islanders used to have a reputation for being tough fighters and the people of Puluwat were probably once the most feared

people in all the central Carolines. Around the late 1800s however, they got religion and then became as gentle as lambs.

Places to Stay

There are no guesthouses on any of the outer islands, but the governor's office on Moen can sometimes make arrangements with island magistrates to help accommodate visitors. Take food as gifts for those who help you.

Getting There & Away

Field Trip Ship Two field trip ships, the *Micro Trader* and the *Micro Dawn*, together make a total of about 60 trips a year, each trip an average of one week long. Separate trips are scheduled to the Lower (and Mid) Mortlocks, the Upper Mortlocks, the Halls and Namonuito, and to Pattiw. The ships can carry 150 people.

It costs three cents per mile on deck or 10 cents per mile plus $2 per night for a cabin. There are only seven two-bunk cabins, however, and they are often reserved for government officials. From Moen it's 170 miles to Satawan, 160 miles to Pulusuk and 80 miles to Murilo.

It's recommended that you take your own food although you can buy breakfast for $3.50, lunch for $4.50 and dinner for $5. You can get a copy of the latest schedule, printed up every three months, from the Transportation Office (☎ 330-2592), Chuuk State Government, Chuuk, FSM 96942.

Boats to the Mortlocks The Mortlocks have two government boats. The *Miss Takular* runs between Moen and the Mid-Mortlocks about once a week for $5 one way. The boat leaves Moen at 8 pm and arrives at 10 am the next day.

The *Miss Lukeisel* goes to the Upper Mortlocks about twice a week. It makes extra trips between May and August, when the water is calmest, and at Christmas. Nama Island, 48 miles and a couple of hours from Chuuk Lagoon, costs $2 one way. Losap and Piis, about 60 miles away, cost $2.50.

Yap

Yap, the land of giant stone money, remains Micronesia's most traditional stronghold.

You know you're in a unique place as you catch your first glimpse of Yap at the airport. Most people dress in Western clothes but a fair number of men and boys wear bright coloured loincloths and some of the women wear only woven hibiscus skirts. Everyone, including the very official-looking customs officers, has a bulge of betel nut in their cheek. The dirt floors of the old airport were so deeply stained with betel nut juice that the designers of Yap's new airport terminal decided to go with the flow and painted the cement floors betel-nut red!

Out in the villages, which are connected by centuries-old stone footpaths, men's houses are still built in the elaborate, traditional style of wood, thatch, rope and bamboo. It's a society where the caste system survives and where village chiefs still hold as much political clout as elected public officials.

The Yapese are a shy yet proud people. They are offended by the occasional tourist who brazenly points a camera at them as if they were subjects in an anthropological museum, yet at the same time they're receptive to travellers who respect their customs and culture.

As the tourist brochure says:

It takes patience, good manners and plenty of understanding to see Yap and observe some of its traditions. Yap is not a world built for tourists, but a world that welcomes visitors.

If you visit Yap on its own terms you won't be disappointed. For the traveller who treads gently, it's still a rare place to see.

History

Pre-European Contact Studies of pottery and other archaeological finds on Map Island date the earliest known Yapese settlement at around 200 AD.

The Yapese once reigned over a scattered island empire, extending from the Marianas in the north to deep into the eastern Carolines. Lengthy ocean-going voyages were not uncommon.

The Yapese empire was built upon magic, rather than conquest. The high chiefs of Yap Proper employed sorcerers who had powers to cause famine, sickness and typhoons. In fear of this sorcery the outer islanders offered an annual tribute to remain in good favour.

Stone Money Legend has it that the ancient navigator Anagumang set sail in search of the ideal stone to be used as Yapese currency. On Palau's Rock Islands he found a hard crystalline limestone that the Yapese then quarried into huge flat discs. Holes were carved in the centre so logs could be slipped through and the stones were then lugged down to barges and towed by canoe the 250 miles back to Yap.

With their weighty cargo, entire expeditions were sometimes lost in storms at sea. The most valuable stones were not necessarily the largest, but those that were transported at the highest cost of human lives. These stones commonly bore the names of the lost mariners.

Stone money, which the Yapese call *rai*, can range up to 12 feet in diameter and weigh as much as five tons. The Japanese civilian government counted 13,281 coins in 1929.

Although single pieces of stone money are commonly seen throughout Yap, most stone money is kept in 'banks' lined up along village pathways. The money is not moved, even when ownership changes. Stone money remains in use today for some traditional exchanges, although the US dollar settles most commonplace transactions.

Caste A complex caste system developed over time as a consequence of warfare between Yapese villages. The victors would demand land ownership rights and patronage of the defeated village. The people of that village retained rights to use the land but were compelled to perform menial tasks for their landlords, such as road construction and burial of the dead.

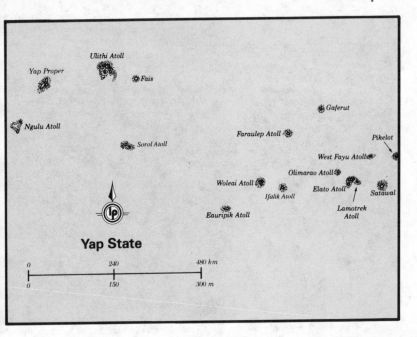

Yap State

```
0        240        480 km
0        150        300 m
```

A village is inhabited by members of the same caste. Every plot of land in the village has a name and rank with the highest ranked plot belonging to the village chief. Even today, the village in which one is born determines one's name and caste.

Depending on how you differentiate them, there are either seven or nine castes in Yapese society today. Each village has its own chief with the paramount chiefs of Yap coming from the three highest caste villages.

It's not really obvious where a village stands in the caste hierarchy just by looking at it. Caste has a more profound effect on people's status than upon their standard of living.

European Contact According to one story, when early explorers first reached Yap the islanders paddled out to meet them. The explorers pointed and asked the name of the island but the Yapese, with their backs to the shore, misunderstood the point. Holding up their paddles they replied *yap* – which was their word for paddle. Ever since, the islands that the local residents call Wa'ab have been known to those outside its shores as Yap.

The first contact with Europeans was in 1526 when the Portuguese explorer Dioga da Rocha landed on Ulithi. The islanders were 'without malice, fear or cautiousness' and da Rocha and his crew remained on the island for four months. Over the next 300 years the rest of Yap's islands were 'discovered' and added to the charts.

Early attempts to settle Yap were half-hearted at best. In 1731 a Spanish Jesuit mission was established on Ulithi but when a supply ship returned a year later they found that all 13 people of the colony had been killed by the islanders.

Apparently Europeans got the hint and for the next 100 years their visits to Yap were few and far between. Strangely however, Dumont d'Urville, the only European known to have visited the main Yap islands in the

Carrying Stone Money

early 1800s, found a people who spoke enough Spanish to request cigars and brandy. It's largely thought that the islanders knowledge of Spanish was the result of their own inter-island commerce with places as distant as the Marianas.

In the 1830s two Spanish ships came to gather beche-de-mer in Yap but at some point during the operation the crews were attacked and brutally murdered. In 1843 the English captain Andrew Cheyne made a similar attempt for a cargo of beche-de-mer. Yapese chiefs seemed cooperative at first, but a brush with would-be assassins and contact with an enslaved survivor of the Spanish massacre convinced Cheyne to drop the venture before suffering a similar fate. It wasn't until the 1860s that regular trade with the West was gradually established. The Germans opened the first permanent trading station in 1869.

Spanish & German Periods Although Spain had long held claim to Yap, it wasn't until the Germans attempted to annex the islands in 1885 that the Spanish established a permanent garrison. Formal colonial occupation of Yap was to continue in one form or another for the next 100 years.

In 1899, in the aftermath of the Spanish-American War, Spain sold Yap to Germany whose interest in the islands was primarily commercial. Concerned about the shortage of labourers to work their plantations and mines, they developed health and sanitation services in hopes of stemming the rapid depopulation. The Germans were the first to use forced Yapese labour, both in Yap and in the phosphate mines on Angaur in Palau.

Japanese Period The Japanese took over in 1914 when the outbreak of WW I forced the Germans to withdraw.

Concern over Yap's transpacific cable station, on line between the US and Shanghai, led the USA to demand access to Yap as a pre-condition to recognising Japan's League of Nations mandate over Micronesia. The two countries signed such a treaty in 1921.

O'Keefe

One of the most colourful characters of Yap's 19th-century history was David 'His Majesty' O'Keefe, a shipwrecked Irish-American who washed ashore in 1871. Near death, the Yapese nursed him back to health and he spent the next 30 years of his life on the islands.

Where the Germans had failed in getting the Yapese to produce copra in quantity, O'Keefe saw his opportunity. He noted that the colourful cloth and trinkets that traders used to entice other Pacific islanders raised little curiosity among the Yapese, who stubbornly preferred traditional hibiscus clothing and grass skirts.

Realising that the enormous stone money the Yapese quarried in distant Palau offered more leverage as a medium of exchange, O'Keefe decided to get into the stone money trade. He went off to Hong Kong to buy a Chinese junk, then returned to Yap and began making runs down to Palau to pick up newly quarried stone money. Yapese chiefs paid for the stone money with copra and O'Keefe soon came to dominate the copra trade in Yap.

O'Keefe's Irish temper and penchant for feuding with colonial administrators made him legendary among the Yapese. In 1901 he disappeared at sea. His former homesite on Tarang Island in Tomil Harbor is now in the Register of National Historic Places, though only a couple of bricks and a stairway remain. ∎

The Japanese then began to arrive in Yap and set up stores, farms and sea-based industries. Their numbers were not as great as in other parts of Micronesia but they nonetheless came to vastly outnumber the dwindling Yapese population.

As WW II approached the Yapese were forced to build airfields and military fortifications. As punishment for non-cooperation the Japanese would smash pieces of Yap's highly valued stone money, sometimes using the broken pieces as road fill.

US forces decided not to invade Yap Proper, although it was bombed during US air raids. Ulithi Atoll was captured and developed into a major Allied support base in 1944.

Geography

Yap Proper consists of the four tightly clustered islands of Yap, Tomil-Gagil, Map (pronounced 'mop') and Rumung. The islands are 515 miles south-west of Guam.

Unlike other high islands in Micronesia which are volcanic in origin, Yap Proper was formed by land upheavals of the Asian continental shelf. Consequently the interior regions are not mountainous, but rather have gentle rolling hills. The highest point, Mt Matade on Yap Island, is 571 feet. Yap Proper has 38.7 sq miles of land, which is 84% of the state's total land mass.

There are also a handful of small islands within Yap Proper's fringing coral reef. Three of these – Pekel, Bi and Tarang (O'Keefe's) – sit in the channel between Tomil-Gagil and Yap islands and total about 10 acres combined. Garim (Bird Island), off the south-east tip of Yap Island, is an uplifted 300-foot-long chunk of coral undercut by the sea.

Strung out some 600 miles to the east of Yap Proper are 134 outer islands, with a combined land area of 7.26 sq miles. Most are mere strands of coral and sand rising precariously above the water. A major typhoon can easily sweep one of these islands clean of its coconut trees and occasionally wash an entire island into the sea.

Trade winds blow onto the north and east sides of the islands, leaving the south and west shores with good sandy beaches.

Climate

Yap has a consistent year-round temperature of about 81°F (27°C) with an approximate 10° variance between noon and night. Humidity is higher during the night and early morning.

Mornings tend to be sunny with a gradual build-up of fair-weather clouds, whose accumulation during the day gives rise to evening showers. This pattern is particularly common from May to December.

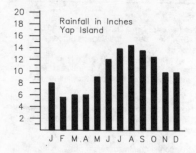

Rainfall in Inches
Yap Island

The average annual rainfall is 121 inches. The north-east trade winds influence Yap from November through June.

Fully developed typhoons are uncommon near Yap, as most of them pass to the north. However, several of the easternmost islands were severely damaged by Typhoon Owen in November 1990.

Government

In addition to an elected state legislature, Yap's constitution establishes two councils of traditional leaders. The Council of Pilung is made up of chiefs from Yap Proper and the Council of Tamol consists of chiefs from the outer islands.

The chiefs pretty much decide who runs and who wins. Although the Yapese can vote for whomever they like for political office, people still generally follow the advice and leadership of their chiefs. The councils have the right to veto any legislation that affects traditional customs.

If the governor is from Yap Proper, then the lieutenant governor must be from the outer islands, and vice versa.

Economy

Yap's moneyed economy is largely reliant upon US funding, with government jobs accounting for the majority of Yapese wage earners.

As most Yapese still make a living in the subsistence economy, the government is trying to develop village-based businesses by distributing free fruit trees, starting chicken hatcheries and the like. They hope to use a 'small is beautiful' approach to go from being an importer of food to an exporter. Presently fish, copra and bananas are exported.

On a different scale, a garment factory that opened in Yap in 1989 is now the first large-scale manufacturing facility in the FSM. A joint Taiwanese-Sri Lankan venture, the factory employs 550 Sri Lankans and 150 Yapese. Most of the garments are shipped to the USA, which gives the FSM duty-free access.

For years Yap has had just 26 hotel rooms, but the opening of two new hotels has doubled that number and Yap's first dive shop is introducing the island to divers, who now account for about half of Yap's visitors. All together, Yap gets about 3000 tourists a year and there is now talk of building a Japanese resort hotel on the north-east coast.

People

The physical characteristics of the Yapese are of western Pacific origin, with traits that indicate Philippine, Palauan and Indonesian influences.

There was little intermarriage with Europeans or Japanese, which makes the Yapese unique among Micronesians. Attempts by the Japanese to assimilate the Micronesian peoples by offering privileges to the offspring of mixed Japanese-Micronesian parents had no impact on the Yapese. They continued to marry traditionally in accordance with their caste system and foreigners remained excluded.

For reasons that are still unclear, the Yapese population dropped by half under the Japanese administration. The population in 1945 was only 2582. With the birth rate among the world's lowest there was serious concern that the Yapese were on the verge of extinction.

The Americans reacted by sending medical teams and a slew of anthropologists. Fortunately the latter needn't have made such haste, for the population slowly edged upwards.

The current population is 11,500, with about 65% living on Yap Proper.

Culture

The Yapese, more than any other Micronesian peoples, have been reluctant to adopt Western ways. Despite four colonial administrations, their culture remains largely undiluted by outside influences and they still proudly retain their own customs and traditions. See also Caste under History earlier.

Food The Yapese grow taro, yams, oranges, bananas, breadfruit, tapioca, papaya and coconuts. They are skilled fishing people using hook and line, nets, spears and traps.

Traditional Dress The loincloth worn by men and boys is called a *thu* and is usually of bright red or blue cotton cloth. Men on the outer islands wear just one layer of cloth, while men on Yap Proper sometimes wear two or three.

Women have two kinds of traditional dress – grass skirts and *lava-lavas*. The latter is a wide strip of cloth woven from hibiscus and banana fibres or from cotton thread. The cotton ones are becoming more common, as they take only about a third of the time to make. Lava-lavas are wrapped around the lower body, extending from the waist to the knee.

Traditionally, neither men nor women wore clothing on their upper bodies, though today T-shirts are coming into style. Western-style clothing is more common than not in Colonia, but both Western and traditional dress are seen all around Yap.

Betel Nut Everyone, but everyone, chews *buw*, as betel nut is called. Small stores do a good business selling zip-lock sandwich bags of betel nuts and pepper leaves for about $1.25 for 'a plastic'.

Betel nut is split open while green, sprinkled with dry lime made from coral, wrapped in pepper leaves and chewed. It produces a mild high that lasts about 10 minutes. Sometimes tobacco, or tobacco soaked in vodka, is added.

Betel nut turns the saliva bright red and stains the teeth red and eventually black. It's the lime that stimulates the flow of saliva. Once called 'a dentist's nightmare' by Westerners, recent findings indicate that chewing betel nut may actually help prevent cavities.

Not that this would sway the Yapese one way or the other. They start chewing buw at a very early age and continue as long as they are able to chew – perhaps even longer:

According to old stories, even ghosts chew betel nut. If a sailing canoe was to stop for no obvious reason in the middle of a lagoon the sailor would prepare a special betel nut mixture, wrap it in extra leaves and tie it up tightly with many knots. He would then throw it overboard and sail away easily, while the ghost who'd been holding his canoe was busy untying the knots.

Traditional Community Houses A *faluw*, or men's house, is a large thatched structure with a sharply pitched roof, supported by heavy wooden pillars and resting atop a stone platform. Traditionally the faluw served as a school for young boys, as quarters for bachelors and as a meeting place for the village leaders.

Pebai are community meeting houses. They often look much like men's houses, only they're larger and have open-air sides. Pebai are mostly built inland whereas faluw are usually by the water.

Once common throughout Yap, women's houses or *dapal* are now only found on the outer islands. When a girl reached puberty she was ushered off to a dapal for initiation and all women in the village went to women's houses to wait out their menstrual periods, using the time to weave, bathe and relax.

Women's Roles Traditionally women have had subservient roles in Yapese society. They did the cooking and tended the fields, harvesting from one plot for male family members and from another for the females. The food then had to be prepared in separate pots over separate fires. Not only could men and women not eat together but neither could members of different castes share the same food.

Although such restrictions are not so strictly adhered to today, perhaps this has some bearing on why there are so few restaurants in Yap.

Avoiding Offence Exploring Yap requires a grasp of Yapese etiquette. Once you step off the road anywhere in Yap, you're on private property. Even some of the stone pathways through villages are private and walking along them is somewhat similar to cutting across someone's backyard. Some villages have areas that women are not allowed to enter.

The official line is that you need to get permission and sometimes a guide to visit most beaches, pebais or villages. Unofficially, the word is that because you're a foreigner and don't know the rules, the Yapese will understand as long as you're considerate and don't overstep the bounds.

The catch-22 is that if you have a guide with you, there are certain things you won't be able to see or do, because the guide knows precisely where he is and isn't allowed to take you.

One couple told us about missing out on photographs because the guide they'd gone out with said he'd get into trouble if they took certain pictures. In Yap this is understandable with photos of people, but he also prevented them from taking more routine shots, including a landscape view because there was a grass shack in the foreground that he said was owned by 'bad people'.

In reality it's not difficult to go off on your own, asking people along the way for directions and permission when appropriate. Smiles go a long way in Yap. In a village you should greet everyone you see so it doesn't look as if you're sneaking around. Be prepared to back off when it's obvious you're intruding, and always ask permission before snapping someone's picture.

To the Yapese, not asking permission is an insult. But they're a very generous people and if you do ask, they'll probably let you go nearly anywhere and see almost anything you want.

Clothing Women should wear clothing that covers their thighs. Otherwise, clothing in Yap is light and comfortable. In fact one of the acts of the first governor was an attempt to pass legislation that would make wearing ties illegal!

Language
The local languages are Yapese, Ulithian, Woleaian and Satawalese. The last three are the languages of outer islanders.

In Yapese, 'hello' is *mogethin*, though you're just as apt to be greeted with a cheery 'good morning.' 'Excuse me' is *siro*, 'thank you' is *kam magar* and 'good-bye' is *kafel*.

Holidays & Festivals
Yap celebrates New Year's Day, Yap Day during the first week of March, FSM Constitution Day on 10 May, FSM Independence Day on 3 November, Yap Constitution Day on 24 December and Christmas Day. Yap Day is the most colourful of these holidays and includes ceremonial dancing and sporting events.

Yap's big traditional celebrations are *mitmits*, all-out feasts accompanied by gift-giving and traditional singing and dancing. One village gives a mitmit for another village to reciprocate for the one they received in previous years. The completion of a major village project such as a new community house is also a time for major festivities.

Activities
Diving & Snorkelling Yap has good diving, including virgin reefs with excellent coral, vertical walls, sea caves, channel drifts, schools of grey sharks and barracuda, sea turtles and a couple of shipwrecks.

The reef off Gilman at the southern tip of Yap Proper slopes gently with extensive branching corals, huge lettuce corals and spectacular coral heads.

Yap's most novel attraction, however, is Manta Ridge in Miil Channel, where a school of manta rays feed. These gentle creatures, which can have a wingspan of 12 feet, swim through the channel as divers cling to a ledge about 30 feet below the surface. The manta rays often come close enough to brush divers with their wingtips.

Yap Divers (☎ 350-2321), Box 177, Colonia, Yap, FSM 96943 at Manta Ray Bay Hotel is Yap's first and only dive shop. It's a well-run operation with boat tours, certification in PADI, dive and snorkel gear for sale and rent, and hotel-dive packages. It costs $65 for a two-tank dive, including lunch on the boat.

They take snorkellers out on the boat too, for $35, but trips are generally geared for divers so ask in advance about destinations and water conditions. A choppy water surface that won't affect divers can make for less than ideal snorkelling. Snorkel sets rent for $5 a day.

Swimming There aren't many good beaches in Yap and even fewer open to use by non-villagers. The most accessible good beaches are Wanyan Beach in Tomil-Gagil and at Bechiyal Cultural Center in Map.

In Yap, although bare breasts are the norm, it's considered vulgar for women to show their thighs. Women may wear a swimsuit in the water but should cover up on the beach.

Organised Tours Guided land and boat tours can be arranged through the hotels or Wave Crest Travel Agency at the Manta Ray Bay Hotel. ESA Hotel charges $50 for a tour by private car for one or two people. It may be cheaper to just rent a taxi for the day however, and use the driver as your guide.

The tourist office should be able to get someone with a motorboat to take you out for about $20.

YAP PROPER

The major islands of Yap, Map and Tomil-Gagil are all tightly clustered and connected by bridges. Yap Island is the westernmost and largest island, with 53% of Yap Proper's land area and 67% of its people. Rumung is separated from the rest of Yap Proper by Yinbinaew Passage and can only be reached

by boat. Rumung is not receptive to visitors however, and outsiders need an invitation to go there. Yap Proper has 10 municipalities with more than 100 small villages.

The landscape of the main islands is mainly rolling hills with a green cover of grass interspersed with sparse pandanus and palm trees. In the south-west, the lowlands have thick growth and a marsh-like jungle floor. Yap Proper has some sandy beaches, but much of the coast is lined with mangrove swamps.

The most interesting sights by far are not WW II relics or scenic views, but glimpses into Yapese culture.

The sparsely populated villages outside the capital of Colonia are quiet, peaceful and tidy. On weekdays, when the children are at school and adults are off fishing or at work either in Colonia or in their taro patches, the villages can look semi-deserted. In a way, it's not a bad time to explore. You'll still see some people, but with fewer folks around it's that many less whose permission you need to seek out.

Bechiyal, a traditional village on a sandy beach at the tip of Map Island, has opened itself to visitors as a living cultural centre. It offers the kind of experience you'd hope to find by journeying to a distant outer island, yet Bechiyal is only an $8 taxi ride away. You can sleep overnight in a men's house, eat breadfruit and freshly speared fish, drink homemade tuba and learn a lot from the villagers about Yapese culture.

Colonia

Colonia is the state capital, the business and administrative centre and the only part of Yap that is the least bit modern. Even so the 'town' of Colonia, which the locals call Donguch, would be considered a village almost anywhere else.

Colonia is built around Chamorro Bay, offering water views most everywhere. The bay, incidentally, got its name after the Germans settled the area with a group of Chamorro labourers who were brought in from Saipan to build the transpacific cable

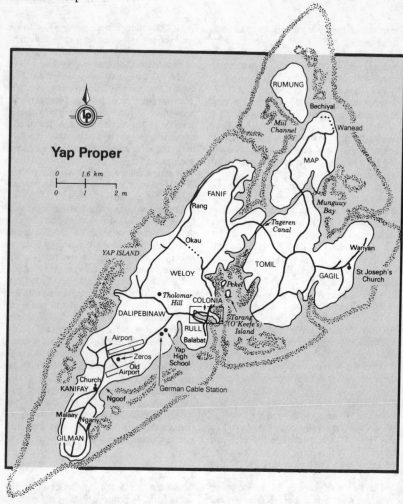

Yap Proper

YAP ISLAND

RUMUNG

Bechiyal

Mill Channel

Wanead

MAP

FANIF

Rang

Munguuy Bay

Okau

Tageren Canal

Wanyan

WELOY

TOMIL

GAGIL

St Joseph's Church

Pekel

Tholomar Hill

COLONIA

DALIPEBINAW

Tarang (O'Keefe's) Island

RULL

Balabat

Airport

Zeros

Old Airport

Yap High School

Church

KANIFAY

German Cable Station

Ngoof

Malaay

Ngariy

GILMAN

0   1.6 km

0   1   2 m

station. These days the south side of Chamorro Bay is home to a sizable Palauan community.

The Yap Cooperative Association (YCA), a jumbled department store, is for all practical purposes Colonia's town centre and a place where Yapese meet to chat. Men in *thus* sit out the front on bamboo benches under thatched awnings, preparing betel nut chews

and watching people come and go. You can even buy a T-shirt inside YCA that depicts the scene, labelling it 'Downtown Yap'.

There's quite a bit to see in the Colonia area and the best of it can be explored on foot: stone footpaths, the trail up Medeqdeq Hill and a walk to the stone money bank and men's house in the nearby village of Balabat. These all make pleasurable strolls and you don't need special permission to do them on your own.

Information The tourist office (☎ 350-2298) is open from 7.30 to 11.30 am and 12.30 to 4.30 pm Monday to Friday.

The public library is open from 1.30 to 4.30 pm Mondays, Wednesdays and Fridays.

Yap has one radio station and one TV station. YCA sells Guam's *Pacific Daily News*. The Land Management office sells USGS maps of Yap and a few other Micronesian islands for $3 each.

The Air Mike office (☎ 350-2127) is next to YCA.

There's a modern public hospital (☎ 350-3446) at the north side of Colonia.

Money The Bank of Hawaii and the Bank of the FSM are both open from 9.30 am to 2.30 pm Monday to Thursday, and to 5 pm on Fridays. The Bank of the FSM doesn't charge a fee to cash travellers' cheques.

Post & Telecommunications Yap Proper's only post office, on the north side of Chamorro Bay, is open weekdays from 8.30 am to 4 pm. Mail goes off-island only twice weekly, on Wednesdays and Fridays.

Long-distance phone calls can be made from hotels or from the FSM Telecommunications building (open 24 hours) near the old airport. You can also make calls by purchasing debit cards for $10 each. There are debit-card phones at ESA Hotel and YCA, among other places.

Government Offices The government administration building is built on the site of the old Spanish fort, of which only remnants of a wall and the foundations remain. The complex holds the governor's Office, the Office for Outer Island Affairs, the field trip ship reservation office and other offices.

Yap State Legislature The state legislature building is on the site of a former Japanese Shinto shrine. The only vestiges of the shrine are the cement torii (pillared gate) in the

middle of the parking lot and a stone lantern near the steps leading to the front door.

Medeqdeq Hill The 482-foot Medeqdeq Hill has a panoramic view of Colonia, the harbour and Yap's east coast. The top of the hill is about a mile up from Colonia on the road past St Mary's, the Catholic church dating back to Yap's first Spanish Capuchin missionaries.

Though the walk starts out on pavement, the last half is along a rough dirt road that's not passable without a 4WD vehicle. Beware of a low-growing ground cover with fuzzy purple flowers and small razor-sharp thorns that draw blood at the slightest touch.

Stone Footpaths There's a lovely traditional stone footpath that starts near the waterfront between the Baptist Mission and Ocean View Enterprises. The path is peaceful and shady, lined with flowering hibiscus and green ti plants much of the way. When the path splits, take the left fork and you'll come out to the paved road just above the Catholic school.

To continue on a second footpath that will bring you down to the north side of Chamorro Bay, turn right and go up the road for about 30 feet. The second path begins beside a dumped car that looks like it'll probably be there forever. This path is not as well-lined with stones as the first, but it does offer some glimpses of taro patches and village houses.

The whole walk only takes about 15 minutes and is a very pleasant way to get across town.

Balabat The mile-long walk to the village of Balabat in Rull Municipality is a good way to see a traditional men's house and stone-money bank without having to drive around the island.

The road starts at the petrol station near the bridge in south Colonia. A few minutes along, you'll pass Madrich, a point of land sticking out into the bay which is home to a settlement of outer islanders. Most people in the village speak Ulithian and traditional dress is the norm. Madrich, once the site of a Spanish trading station, was named after Madrid.

The walk continues along the waterfront until it reaches Rull municipal office, where the road is lined with an impressive collection of stone money.

There the pavement ends and the road curves to the right. A little less than five minutes past the municipal office, look on the left for a dirt road that is about as wide as the main road. It's just a couple minutes down that road to more stone money and a seaside faluw in a setting of coconut palms.

The main road ends at two raised stone platforms used for community gatherings. Traditional dances sometimes take place on the pathway between the platforms. The village of Balabat is neatly landscaped with betel nut trees, taro patches, hibiscus and lilies. You can usually spot bright-red cardinal honeyeaters in the trees along this walk.

Around Yap Island

German Cable Station In 1905, the German communications station in Yap completed a link to Shanghai through Guam and the Phil-

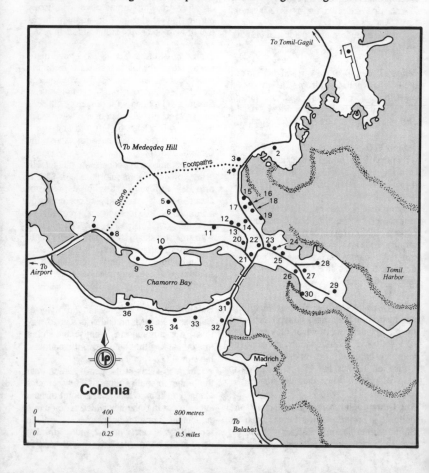

ippines via an undersea cable system. In August 1914, shelling from a British warship destroyed the station's 200-foot steel radio tower, breaking Germany's communications link to its Pacific territories and marking the start of WW I activity in Micronesia.

To see the graffiti-decorated concrete remains of the station, one of the few remnants of German occupation in Yap, head west out of Colonia on the road to the airport. Pass the pond that serves as the town's water reservoir on the right, then turn left onto the unmarked dirt road that leads up to Yap High School. The station remains are opposite the school's parking lot.

Japanese Zeros The base camp of a small contingent of US Navy Seabees who work on public construction projects is on the left just past the high school. The entrance to the new airport is a mile farther down on the right.

One mile beyond that, take the road to the left to see the remains of some Japanese Zero planes. The two planes that are best preserved and easiest to see are just behind the weather station. You can see the remains of a couple of others along the left side of the driveway leading up to the next door FSM Telecommunications building.

The Zeros were destroyed on the ground by US aerial bombings during WW II. The planes are missing engines and other parts that were taken away by Japanese collectors, but they're still interesting to see. The area around the planes is a good place to find low-growing, insectivorous pitcher plants.

There's a well-preserved Japanese anti-aircraft gun under a big mahogany tree on the weather station lawn about 20 feet from the road, just beyond the little chain-link enclosure.

The road continues down to an old 5000-foot airstrip built by the Japanese. The old thatched-roof terminal still stands, but it's difficult to spot the remains of the 727 that landed short of the runway in 1980, lost a wheel and skidded off into the bush at the east end of the airstrip.

You can turn right onto the runway to get back to the main road that goes to Gilman.

Southern Tip of Yap South of the old airport is the village of Ngoof with the brightly painted St Ignatius of the Loyola church. About half a mile beyond that there's a turn-off to the left which takes you along a rather rough coastal road south to Ngariy.

On the left side of the road in the village of Ngariy there's a faluw, pebai and a couple of *wunbey*, or meeting platforms. There in the open air the elder men of the village have their meetings, sitting against stone back-

1	Hospital
2	Family Chain Store
3	Ocean View Enterprises
4	Baptist Mission
5	St Mary's Elementary School
6	St Mary's Catholic Church
7	Aces Mart
8	Bahai Center
9	Lagoonia Store
10	Post Office
11	Rai View Hotel & Restaurant
12	Land Management Office
13	Peace Corps
14	Tourist Office
15	Manta Ray Bay Hotel & Restaurant/Yap Divers
16	Laundromat
17	YWA Handicraft Shop
18	Playground
19	Waab-Mak'uuf Market
20	Police Station
21	Bank of Hawaii
22	Courthouse
23	Bank of the FSM
24	Yap Co-op (YCA)/Cool Corner
25	Air Micronesia
26	Marina Restaurant
27	Government Offices
28	Commercial Dock/Waab Transportation
29	Yap State Legislature
30	Library
31	Petrol Station
32	Laundromat
33	Blue Lagoon Store
34	The Pathways Hotel
35	Yap Evangelical Church
36	ESA Hotel & Restaurant

rests. A low platform in the centre is for holding food and betel nut which young men sitting around on the edges serve to the elders.

Gilman, at the southernmost tip of the island, has a rocky beach. There are some attractive traditional houses in this area, landscaped with stone money, hibiscus hedges and chenille plants with velvety red tails.

The road going up the west side skirts the mangrove-studded coast, in places narrowing to just one lane elevated a few feet above the swamps. Tiny lipstick-red fiddler crabs are easy to spot running around in the black mud between the sharp spikes of the mangrove shoots, and sometimes you can also see edible mangrove crabs and monitor lizards. The lizards, which can reach a length of several feet, were introduced onto Yap and Ulithi by the Japanese to control the rat population and as a food source.

At Malaay village an extensive moss-covered Japanese stone wall, part of WW II defence fortifications, runs along the right side of the road.

Okau Village The village of Okau in Weloy has one of Yap's best meeting houses and stone money banks at the end of a very pleasant walk down a stone footpath.

To get there from Colonia you take the road west, as if heading towards the airport, but instead of turning left with the main paved road take the right fork, which is three-quarters of a mile from the westside bridge on Chamorro Bay.

When the road forks again, keep to the right. The stone pathway is 3¼ miles from the airport road and starts on the right side of the road opposite a stone platform, just before two small houses.

One section of the path meanders alongside taro patches, while another part is lined with hibiscus and lush variegated plants. Mosses grow in the cracks between the stones. It's very quiet and peaceful, almost like walking through a Zen garden.

The large pebai, about 10 minutes down the pathway, is built on a raised stone plat-

form. The supports are made of mahogany, the inside floor planks of betel nut and the roof is nipa palm lashed onto bamboo.

Yap's most valuable stone money is generally thickest in the middle and thinner at the edges, with circular gouge markings across the face. You can see this type of money in front of the pebai to the left.

Fanif From Okau, the road continues through Fanif Municipality around the northern tip of Yap Island. The dirt road, which is in reasonably good condition, skirts sandy beaches and mangroves, crosses little bridges and passes through a few sleepy villages.

Rang Beach is a brown sand beach which begins about two miles north of Okau. Swimming might be good at high tide, but at low tide it's all sea grass and sand flats. If you want to use the beach, it's proper to first seek out the village chief and ask his permission.

About a half-mile after the road curves inland, you'll pass a church on the right. Continue on the main road for another two miles. At the crossroads, take the right fork to go back to Colonia or the left to continue on to Tomil-Gagil.

Tomil-Gagil Island
Tomil-Gagil was once connected to Yap Island at the upper end of Tomil Harbor by mangrove-covered swampland. During the German occupation the shallow Tageren Canal was dug between the islands to allow boat passage to Map and Rumung from Colonia.

Most visitors to Tomil-Gagil are on their way to the beach in Wanyan or to Bechiyal on Map Island. For the most part it's a dry area of open rolling meadows and dusty red earth.

Shortly after crossing the Tageren Canal you'll go by the Seventh Day Adventist school. When the road forks a mile further, turn left. The road north to Bechiyal will come in after a quarter of a mile, but to get to Wanyan continue straight ahead. The Wanyan road runs through the former US

Coast Guard Loran Station, now converted to a maritime academy.

Gacham Hill, south of the road near the academy, is a sacred place considered to be the centre of Yapese wisdom and the spot where Yap is said to have been formed.

Wanyan

Yap's largest piece of stone money is on the island of Rumung, but since the people of Rumung have decided they're not ready for foreign visitors, you'll probably have to settle for number two, which is in the centre of Wanyan Village.

Upon entering Wanyan, you'll pass St Joseph's Catholic Church which is interesting for the mural painted above its door showing Yapese men presenting gifts of stone money, lava-lavas, food and storyboards.

A little further on, you'll pass a meeting house and will then see two huge rai standing along the roadside. The piece on the left is Yap's second largest.

Wanyan Beach One of Yap's most accessible beaches is Wanyan Beach (also called Coast Guard Beach), at the end of the road. This brown sand beach is backed by lots of loaded coconut trees – if you're driving, be careful where you park! There's a thatched picnic shelter, a volleyball net and sometimes a $1 user fee. A freshwater shower is just past the far end of the beach.

Swimming is best at high tide, as otherwise the water is shallow and there's lots of sea grass near the shore. About halfway out to the reef there are several circular drop-offs with good fish and coral. If you look straight out from the beach, you can identify these snorkelling holes by the water colour, which changes from dark blue to aqua. The closest is directly out from the beach at 11 o'clock and takes about 10 minutes to swim out to.

There are plans to put up a few island-style guest cottages near the beach. If you want to find out if the cottages have been built, write to Bill Yamnang, Box 308, Colonia, Yap, FSM 96943.

Bechiyal Cultural Center

Bechiyal is a special place. This friendly seaside village at the northern tip of Map has not only decided to accommodate overnight visitors, but has set itself up as a cultural centre.

This is a wonderful way to experience traditional Yapese village life. Many villagers will take the time to share stories or skills (such as fishing or weaving) with visitors who spend some time in Bechiyal.

Getting there is part of the experience. Drive or take a taxi to the end of the road (or, if you're overnighting, take the public school bus) and walk across the log footbridge. The path passes through Wanead and Toepuw, two traditional villages with thatched houses spread out along the coast, then leads through a jungle setting with lots of bird calls before ending at Bechiyal, a mile away. There's a little unmarked store on the left in Wanead where you can get soda and drinking coconuts. The store owner, a former chief, is a great storyteller who can converse easily in both English and Japanese.

Bechiyal is on a lovely beach, one of Yap Proper's best, though you'll need to wade out for about 10 minutes to reach water deep enough for swimming. Between the coastline and reef are two large V-shaped stone fishtraps of ancient origins. When the tide goes out the bigger fish get stuck in the narrow end of the traps, making it a cinch for villagers to go out and spearfish their next meal.

Visitors are welcome to use the beach in front of the men's house, though the beaches just beyond the village are even nicer, and as they're more secluded women can sunbathe without having to worry about offending anyone. There's a freshwater shower in the village. Masks and snorkels are rented out for $2 a day. For $15, they'll take snorkellers out by boat to the channel where the manta rays feed and even do a scenic loop around the forbidden island of Rumung on the way back.

Bechiyal's pebai is the largest on Yap. Inside are glass cases from Colonia's now-defunct museum containing shell money called *yar*, war spears, a pig's tooth necklace worn by boys, shell adzes and other artefacts.

The faluw, on a high stone platform above the beach, is one of the oldest on the island. It's crafted in the centuries-old manner with openings that hinge in and out, and thatch that catches the cooling ocean breezes. Inside, a carved wooden figure represents the *mispil*, which in times past was a woman captured from a neighbouring village and used as the mistress for the faluw.

The entrance fee to Bechiyal is $2.50 for adults, $1.25 for children, and includes a guided tour by one of the villagers if you visit on weekdays. There's no extra charge for still photography, but previous negative experiences with video cameras makes their use frowned upon and there's a fee to use one. Taking shells is strictly forbidden.

Meals are available for $3 to $4 each, but should be arranged a day in advance. Dinner might well be a hardy Yapese meal of fish or crab, breadfruit, taro and fried banana, all from the village. Coconuts to drink from and coffee cost 35 cents and bananas, oranges and soursop are available in season. Bechiyal's tuba has such a good reputation that Rumung islanders regularly come ashore to buy it.

The handicrafts for sale in Bechiyal, typically woven bags and grass skirts, are often cheaper than those found in Colonia.

Places to Stay

Camping Camping can be complicated on Yap as every speck of land is privately owned. If you do insist on communing with nature, you'll need to get permission from a landowner. The tourist office may be able to help if you aren't successful on your own.

For the most part people think camping is a bit odd and may insist you pitch your tent in their backyard where they can keep an eye on you. They'll need to explain it all to the neighbours and will most probably breathe a sigh of relief once you've gone.

The one notable exception is Bechiyal Cultural Center in Map, where arrangements have been made to accommodate campers. It costs $5 per person to pitch a tent and the location can't be beaten.

Guesthouses The tourist office maintains a list of Yapese families who are interested in taking travellers into their homes. To arrange this, you should write to the tourist office a month or so in advance to let them know when you're coming, how long you'd like to stay with a family and maybe a little about yourself. When you arrive, the tourist office will arrange for you to visit a few homes so you and the families can check each other out. You should plan to stay in a hotel for one or two nights first until arrangements are complete. Rates are negotiable between you and the family, and there's no charge by the tourist office.

This is a new concept in Yap and these are not established guesthouses by any means so this could be a good opportunity to experience authentic Yapese home life, while possibly saving a little on hotel costs.

In Bechiyal for overnight guests, there are two simple cottages on stilts, one with a loft and glass louvred windows all around. Guests are provided with thin sleeping mats to put on the floor, pillows, towels, sheets, mosquito coils and kerosene lanterns. The cost is $15 per person.

Visitors can also stay overnight at the men's house, where a Peace Corps volunteer and a couple of village boys sleep. It costs $10 for mat space on the floor. Accommodations cost half price for children.

If you want to do your own cooking, you can borrow pots, pans and a kerosene stove, and purchase kerosene for a small fee.

Reservations for overnight stays can be made by writing to Chief John Tamag, Bechiyal Cultural Center, Box 37, Colonia, Yap, FSM 96943, or through the tourist office.

Hotels There are four hotels in Yap Proper, all in Colonia, and cottages at Bechiyal. All Yapese hotels are small, locally owned operations and all meet guests at the airport. Yap has a 10% hotel tax. Only the Manta Ray Bay Hotel takes credit cards.

The *Rai View Hotel* (☎ 350-2279), Box 130, Colonia, Yap, FSM 96943, has 10 very basic rooms which cost $20/28 for singles/doubles with a shared bathroom or $25/30 with a private bathroom. Rooms have TV and air-con, but little appeal. Airport transfers are $4 round trip.

The *ESA Hotel* (☎ 350-2139), Box 141, Colonia, Yap, FSM 96943, run by a Palauan family, overlooks Chamorro Bay and is a little nicer than the Rai View. There are 16 simple but clean rooms with air-con, private bathrooms and TVs. The rate is $40 for singles or doubles. They charge $6 per person for round-trip airport transfers.

The *Pathways Hotel* (☎ 350-2253/3310), Box 718, Colonia, Yap, FSM 96943, consists of free-standing hillside cottages that finely balance modern comforts and traditional Yapese aesthetics. Each is crafted from native materials, with nipa palm thatched roofs, split bamboo walls and Yapese mahogany beams tied with coconut fibre rope. There are ceiling fans and screened windows to catch the breeze. Sitting verandas give clear views of Chamorro Bay. Modern amenities are hidden from view; the silent refrigerators are behind wood cabinets and the air-con is concealed by louvres. The cottages are in a garden-like setting, connected by wooden walkways. The management is very knowledgeable and friendly and with all things combined this is one of the nicest places to stay in Micronesia. Rates are $50 and include tax and airport transfers.

The new *Manta Ray Bay Hotel* (☎ 350-2300) Box 177, Colonia, Yap, FSM 96943, has 15 large attractive rooms with rattan furnishings and modern conveniences such as thermostat- controlled air-con, VCRs, mini-bars and purified water. All rooms have two queen-sized beds, with waterbeds on the 1st floor. Rates are $85 for street-side rooms and $95 for rooms with verandas facing the bay. If you're paying this much, it's worth the extra $10 for the water view. For high rollers, there's a huge luxury suite with a spiral staircase leading to a private rooftop jacuzzi for $250. Airport transfers are $5.

Places to Eat

Cool Corner, at the left side of YCA, is one of Yap's best food values and a favourite eating plate of Colonia's workers. You can get two eggs, toast and coffee for $2. Lunch specials often include an excellent fresh fish plate with rice and potato salad for $3.50. Hamburgers or ramen cost $1.35. It's open from 7 am for breakfast daily and for lunch (until 4.30 pm) Monday to Friday.

Waab-Mak'uuf Market, open Monday to Friday, sells locally grown fruits and vegetables, boiled eggs and smoked fish. Lunch is served at picnic tables on a covered porch at the rear of the market where there's usually a breeze coming off the bay. The menu changes daily, but fried fish, pork or chicken with boiled taro and rice for $3.50 is common.

The *ESA Restaurant* is unexciting but acceptable, with pancakes for $1.10 or bacon, eggs, toast, juice and coffee for $3.75. The fried fish plate costs $4 at lunch or $6 at dinner. Chicken and beef dishes are a little bit more and they have reasonably priced sandwiches and ramen.

The best thing about the *Rai View Restaurant* is the fact that they have chilled drinking coconuts served with a straw for 35 cents. Their blackboard menu changes from day to day. The price range is similar to ESA, though overall the food is not as good.

Colonia's new marina complex contains a relaxed open-air restaurant, as well as a dock with slips for visiting yachts. The *Marina Restaurant* has good food, with fish, pork and chicken specials averaging $5 at lunch and a few dollars more at dinner. The fish sandwich, served anytime, is made with a big chunk of fresh fish and is a good deal at $1.75. The Marina is open from 11 am to 8.30 pm.

The *Manta Ray Bar & Grill* has both indoor and veranda seating with a bayside view. You can get a good cheeseburger with onion rings for $5.50 and fish or chicken dishes for about $8. The pizza, which can be recommended, is loaded with cheese and the large size ($9 plain) will fill two people.

There are no restaurants outside Colonia, though the outlying villages often have small stores. However, they're almost invariably unmarked, so you'll need to ask.

YCA is Yap's biggest grocery/general store. Others are Aces Mart, Family Chain Store and the Blue Lagoon Store. You can get a variety of liquor at reasonable prices at the little store to the left of YCA.

Colonia's water is not safe to drink from the tap. A gallon of bottled water costs $2.25 at Blue Lagoon Store.

Entertainment

There's not much to do in the evening around Colonia in terms of standard entertainment. Yap has no movie theatre, though the Seabees Camp shows free movies several nights a week.

Colonia's two best restaurants have open-air bars with good water views. The *Marina Restaurant* has beer for $1.50 and the *Manta Ray Bar & Grill* sells wine or beer for $2 and tropical drinks for $5.

Things to Buy

Yap has some fine handicrafts. Lava-lava skirts hand-woven of cotton or hibiscus and banana-tree fibres can make attractive wall hangings or table mats. They generally sell for $20 to $50. Other interesting crafts are handbags or betel nut pouches woven of pandanus leaves, shell jewellery, wood carvings of outrigger canoes and 'grass' skirts made of brightly dyed hibiscus bark.

Two places selling handicrafts are the Yap Women's Association (YWA) shop, near Waab-Mak'uuf Market, and the Lagoonia Store on the north side of Chamorro Bay. YWA is open from 8 am to 4.30 pm Monday to Friday and Lagoonia is open daily except Sundays.

YCA is the best place to get T-shirts with Yapese designs. It's open from 8 am to 5.30 pm Monday to Friday and from 8.30 am to early afternoon on weekends.

Getting There & Away

Air Mike, the only airline which services Yap, flies on Sundays, Wednesdays and Fridays. The flight originates in Guam, touches down on Yap on the way to Palau, and lands again on Yap on the return to Guam.

The full fare between Guam and Yap is $208, though on Sundays tickets cost just $120. The regular one-way fare between Palau and Yap is $141. The Sunday flight from Palau to Yap costs $80. Also note that on the regular round-trip ticket between Guam and Palau you can stop over on Yap in either direction.

Airport The airport is 2½ miles from town. There are restrooms, but no car rental booths or other services, and you're unlikely to find a taxi. There is a pay phone, though it doesn't use coins but rather a debit card that must be purchased in advance for $10. If you need to call for a ride you can try asking to use the phone at the Air Mike desk. A van in the parking lot sells soft drinks, bags of betel nut and a few snacks.

Micronesian Fan

Getting Around
There are a few paved roads around Colonia and most of the island's dirt roads are in good condition by Micronesian standards. The road heading north from Colonia to Map is scheduled to be paved.

Bus School buses run between Colonia and outlying villages transporting students and commuting workers. They generally run towards Colonia in the early morning and back to the villages in late afternoon. Visitors can use them on a space available basis for 30 cents. If you're going to Bechiyal, that bus leaves Colonia at 2.30 and 5 pm and returns from Bechiyal at 7 am and 3 pm.

Taxi Yap's taxis are radio dispatched, not hailed down by the side of the road. Rides around the Colonia area are 50 cents. Fares quoted are per taxi, not per person.

Nanyo Taxi (☎ 350-2120), in a small store on the left side of YCA, charges $2 to the new airport and $2.50 to the old airport, but doesn't go much farther than that. Mid-land Taxi (☎ 350-2405), at the right side of YCA, charges $3 to the new airport, $5 to Okau, $7 to Gilman or Wanyan and $8 to Bechiyal.

Car ESA Hotel, Pacific Bus Co (☎ 350-2288 or 350-2266) and Rai View Hotel rent sedans for $35 a day, plus 10% tax. None of them has a booth at the airport.

Hitching There isn't enough traffic outside of Colonia to really depend on hitching, though if you're walking along the road you might get offered a ride. Sticking out a thumb is not a custom here.

OUTER ISLANDS
The outer islands are made up of 11 atolls and four single islands. Of these 15 outer island groups, 11 are populated.

Yap's outer islanders are some of the most isolated people on earth. Little is known of their origins although it's believed that their islands were settled quite independently of Yap Proper. Yap's easternmost islanders and Chuuk's westernmost islanders have more physical, cultural and linguistic similarities with each other than they do with either of their district centres.

Most outer islanders live the same way they have for centuries, wearing thus and lava-lavas and living in thatched huts. Some of the elderly men still have elaborate body tattoos, though the practice has been all but abandoned by younger generations.

For the most part the outer islanders maintain a subsistence livelihood of fishing and farming. To earn a little money, many of the islanders produce copra which they load onto the field trip ship when it stops by.

Uninhabited islands are visited in outrigger canoes to gather turtles, turtle eggs and coconuts. On Lamotrek, for instance, turtle meat is the staple food between April and August.

Some of the smaller atolls have so little land that every spare bit is used for growing crops. During severe dry spells some islanders are forced to rely solely on drinking coconuts when they run out of catchment water.

Ulithian is the native language on Ulithi, Fais and Sorol. Satawal islanders speak Satawalese, which is closely related to the language of Chuuk's western islanders. The native language on Yap's other outer islands is Woleaian.

Ulithi Atoll
Ulithi Atoll, 100 miles north-east of Yap, has the most land and the most people of any of the outer islands. Its huge lagoon, which encompasses 209 sq miles, is the world's fourth largest. All in all, there are 49 islands with a total land mass of 1.79 sq miles. Ulithi played an important role in WW II. The Japanese came in numbers that must have seemed enormous to the Ulithians – that is until the USA moved in with temporary population densities rivalling major cities.

The Japanese had established a seaplane and naval base as well as a radio and weather station on Ulithi. When the Americans got close, the Japanese evacuated to Yap Proper taking most of the able-bodied Ulithians along with them.

In September 1944 the Americans landed on Ulithi unopposed. They quickly constructed an airstrip on Falalop Island, a hospital, and a recreation centre on Mogmog Island that eventually entertained as many as 20,000 soldiers a day.

Strategically located, Ulithi served as a major anchorage and supply and repair base for the final six months of the war. Its extensive lagoon held 617 Allied naval vessels prior to the Okinawa invasion.

Somehow folks on Ulithi survived these encounters with uninvited visitors from the 'civilised' world. These days if you want to visit the atoll you have to seek permission.

Ulithi is the most developed of the outer islands. It has the only outer islands high school, public electricity and even a new laundromat built with Australian aid. Concrete houses are more common than thatched houses. Partly because the US military left so much corrugated metal, there are more tin roofs on Ulithi than any of the other islands.

Ulithi's inhabited islands – Falalop, Mogmog, Asor and Fassarai – have a total population of 850. All have nice sandy beaches. The only airstrip is on Falalop and the terminal building has Yap's only outer island post office.

Flights between Yap and Guam often fly over Ulithi. It's quite an impressive sight from the air, with islands spread so far apart that they scarcely seem related.

Woleai Atoll

Of the outer atolls, Woleai ranks a close second to Ulithi both in land size and population. About 800 people live on five of Woleai's 22 islets and the atoll has a junior high school. Several of the islands are clustered close together, some separated only by narrow mangrove channels and others joined at low tide by sand bars.

The Japanese fortified much of Woleai and wrecked ships and planes, old tanks, bunkers, field guns and monuments are all around the islands. Even the airfield used by PMA is a former Japanese fighter airstrip. Woleai has beautiful sandy beaches and canoes are favoured over motorboats.

Fais Island

Fais is a single island of raised limestone with just over one sq mile of land. It has a partial fringing reef, sandy beaches, cliffs and sea caves. With an elevation of 60 feet, Fais is the highest of Yap's outer islands and was once known for its agricultural production.

Both the Germans and the Japanese had phosphate mines on Fais. You can find the remains of a Japanese dock hit by American bombers during WW II, parts of a steel observation tower and the base of a shore defence gun. Fais has one village, a population of 250 and a new 3000-foot crushed coral airstrip. The women are known for their skilled weaving of lava-lavas, many of which are created during their stays in the village menstrual house.

Satawal Island

Satawal is home to some of the world's most skilled traditional navigators who still sail vast expanses of ocean in outrigger canoes without charts or compass, relying on their knowledge of star positions, ocean swells and other natural phenomena. It was Satawal master star-path navigator Mau Piailug who was chosen to navigate the double-hulled sailing canoe *Hokulea* on its historic journey between Hawaii and Tahiti in 1976. Using traditional navigational skills preserved in Satawal but long forgotten elsewhere in the Pacific, the trip retraced the ancient routes of the early Polynesian seafarers who settled Hawaii.

Satawal is a single raised island of half a square mile of land. It has a fringing reef and sandy beaches. The population is 465. After Typhoon Owen hit in November 1990, only nine of the island's 90 houses were left standing.

Lamotrek Atoll

Lamotrek has seven small islets totalling 0.38 sq miles, 285 people, a good beach and an abundance of land crabs and fruit. The Japanese occupied the island and the remains of WW II planes can still be found.

The 27-minute documentary *Lamotrek:*

Heritage of an Island by Eric Metzgar focuses on the traditional skills of the Lamotrek islanders, including dancing, chants and crafts. The film is available on video cassette for $30 plus postage from Canyon Cinema (☎ 415-626-2255), 2325 Third St, Suite 338, San Francisco, CA 94107.

Ifalik Atoll

This atoll has long white sandy beaches, lots of coconut palms and a lagoon in a near-perfect circle. The two inhabited islands were one island until a typhoon hit and broke a narrow channel through the middle. With a land area of just over half a sq mile, Ifalik is home to 485 people. The atoll is very traditional. There's a taboo area in the main village where no one may enter and the chief reportedly won't allow motorboats into the lagoon.

Faraulep Atoll

Faraulep Atoll has a small lagoon and five islets totalling just 0.16 sq miles, with most of the 195 residents living on Faraulep and Pig. A large sand spit has built up on the south side of Faraulep islet and the field trip ship cannot enter the lagoon.

Eauripik Atoll

This has 140 people living on a mere 0.09 sq miles of land, giving it the highest population density of any of Yap's outer islands. Every speck of the island is used either for homesites or food crops. Copra is not made as all coconuts are eaten. Houses are built on raised stone platforms and the church is one of only two on the outer islands still of traditional-style construction.

Elato Atoll

Elato has seven islets, comprising 0.2 sq miles of land, in a lovely lagoon setting with a curved sandy beach. From its shores you can see Lamotrek, 13 miles to the east. There is a relatively large area set aside for copra production, though food is sometimes scarce. Elato has about 70 people.

Sorol & Ngulu Atolls

These have small land areas and only about 25 people each. Ngulu has a very large lagoon of 148 sq miles, with nesting areas for sea turtles and excellent commercial fishing.

Gaferut, West Fayu, Pikelot & Olimarao

These atolls have no permanent inhabitants and are nesting grounds for turtles and birds.

Permission

There's concern that Yap's more isolated outer islands may be very vulnerable, should the 20th century suddenly appear upon their shores clad in a bikini and grasping a video camera. It's largely because of this that visitors are screened.

In a recent government survey, outer islanders were adamant that visitors come only with prior permission and 99% thought visitors should be accompanied by a Yapese guide. The saving grace of all this is that 96% said they would like to share their knowledge of Yap's traditional culture and their present lifestyle with outsiders.

In response to this, the Governor's Office and the Council of Tamol (composed of chiefs from the outer islands) have established a formal set of guidelines for visiting the outer islands. The guidelines aren't meant to discourage 'appropriate' visitors, but rather to make the process smoother for everyone and assure that traditional ways are respected.

You should make a request to the Special Assistant for Outer Islands Affairs (☎ 350-2108), Office of the Governor, Colonia, Yap, FSM 96943, at least a month before the date you're hoping to visit. The office will then take the request to the chief of the island you want to visit. Upon the chief's approval, the office will issue a pass authorising the visit and stating the length of stay. You need this pass to purchase a ticket from either the field trip ship or PMA. Upon landing the pass needs to be presented to the island chief, along with a visitor fee of $20.

Places to Stay

None of the outer islands have established accommodation for visitors. Overnight visitors will probably end up staying at a men's house or with a host family. Where you stay and what it will cost will be the chief's decision, and won't necessarily be cheaper than staying in a hotel on Yap Proper. Gifts of coffee, bread or other food items unobtainable on the islands are welcome. Plan also to bring enough food and supplies for the duration of your stay.

Getting There & Away

Air Pacific Missionary Aviation (☎ 350-2360), Box 460, Colonia, Yap, FSM 96943 flies a nine-passenger plane to Ulithi, Fais and Woleai.

Flights to Ulithi and Fais are on Mondays, Wednesdays and Fridays, departing Colonia at 8.45 am and returning in the early afternoon. The one-way fare is $50 between Yap and Ulithi, $25 between Ulithi and Fais, and $70 between Yap and Fais. When there are enough passengers, PMA sometimes has two flights a day or adds one on the off-days.

Flights to Woleai are expected to start up in late 1991, with the schedule not yet fixed. One-way fares are expected to be about $140.

Sea The Waab Transportation Company (☎ 350-2301), Box 177, Colonia, Yap, FSM 96943 runs the field trip ship *Micro Spirit* between Yap Proper and all the populated outer islands. The full trip takes a good two weeks. They make about 10 trips a year.

The deck fare costs three cents per mile and the cabin fare is 15 cents per mile. One-way deck fare from Yap is $3.10 to Ulithi and $11 to Woleai. It's $3 for breakfast, $4 for lunch and $4.50 for dinner but the food doesn't have the best reputation.

The field trip ship office is in a metal shed at the north-west corner of the government offices.

You can get a schedule from the company, and they're good about answering inquiries by mail, but as with most Micronesian ships it runs when the captain and crew are ready to go.

Top Left: Beach Morning Glory
Top Right: Barringtonia flower
Bottom Left: Plumeria
Bottom Right: Hibiscus

Top: Fort Soledad sentry post & Umatac Bay - Guam
Bottom: Taga Beach - Tinian

Republic of Palau

Palau features Micronesia's richest flora & fauna, both on land and underwater. The islands are inhabited by exotic birds, crocodiles live in the mangrove swamps and orchids grow freely in people's yards.

Palau's waters contain an incredible spectrum of coral, fish and other marine life, including giant clams that weigh up to 1000 pounds and many rare sea creatures found in few other places.

The scenic Rock Islands have some of Micronesia's finest snorkelling and diving just off their shores. Beyond them lie the sleepy southern islands of Peleliu and Angaur with their own special appeal to independent travellers.

The native name for the islands is Belaù, though the new nation calls itself the Republic of Palau. Of all the political entities to come out of the Trust Territory, Palau is the smallest in terms of population. Koror has the bulk of the nation's 14,000 people and by Micronesian standards it's a busy town.

Palau, however, is the one emerging Micronesian nation that has not yet emerged. Until critical conflicts are resolved concerning Palau's pro-nuclear compact with the US and its anti-nuclear constitution, Palau remains the sole district still under Trust Territory administration.

History

Pre-European Contact It is generally believed that the first inhabitants of Palau came from eastern Indonesia. Carbon dating has established that the Rock Islands were settled around 1000 BC.

Traditionally the women of Palau tended the taro swamps and the men fished the reef and harvested breadfruit and betel nut. With a fairly vast land area offering an abundance of vegetation Palauans were not compelled to journey beyond their shores. They spent their leisure time working on projects such as the construction of *bai*, or men's meeting houses, with each village having its own skilled artisans to do the tasks of woodworking and thatching.

The Palauans developed fairly complex social systems. The culture was matriarchal and matrilineal, with property inherited by women, though owned by the clan. Men needed women's permission to spend money.

The accumulation of land and money has always been very important in Palauan society, with clans ranked according to their wealth. Villages were typically settled by seven to 10 clans and the chief of the highest-ranking clan was the village leader.

Uab

Palauan legend tells of the creation of the islands in this way:

In ancient times an island woman gave birth to a son named Uab who grew so quickly and had such an insatiable appetite that it soon became the primary chore of the islanders to keep the boy fed. The more they fed him, the more food he demanded and the larger he grew, until one day he was taller than the coconut trees and had eaten all the food on the island. The villagers reluctantly decided they must destroy the giant boy in order to survive and one night set fire to the men's meeting house where he slept. Uab's bloated body exploded and parts of it were flung in all directions. Kayangel was created from his head, Babeldaob from his body, Peleliu from his legs, Angaur from his feet and all the little rock islands from his fingers and toes. The people then settled the new islands believing that as they had fed Uab, he would now feed them. ∎

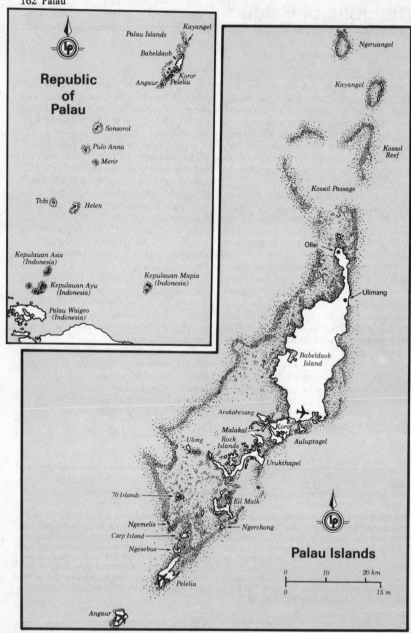

Republic of Palau

Palau Islands
Kayangel
Babeldaob
Angaur Koror Peleliu
Sonsorol
Pulo Anna
Merir
Tobi Helen
Kepulauan Asia (Indonesia)
Kepulauan Ayu (Indonesia)
Kepulauan Mapia (Indonesia)
Palau Waigeo (Indonesia)

Palau Islands

Ngeruangel
Kayangel
Kossol Reef
Kossol Passage
Ollei
Ulimang
Babeldaob Island
Arakabesang
Malakal
Ulong
Rock Islands
Koror
Auluptagel
Urukthapel
70 Islands
Eil Malk
Ngemelis
Ngerchong
Carp Island
Ngesebus
Peleliu
Angaur

| 0 | 10 | 20 km |
| 0 | | 15 m |

Palauan Money Beads, called *udoud*, were the most common type of traditional Palauan money. The beads were made of clay or glass and were usually yellow or orange in colour.

Common round beads were used for daily transactions, while beads which were oval, faceted or cylindrical were more prestigious and valuable. The beads were not made in Palau and although no one today knows exactly where they came from, it is thought they may have originated in Indonesia or Malaysia.

One legend, however, says they came from a mysterious Yapese island called Kablik. Kablik was said to be so magical that stones thrown from the island toward the sea never touched the water, but returned instead to the thrower.

The beads still have value but are in limited use today. Strings of udoud are worn by high-ranking women on special occasions and it's common to see women wearing a single bead on a black cord as an heirloom necklace.

Another kind of money was *toluk*, made by steaming tortoise shell and pressing it into a wooden tray-shaped mould.

Early European Contact The first European to sight Palau was probably the Spaniard Ruy Lopez de Villalobos in 1543. He named the islands Arrecifos, which means 'the reefs'. Spain claimed authority over Palau in 1686 but did nothing to develop the islands.

It wasn't until 1783, when English captain Henry Wilson wrecked his ship the *Antelope* on a reef off Palau's Ulong Island, that any real contact began between Palauans and Westerners. The crew was treated well by Chief Ibedul of Koror who helped them rebuild their ship from the wreckage and then sent his young son, Prince Lebuu (Lee Boo), back with Wilson to England for schooling.

Gifts from the Palauans, which the British called the 'Pelew Curiosities', included a bracelet made from a dugong vertebrate, a dagger made from a stingray stinger and tortoise shell dishes. These are now in the British Museum.

The prince died of smallpox less than six months after arriving in London and the tragedy touched many of the British and piqued their interest in Palau. There was even a romantic melodrama called *Prince Lee Boo* that played on London stages at the time.

The story of Wilson and his crew was immortalised in the popular book *An Account of the Pelew Islands* by George Keate, published in 1788, which further whetted Britain's appetite for trade between the two nations. Unfortunately, favoured trade items included guns and other weapons which served to increase hostilities among local tribes and, at times, against European traders.

The British were Palau's main trading partners until Spain moved in and kicked the British out in 1885. Spanish missionaries managed to introduce Christianity and a written alphabet before Spain sold Palau to Germany following the Spanish-American War.

German Period The Germans were more interested in making money than saving souls. By the time they had taken control in 1899 only about 4000 Palauans had survived the diseases introduced by Western explorers, a drastic drop from the estimated pre-European contact population of 40,000. The Germans took steps to contain contagious diseases by providing innoculations and instituting sanitary controls. They then used forced Palauan labour to start coconut plantations and other business ventures.

Japanese Period The Japanese occupied Palau from 1914 until the end of WW II. It was during this time that Palauan culture went through its most radical transformation, as the Japanese attempted to replace it with their own. Free schools taught the Japanese language, albeit a subservient dialect, and village chiefs lost power to Japanese bureaucrats.

Japan continued and expanded the commercial ventures started by the Germans and developed many more. Thousands of Japanese, Korean and Okinawan labourers were brought in to work in phosphate mines, rice fields, pineapple plantations and other lucrative businesses. Traditional inheritance patterns were shattered as Palauans lost their land, either through sale or confiscation.

From 1922 all of Japan's Pacific possessions were administered from Koror, which the Japanese developed into a bustling modern city complete with paved roads, electricity and piped-in water. Out of 30,000 residents only 20% were Palauan.

In the late 1930s, Japan closed Palau to the outside world and began concentrating on military fortifications.

WWII US air bombings of Malakal Island and Airai State in March and July 1944 destroyed a large number of Japanese ships, planes, fuel tanks and military facilities. However the real fighting in Palau took place in September of that year on the islands of Peleliu and Angaur.

Before the USA's invasion of the two southern islands, most Palauans were rounded up and sent to central Babeldaob. As elsewhere in Micronesia, the reason for the forced relocation is not entirely clear. Some islanders insist that the Japanese had plans to kill the Palauans and even had ditches dug to use as mass graves. Nonetheless, history books tend to credit the Japanese for getting the islanders out of harm's way and undoubtedly the action did save many Palauan lives.

Koror and Babeldaob were never invaded and the 25,000 Japanese soldiers stationed on those islands remained there until the war's end.

Modern Palau In July 1978 Palauans voted against becoming part of the Federated States of Micronesia. In July 1980 they adopted their own constitution and their first president, Haruo Remeliik, took office in January 1981.

Koror was named the provisional capital, although Palau's constitution requires that the capital eventually be moved to Melekeok State in Babeldaob.

The decade since Palau inaugurated its first president has been a troubled one.

President Remeliik was assassinated in June 1985. Though the son of his most powerful political opponent was convicted of the murder, he was later acquitted and the case remains unsolved.

In August 1988 Remeliik's successor, Lazarus Salii, was found shot to death, an apparent suicide. His administration had been marred with accusations of bribery and corruption and the president himself was under investigation at the time for accepting huge payoffs involving a scandal-ridden power plant deal.

Palau's current president, Ngiratkel Etpison, took office in January 1989.

Nuclear Issues & the Constitution In 1979, Palauans wrote into their constitution a provision which declared Palau nuclear-free. This nuclear ban, while hailed by environmentalists throughout the Pacific, was unacceptable to the US government which had long been eyeing Palau as a potential military site. For Pentagon officials, Palau was seen as part of a 'defensive arc', along with Guam and Tinian, to be used in the event that the USA lost its bases in the Philippines.

Disregarding the constitution's anti-nuclear provision, the USA went ahead and drew up a Compact of Free Association which would not only allow it to bring nuclear weapons into Palau, but also gave it the right of eminent domain over virtually all Palauan territory. In exchange, the USA offered Palau millions of dollars in aid.

If the compact had been written to abide by Palau's constitution, it would have required approval by only 50% of Palauan voters. But with the USA insisting on unrestricted military access, the only way the compact could be approved was for Palauan voters to override the anti-nuclear provision in their constitution, which required 75% of the popular vote.

In seven referendums in as many years,

the compact vote has failed to reach the 75% approval margin. The US government has tried everything from election-eve 'voter education programmes' with free beer and barbecues to upping the total compact aid package to $1 billion, but such measures haven't been enough to swing the vote.

In 1986 the USA tried to make the compact more palatable by dropping one of the more offensive provisions that would have given the US military direct access to one-third of Babeldaob for training American GIs in guerrilla warfare.

In June 1987, after an election once again failed to get 75% approval, the USA tried the big stick approach, levelling off Palau's operational funding and thereby forcing the Palauan government to lay off the vast majority of its employees. Hundreds of those affected by the layoffs camped outside the Palauan legislative building to demand another referendum, this time to change the constitution.

An election was hastily called on 4 August to amend the constitution 'for the purpose of avoiding an inconsistency with the compact'. Though voter approval was only 73.33%, the government declared that the 75% voter approval requirement in the constitution had been eliminated. On August 21 a second referendum was held, this one to vote on the compact, which now apparently required only a simple majority. It received 73% of the vote.

The Palauan government immediately declared the compact ratified and submitted it to the US Congress for approval. Traditional Palauan leaders countered by filing a lawsuit to block the action. The August elections, which had been marred by violence, were eventually declared invalid and the 75% rule reinstated.

The next election wasn't held again until February 1990, at which time the compact was rejected by the largest margin ever.

At the end of 1990 the US Interior Department, which administers the Trust Territory, began to reassert its authority by declaring veto power over Palauan legislation, suspending the 1991 budget approved by Palau's Congress and enacting strict restrictions on how US funding could be spent.

On 22 December 1990, at the same time the USA was bringing Palau back under direct rule, the UN Security Council dissolved the trusteeship for the rest of Micronesia, leaving Palau as the world's only remaining UN Trust Territory.

Geography

The tightly clustered Palau archipelago consists of the high islands of Babeldaob, Koror, Peleliu and Angaur; the low coral atoll of Kayangel; and the limestone Rock Islands, of which there are more than 200. The islands run roughly from north to south, covering about 125 miles. Except for Kayangel in the north and Angaur in the south all islands in the Palau group are inside a single barrier reef.

The nation's boundaries also encompass five other small, isolated islands: Sonsorol, Pulo Anna, Merir, Tobi and Helen. They are spread out 370 miles south-west from the main Palau Islands, reaching almost as far as Indonesia.

Babeldaob, the largest island in Micronesia after Guam, is 27 miles long and has a land area of 153 sq miles. All the other Palauan islands together total just 37 sq miles.

Palau, which is part of the western Caroline Islands, is the westernmost part of Micronesia, 470 miles east of the Philippines.

Climate

In Koror, the average daily high is 87°F (30°C) and the average daily low is 75°F (24°C). Humidity averages 80% and the annual rainfall is 147 inches. February and March are the driest months, with about eight inches of rainfall each, and June to August is the wettest period with about 15 inches monthly. June is a month for thunderstorms which have been known to drop as much as an inch of rain in 15 minutes. Although Palau lies outside the main typhoon tracks, it occasionally gets hit.

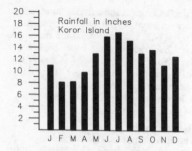

Rainfall in Inches
Koror Island

J F M A M J J A S O N D

Government

A stalemate between Palau and the USA has left Palau the only remaining district of the original Trust Territory of the Pacific Islands.

Palau's national congress, a two-house legislature with 30 members, is called *Olbiil Era Kelulau* which means 'meeting place of whispers'. There's also a Council of Chiefs, comprised of one traditional chief from each state, which advises the national government on legislation affecting Palauan customs.

The USA did a good job of introducing its brand of democracy. Palau has a political framework similar to both the US federal and state governments – except that its population is not 250 million but a mere 14,000. Some of Palau's 16 states have fewer than 200 people, yet each has a governor, a legislature and a state office. It would be hard to find another nation where so few are governed by so many.

Economy

Palau is almost totally dependent upon US aid. The government employs approximately 1700 people, which is about half of the Palauan labour force.

Although the land is quite fertile, Palau imports more food than it produces. The largest cash crop is said to be marijuana.

Palau is located in one of the richest fishing grounds in the western Pacific and collects about $1 million annually in licensing fees from foreign ships that fish within Palauan waters.

PITI, a private fisheries operation in Palau, has its own DC-8 that flies about 30 tons of fresh tuna to Japan every week. PITI is supplied fish from about 60 Taiwanese long-line fishing vessels that operate in Palauan waters and employs about 150 Palauans in its fisheries plant.

Palau is beset by major financial problems, many related to ill-planned government projects. On its massive new power plant alone it has racked up $50 million in unpaid debts.

The power plant, which was built in remote Aimeliik, has been surrounded by controversy from the start. Until 1982 Palau got its power from three diesel generators on loan from the US military. When the military abruptly decided the generators should be pulled out, the Palauan government found itself in need of a new source of power and signed a contract for a 16-megawatt plant with the British company IPSECO.

Palauans were told the huge plant would pay for itself with the power it would generate – a very unrealistic claim. The US Interior Department assured IPSECO's financial backers that funds would be available to pay for the plant through compact money, even though the compact hadn't been approved. Those funds never became available and the loan on the power plant has been declared in default.

The plant, which provides Koror's power, operates at a huge loss, in part because of its enormous over-capacity though it's also poorly designed. The Palauan government, trying to get out from under the debt, has

recently attempted to sell the power plant to private companies, but to no avail.

As in the Marshalls, Palau is being tempted with huge sums of money in exchange for becoming a toxic-waste site. In this case an Australian company wants to build an incinerator in western Babeldaob to burn industrial waste from South-East Asia and Australia. The plant would generate electricity (not that Palau needs more!) and the idea is generating a lot of support among Palauan politicians who are finding it difficult to resist the multi-million dollar annual income that the plant would bring in. Environmental groups are busy in Palau trying to convince the government otherwise and to educate islanders to the potential hazards.

People

In 1988, Palau's population was 14,206. There are also about 1900 foreigners living in Palau, the majority of them Filipino labourers.

The people of Palau are among the most Westernised of all Micronesians and you'll have to look close to find evidence of the indigenous culture.

Palauans place an emphasis on education and a large percentage of high school graduates continue their studies, often at overseas colleges and universities. They hold few qualms about travelling in search of economic opportunities and throughout Micronesia you'll find a scattering of Palauans who have gone further afield.

Customs & Behaviour Though not as widespread as in Yap, many Palauans chew betel nut and subsequently spit a lot. Betel nut chewers often carry their supplies in woven pandanus handbags.

Palauans wear Western clothing and are quite casual in their dress, though short shorts are frowned upon, especially in villages outside Koror. People remove their shoes when entering private homes and even a few public buildings such as the library.

In some parts of Palau there are prohibitions on fishing and camping. The collection of live shells and coral is prohibited most everywhere.

Religion

Most Palauans are Christian, with both the Catholic and Protestant churches well established. Seventh Day Adventists have a noticeable stronghold, while Jehovah's Witnesses and Bahai also have a presence.

Many Palauans still hold some form of traditional beliefs, based on nature spirits, ghosts and village gods. *Modekngei* is the newer name for the traditional religion.

Language

Palauan is the local language, though English is most commonly spoken in business and government, and schools teach in both languages. Most older Palauans still remember Japanese. The south-west islanders speak Sonsorolese, a language that's more closely related to a Chuukese dialect than to Palauan.

In Palauan, 'hello' is *alii* and 'thanks' is *sulang*.

Many Palauan words begin with 'ng' – which is a nasal sound, pronounced like the ending of the word 'bring'. The 'ch' spelling is pronounced 'uh'.

Holidays

Palau celebrates New Year's Day, Youth Day on 15 March, Senior Citizens Day on 5 May, Constitution Day on 9 July, Labor Day on 24 October, Thanksgiving on the last Thursday in November and Christmas Day.

Youth Day features concerts and sporting events, while Senior Citizens Day features a parade with floats, handicraft exhibits and a dance competition. The Belau Arts Festival, which is held on Constitution Day, includes craft exhibits, dances and cooking contests.

Koror

Koror is both the economic centre and capital of Palau and has two-thirds of the republic's population. Many of the 9500

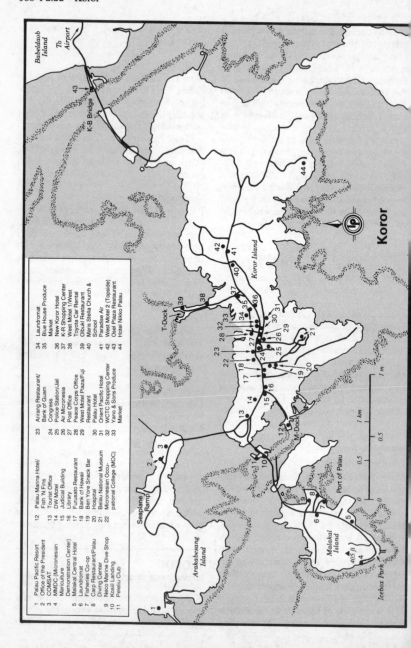

Koror

1 Palau Pacific Resort
2 Office of the President
3 COMSAT
   MMDC (Micronesian
   Mariculture
   Demonstration Center)
5 Malakal Central Hotel
6 Laundromat
7 Fisheries Co-op
8 Carp Restaurant/Palau
   Diving Center
9 Neco Marine Dive Shop
10 Kossil Landing
11 Peleliu Club

12 Palau Marina Hotel/
   Fish N Fins
13 Tourist Office
14 MW Motel
15 Judicial Building
16 Library
17 Funusato Restaurant
18 Bank of Hawaii
19 Ben Yore Snack Bar
20 Hospital
21 Belau National Museum
22 Micronesian Occu-
   pational College (MOC)

23 Arirang Restaurant/
   Bank of Guam
24 Congress
25 Police Station/Jail
26 Air Micronesia
27 Post Office
28 Peace Corps Office
29 West Motel Plaza/Fuji
   Restaurant
30 Palau Hotel
31 Orient Pacific Hotel
32 WCTC Shopping Center
33 Yano & Sons Produce
   Market

34 Laundromat
35 Blue House Produce
   Market
36 New Koror Hotel
37 K-R Shopping Center
38 West Motel 1/West
   Office
39 Toyota Car Rental
40 Olbuil Restaurant
41 Maris Stella Church &
   School
42 Paradise Air
43 West Motel 2 (Topside)
44 Osei Plaza Restaurant
44 Hotel Nikko Palau

Babeldaob Island
To Airport
K-B Bridge
Koror Island
T-Dock
Seaplane Ramp
Arakabesang Island
Port of Palau
Malakal Island
405 ft
Icebox Park
M-Dock

0   0.5   1 km
0   0.5   1 m

people who live in Koror have been drawn from their home villages by employment opportunities.

In prewar days Koror, with three times the current population, was jammed not only with homes, restaurants, office buildings and military facilities, but also with geisha houses, Shinto shrines, kimono tailors and public baths.

It's a more nondescript and less crowded Koror one sees today, with a pace more typically Micronesian and no particular penchant for hustle and bustle. The greater Koror area is good for maybe a day of exploration, but after that it's best used as a base for trips to the Rock Islands, Peleliu, Angaur and other islands.

Orientation

Koror is connected to neighbouring islands by an impressive array of bridges and causeways, including the K-B Bridge between Koror and Babeldaob. The airport in Airai State on Babeldaob is a 15-minute drive from central Koror. The east side of Koror, between the town centre and the K-B Bridge, is called Topside.

Information

The Palau Visitors Authority (☎ 488-2793) has a tourist office at the west side of town which is open from 8 am to 4.30 pm Monday to Friday and a booth at the airport that's open during flight times.

The *Palau Tribune*, which is a version of the *Guam Tribune* with Palauan news up front, comes out on Fridays. This and Guam's *Pacific Daily News* are sold at the WCTC Shopping Center and other large stores.

Koror has a couple of TV stations, including Cable News Network (CNN) which broadcasts 24 hours a day. The government radio station broadcasts Voice of America and other overseas newscasts several times a day.

The Air Mike office (☎ 488-2448), which is behind the post office, is open from 8 am to 4 pm Monday to Saturday and from 12.30 to 4.30 pm on Sundays.

Ben Franklin in the WCTC Shopping Center sells both print and slide film.

Koror's water is shut off between 9 pm and 6 am daily.

Visas As elsewhere in Micronesia, immigration officials at the airport usually ask you how many days you intend to stay and write that number in your passport. It's a good idea to ask for the maximum of 30 days, or at least give yourself a buffer, as visa extensions cost $50!

Money The Bank of Hawaii and the Bank of Guam, both on the main road in central Koror, are open from 9.30 am to 2.30 pm Monday to Thursday, to 5 pm on Fridays. Credit cards are accepted at many hotels, car rental agencies, dive shops and larger restaurants.

Post & Telecommunications Palau's only post office is in central Koror. It's open from 8 am to 4 pm, Monday to Friday. Palau issues attractive postage stamps of tropical fish, flowers and shells as well as commemorative stamps of historic events.

International phone calls can be made from the COMSAT station on Arakabesang Island and from most hotels.

Medical Services Dr Yano's clinic, Belau Medical Clinic, next to Yano & Son's produce market, is recommended if you need medical attention. Koror's ageing MacDonald Hospital is sometimes referred to locally as 'the morgue', though a new hospital is being built on Arakabesang Island, just over the causeway from Koror. The hospital has a decompression chamber for divers who get the bends.

Snorkelling

The beach fronting the Palau Pacific Resort has some of Koror's best snorkelling. The water is calm, shallow and clear. You can find colourful tropical fish, platter and mushroom corals, and tridacna clams with fleshy mantles in beautiful mottled designs of browns, greens and iridescent blues. Breakfast in the open-air restaurant, followed by a morning of snorkelling from the beach, isn't a bad way to kick off the day.

Snorkelling is also good off Icebox Park and the MMDC grounds on Malakal Island. There's no beach, but rather concrete retaining walls with steps leading into the clear water. The waters are deeper and the fish are larger than at the resort and several groups of clownfish hide in anemone shelters. From Icebox Park, the best snorkelling is to the right toward MMDC where giant clams are lined up in underwater cages just offshore. Watch out for the spiny urchins that cling to the sides of the wall.

If you're stuck in town, snorkelling is OK in the shallow water between the long breakwater and the Malakal bridge, half a mile from the tourist office. There are tiny tropical fish and some low thickets of coral.

On the other hand no one really comes to Palau to snorkel in Koror. The real action is in and around the Rock Islands – and it's worth whatever it takes to get yourself out there!

Belau National Museum
A good starting place for understanding Palauan history and culture is the Belau National Museum. The sights begin at the door, which is intricately carved like a storyboard. The museum has bead and tortoise shell money, a model village and displays of artefacts and crafts. As you climb the stairs you'll be greeted by the head of a 15-foot crocodile, the largest found in Palau since WW II.

To get to the museum, turn off the main street by the baseball field, veer to the left past the hospital and continue on the main road to its end. The museum is open from 8 to 11 am and 1 to 4 pm Monday to Friday, and from 10 am to 3 pm on Saturdays. Admission is $2.

A new bai on the museum grounds is a replacement for a more traditional bai which burned down in 1979. The museum building was once a Japanese weather station and there are still a few anti-aircraft guns and other Japanese-era artefacts on the grounds.

Next to the museum is a research library, with a good collection of books on Palau and Micronesia, which museum officials will open upon request.

Hotel Nikko Palau
For a superb view of the Rock Islands head in the direction of the airport and when you get out of central Koror take the paved road to the right that winds down to the Hotel Nikko. The view from the hotel is worth catching at any time of day, but it's particularly nice at sunrise.

Other attractions include the remains of a pre-war Japanese Shinto shrine near the beginning of the hotel driveway and some live crocodiles caged in front of the hotel office. Follow the stairs up past the swimming pool to the top of the hill to see two anti-aircraft guns and get a sweeping view of the Rock Islands.

Malakal Island
Malakal Island, across a causeway from

Magic Breadfruit Tree
A popular Palauan legend tells of a woman who owned a magic breadfruit tree with a hollow trunk and roots that went deep into the sea. Whenever the people of the island were hungry, they would call on the woman and a wave would come up through the trunk, bringing with it fish for everyone to eat. Over time some of the islanders became jealous of the woman and cut down the tree. Water then rushed in through the hollow trunk and flooded the island which sank into the depths of the ocean. It is said the outline of the island can still be seen off the coast of Ngiwal on Babeldaob Island.

This legend is painted onto the front of the Bureau of Community Services in Koror. It's the building with a traditional high-pitched roof, at the end of the drive past the police station. ■

Koror, has the Fisheries Co-op, the deep-water commercial port, small boat docks and other marine businesses.

Icebox Park, at the southern tip of the island, was the site of an ice-making plant during the Japanese era. It's now a grassy public park and although there's no beach there's access to the clear waters for swimming and snorkelling.

MMDC The Micronesian Mariculture Demonstration Center (MMDC), at the end of the road on Malakal Island, is a research marine laboratory where work is carried out on conservation and commercial projects. Their main projects are with the threatened giant tridacna clam.

These giant clams regularly grow more than four feet in length and can weigh half a ton. Despite their notoriety at the hands of science fiction writers, the probability of a giant clam trying to swallow your leg while you're out diving is nil. On the other hand it's probably not a good idea to stick your toes or fingers in to find out!

Palauans eat the meat of the clams, sell the huge shells to tourists and grind up the smaller shells for lime powder to chew with betel nut. But it is not these practices which are threatening the clams.

Rather it is outside poachers, mainly from Taiwan, who are wiping out the tridacna on coral reefs around the Pacific, overharvesting to a point where few are left for breeding. The poachers take only the profitable adductor muscle of the clam which is considered to be a delicacy and aphrodisiac in the Orient. The rest of the clam is left to rot.

The MMDC is raising hundreds of thousands of seed clams to be planted in reefs around Palau and other islands in Micronesia, especially in places which can be guarded against illegal harvesting. The hope is that someday Micronesian nations will not only have the clams as a food source, but will themselves be able to profit from the adductor muscle trade without destroying the species.

You can wander around the MMDC complex from 8 to 11 am and from 1 to 4 pm on weekdays and peer into the tanks of fish, giant clams and hawksbill turtles. Scientists or students interested in doing research there may write for information to MMDC, Box 359, Koror, Palau 96940.

Malakal Hill You can get an excellent view of the nearby Rock Islands by going halfway up Malakal Hill, where the road ends at a water tank. After leaving Icebox Park, take the dirt road to the left just past the green sewage plant. The road is steep and narrow, with sharp drops on both sides, but should be passable in a sedan. It also only takes about 10 minutes to walk up.

It's possible to continue hiking to the top of the 405-foot hill for even better views. It takes about 15 minutes of hard climbing from the water tank, though there really isn't much of a path and you may need a guide to show you the way.

Arakabesang Island
Once a Japanese military base, Arakabesang Island is now a 'suburb' of Koror. On the south side of the island there's a village settled by people from Palau's South-west Islands, complete with traditional outrigger canoes.

After crossing over the causeway from Koror, the first road to the right past the COMSAT station leads to the Office of the President and other national government offices.

If you're interested in WW II sites, make note of the concrete pillars flanking the entrance to this road because the next road to the right with similar pillars is the turn-off to one of the Japanese-era seaplane ramps. There's another seaplane ramp on the beach at the Palau Pacific Resort, a luxury hotel complex at the west side of the island.

Places to Stay
Koror hotels can get booked out during the Japanese New Year holidays which run from about Christmas to mid-January and during their Obon holidays from late July through August. Room rates are the same for singles and doubles unless otherwise noted. Credit

cards are accepted at most hotels, including D W Motel, Palau Marina Hotel and the West Motels. Koror has a 10% room tax.

Places to Stay – bottom end The *D W Motel* (☎ 488-2641), Box 738, Koror, Palau 96940, is a family-run operation popular with independent travellers. Owner Dave Williams is a former language instructor for the Peace Corps. The 17 rooms are rather large and have refrigerators, air-con and private bathrooms. The 2nd floor rooms have comfortable foam mattresses, but avoid the room across from the lounge which has sheer curtains that offer no privacy and let the hall lights shine through all night long. There's free coffee and tea in the lounge and free transport to and from the airport. Dave's son, Wilfred, meets nearly every flight. Singles/doubles cost $25/30.

The *Orient Pacific Hotel* is behind the Palau Hotel, on the road that parallels the main street. This small hotel has eight quite sufficient rooms with air-con and private bathrooms, and is a good deal at $25 a double.

The four-storey *Palau Hotel* (☎ 488-1703), Box 64, Koror, Palau 96940, central Koror's largest hotel, has 38 rooms with air-con, refrigerators, bathtubs and telephones. It's a rather standard-looking hotel, comfortable enough but with no special character. Singles/doubles cost $35/40.

The West Motel (☎ 488-1780), Box 280, Koror, Palau 96940, has three separate locations. *West Motel I*, a nine-room motel at T-Dock, is a little out of the way, but it's nice enough and is the cheapest of the three. The rooms are spacious, have TV and refrigerators, and cost $40 with a kitchenette, $35 without.

West Motel II, an 11-unit building in Topside, is on the outskirts of town in the midst of a residential area and has the overall feel of being in a housing complex. All units have kitchens. Rates start at $40 and go up to $65 for two-bedroom units.

West Motel Plaza is a new, modern, 22-room hotel in the centre of town. The management is friendly and the rooms,

which are large and nicely furnished, have TVs, in-house videos, refrigerators and phones. Rates are $65 with a kitchenette, $55 without.

The *New Koror Hotel* (☎ 488-1582), Box 339, Koror, Palau 96940, has cheerless rooms for $33 and is best considered as a last resort.

Places to Stay – top end The new three-storey *Palau Marina Hotel* (☎ 488-1786), Box 142, Koror, Palau 96940, on the water at M-Dock has 27 rooms with rattan furnishings, balconies, TVs, refrigerators and phones. It's managed by Fish 'N Fins owner Francis Toribiong and geared for divers, who can practically step out of their rooms and into the dive boat. Rooms cost $75.

The *Hotel Nikko Palau* (☎ 488-2486), Box 310, Koror, Palau 96940, which is owned by Japan Air Lines, was Palau's premier hotel until the Palau Pacific Resort opened, drawing most of the high-spending tourists away. Though no longer as spiffy as it could be, the hotel has a gorgeous hillside setting overlooking Palau's northernmost Rock Islands. Most of the 51 rooms cost $95, but if you're spending this much it's well worth the extra $10 to stay in A-block which has fantastic views from the verandas. The hotel has a swimming pool, bar and restaurant.

The *Malakal Central Hotel* (☎ 488-1075), Box 6016, Koror, Palau 96940, down by the dock on Malakal Island, is a large modern hotel. The completed hotel annex, above a bar and restaurant, has nice rooms with wooden floors, ocean-view balconies, TVs with VCRs and other modern amenities. Rates are $140 during Japanese vacation times and $100 during the rest of the year, plus 5% service charge.

If you're rolling in money, there's the 64-acre *Palau Pacific Resort* (☎ 488-2600), Box 308, Koror, Palau 96940, which may well be Micronesia's best resort hotel. Its protected white sand beach is certainly Koror's finest. The 100 rooms have rattan furniture, block prints and private lanais. Rates are from $160 to $230. There's a beachside swimming pool, tennis courts and a dive shop. Local events such as islander dance competitions and the presidential inaugural ball also take place at the Palau Pacific.

Places to Eat

Seafood, especially fish, crabs and shellfish, is an important part of the Palauan diet. Crocodile, giant clam, pigeon and fruit bat are some of the more unusual local delicacies, though these are unlikely to appear on restaurant menus. Most places in Koror serve both Japanese and Western dishes.

Places to Eat – bottom end & middle

The *Ben Yore Snack Bar*, opposite the baseball field, has inexpensive breakfasts, hamburgers, fried noodles and ice cream.

Blue House, a small market on Lebuu St, sells produce and other local food. Papayas and pineapple are 50 cents a pound, boiled eggs cost 25 cents and fried bananas are a dime. A whole smoked fish costs $2.50 a pound.

Yano & Sons, diagonally opposite the Palau Hotel, also sells produce and freshly cooked Palauan-style food by the piece. You could easily put together a meal from the fried fish, sweet tapioca, coconut candy and bananas which are sold out of bulk containers.

The *WCTC Shopping Center* has a big modern supermarket with surprisingly reasonable grocery prices.

The *Carp Restaurant*, out on Malakal Island, has good Japanese food, such as tofu vegetable stew or fried fish for $4. Tempuras range from $5 for vegetable to $15 for shrimp. Meals are served with fresh fruit, which is a welcome treat.

The *Furusato Restaurant*, which is an easy walk from the D W Motel, is a popular local eatery. Beef, pork and fish dishes average $5 to $6. Teriyaki chicken or oyako domburi are $4.50. Furusato opens for breakfast from 6 am daily and stays open later than most Koror restaurants, closing at 10 pm.

The *Olbukl Restaurant* on T-Dock has reasonably good and relatively inexpensive food, but you have to sit through the B-grade video movies that run nonstop. Fried fish or chicken dinners cost $5.

Southern Cross, at the Palau Marina Hotel, has a fine view right on the water at M-Dock and the food is quite good as well. Lunch is the best deal, with fish & chips a good choice for $5, and sandwiches with fries from $4. Dinner ranges from $7 to $20 for fish, steak and Japanese dishes. They also have breakfast at moderate prices.

Some of Koror's best food can be found at *Osel Plaza*, which has a nice atmosphere with an outside patio by the water and a fine sunset view. Meals cost from $5 to $13 with most dishes, including vegetable tempura, around $7. It's open from 6 to 10 pm daily for dinner only, but it occasionally closes down for private parties. From Koror centre, take an immediate left at the end of the K-B Bridge just before reaching Babeldaob.

The *Fuji Restaurant*, in the same complex at West Motel Plaza, is a sister restaurant of Osel Plaza and has a good reputation. The sweet and sour fish can be recommended at $6, though the tempura at $10 is ordinary. Meals end with a piece of fresh fruit. It's open daily except Sundays for dinners only.

Places to Eat – top end

The *Arirang Restaurant* is a Korean barbecue where you cook the food at your table, but it's rather expensive, with dishes around $13.

The open-air restaurant at *Palau Pacific Resort* has average food at higher-than-average prices. Dinners range from $12.50 for reef fish to $20.50 for filet mignon. At breakfast there's a buffet for $12 or you can order from the menu. Lunch specials are about $10.

The *Hotel Nikko Restaurant* has a water view and is open from 7 am to 9.30 pm daily. Continental breakfast is $4.50 and sandwiches are $6 at lunch. Full-course dinners start at $17, though you can get a simple fish or chicken plate for $9.

Drinking Water

In Koror, be wary of drinking tap water as water and sewage lines lay side by side and when the water's turned off for rationing, cross-seepage can occur. Ice and water are OK in most restaurants.

Entertainment

Many restaurants have bars and serve drinks; the one at the Palau Marina Hotel has a nice atmosphere and a water view. The drinking age is 21 and all bars close at midnight.

Kosiil Landing, along the causeway to Malakal Island, is Koror's hottest dance spot. It's open nightly except Mondays and usually has a band that plays both rock and local cha-cha music. The nearby Peleliu Club has a live band nightly except Wednesdays. Other places with live bands include Olbukl on T-Dock and the lounge in the basement of the Palau Hotel.

There are no movie theatres on Koror, though there are plenty of video shops.

Traditional dance shows can be arranged through the tourist office for about $100 a performance. Dancers in brightly dyed 'grass' skirts usually perform in a line, with Palauan dances typified by rhythmic movements and chanting in unison. The Belau National Museum sponsors one of Palau's best dance troupes and you can sometimes catch them practising on the museum grounds.

Things to Buy

Palau's most unique art form is the storyboard, which is a smaller version of the carvings of legends and historic scenes that have traditionally decorated the beams and gables of men's meeting houses. A revival of this type of carving was initiated in 1935 by Japanese anthropologist Hisakatsu Hijikata who suggested making the smaller boards as a way to keep the art form and legends from dying out. Many of the scenes depicted on the storyboards are quite erotic.

A good way to see what top-quality storyboards look like is to check out the collection on display in the Belau National Museum. Though not the same calibre as those in the exhibits, the gift shop at the museum sells nicely carved storyboards, plus T-shirts, woven baskets and purses, commemorative stamps and a few books on Palau.

Some of the best storyboards are made by the inmates of the local jail, next to the police station. You can go and watch them work from 1 to 3 pm daily and then bargain for a storyboard.

Both the Hotel Nikko and Palau Pacific Resort have overpriced gift shops. It's been said that storyboards that fail to sell for $60 at the museum get shipped up to the resort with a $120 price tag slapped on them.

The Senior Citizen Center is a good place to find handicrafts. The women sit outside during the day and weave hats, baskets, purses and cigarette cases out of pandanus and coconut palm. The centre, which is painted to resemble a traditional bai, is next to D W Motel.

Ben Franklin, in the WCTC Shopping Center, sells storyboards for about $65 to $600, a wide selection of handicrafts of varied quality, T-shirts with Palauan designs,

Palauan storyboard carved with legends

sea shells and cassette tapes of Palauan music.

The Palau Islands by Mandy Thyssen, a comprehensive 167-page book about the history and culture of Palau, has good colour photography and would make a fine souvenir. It can be found in many shops around Koror, though the price ranges from $20 to $30. As Neco Tours publishes the book, one good place to pick it up would be the Neco Marine Dive Shop. The book can also be ordered by mail (USA addresses only) by sending $20, which includes airmail postage, to Neco Marine, Box 129, Koror, Palau 96940.

Keep in mind that sea turtles are endangered and the turtle shell jewellery which is sold in Palau cannot be brought in to Guam or most Western countries.

Getting There & Away

Air Air Mike, the only airline servicing Koror, has daily flights from Guam. The regular Guam-Koror fare is $320, though discounted flights on Sunday, Monday and Thursday evenings cost $166.

Air Mike flies from Yap to Koror on Sundays, Wednesdays and Fridays. The regular fare is $141, though the Wednesday flight is $80.

Air Mike also flies from Manila to Koror on Tuesdays, Thursdays and Saturdays for $173.

Round-trip Air Mike tickets to Koror are double these one-way fares.

Paradise Air (☎ 488-2348) Box 488, Koror, Palau 96940, flies a six-seater Cessna from Koror to Peleliu and Angaur, passing over the Rock Islands en route. Day trips are possible, as there are two return flights a day, leaving Koror at 9 am and 3.30 pm and coming back from the islands about an hour later. Sometimes extra flights are added if there's a demand. Wednesdays are usually reserved for charter flights and there's only a morning flight on Saturdays. Paradise Air provides free transportation between the airport and its office in Koror.

Airport Koror's warehouse-like airport terminal has car rental booths, a Palau Visitors Authority booth, a couple of gift shops, a snack bar, restrooms and a phone. The departure tax for non-Palauans is $10.

Boat Because Koror is the nation's commercial centre, Palauans commonly commute between Koror and their home villages by private speedboat. You might be able to hitch a ride with someone by offering to help pay for petrol. Abby's Marine Shop near the Fisheries Co-op is where most of the speedboats fill up, so check there first. T-Dock and M-Dock are other possibilities.

Getting Around

Koror is a sprawling town and it's not very convenient trying to get around solely on foot.

Taxi Taxis are plentiful and can be flagged down. Koror taxis are private, not the shared group kind, and though they have no meters, the going minimum rate of $2 covers most places around town. Expect to pay about $10 from the airport to town, but ask around first and beware of overcharging.

Car West Toyota Car Rental (☎ 488-1780), Box 280, Koror, Palau 96940 and King's U-Drive (☎ 488-2964), Box 424, Koror, Palau 96940, have booths at the airport and offices in central Koror. They'll also deliver cars to your hotel. West has some cars without air-con for about $20 and newer cars with air-con from $32.50. King's has cars with air-con from $32.50. D W Motel has a few tired older cars without air-con for $20 and a couple of new ones with air-con for $35.

Around town, watch out for dips and bumps and sharp V-shaped rain gutters that can tear up car bottoms. The maximum speed limit is 25 miles per hour and passing is not allowed.

Hitching Hitching is not common, but if you start walking over the causeways to either Arakabesang or Malakal islands chances are good that someone will stop and offer you a ride. Likewise, it shouldn't be too difficult to get a ride back to Koror from the MMDC or Palau Pacific Resort.

The Rock Islands

The Rock Islands are Palau's crowning glory.

More than 200 of these rounded knobs of limestone, which are totally covered with green jungle growth, dot the waters for a 20-mile stretch south of Koror. The bases of the islands are narrower than the tops, having been undercut by water erosion and by grazing fish and tiny chitons that scrape at the rock. The islands are often likened to emerald mushrooms popping up above vivid turquoise blue seas.

From the air they are an absolute knock-out! Even if you don't want to go anywhere, flights from Koror to Angaur or Peleliu are worth the airfare for the scenic overview of the Rock Islands alone.

But that's only half of it, for the waters that surround the Rock Islands contain some of the most abundant and varied marine life to be found anywhere.

The islands are also home to crocodiles and fruit bats and are rich with bird life, including kingfishers, reef herons, black noddies, white-tailed tropicbirds, black-napped terns and introduced cockatoos and parrots.

Most of the islands have been undercut all the way round and have no place for boat landings, but others have beaches where soft white sands have washed up and stayed. Ancient rock paintings can be found on Ulong Island and half-quarried Yapese stone money can be seen in a limestone cave near Airai Channel. Other islands have caves with dripping stalactites, rock arches and underground channels.

The Rock Islands are a superb place to lose the rest of the world for a while, hanging out on a speck of paradise and snorkelling the clear waters at whim.

Diving & Snorkelling
Palau is one of the world's truly spectacular dive spots. If coral reefs in crystal clear waters, blue holes, WW II wrecks and hidden caves and tunnels aren't enough, consider the more than 60 vertical drop-offs.

Palau is the meeting place of three major ocean currents that merge with their abundant food supplies to support an enormous variety of marine life. The waters surrounding the Rock Islands are literally teeming with over 1500 varieties of reef and pelagic fish. There are four times the number of coral species in Palau than there are in the Caribbean, including immense tabletop corals, interlocking thickets of staghorn coral and soft corals of all types and colours.

Divers can see manta rays, sea turtles, moray eels, giant tridacna clams, grey reef sharks and sometimes even a sea snake or a rare dugong. The sea temperature averages about 82°F (27°C).

The **Ngemelis Wall**, also called the 'Big Drop-off', is widely considered the world's best wall dive. Starting in water just knee-deep, the wall drops vertically nearly 1000 feet. Divers can free float past a brilliant rainbow of sponges and soft corals whose intense blues, reds or pure whites form a backdrop for quivering nine-foot orange and yellow sea fans and giant black coral trees.

Blue Corner, one of Palau's most popular dives, is known for its sheer abundance of underwater life. You can expect to be totally bedazzled by the incredible variety of fish, including barracudas and sharks, as well as hard and soft corals. Strong tidal currents nourish this chain of life, but also render it a dive for the more experienced.

Both the **German Channel** and **Turtle Cove**, at the edge of the Rock Islands north of Peleliu, offer dives that novices can feel comfortable with. Snorkelling is also good from the beach at Turtle Cove.

Jellyfish Lake, popularised by the National Geographic television special *Medusa*, is a different kind of experience. You'll need to hike up over a hill a little way through the jungle to reach this mangrove-bordered lake. Mark your entry point into the lake to avoid having a problem finding your way back out and be careful of slippery rocks around the shoreline where the water is murky and green. Further out, the water clears up and millions of harmless transparent jellyfish swim en masse following the sun. Snorkelling in this pulsating mass is an unearthly, somewhat eerie sensation.

Crocodiles are generally nocturnal creatures, but should you hear a low 'harrumph' you just might want to head quickly in the opposite direction – unless you plan to test the theory that the crocodiles in Jellyfish Lake are more afraid of people than vice versa.

Dive Shops Generally the dive boats leave Koror around 9 am and come back around 4 pm, breaking for a picnic lunch on a Rock Island between the morning and afternoon dives. All the dive shops listed also offer night diving.

Fish 'N Fins (☎ 488-2637) Box 142, Koror, Palau 96940, owned by respected divemaster Francis Toribiong, is on M-Dock in Koror. A day's worth of diving around the Rock Islands, including lunch, costs $85 if you have your own equipment, $95 if you just show up in a swimsuit. Snorkellers pay $45 to go out with divers. Francis can certify divers in NAUI in three days for $450, which includes full-day dive tours in various locales around Palau.

The Neco Marine Dive Shop (☎ 488-1755), Box 129, Koror, Palau 96940, is a large dive operation at a marina on Malakal Island. It costs $55 for a single tank dive, $85 for two. Trips to Jellyfish Lake can sometimes be arranged between dives. They provide free transportation to and from Koror hotels.

The Palau Diving Center (☎ 488-2978), Box 5, Koror, Palau 96940, is a Japanese operation next door to the Carp Restaurant on Malakal Island. Single tank dives cost $65 and double tank dives cost $85. The company owns Carp Island Resort, which is a base for many of their divers. The boat leaves each day from Koror, however, with free transportation provided to and from Koror hotels.

Sam Scott of Sam's Tour Service (☎ 488-1471), Box 428, Koror, Palau 96940, offers small, personalised tours. Sam charges $75 for a two tank dive, or $50 for a snorkelling trip. He can also arrange Babeldaob excursions and overnight camping trips, with prices varying according to the destination.

Live-Aboard Dive Boat The *Sun Tamarin*, a six-passenger, 60-foot yacht with three aircon double cabins, offers live-aboard dive vacations. The boat leaves Koror each Tuesday. The cost for seven nights, including all meals and unlimited day and night diving, is $1695. Bookings can be made through Tropical Adventures (☎ 800-247-3483) 111 Second Avenue North, Seattle, WA 98109, or See & Sea Travel Service (☎ 800-348-9778) 50 Francisco St, Suite 205, San Francisco, CA 94133.

Day Trips For day outings, the dive boats can drop you off on a Rock Island beach in the morning and pick you up in the afternoon after their last dive, usually for the same price as a snorkelling tour.

Palau Diving Center and Neco Marine Dive Shop usually take you to their own islands, Carp Island and Neco Island respectively. If you just want to laze around for the day, Carp Island is a good choice and as it's quite far south you get a long scenic ride through the Rock Islands coming and going. If you want to snorkel as well, Neco is the better bet, though you'll see only about half as many Rock Islands on the boat ride down.

Carp Island Ngercheu Island, more commonly called Carp Island, is primarily a divers' base camp for the Palau Diving Center.

A motorboat leaves Koror around 8 am, zips through the Rock Islands and arrives on Carp an hour later. There it picks up divers who have stayed on the island and takes them out for the day, leaving you and a couple of friendly groundkeepers alone. When the boat brings the divers back in the late afternoon, they take you back to Koror. The boat ride costs $30 return.

Carp Island is very peaceful, with a white sand beach lined with coconut palms, and hammocks tied to shady ironwood trees. At high tide the Rock Islands across from Carp seem to be floating on the sea, but as the water recedes they become encircled with beaches and linked by sand bars, and all around Carp Island beautifully rippled shoals of sand appear.

If the tide is right and the staff isn't busy, someone might give you a boat ride to a reef where there's good coral. Otherwise, snorkelling is not very good around Carp Island itself, as the water is shallow and about all you'll see is sea grass, goatfish and sea cucumbers. (If you want to go snorkelling with the divers instead of staying on the island, it costs an additional $30!)

Neco Island Neco Marine Dive Shop charges $45, including lunch, for an outing on the beach at Neco Island. As their divers usually have lunch on Neco Island, you can choose between staying on the island all day, or spending half the day on the island and the other half out snorkelling with the divers, at no extra charge.

Organised Tours

The Japanese-operated Rock Island Tour Co (☎ 488-1573) has a large, modern boat with underwater glass windows on a lower deck which allow the viewing of corals and fish. Its cruise of the Rock Islands includes snorkelling at a couple of locations, lunch, drinks and the use of snorkelling gear for $95. Tours last from 9 am to 4 pm and include hotel transfers. The office is at the north end of Malakal Island.

Several other tour agencies can arrange full-day Rock Island boat tours that stop on an island for lunch and a bit of snorkelling. They generally charge about $65 per person, but if they don't have a minimum number of people (often three or four), they'll charge by the boat, usually $150 to $200. The tourist office maintains an updated list of tour operators.

Marine Lakes

The Rock Islands hold about 80 marine salt lakes, former sinkholes now filled with saltwater with a limited exchange to the sea. Variations in algae give them different colours and some have soft corals, fish, sponges or jellyfish.

The heavily forested island of **Eil Malk** contains **Spooky Lake** which has stratified layers of plankton, hydrogen sulphide and gases and **Jellyfish Lake**, filled with jellyfish which have lost the ability to sting. Eil Malk also has a hot water lake that reaches 100°F (37.4°C) just 15 feet down, as well as Palau's largest salt lake, **Metukercheuas Uet**, which is 1½ miles long and 200 feet deep.

Each lake is a different ecosystem, providing unique habitats for creatures that have evolved in their waters over the millennia. Travellers rarely get in to see them but marine biologists love 'em.

70 Islands (Ngerukuid)

Ngerukuid, also known as 70 Islands, is an extremely scenic part of the Rock Islands popular with aerial photographers. It is a nesting site for hawksbill turtles and seabirds and has been set aside as a wildlife preserve. Visits by divers, tourists and fishermen are prohibited.

Places to Stay

Camping The Rock Islands are possibly the best place for camping in all of Micronesia and the star gazing is tremendous. Some of the islands have shelters and picnic tables (and some have enormous piles of Budweiser cans!), though none have water and you'll need protection from biting sand gnats. There are no fees to camp.

You can make arrangements for one of the dive shops to drop you off on a deserted island and then pick you up later at an arranged time. Fish 'N Fins charges $35 for this service. Plan to have water dropped off as well.

Fish 'N Fins will also pick you up on your Rock Island so you can join one of their diving or snorkelling tours. The rates are the same as if you got on the boat in Koror. They weave through the Rock Islands for most diving tours anyway, and on the return they can drop you back off at your rock. This is definitely one up on the free hotel pick-up service, as without the hotel bills the diving fees aren't as painful.

A Palau Visitors Authority brochure notes:

An unsurpassable experience includes spending the night on an islet during the full moon. The white beaches sparkle in the moonlight and a romantic atmosphere privates the whole evening.

Hotels *Carp Island Resort*, booked through the Palau Diving Center, has six rooms in duplex cottages, each with two single beds, a shared indoor toilet and a porch overlooking the beach. The cost is $55/65 for singles/doubles. There's also a divehouse with 40 beds in 10 rooms that costs $22 per bunk. Electricity comes on at night via a generator that is far enough away so as not to keep you awake. All accommodation is rustic but sufficient and clean. Showers are outdoors. There's an informal restaurant but choices are limited and meals cost $7.50 for breakfast or lunch, $20 for dinner. You can bring your own food and use the kitchen facilities at no charge. Most of the guests are young Japanese divers.

The *Ngerchong Boat-el* (☎ 488-2691) Box 94, Koror, Palau 96940, on Ngerchong Island, has eight simple rooms for $30. There's a small restaurant and boat transportation can be arranged for about $80.

Babeldaob

Babeldaob, or Babelthaup, is the second largest land mass in Micronesia, three-quarters the size of Guam. It has 10 states but a total population of only about 3500, with many of the younger people making an exodus to Koror in search of jobs.

Melekeok, a state with just 250 people, has been designated in the constitution as the future site of Palau's new capital. The architectural renderings for the grandiose new capital complex can be seen in the Melekeok state office in Koror, though many people doubt the expensive complex will ever be built.

Although Babeldaob is a high volcanic island, the highest of its gently rolling hills, Mt Ngerchelchuus, has an elevation of only 713 feet. Babeldaob's Lake Ngardok, which is about 3000 feet long and 12 feet deep, is one of the few freshwater lakes in Micronesia. Parts of the island's dense jungle interior are virtually unexplored.

There are beautiful stretches of sandy beach on the east coast, particularly from Ngiwal to Ngaraard, while the west coast is largely mangrove-studded shoreline. Many of the villages are connected by ancient stone footpaths.

Ngarchelong State, at the northernmost point of Babeldaob, has an open field with rows of large basalt monoliths known as Badrulchau. Their origin is unknown, but there are many stories. One legend says the gods put them there to support a bai that held thousands of people. There are 37 stones in all, some weighing up to five tons.

Many of Babeldaob's hillsides were once elaborately terraced into steps and pyramids. Although their purpose remains a mystery, archaeological research suggests they were probably started around 100 AD and abandoned around 1600. Quite mysteriously, few villages seem to have been located close to these terraced hillsides. Badrulchau is the only known exception.

Organised Tours

Mera Koror Corporation (☎ 488-2675) Box 6029, Koror, Palau 96940, has a five-hour tour of Babeldaob from Koror. The cost is $55 per person, with a minimum of four people, and includes lunch.

Ngaraard Traditional Resort (☎ 488-1788) offers guided tours around northern Babeldaob, leaving from Ulimang. One that includes the stone monoliths of Badrulchau costs $25. A boat tour to Ngardmau, followed by an hour-long hike to Palau's largest

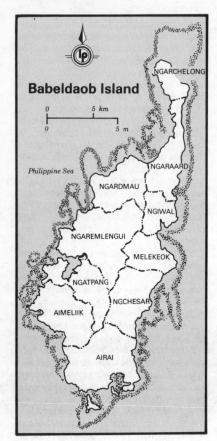

Babeldaob Island

0   5 km
0   5 m

Philippine Sea

NGARCHELONG

NGARAARD

NGARDMAU

NGIWAL

NGAREMLENGUI

MELEKEOK

NGATPANG

NGCHESAR

AIMELIIK

AIRAI

waterfall, costs $30. Make tour reservations in Koror before going to Ngaraard.

Airai State

Airai, at the southern end of Babeldaob, has Palau's international airport. The state's relatively good roads and its proximity to Koror, makes it a good area for exploration. The most visited attractions are two bais, one old and one new.

Airai and Koror are connected by the 1272-foot cantilevered K-B Bridge which at the time of construction was the longest bridge of its type in the world.

There are some crocodile pens behind a store next to the Wash Land Laundromat, 1¼ miles after crossing over the K-B Bridge from Koror. The storekeeper charges 50 cents for viewing and will toss fish to the crocs or spray them with water to liven up an otherwise sleepy show. The Mobil petrol station opposite the laundromat is the last place to get gas before the airport.

The paved road to the airport comes in on the left about half a mile ahead, but to get to the bais continue straight on.

The bombed-out shell of a Japanese administration building is two miles from Wash Land, on the left just after the pavement ends. If you drive behind it you can see another old building which is now an auto repair shop. The ruins of two generations coexist here, where dismantled cars sit inside the bombed building and a Japanese tank and gun rust in union with a heap of car parts outside.

Continue down the main road, where there's tall grass, red soil and an occasional ocean view. Just past a security gate the road splits. Take the road to the left to get to the new bai, which is on the right, 4½ miles from the K-B Bridge. This bai is made mostly of concrete though it incorporates traditional features.

Just beyond, turn left at the T-junction and after a few hundred yards the road will end at Palau's only remaining traditional bai. The bai, which is about 100 years old, is 70 feet long and 20 feet wide with a high-pitched roof reaching a height of 40 feet. It was constructed without nails using native materials of wood and thatch on a stone platform.

Chances are good that as soon as you start walking up the path, the keeper of the bai will appear. You'll have to pay if you want to photograph the bai – probably $5, though in the past it's been as high as $10. There used to be a fee to visit the bai as well, though when we went back this last time there was no charge to look around.

There are traditional scenes and symbolic designs painted inside and outside both bais.

Ngaraard State

Ngaraard has villages on both the east and west coast and a road running across the state to connect them. Some of Babeldaob's prettiest beaches are on Ngaraard's east coast, as is the island's only established visitor accommodation. Though Ngaraard has only 475 people, that's enough to make it the second most populated state in Babeldaob (after Airai).

Ngaraard residents are used to seeing foreigners. Peace Corps volunteers train in this state and Bethania High School, a Christian girls school which takes students from throughout Micronesia, has some American teachers.

Places to Stay

Camping This could be a problem on Babeldaob as people think it's strange and you'll probably have to deal with the local drunks.

The Babeldaob state offices in Koror can sometimes help you make arrangements for places to stay elsewhere on the island, though often if you just show up in a village someone will put you up. Local school principals might let visitors stay in classrooms during school holidays. Appreciated gifts include bread, coffee and canned meat.

Guesthouses *Ngaraard Traditional Resort* (☎ 488-1788) Harson Shiro, Box 773, Koror, Palau 96940, has three cottages in a natural beach setting in Ulimang Village in Ngaraard. The cottages are built in traditional local style with thatched roofs and rough-hewn beams and each has two bedrooms with double beds and mosquito nets, an ice cooler and kerosene stove. Showers and toilets are outdoors. The cost is $25/45 for singles/doubles, plus 10% hotel tax.

You can bring your own food or, with a day's notice, local women will fix native dishes such as reef fish, mangrove crab, taro greens, fruit and coconuts. Meals cost $3.50 for breakfast, $5.50 for lunch and $10 for dinner.

Getting There & Away

Private speedboats and fishing boats going to Babeldaob generally leave from Koror's T-Dock or the Fisheries Co-op. If you're adventurous just go to the docks and ask when someone is going. They'll generally charge about $5 to go anywhere, though it often costs less for women.

Ngaraard Traditional Resort can arrange a speedboat from Koror to Ulimang at $75 per boat for the round trip. The 25-mile ride takes a little over an hour each way.

Getting Around

Car You can easily get from Koror to the bais in Airai in a sedan, but beyond that you'll probably be better off with a 4WD vehicle and a local guide. It is possible to drive from Airai as far as Melekeok on rough dirt roads.

Babeldaob has only a few vehicle roads, generally following the paths of the once-extensive road system constructed during the Japanese era. Some states have just a mile or two of roads which go through a main village and then stop. Because each state works on its own road projects, roads in one state don't always connect up with roads in the next.

Peleliu

Peleliu was the site of one of the bloodiest battles of WW II. The death toll from two months of fighting on this island, that measures only 24 sq miles was 12,000 – almost equivalent to the current-day population of all Palau. Many of Peleliu's visitors these days are survivors of that campaign.

History

WW II The battle for Peleliu was conceived by US military tacticians who were worried that Japanese attacks from bases in Peleliu and Angaur might prevent a successful retaking of the Philippines. By mid-1944, however, American air bombings had reduced Peleliu to a negligible threat and it should have been bypassed, as were other islands held by the Japanese. Instead Peleliu

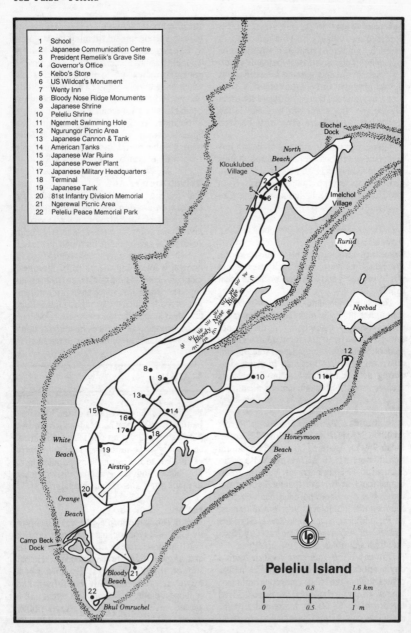

1 School
2 Japanese Communication Centre
3 President Remeliik's Grave Site
4 Governor's Office
5 Keibo's Store
6 US Wildcat's Monument
7 Wenty Inn
8 Bloody Nose Ridge Monuments
9 Japanese Shrine
10 Peleliu Shrine
11 Ngermelt Swimming Hole
12 Ngurungor Picnic Area
13 Japanese Cannon & Tank
14 American Tanks
15 Japanese War Ruins
16 Japanese Power Plant
17 Japanese Military Headquarters
18 Terminal
19 Japanese Tank
20 81st Infantry Division Memorial
21 Ngerewal Picnic Area
22 Peleliu Peace Memorial Park

Elochel Dock

North Beach

Klouklubed Village

Imelchol Village

Ruriid

Ngebad

Bloody Nose Ridge

White Beach

Honeymoon Beach

Airstrip

Orange Beach

Camp Beck Dock

Bloody Beach

Bkul Omruchel

Peleliu Island

0   0.8   1.6 km
0   0.5   1 m

was captured at a terrible, unanticipated cost, with more than 8000 US casualties.

About 10,000 Japanese soldiers were holed up in the natural and people-made caves honeycombed into Peleliu's jagged limestone ridges. Their goal was not to win, but to stall defeat. Far away from the beaches and the reach of naval bombardment, they tenaciously defended these caves to their deaths.

Rather than the expected quick victory, it took 2½ months for the Americans to rout out the last of the Japanese forces – often one by one with the use of flame throwers.

In the late 1950s, a Japanese straggler who had been hiding in the jungle was discovered by an old woman as he entered her garden. Crouching low to see who had been stealing her tapioca, the woman froze and then screamed, thinking she was seeing a ghost. The man's uniform was torn into shreds, his hair matted and teeth streaked black. Police from Koror hunted the straggler down, bound him with rope and paraded him around for everyone to see. In that way, the last soldier left Peleliu.

Peleliu Today In prewar days there were settlements scattered around Peleliu, but upon returning from Babeldaob after the war, the people all resettled on the northern tip of the island. The population is now about 550.

Several areas in Peleliu have been renamed in recognition of their military usage. Koska, at the southern end of Klouklubed, is not really a separate village but is the area where the Coast Guard, or the *kos ka*, personnel once stayed. Ngerkeyukl, the former village north of Orange Beach, is now called Sina, which is the Palauan word for China, and is named after the Nationalist Chinese that came to that area to buy jeeps and other WW II surplus.

During the fighting Peleliu's forests were bombed and burned to the ground. Today the island is alive with the whistles and songs of a great number of tropical birds that thrive on the secondary jungle growth of vines and leafy foliage that have grown up to cover the battle scars. If there weren't the occasional pillbox, rusting tank or memorial to stumble across, there'd be no immediate sense of this island's place in war history.

Peleliu is also known, in other circles, for its high-quality marijuana. Fertile soil is brought in from Babeldaob for pot planting in 50-gallon oil drums. Raids by US agents from Guam some years back outraged the locals, who were indignant that anyone would consider such an attack on their economy.

Peleliu has much more to offer than just war relics. It's a fine place to kick back and take life easy for a while. The old name for Peleliu was *Odesangel* which means the 'beginning of everything'.

Orientation
The coral-surfaced 6000-foot airstrip, dating from WW II, is about five miles from the village. Sometimes there's a minibus that will give you a ride into town for a dollar or so. If not, get a lift from one of the people meeting the plane.

Many of the remnants of war are clustered north of the airport amidst a criss-cross of roads that can be confusing. It's helpful to have a guide, but if you don't care about seeing each and every war relic, you can explore on your own as the coral and concrete roads are in good condition. Peleliu is too big to thoroughly cover on foot, but bicycling is a good option if you don't want to rent a car. The island still has a scattering of live ammunition, so take care if you go off the beaten path.

Most of Peleliu's best beaches are to the south.

Diving & Snorkelling
Peleliu Wall is one of the world's finest dives, an abrupt 900-foot drop that starts in about 10 feet of water. It's a veritable treasure-trove of sharks, hawksbill sea turtles, black coral trees, mammoth gorgonian fans and an amazing variety of fish. The wall is to the south-west of Peleliu.

Many of Palau's best dive spots are in fact closer to Peleliu than Koror, but most people start from Koror because that's where the diving services are.

Both White Beach and Bloody Beach have coral and good snorkelling.

Klouklubed

The main village of Klouklubed is interesting more for its small-town atmosphere than for any particular sights, though there are a couple.

Palau's first president, Haruo Remeliik, who was killed by an assassin in 1985, was from Peleliu. His grave is directly opposite the governor's office.

A multistorey bombed-out Japanese communications centre is right in the middle of the village, tangled with vegetation and encircled by homes. Kids play inside the building and its roof is now a forest floor.

There's a small US military monument opposite Keibo's store. Heading towards the dock you can spot a cave and pillbox on the right, opposite a sandy beach.

WW II Ruins

North of the airport are the bombed-out shells of the Japanese power plant buildings, which are almost completely draped with vines hanging down from the upper ledges. Watch out for the wasp nests inside. The seemingly orchestrated chorus of birds in the background is amazing and the whole place has an eerie feeling of abandonment.

Nearby are two-storey buildings that served as Japanese military headquarters, now in a state of decay with concrete crumbling around the steel reinforcement rods. There are two rusting Quonset huts behind the main building.

Not far away, a small rusted Japanese tank sits at the convergence of three paths, all once paved roads. Other war wreckage in the general area includes a larger US tank with ferns and grass growing out the sides, two rusting US amphibs by the side of the road and a Japanese cannon guarding the entrance of a cave near a tiny Shinto shrine.

Bloody Nose Ridge

Below Bloody Nose Ridge, a sign points to

a US Marine Corps monument in a clearing to the right, from where there's a nice view.

To get to the top of Bloody Nose Ridge, head uphill behind the sign, taking the path to the left. It starts as a rough road and soon changes to steep narrow stairs with a chain alongside to use as a handrail. The climb to the top takes about five minutes and the remains of some munitions can be seen along the way.

At the top of the ridge there's a monument, a machine gun and a spectacular 360° view. There were once more than 500 caves dug into the limestone cliffs of Peleliu, many of them on this ridge.

Orange Beach

The first US invasion forces to land on Peleliu came ashore at Orange Beach on 15 September 1944. From concrete pillboxes the Japanese machine-gunned the oncoming waves of Americans as they hit the beaches. Despite the barrage, 15,000 US soldiers made it ashore on the first day.

Today Orange Beach is a quiet picnic spot with a barbecue grill, sandy beach and water that's calm, clear, shallow and warm.

Just before the beach there are two grey coral monuments with plaques, metal crosses and rusting helmets, dedicated to the US Army's 81st Infantry Wildcat Division. There's a striking sense of stillness at this site.

Camp Beck Dock

Behind Camp Beck Dock, where the water is a creamy aqua, you'll find a huge pile of mangled WW II plane engines, cockpits, pipes, tubing, fuselages, anchors and who knows what, all compacted into blocks of twisted aluminium and steel.

South Beaches

At Bkul Omruchel, the south-west tip of the island, the Japanese have constructed half a dozen chunky concrete tables and named the area Peleliu Peace Memorial Park. There are some small blowholes on the shore and you can see Angaur Island to the south. Aside from the crashing surf it is very peaceful.

Bloody Beach, despite its name, is a calm circular cove with a nice sandy beach. Nearby is the Ngerewal picnic area.

Northeast of the airport is Honeymoon Beach, a long stretch of beach with good seasonal surf.

At the eastern tip of the island is the Ngurungor picnic area, with some mangroves and tiny rock island formations just offshore.

Heading back from Ngurungor, off a grassy road to the right, there's a small swimming hole of half-salt, half-freshwater that bobs up and down with the tides. A metal ladder hangs down the side of the tiny pit, but local kids just jump in from the top.

Places to Stay & Eat

Camping Camping is easy and acceptable on Peleliu. Some of the beach picnic sites have open-air shelters, tables, barbecue pits and outhouses, but you'll need to take drinking water. You'll also need a close-knit screened tent or insect repellent to keep the bugs at bay.

No permission is needed to camp, though it's a courtesy to check in first at the governor's office. You can arrange in town for a car to drop you off and pick you up.

Ngurungor picnic area is a good choice for camping. It's close to the swimming hole and it usually has a refreshing breeze. Beware, though, that there have been reports of crocodile tracks on the shore!

Honeymoon Beach is not recommended as it's littered and has a serious infestation of sand gnats that bite hard and can make for a totally sleepless night.

Orange Beach is another possibility for camping, though the west coast doesn't catch many breezes, and it can be hot and muggy.

If you want to camp in Klouklubed, the Wenty Inn lets campers pitch a tent in the yard for $10 per day. This includes the use of shower rooms and rest rooms.

Guesthouses The *Wenty Inn*, run by Emery Wenty, has six rooms in a new guesthouse for $15 per person. Meals cost $5 for break-

fast, $7 for lunch and $8 for dinner. There's a nice beach when the tide is in. Reservations can be made by mail by writing to Wenty Inn, Peleiliu State, Republic of Palau, 96940.

Mayumi and Keibo Rideb rent three rooms next door to Keibo's store. The rate is $15 per person.

The Paradise Air Agent, Reiko Kubarii, sometimes rents rooms in her house a few doors down from the governor's office, for $15 per person.

All rooms on Pelelieu can be booked through Paradise Air if you're flying in with them.

Peleliu has some small food stores but no restaurants. Electrical power is on only at night, from 6 pm.

Getting There & Away

Air Paradise Air (☎ 488-2348) flies to Peleliu from Koror for $20 and from Angaur for $15. Flights leave Koror at 9 am and 3.30 pm and arrive on Peleliu 20 minutes later. Flights leave Angaur at 9.45 am and 4.10 pm and take 10 minutes to get to Peleliu. There are no flights on Wednesdays and only morning flights on Saturdays.

Boat The state boat runs between Elochel Dock in Klouklubed and the Fisheries Co-op on Koror. It leaves Koror on Monday and Friday mornings and returns from Peleliu on Thursdays and Sundays. Reservations are not necessary. The two-hour ride costs just $1.50 each way, and taking the boat gives you the chance to meet islanders on the way.

Private speedboats commute between Klouklubed and Koror, so you might be able to get a ride by asking around at the Fisheries Co-op. Kosiil Landing, on the causeway between downtown Koror and Malakal Island, is a hangout for Peleliu islanders, and someone there might also know of boats going down.

Getting Around

Car & Guides You can rent a pick-up truck, with or without a guide, for about $30. A guide and minivan costs about $40. It may be possible to politely negotiate $5 or so off those rates or arrange for less than the full-scale tour. Cost is per vehicle, so the more people you pile inside, the cheaper it is. Make arrangements through the Peleliu guesthouses or in advance through the airline.

The Wenty Inn rents cars for $50 a day.

Bicycle Wenty Inn rents bicycles for $5 a day. It would take two or three days to see most of Peleliu's sights by bike. The road running down the east side of Bloody Nose Ridge is best for cyclists as it's shady and less frequented by cars.

Angaur

For the independent traveller looking to get off the beaten track, Angaur has a certain timeless South Seas charm. It's a tranquil, hassle-free island with only one village and a population of just over 200.

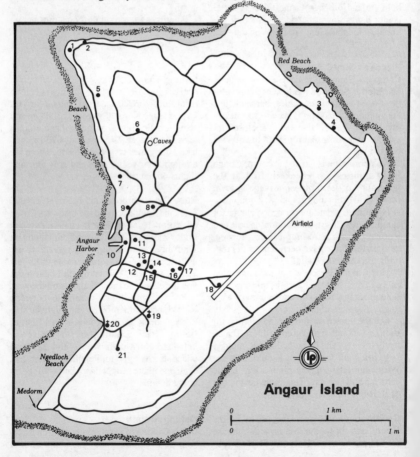

Angaur Island

Angaur, seven miles south-west of Peleliu, is outside the protective reef that surrounds most of Palau's islands. Open ocean pounds the north coast where in places the sea explodes through blowholes. The south end of the island is calm with sandy beaches.

The only monkeys in Micronesia are on Angaur. The island has about 600 crab-eating macaques, the descendants of a couple of monkeys accidentally introduced by the Germans in the early 1900s. The macaques cause some agricultural damage and there is occasional talk of eradication programmes.

Orientation

If you arrive by air you'll be greeted by a weathered 'Angaur International' sign hanging from a tiny open-air shelter. The 7000-foot paved airstrip dates from WW II. You may be able to get a ride from someone meeting the plane, though the village is only a 10-minute walk from the airport.

The coastal road circling the island is mostly level and in good condition. Angaur is just 2½ miles long, making it easy to get around on foot.

1	Virgin Mary Statue
2	Buddhist Memorial & Blowholes
3	Former Coast Guard Station
4	Aeroplane Graveyard
5	Shinto Shrine
6	Overview of Ponds
7	Lighthouse
8	Phosphate Plant Ruins
9	Phosphate Conveyor Belt Ruins
10	Dispensary
11	Elementary School
12	Bai
13	Masao Endo's Guest House
14	Kazuo's Guest House
15	K Family Store
16	Governor's Office
17	School
18	Terminal
19	Catholic Church
20	Catholic Priest's House
21	Cemetery

If you're on a day trip, however, you'll probably want to rent a vehicle or be content with walking around just a portion of the island. Though it's possible to walk the entire coastal road in a day, the heat and humidity don't make it tempting – at least not at midday. The hottest walking is around the village where the sun reflects off the crushed coral streets. Outside the village tall trees and tropical growth close in, allowing for shady strolls.

Diving

There's good diving around Angaur between January and July, but the rest of the year the water's too rough. You need to make arrangements in Koror, as there are no facilities on Angaur.

Angaur Harbor

Angaur's well-protected harbour is so nearly enclosed that the calm waters look like a big swimming pool. There's good swimming inside the boat basin and you can snorkel outside.

Phosphate Mines & Ruins

The Germans started mining phosphate for agricultural fertiliser in 1909, with operations later taken over by the Japanese. Following a break during the war, mining resumed for another decade. There is occasional talk of reopening the mines, but it's questionable whether there's enough phosphate remaining to make it worthwhile.

To get to the old mines, turn inland north of the harbour, take the left-hand road at each of three forks and then look closely on the right for a low horizontal iron ramp. It's not the mines that are visible below, but cool green ponds which formed when the excavations filled with water after the mining. The water is just a little salty, which is apparently how the resident crocodiles like it.

Back on the coastal road, look for the tall rusting iron girders of the conveyor belt that moved the phosphate down to the nearby harbour.

Japanese Lighthouse
Up ahead, there's an old Japanese lighthouse hiding in the jungle on a hill to the left of the road. It takes a sharp eye to find it, but when the road nears a hill with dense vegetation walk back toward the village about 50 yards and look for the rough start of a trail. The crumbling coral steps give way to concrete ones leading up to the lighthouse, which is a five-minute walk from the road. There's a good view from the lighthouse, though the uppermost tower has toppled off. Wasps have made thousands of little mud homes on the inside but they don't seem bothered by visitors.

Shrines & Monuments
Further north there's a miniature wooden Shinto shrine, no more than four feet high. It's set off to the right with jagged rock formations and twisting plant roots making an interesting backdrop. There's a nice beach across the way.

Around the north-west tip of the island is a statue of the Virgin Mary, erected to protect Angaur from stormy seas. A Buddhist memorial with markers honouring fallen Japanese soldiers is just ahead and if you walk down towards the ocean and look to the right you'll see a big blowhole.

Red Beach
On 18 September 1944, after five days of bombing, US Army troops stormed Angaur at Red Beach on the northern coast. The landings were unopposed. The USA declared the island secured two days later, though hundreds of Japanese soldiers had merely retreated to caves in the north-west corner of the island.

Although the Americans were able to immediately move in and start building airfields, fighting continued until 23 October. By then 1500 Japanese and 240 US soldiers had been killed.

Coast Guard Station
The well-manicured grounds of the former Coast Guard station have been returned to the former landowner who now lives in one of the buildings. He occasionally lets campers stay on the property and there has been some talk of turning the site into a small hotel.

Aeroplane Graveyard
Look closely into the dense jungle left of the road about halfway between the Coast Guard station and the northern end of the airstrip to find the aeroplane graveyard. Pieces of wrecked WW II planes are blanketed with the soft needles of towering ironwood trees. A Corsair plane with both wings still intact is the most recognisable, but the incredible root structure of the trees and the dream-like setting are as interesting as the plane.

Swimming Cove
On the south-west side of the village there's a quiet swimming cove near the Catholic priest's house. A concrete slab and rock under a large shade tree are used to crack tasty Palauan almonds found scattered on the ground. The beach from this cove to the southern tip of the island is called Ngedloch or sometimes Waikiki.

Spirit Respites
Beyond the priest's house is a cemetery with Palauan, Japanese and German graves and nearby, quite coincidentally, is an area where the souls of all Palauans go after death.

There's usually nothing to see, but within one or two days after a death it's said that a small waterhole appears so the spirit of the deceased can wash off all traces of earthly trappings and become totally free. The spirit then makes its way to Medorm at the south-west tip of the island, ascends a huge banyan tree and shoots off into the heavens. Fishermen in the area at night sometimes report seeing streaks of fiery light in the sky.

Places to Stay & Eat
Camping Camping is easy and acceptable though there are no developed facilities. Take water and protection from insects. For the most part no permission is necessary and you can pick your own beach.

Guesthouses There are two guesthouses, both in modern concrete homes a short walk from the airport.

Masao Endo's Guest House has one bedroom for a single person or couple and mats on the floor in a larger room for groups. Either way it's $10 per person. Meals cost $4 for breakfast, $5 for lunch and $6 for dinner and the food's quite good. Reservations are made through Paradise Air.

Kazuo's Guest House Box 261, Koror, Palau 96940, has three rooms with shared bathroom that cost $15/25 for singles/doubles.

Electricity is only on for six hours a day, from 5 to 11 pm. Angaur has a couple of small stores with basic provisions, but no restaurants. Locals proudly claim their fertile soil produces the best pot in Micronesia.

Getting There & Away

Air Paradise Air (☎ 488-2348) flies between Koror and Angaur for $26 and between Peleliu and Angaur for $15. Flights leave Koror at 9 am and 3.30 pm, stopping on Peleliu en route. There are no flights on Wednesdays and only morning flights on Saturdays.

Boat A state speedboat makes the 1½ hour trip between Angaur and Koror about once a week, usually on Fridays. Check at the Fisheries Co-op or the Angaur state office in Koror for details and expect to pay about $10 one way. Private speedboats sometimes commute between Koror and Angaur, but not nearly as often as between Koror and Peleliu. The channel between Angaur and Peleliu can be very rough.

Getting Around

If you don't want to explore on foot, ask at the guesthouses about hiring someone to take you around in their pick-up truck. People usually ask about $25 but it's often negotiable. Although you might be able to rent a truck without a driver to go off on your own, it probably won't be cheaper.

Kayangel

Kayangel, 15 miles north of Babeldaob, is a picture-postcard coral atoll. It has four islands with sun-bleached beaches circling a well-protected aqua blue lagoon. There's just one quiet village of 150 people, a predominance of tin houses, two small stores, no vehicles and no electricity. The main island is only half a mile wide and three-quarters of a mile long, yet there are two chiefs – one for each side.

Kayangel is still fairly traditional. Visiting women should wear a T-shirt and shorts over their bathing suit for swimming and neither men nor women should wear shorts in public.

Woven handbags and baskets from Kayangel are in demand as they're made of a high quality pandanus leaf imported from Saipan. An average handbag costs $35 and lasts a couple of years.

Places to Stay

There are no hotels but you can ask at the Kayangel governor's house in Koror about the possibility of camping or staying with a family. Take rice, coffee or other provisions to give to people who help you. Bread is appreciated as there is none on Kayangel.

Getting There & Away

State diesel boats called *bilas* leave Kayangel for Koror every other Thursday, returning to Kayangel from T-Dock the following Saturday.

Kayangel's fishing boat travels to Koror about every five days. The schedule is irregular but the Fisheries Co-op will know if it's in. It's a smoother ride than on the state diesel boats.

Both take seven to eight hours and charge $6. Private speedboats, if you can find one, take about three hours.

South-West Islands

The tiny islands to the south-west stretch for 370 miles beyond the main Palauan islands towards Indonesia. There are five groups, each covering less than one sq mile of land. Sonsorol has two islands, named Sonsorol and Fana, while Pulo Anna, Merir, Tobi and Helen are single islands.

People from the south-west islands are related culturally to the central Carolinians and have more in common with Yapese and Chuukese outer islanders than with people from the main islands of Palau. Their language is Sonsorolese. This is traditional island life at its purest, with thatched houses, carved canoes and fishing as a livelihood.

Sonsorol has about 80 people, Tobi about 70, Pulo Anna a dozen or two. The only inhabitants on Merir and Helen are birds and sea turtles.

Getting There & Away
There's no official field trip ship to the south-west islands, though a Palauan fishing patrol boat heads that way on occasion.

Guam

Guam is the metropolis of Micronesia. It's the region's largest island, covering 212 sq miles, and with about 127,000 people it also has the largest population. In appearance and in style it's not unlike a 'little Hawaii' mixed with the Americanised Hispanic flavour of East Los Angeles.

Guam has traffic jams, fast food restaurants, large shopping centres, a university, busloads of package tourists who stay in a row of resort hotels, and a substantial US military presence.

It also has tropical forests, sleepy villages, a mountainous interior, good sandy beaches and an abundance of butterflies and rainbows.

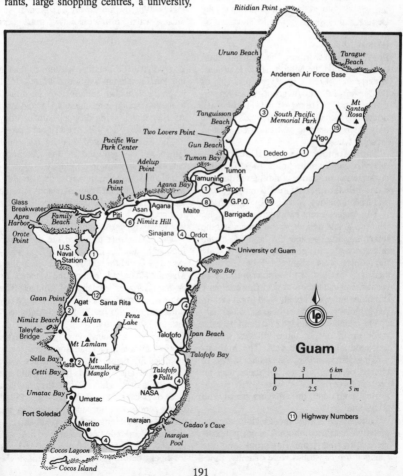

Ritidian Point

Uruno Beach

Taragua Beach

Andersen Air Force Base

Tanguisson Beach

Two Lovers Point

Pacific War Park Center

Gun Beach

Adelup Point

Tumon Bay

Asan Point

Agana Bay

Tamuning

Tumon

U.S.O.

Asan

Agana

Airport

Glass Breakwater

Piti

Nimitz Hill

Maite

G.P.O.

Apra Harbor

Family Beach

Sinajana

Ordot

Barrigada

Orote Point

U.S. Naval Station

Yona

University of Guam

Gaan Point

Agat

Santa Rita

Fena Lake

Pago Bay

Nimitz Beach

Mt Alifan

Ipan Beach

Taleyfac Bridge

Mt Lamlam

Talofofo

Sella Bay

Vista

Mt Jumullong Manglo

Talofofo Bay

Cetti Bay

Talofofo Falls

Umatac Bay

NASA

Fort Soledad

Umatac

Inarajan

Gadao's Cave

Merizo

Inarajan Pool

Cocos Lagoon

Cocos Island

South Pacific Memorial Park

Mt Santa Rosa

Yigo

Dededo

Guam

| 0 | 3 | 6 km |

| 0 | 2.5 | 5 m |

Ⓛ Highway Numbers

The way you view Guam depends on the direction from which you're coming. If you've just been island hopping through the less developed FSM then Guam is big time, and perhaps spoiled and overdeveloped. It's a consumer playground and a place for a salad fix for those expatriates living on the outer islands.

On the other hand if you've just flown in from New York, Sydney or Tokyo, Guam is likely to appear slow, rural and laid back.

Guam's prolific tourist bureau promotes the island both as 'Where America's Day Begins' and as the 'Gateway to Micronesia'.

History

Pre-European Contact The ancient Chamorros inhabited the Mariana Islands at least as early as 1500 BC. They were probably of Indonesian-Filipino descent, sharing language and cultural similarities with South-East Asians. The Chamorros were the only Micronesians to cultivate rice prior to Western contact.

Their society was matrilineal, with extended family households. Most farming, construction and canoe building was done by men while the cooking, reef fishing, pottery and basket making was done by women.

The social system had three main classes. The *matua* and *achoat*, or the nobles and the lesser nobility, owned the land while the *manachang*, or lower class, worked it. Only the nobles were allowed to be warriors, sailors, artists and fishermen. The manachang had to bow down in the company of nobles and were not allowed to eat certain foods including such basics as saltwater fish.

The island was divided into districts, each made up of one or more villages, mainly scattered along the coasts. The highest-ranking district noble, the *chamorri*, was in charge of local affairs but there was no central leader. The districts often fought against each other, the villagers armed with slings and spears.

Latte stones are the most visible remains of early Chamorro culture. The upright posts were quarried from limestone and the rounded top capstones were of either limestone or brain coral. The stones are of such antiquity that at the time of the first Western contact the islanders no longer knew what their purpose had been. Historians now believe the stones were used as foundation pillars for men's houses and the homes of nobility. Latte stones vary from a few feet high to as tall as 20 feet.

Chamorros were a tall, handsome and well-built people. Before the arrival of Europeans the men wore no clothing at all, except occasionally hats or sandals made of palm leaves. When women wore anything, it was only a waist cord with a thin grass skirt attached.

Spanish Period The first Western contact in the Pacific islands was on 6 March 1521 when the *Trinidad*, captained by Ferdinand Magellan, sailed into Guam's Umatac Bay. As Magellan's ships dropped anchor, they were greeted by a flotilla of outrigger canoes.

The Spaniards noted that the triangular lateen sail design used on the Chamorro canoes was superior in efficiency to the conventional European sails of the day. Magellan named the chain of islands *Islas de las Velas Latinas*, Islands of Lateen Sails. He retained the local name *Guahan*, meaning 'we have', for the island of Guam.

The Chamorros provided the crew with food and water but in return they took whatever they could find on the ships, prompting Magellan to quickly rename the islands *Islas de los Ladrones* – Islands of Thieves. The name Ladrones was still being used by sailors to refer to the Mariana Islands well into the 20th century.

To the Guamanians, what the Europeans saw as theft was in fact traditional reciprocity practised in Chamorro society between hosts and guests. The Spaniards however, did not take the matter lightly. Before they had left three days later, Magellan's crew had killed seven people and burned 40 houses in the process of retrieving a stolen rowboat.

Miguel Lopez de Legazpi arrived in Guam in 1565 and officially claimed the Marianas for Spain before going on to establish the

Top: Japanese Train & Sugar Mill - Rota
Bottom Left: Suicide Cliff - Saipan
Bottom Right: Mural - Guam

Top: Natural swimming hole - Rota
Bottom: Overview of Agana - Guam

trade route between the Philippines and Mexico.

For the next 250 years Spanish galleons stopped at Guam to take on provisions during annual runs between Manila and Acapulco. In addition to galleon layovers, there were occasional visits by Spanish, English and Dutch explorers. Yet almost 150 years passed between Magellan's landing and any real attempt at European settlement.

In 1668 the Jesuit priest Diego Luis de Sanvitores arrived with a small Spanish garrison and established a Catholic mission in the village of Agana. At first the mission was welcomed and Catholicism began to spread.

As the missionaries gained influence they became more outspoken in opposing traditions such as ancestor worship and the sexual initiation of young women in the communal men's houses. They insisted the islanders wear clothing and blurred traditional caste lines by accepting converts from all classes.

It took only a few years for the islanders to realise that their culture was being subjugated and this sparked rebellions and warfare that lasted for the next 25 years. Sanvitores was killed in 1672 after he baptised a chief's infant daughter against the chief's wishes. Spain sent reinforcements and the battles escalated.

By 1695 the fighting was over, but only because there were no more Chamorro men left to fight. Between the bloodshed and epidemics of smallpox and influenza, the Chamorro population had dropped from perhaps 100,000 to fewer than 5000, virtually all of them women and children.

Spanish soldiers and Filipino men brought in to help re-populate the islands intermarried with Chamorro women, marking the end of the pure Chamorro bloodline.

As was the custom at that time, men moved into their wives' houses after marriage. This gave the women the chance to raise their children with some Chamorro influence. If not for this, the children would undoubtedly have grown up speaking Spanish and all traces of Chamorro culture would have been lost.

In addition to religion and disease, the Spanish introduced a written language, set up schools and taught construction and farming skills.

US Period Although whaleships visited the Marianas as early as 1798, it wasn't until 1822 that any stopped at Guam. Some of the whalers were British, but most were American, and during the peak whaling years of the 1840s there were hundreds of ships passing through.

In April 1898 the USA declared war on Spain. Two months later Captain Henry Glass sailed into Guam's Apra Harbor with guns firing. He was greeted warmly by the Spanish authorities who, having no idea that their two nations were at war, apologised for not having enough ammunition to return the salute. The next day the Spanish governor officially surrendered.

In August 1898 the Treaty of Paris ceded Guam (as well as Puerto Rico and the Philippines) to the USA who maintained a largely unfortified naval control over the island until 1941.

Japanese Occupation Japanese bombers attacked Guam from Saipan on 8 December 1941, the same day as the Pearl Harbor attack across the International Date Line. Guam was an easy and undefended target. On 10 December, within hours of 5000 Japanese invasion forces coming ashore, Guam's naval governor surrendered.

In anticipation of such an event, many Americans on Guam had been sent home just two months earlier. Those that remained were taken prisoner and sent to labour camps in Japan.

The Japanese administration in Guam immediately began the task of teaching the Chamorros the Japanese language. They renamed the island *Omiyajima* which means 'Great Shrine Island'. Guam became part of an empire that the Japanese said would last for a thousand years. They held it for just 31 months.

In the beginning the Chamorros were mostly left alone. Food supplies were rationed, but islanders could live where they liked and workers were paid low wages for their labour.

Toward the end of Japanese control the military rule became quite harsh. Guamanians were placed in work camps to build fortifications and forced into farming to provide food for Japanese troops.

On 12 July 1944 the Japanese military command ordered all Guamanians be marched into concentration camps on the eastern side of the island. The people didn't know where they were going or why but, alarmed by a number of recent atrocities, many feared the worst. Particularly for some of the elderly and the sick it did indeed become a death march.

As it turned out the move saved many lives by concentrating the Guamanians away from the American invasion bombardment and subsequent fighting on the south-west side of the island.

In the final hopeless days there were several incidents of massacres. The Japanese, hoping to kill as many Americans as possible before dying themselves, also took the lives of the Chamorros who they thought might compromise that aim.

In one incident, 40 Chamorro men were taken abruptly at night from their camp to carry provisions as the Japanese retreated to the north. After arriving in Tarague, rather than allow the men to go back to their camp and give away their positions to the advancing US forces, the Japanese tied them to trees and beheaded them.

US Returns Pre-assault bombings by the USA began on 17 July 1944. The US invasion came on 21 July, when 55,000 US troops hit Guam's beaches at Agat and Asan. The USA secured Guam on 10 August after fierce fighting, with 17,500 Japanese and 7000 US casualties.

Agana was a city in ruins and many smaller villages were also destroyed. The population swelled tenfold, as 200,000 US servicemen moved in to prepare for the invasion of Japan.

Large tracts of land, comprising roughly one-third of Guam, were confiscated by the US military at the time. When the war ended the military kept the land.

In 1986, a class action lawsuit for dispossessed landowners won a multimillion dollar settlement from the US government, though many found the terms unsatisfactory. To rub salt into old wounds, the military is now considering leasing out some of the land for farming – not to the families who were kicked off those farms, but to the highest bidders.

Twenty years after WW II, Guam's Andersen Air Force Base was a centre for B 52 bombing raids over Indochina during the Vietnam War. In 1975 more than 100,000 Vietnamese refugees were flown to Guam under the 'Operation New Life' programme before going on to the USA. A decade later, a deposed Ferdinand Marcos took a similar route to the States, stopping long enough on Guam for his entourage to run up sizable unpaid bills at the base commissary.

Geography

Guam is about 30 miles long and nine miles wide. It narrows to about four miles in the centre so it's shaped a little like a bow tie. It is the southernmost island in the Marianas chain.

The northern part of Guam is largely a raised limestone plateau, with some steep vertical cliffs dropping 300 to 600 feet to the sea. The south is a mix of high volcanic hills and valleys containing numerous rivers and waterfalls.

Reef formations surround much of the island. The beaches on the west side tend to be calmer than those on the east coast which get heavier seas. The southern tip of the island has a number of protected bays.

Climate

Guam's climate is uniformly warm and humid throughout the year. Daily temperatures average a low of 72°F (22°C) and a high of 85°F (30°C).

Guam's annual rainfall averages 98 inches. The most pleasant weather is during the dry season from January to the end of April when the dominant trade winds, which

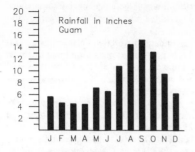

20
18
16
14
12
10
8
6
4
2

Rainfall in Inches
Guam

J F M A M J J A S O N D

blow year-round from the east or north-east, are strongest. The humidity is also slightly lower then and the rainfall averages just 4½ inches monthly.

Guam lies in the path of typhoons and strong tropical storms, which are most frequent in the last half of the year but can occur in any month. To get the latest pre-recorded weather forecast call ☎ 343-2991.

Government

Guam is an Unincorporated Territory of the United States of America.

The Organic Act of Guam in 1950 installed a civilian government to replace the navy and granted all Guamanians US citizenship. In 1962 security clearance restrictions on travel to Guam, which had been imposed by the US Navy, were lifted.

Guam's government includes a 21-seat legislature and a judicial system with limited powers. Guamanians chose their first elected governor, Carlos Camacho, in 1970. Although a part of the USA, Guam does not have a voice on par with the 50 states. The islanders cannot vote in national elections and though in 1972 they were finally given the right to send a representative to the US Congress, he also has to sit on the sidelines without a vote.

With the USA paying millions of dollars in leases for bases in the Philippines, some Guamanians question whether they're not being taken for a ride – token citizenship in exchange for free land use.

Many Guamanians feel that the Micronesian islands of the former Trust Territory have had more opportunities to develop self-government than has Guam. In an effort to redefine their relationship with the US, Guam voters approved a draft Commonwealth Act in a 1987 plebescite which, if enacted into law, would change their status to that of a US Commonwealth. The bill has been bogged down in the US Congress, ostensibly over a provision that grants the right of self-determination exclusively to Guam's Chamorro minority. Perhaps more troublesome for Washington are provisions that would give Guamanians more control over federally held land on their island and allow Guam to make treaties with other nations.

Graft and payoffs have been so widespread on Guam that in the late 1980s a federal investigation of local government resulted in more than 100 indictments, including many against department heads and Governor Ricardo Bordallo himself. In January 1990, just hours before he was to fly to the US mainland to begin a four-year prison sentence on corruption charges, Bordallo chained himself to the Chief Quipuha statue in Agana and shot himself dead.

Economy

Before WW II Guam's economy was based largely on subsistence agriculture. The establishment of large post-war military bases, however, opened up jobs in construction and support services.

The 1960s saw the beginning of economic growth and a rise in the standard of living. In

1962 Typhoon Karen hit Guam hard, destroying more than 60% of the buildings and levelling much of the vegetation. Reconstruction aid and the building boom that followed gave a big boost to the economy.

The Vietnam War and its related military expenditures provided more jobs and pumped in more money. Today the military is Guam's largest industry.

Among Guam's large naval and air force stations is a nuclear submarine base and a US Strategic Air Command headquarters. Guam is also a storage depot for an estimated 450 nuclear warheads, the largest stockpile of US nuclear weapons in the western Pacific.

The lifting of the security clearance in 1962 and the start of jet service in 1968 opened Guam to tourism. Neighbouring Japan, then emerging as an economic power, provided the customers. Today Guam gets about 800,000 tourists annually, with about 80% of those visitors from Japan.

GovGuam, as the local government is called, is an over-loaded bureaucracy employing 25% of the work force. If you add those on military bases as well as other federal jobs, the government payroll swells to include about 50% of all workers.

Guam is in the midst of a construction boom, with hotels, shopping centres and the like going up everywhere. In addition, Japanese developers are busy scooping up large tracts of land to build golf courses, most with adjoining resort hotels or condo complexes. Over a dozen golf course projects are currently under way and more are planned.

Though unemployment is low, salaries are not very high and the tourist development that's heated the economy has spurred double-digit inflation. Many islanders from less-developed Micronesian islands are drawn to Guam in hopes of landing a minimum wage ($3.75 an hour) job in one of the hotels. Faced with a high cost of living and unfamiliar with Guam's fast pace, not all fare well and quite a few end up in skid-row conditions.

People

When the US opened Guam to settlement in 1962 it was largely Asians, not Americans, who started pouring in. The current population is 127,000.

Although the 58,000 Chamorros are still the largest ethnic group, indigenous rights groups are concerned that Chamorros will end up losing control of their island to outsiders.

About 33,000 residents are from the US mainland, 10,000 of them permanent and 23,000 of them military workers and their families. The next largest groups are Filipinos (28,000) and Micronesians (3000). Guam is also home to sizable groups of Koreans, Chinese and Japanese and a smattering of other Pacific peoples.

About 90% of the population is Roman Catholic.

Language

Spanish never completely replaced the Chamorro language, although more than 75% of modern Chamorro words are derived from Spanish. Though it has more guttural and repeated rhythmic sounds, Chamorro sounds a lot like Spanish too.

Chamorro was first written by Spanish missionaries who, using their own language as a base, used 'y' for the Chamorro article 'the'. Western scholars later started writing it as 'i'.

Chamorro also has a unique sound that's something like 'dz', which is spelt 'y' in the Spanish style and 'j' in the Western style. These two systems for spelling Chamorro words are still in use, so you can expect to see both.

In theory Chamorro and English are both official languages as both are taught in schools and used in government documents. In practice, however, English is taking over as the language of choice.

Many common Chamorro phrases are the same as in Spanish. 'Good morning' is *buenas dias* and 'goodbye' is *adios*.

The common Chamorro greeting is *hafa adai* (pronounced 'half a day'). Literally, it means 'what?' but it's sort of a 'hello', 'what's up?' and 'how are you?' all combined. *Hafa adai* is sometimes shortened to *hafa* or *fa*. 'Thank you' is *si yuus maasi*.

Holidays & Festivals

Guam's public holidays are:

New Year's Day
    1 January
Martin Luther King's Birthday
    3rd Monday in January,
President's Day
    3rd Monday in February
Guam Discovery Day
    1st Monday in March
Good Friday
    Last Friday of Lent,
Memorial Day
    Last Monday in May
US Independence Day
    4 July,
Liberation Day
    21 July,
Labor Day
    1st Monday in September
Columbus Day
    2nd Monday in October
Veterans Day
    11 November,
Thanksgiving
    4th Thursday in November
Lady of Camarin Day
    8 December
Christmas Day
    25 December

Guam Discovery Day, which celebrates Magellan's landing at Umatac, is one of the big events of the year. Activities are centred in Umatac. The historical recreation of the 'discovery of Guam' is so complete that it includes building thatched huts on the beach and later torching them as Magellen's crew did to the village in retaliation for the theft of a small boat. Other activities during the four-day event are cultural dances, sports competitions, arts and crafts and tuba making.

Liberation Day celebrations include feasts, fireworks and the largest parade of the year.

New Year's Eve is wild. Some Guamanians sit in their backyards shooting off guns and either the Guam Hilton or the Pacific Star Hotel has a fireworks display.

The Guam Visitors Bureau publishes a free calendar of events, including fiesta dates, which is updated quarterly.

Fiestas Nowhere is the Spanish influence so evident as in Guam's Catholic traditions, particularly in its fiestas and celebrations.

Each village's annual fiesta honouring its patron saint is a community affair with feasting, games, music, traditional mass and a parade around the village with the statue of their saint.

Fiestas are celebrated on the weekend closest to the saint's feast day so the dates vary slightly each year. If you're lucky enough to be in Guam during fiesta time, it's worth checking out. The idea is to attract as many people as possible to the festivities, so everyone is welcome.

Fiestas are held in the following places:

January
    Asan, Tumon, Chalan Pago
February
    Yigo, Mongmong
March
    Inarajan
April
    Barrigada, Merizo
May
    Inarajan, Malojloj
June
    Tamuning, Toto, Ordot
July
    Agat, Nimitz Beach, Tamuning
August
    Piti, Barrigada, Agat
September
    Agana, Canada, Talofofo
October
    Mangilao, Yona, Umatac, Sinajana
November
    Agana Heights
December
    Dededo, Agana, Santa Rita

Orientation

The airport is in Tamuning about a mile up from Route 1, which is also called Marine Drive. From the intersection of the airport road and Route 1, Agana centre is to the left. Tumon Bay, Guam's main resort area, is immediately below you, though you must first turn onto Route 1 (either way) before heading down to the bay.

The four-mile stretch of Marine Drive from Tamuning to Agana has four-lane roads that get jammed with rush hour traffic. The ever-present road construction and detours compound the congestion.

A 50-mile road circles the lower half of the island, which is the most scenic and historic part of Guam.

Most of the driving around Guam is on excellent paved roads, but tourist attractions are often poorly marked and street signs are scarce. It's more common to see signs pointing the way to 'Maria's Christening Party' or 'Roasting Pigs 4 Sale' than to a viewpoint or village.

Information

Most of Guam's main tourist and business facilities are centred in the adjacent areas of Tumon, Tamuning and Agana.

The Guam Visitors Bureau (☎ 646-5278) on San Vitores Rd in Tumon has free brochures and maps. Be sure to ask for the detailed highway map put out by the Department of Public Works.

Guam Now is a free bilingual promo booklet with restaurant and entertainment listings, airline schedules and a calendar of events. It can be found at the larger hotels.

The *Guam USO Handbook* is another free booklet with feature articles and useful information about Guam, though it's geared more toward newly arrived GIs than tourists. You can pick one up at the USO in Piti.

Guam has two newspapers, the *Pacific Daily News* and the *Guam Tribune*, as well as several weekly and monthly publications.

Money Bank of Guam, Bank of Hawaii and First Hawaiian Bank are the biggest banks and together have about 30 branches around Guam. Banking hours are 9 am to 3 pm Monday to Thursday, to 6 pm on Fridays. Credit cards are widely accepted all around Guam.

Post All mail sent to Guam c/o General Delivery (even mail marked Agana) is delivered to the less-than-central Barrigada post office and can be picked up between 9 am and 5 pm Monday to Friday and from 1 to 4 pm on Saturdays. Mail should be addressed to General Delivery GMF, Barrigada, Guam 96921.

There are also post offices in central Agana on Chalan Santo Papa and in Tamuning behind the ITC Building. You can get inexpensive boxes and padded envelopes useful for mailing things home at any of the post offices.

Telephone International calls can be made from hotels or via pay phones using a credit card. There are two companies, IT&E (☎ 013) and RCA/MCI (☎ 472-2228). Calls to Australia, Canada and Hong Kong cost $2.50 per minute. Three-minute calls cost $2.40 to the Marianas and $11.25 to Palau, the Marshalls or the FSM. Calls to the USA cost 95 cents to $1.25 per minute depending on the time of day. It's possible to dial direct, without operator assistance; see the pink pages in the front of the phone book for instructions and detailed rate information.

Consulates Four nations maintain consulate offices in Guam. Their addresses are:

Japan
    6th Floor, ITC Building, Route 1, Tamuning (☎ 646-5220)
The Philippines
    4th Floor, ITC Building, Tamuning (☎ 646-4620)
Republic of Korea
    305 GCIC Building, opposite Agana Marina (☎ 472-6488)
Nauru
    Pacific Star Hotel, Tumon (☎ 649-8300)

Art Galleries Guam has three art galleries with changing exhibits. The gallery in the Bank of Guam, at the corner of Route 4 and Chalan Santo Papa in Agana, is open from 10 am to 3 pm Monday to Friday.

The ISLA Center for the Arts at the University of Guam is open from noon to 6 pm weekdays, and to 9 pm on Thursdays.

The CAHA Gallery (☎ 472-7413) in Maite, operated by the Guam Council on

Arts and Humanities Agency, is open from 8 am to 5 pm Monday to Friday and from 11 am to 2 pm on Saturday.

In addition, Guam has a new law requiring most government buildings and hotel developments to spend 1% of new construction or renovation costs on local artwork, which should give a considerable boost to Guamanian art around the island.

Libraries The Agana public library (☎ 472-6417), on the corner of Route 4 and West O'Brien Drive, is open from 9.30 am to 6 pm or later on weekdays, from 10 am to 4 pm on Saturdays and from noon to 4 pm on Sundays. There are other public libraries in Barrigada, Dededo, Agat and Merizo. The University of Guam has a good general library in addition to the collection in its Micronesian Area Research Center.

Bookshops Faith Book Store in the Agana Shopping Center has a good selection of books on Guam and Micronesia.

Airlines Some airlines, including Continental Air Micronesia, centre their customer services at the airport. Japan Air Lines has an office on the 1st floor of the ITC Building in Tamuning and Korean Airlines is on Route 1 in Tamuning.

Continental Air Micronesia – ☎ 646-0220
Japan Air Lines – ☎ 646-9195
Korean Airlines – ☎ 649-9682
Northwest Orient – ☎ 477-7811
All Nippon Airways – ☎ 646-9057

Emergencies For police or fire emergencies, dial 911. The Guam Memorial Hospital (☎ 646-5801) is in Tamuning, at the west end of Tumon. Divers with the bends are sent to the SRF Guam Recompression Chamber (☎ 339-7143).

Activities

Diving Guam has a rich marine habitat with more than 800 species of fish and 300 species of coral.

There are a couple of dozen popular dive spots on the west coast alone, many in or south of Apra Harbor. One of the best known, for advanced divers, is the Blue Hole at the end of Orote Peninsula. At about 60 feet a perpendicular hole in the reef can be descended by divers in a free fall. At about 130 feet there's a window that allows divers to exit. The area is known for its large fish and sea fans, and has good visibility.

One of the more unusual dives is to the *Tokai Maru*, a Japanese freighter bombed during WW II. It sank and landed on top of the *Cormoran*, a German cruiser scuttled during WW I, which is resting upside down on the ocean floor. At about 95 feet you can have one hand on each war.

Dive Shops The *Micronesian Divers Association*, Box 24991 GMF, Guam 96921 has its main shop on Route 2 in Agat (☎ 565-2656), with other locations in Tumon (☎ 649-9870) and Yigo (☎ 653-1665). Full-day diving (two dives and snorkelling) costs $85 including lunch and hotel transfers. Snorkellers are charged $50 and an introductory scuba dive for the non-certified costs $95. They can also arrange Snuba outings, a kind of scuba diving for snorkellers using long air hoses attached to a tank on a raft.

Guam Divers (☎ 477-2774), Box 3361, Agana, Guam 96910 is on Marine Drive opposite Ace Hardware. Two boat dives cost $85 and two daytime beach dives or one night dive costs $65. They provide free pick-up and drop off, and rent snorkel gear for $10.

Papalagi Divers (☎ 472-3232), 110 West Soledad, Agana, Guam 96910, on the corner of Marine Drive and Route 4, has similar rates and caters almost exclusively to Japanese divers. Snorkel gear rents for $7.50.

Nautical Charts The Coral Reef Marine Center (☎ 646-4895), behind the ITC building and the Tamuning Post Office sells US Defense Department nautical charts and maps for all parts of Micronesia. Coral Reef also sells and services dive and marine equipment.

Swimming The best swimming conditions are usually along the west coast, with the greater Tumon Bay area having some of the busiest beaches. There are no fees to use Guam's beaches or any of the island's 20 beach parks, many of which have showers, toilets and picnic tables. Before entering the water, check for jellyfish that occasionally float in, especially during trade wind months.

There's also a large public swimming pool in Agana (☎ 472-8718) opposite the Agana Shopping Center. It's open from 11 am to 8.30 pm weekdays, from 11 am to 7.30 pm on weekends, and admission is free.

Surfing In Guam it's best between December and June. Beginners might prefer to start off at Talofofo Bay, while the more experienced surf the channel at Agana Marina.

The Marianas Yacht Club, Box 2297, Agana 96910, at Apra Harbor sponsors several races throughout the year. These include the Guam-Japan Goodwill Regatta in February, the Round the Island Race in April, and the Rota and Return Race on Memorial Day weekend. The club also has information about charter boats and sailing lessons.

Tumon Bay hotels and shops rent paddle boats, outrigger canoes, snorkelling gear, inflatable rafts, windsurfing gear and other water sports equipment.

Windsurfing This is popular in Tumon Bay and around Merizo. Cocos Lagoon, between Merizo and Cocos Island, is also a popular place for water skiing, snorkelling, diving and other water sports.

Fishing Deep sea fishing boats leave from Agana Marina, Apra Harbor and Merizo Pier on the search for marlin, wahoo, yellowfin tuna, sailfish, barracuda and mahi-mahi. A 1153-pound Pacific blue marlin, caught off Ritidian Point by a Guamanian in 1969, broke the world record at the time.

For information on the Marianas Fishing Derby held in late July write to the Guam Fishing & Boating Association, Box 24023 GMF, Guam 96921.

Submarine Atlantis Submarine (☎ 477-4166) runs 10 dives a day to Gab Gab Reef II in Apra Harbor. The 65-foot sub carries 46 passengers and has 26 viewport windows. Dives last about 45 minutes and range from about 40 to 80 feet in depth. Rates are $85 for adults, $50 for children ages four to 12, and they include hotel pick-up.

Hiking, Cycling & Running The USO in Piti (☎ 333-2022) sponsors 'boonie stomps' around Guam every Saturday and if you're at the USO by 12.30 pm and have $1 you can go along. They usually return by 5 pm. The location and difficulty of each week's hike is written up in a monthly schedule that can be picked up at the USO (or call and ask). These folks know their hikes well, making this a great way to explore the backwoods of Guam. They also get to hike into some interesting wilderness areas under military control which are normally off-limits.

The Athlete's Foot (☎ 472-1514), in the Agana Shopping Center, has information on the Guam Running Club and upcoming road races.

The bicycling club (☎ 477-9711; ask for the sports department) meets for rides on the first Sunday of the month and sponsors a number of races.

Organised Tours A score of tour companies provide all sorts of tour options, though most are in Japanese only. Discover Guam (☎ 649-8687),Box 2860, Agana, Guam 96910, is a local company that has tours for English-speaking visitors, including a half-day island sightseeing tour for $35.

For something different, there's the Adventure River Cruise (☎ 646-1710) on a catamaran-style riverboat which goes up the Talofofo River and visits an ancient latte stone site where craft demonstrations are given. The trip costs $47 for tourists and apparently $15 for locals.

AGANA

The capital city of Agana (pronounced a-GHAN-nya) has been the centre of Guam since the Spanish period. With its parks and historic sites it's a pleasant place to spend an afternoon. If you have a car, it's easier to park in the public lot by the museum and visit many of the sites on foot rather than deal with the traffic.

Plaza de Espana

Plaza de Espana, in the heart of Agana, is a peaceful refuge of Spanish-style buildings, old stone walls and flowering trees.

The plaza was the seat of Spanish administration from 1669 and the centre of religious, government and cultural activities. Buildings once completely surrounded the central park area and included schools, a hospital, priests' quarters, governor's residence, military compound, arsenal and town hall. Most of the buildings were constructed of ifil wood and a concoction of lime mortar and coral called *manposteria*. They were roofed with clay tiles. Only a few of the

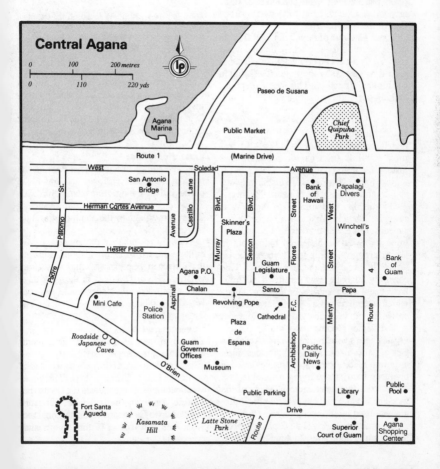

Central Agana

buildings survived the US pre-invasion bombings in July 1944.

The Garden House, now the site of the Guam Museum, formerly served as a storage shed and servants' quarters.

The Chocolate House, the small white circular building with the pointed tile roof, was where the wives of Spanish governors served hot chocolate to their guests.

All that remains of Casa Gobierno, the Governor's Palace, is the raised, open-air terrace (west of the Chocolate House) called the Azotea. The small pavilion in the centre of the plaza is the Kiosko and the three stone arches, which date from 1736, were part of the Almacen, or arsenal.

There's a statue of Pope John Paul II north of the plaza on the site where he held Mass in 1981. Don't get disoriented if you find that each time you go by the statue it's facing in a different direction. This pope revolves, making one complete turn every 24 hours.

Guam Museum

Guam's small museum (☎ 477-8320) features exhibits on Chamorro culture and history, including pottery and other archaeological finds. There are also displays of sea shells and other aspects of natural history.

One display is dedicated to the WW II straggler Shoichi Yokoi, a sergeant in the Japanese army, who was discovered and captured in 1972. He had been hiding out in Guam's rugged interior for 28 years because no one had told him the war was over. One can only imagine how confused he must have been when he was brought to Agana which is cluttered with signs in Japanese and crowded with busloads of Japanese tourists!

The display records Yokoi's talent for survival. There's a skilfully woven jacket and a pair of pants made from wild hibiscus fibre, a rat trap made from wire (rat liver was his favourite food) and a frying pan cut from a discarded army water canteen. Many of the foods he ate and tools he made were similar to those used by the ancient Chamorros.

The museum, in Plaza de Espana, is open from 9 am to noon and 1 to 4 pm Monday to Saturday. Admission is $1 for adults, free for children under 12.

Dulce Nombre de Maria Cathedral

The cathedral in the Plaza de Espana was first built in 1669, although the current building dates from 1955. Chief Quipuha and other Chamorro chiefs and church leaders are buried beneath the floor.

Above the main altar is a 12-inch statue of Santa Marian Camarin, which is carved of ironwood and has natural hair and a face made of ivory.

Local lore says that it was found off the waters of Merizo in the early 1800s by a fisherman who watched as the figurine was guided to shore by two gold crabs, each with a lighted candle between its claws.

The church is the main scene of activity during Agana's two annual fiestas, honouring the 'Sweet Name of Mary' in early September and the 'Feast of the Immaculate Conception' on 8 December.

Latte Stone Park

The latte stones in Latte Stone Park, at the base of Kasamata Hill, are thought to be house pillars dating from about 500 AD. They were moved to this site from an ancient Chamorro village in the south-central interior of Guam.

There are a number of Japanese caves, built by forced Chamorro labour, dug into the hillface in the park and further west along O'Brien Drive. The ones in the park have been reinforced with cinder blocks and converted into fallout shelters.

Government House

The governor's residence, called Government House, is a Spanish-style building built in 1952 on Kasamata Hill, one-third of a mile up Route 7 from O'Brien Drive. There's an excellent view of Agana from the lawn at the rear. If you're on foot, it takes about 10 minutes up to Government House from Latte Stone Park, and another 10 minutes to nearby Fort Santa Agueda.

Fort Santa Agueda

All that remains of Fort Santa Agueda is part of its stone foundation, built of coral and burnt limestone. The fort, which once had 10 cannons, was built in 1800 as a lookout, which is the best reason to visit it now – the view of Agana and the turquoise bay can't be beaten!

This is also the site of Guam's first mission, established in 1668, though nothing remains to be seen. The fort is at the end of the first road on the right after heading uphill from Government House.

Skinner's Plaza

Guam's first civilian governor, Carlton Skinner, lends his name to this neglected park that contains a few vandalised memorials to Guam's war heroes. The most interesting is a bust of General Douglas MacArthur, complete with snazzy green sunglasses, but minus his trademark pipe, which has been stolen.

San Antonio Bridge

The San Antonio Bridge, also known as the 'Old Spanish Bridge' or *To lai Achu*, was built of cut stone in 1800 to cross the Agana River which had been diverted to this location. The river was filled in after WW II and the bridge now spans just a stagnant pool, though the park-like setting with colourful flame trees is quite pretty. A stone plaque on the bridge honours St Anthony of Padua.

In front of the bridge, beside the pool, is a statue of the mermaid Sirena.

According to legend Sirena was a young girl of Agana who went swimming instead of gathering coconut shells as her mother had asked. When she didn't return on time the mother cursed her daughter saying, 'If the water gives Sirena so much pleasure I hope she turns into a fish!' Sirena's godmother intervened in time to say, 'Let the part that has been given to me by God remain human.' Sirena thus became a mermaid – half fish, half human.

Paseo de Susana

Paseo de Susana, the peninsula north of central Agana, was built during the reconstruction of the city after WW II by bulldozing all the rubble and debris of Agana to this area.

The Public Market with its food stalls and flea market is close to Marine Drive and behind it is the baseball stadium used by Guam's major league teams. The stadium is also where the Yomiuri Giants, a top Japanese major league baseball team, trains each January. The Agana Marina (also called the Agana Boat Basin) is along the west side of the park. At the park's northern tip there's a tacky miniature replica of the Statue of Liberty and beyond that a breakwater where you can walk out and watch local surfers challenge the waves.

In the south-east section of the park, a statue of Chief Quipuha stands forever condemned to survey Agana's congested traffic on Marine Drive. Quipuha was Agana's highest ranking chief when the first mission was built on Guam and he was the first Chamorro adult to be baptised. Quipuha donated the land for Guam's first Catholic church, the site of the present Dulce Nombre de Maria Cathedral.

TUMON BAY & POINTS NORTH

Tumon is the tourist centre of Guam, jammed with hotels, nightclubs, restaurants, souvenir shops and all the usual trappings of resort life.

Ypao (Ipao) Beach Park

Ypao Beach is a large public beach park in the midst of the resort hotels. It was once an ancient Chamorro village and in the late 1800s was the site of a penal and leper colony.

The park has an expansive beachfront with white sand and turquoise waters and is a popular place for local families and other picnickers.

Zoo

Jimmy Cushing runs a small funky zoo and aquarium on Tumon Bay, opposite the Church of the Blessed Diego. Tourists largely bypass it, as it's geared more towards local kids, but it's a good place to see animals from around the islands, including a nine-

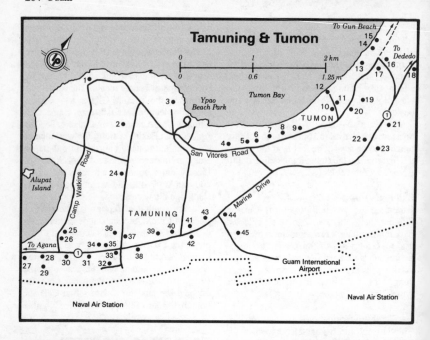

Tamuning & Tumon

Tumon Bay

Ypao
Beach Park

TUMON

San Vitores Road

Alupat
Island

Camp Watkins Road

Marine Drive

TAMUNING

To Agana

Guam International
Airport

Naval Air Station

Naval Air Station

To Gun Beach

To
Dededo

foot saltwater crocodile from Palau, brown tree snakes, monitor lizards, coconut crabs, Guam deer, small sharks, moray eels, tropical fish, a variety of birds and the largest carabao in Micronesia. It's open from 10 am to 5 pm daily. Admission costs $1.50 for adults, 75 cents for children.

Gun Beach

Gun Beach is one-third of a mile down the washed-out but passable coral road that goes by the new Hotel Nikko. It's named for the rusted Japanese gun that is half-hidden in jungle growth at the foot of the northside cliff, behind the remains of a pillbox.

From the beach, there's a cut in the reef that was made for the placement of underwater cables. It's convenient for divers and snorkellers who can follow the cable run out to deeper waters, where conditions are quite good when the surf's not up.

The sand at Gun Beach is largely com-

prised of tiny orange grains with little star-shaped points. Known as star sand, it's actually the calcium carbonate shells of a common protozoan found on Guam's reefs.

Gun Beach is OK but past the gun and around the point to the north is an even nicer crescent of white sand. At low tide it's possible to wade right around or at high tide you can swim or snorkel. There was once an old Chamorro village in this area and latte stones can be found by following an overgrown trail heading inland.

Two Lovers Point

Two Lovers Point, or Puntan Dos Amantes, is at the top of a 410-foot cliff just north of Tumon Bay.

Heading north on Route 1 toward Dededo, turn left on the road across from the Micronesia Mall, continue down past a golf driving range and turn left at a little green cinder-block building. Beware of the unmarked speed bumps as you drive down to the point!

1	Guam Memorial Hospital
2	Guam Greyhound Track
3	Guam Hilton
4	Pacific Islands Club
5	Pacific Star Hotel
6	National Car Rental
7	Guam Dai-Ichi Hotel
8	Sotetsu Tropicana Hotel
9	Zoo
10	Fujita Tumon Beach Hotel
11	Terraza Tumon Villa Hotel
12	Beach House
13	Guam Reef Hotel
14	Guam Hotel Okura
15	Hotel Nikko
16	Hotel Sun Route Guam
17	Guam Plaza Hotel
18	Guam Horizon Hotel
19	Guam Visitors Bureau
20	Micronesian Divers Association
21	Laundromat
22	St John's School
23	Pagoda Hotel
24	Golden Motel
25	Lights Disco
26	Sub Station II
27	Tamuning Plaza Hotel
28	Ben Franklin department store
29	Mid-Town Hotel
30	Pizza Hut
31	Taco Bell
32	Tamuning Post Office
33	TC Building
34	Marty's Mexican Restaurant
35	Shakey's Pizza
36	Gibson's shopping centre
37	Marianas Trench
38	Hafa Adai Exchange
39	Denny's Restaurant
40	Winchell's Doughnut Shop
41	Korean Airlines
42	Hafa Adai Motel
43	McDonald's
44	Exxon petrol/Thrifty Car Rental
45	Hotel Mai'Ana

As the story goes, two young Chamorro lovers entwined their hair and jumped to their deaths from the jagged limestone cliff while being hunted down by the Spanish captain who had been promised the girl in marriage. A giant gilt statue on this site that graphically showed the two lovers entwining more than just their hair was knocked down by a typhoon, but a new recast is on the way.

The top of the cliff is a good vantage point for views of Tumon Bay and the coral gardens below. Another attraction at the point is a very deep basalt cave which drops down to the ocean. It's enclosed by protective fencing but you can look down into it.

Northern Beaches

Two of Guam's best beaches are Tarague Beach and Uruno Beach, on the northern tip of the island. However, although these beaches are public the only land access to them is through Andersen Air Force Base and without a visitor's pass non-military types can't get to them. On the other hand if you approach from the sea you're allowed to land.

One of the few stretches of northern coastline with public access is Tanguisson Beach, also known as NCS Beach. To get there, take the turn-off from Route 1 towards Two Lovers Point but instead of taking the final turn-off to the point follow the paved but potholed road past the sewage treatment plant. When the road forks, bear left and wind down to the shore. Tanguisson is a popular place for local picnics but a huge power plant at the south end of the beach mars the view. There are pit toilets and outdoor showers, but no changing rooms.

Heading north from Tanguisson Beach there's a dirt road that runs parallel to the ocean which you can drive at least part way down, though how far depends on recent rain and road conditions. You could also park at Tanguisson Beach and walk, which is probably safer for your car. There are good sandy beaches along the way. The final one, which is about two miles north of Tanguisson and is called Shark's Hole, has a turquoise hole with very good snorkelling. There are two channels into the hole so beware of currents.

South Pacific Memorial Park

This park in Yigo is a memorial site for those who died during WW II. The main monument is a 15-foot abstract sculpture of large white hands folded in prayer, which is surrounded by personalised memorial plaques in Japanese script. A small chapel called the

Queen of Peace is staffed by Japanese priests and nuns.

Steps lead down the hill from the monument to four caves which served as the last Japanese Army command post. On 11 August 1944 American soldiers detonated 400-pound blocks of TNT at the opening of the caves. When the caves were reopened a few days later more than 60 bodies were removed, including that of the Japanese commander, Lieutenant General Hideyoshi Obata, who had taken his own life. The caves are surrounded by a bamboo forest which creaks in the wind and is spooky enough to conjure up images of restless spirits.

The park, on Route 1 in Yigo, is open from 8 am to 5 pm daily.

University of Guam

The University of Guam, which is in Mangilao on the east coast, offers both undergraduate and graduate programmes. It is noted for its work in marine biology. The university's Micronesian Area Research Center (☎ 734-2921) has an excellent collection of books, maps and documents on the Pacific region and the library staff are very helpful if you're interested in research.

Guam's two-year community college is just to the north of the university.

SOUTHERN GUAM

If you had only one full day on Guam, you couldn't do better than to rent a car, circle the southern part of the island and take time to stroll through historic sites and catch the scenery along the way. Southern villages such as Umatac and Inarajan give a glimpse of a more rural Guam whose character remains unaffected by tourism.

If you start in Agana and go down the west coast in the morning and up the east coast in the afternoon you'll keep the sun at your back for photography and views.

GovGuam at Adelup Point

South of Agana on the western coastal road is Adelup Point, site of the attractive new Spanish-style government administration offices. From the east side of the complex

there's a little beach park with picnic tables and a broad view of Agana Bay and on the west side there's a very small sand beach with protected waters.

Route 6 Side Trip

At another time you might want to take the five-mile Route 6 loop from Adelup Point through the Nimitz Hill area to Piti. You'll get some views of the west coast as well as glimpses into the island's interior.

About 1½ miles up Route 6 there are two bunkers in the hillside, visible on the right side of the road, which once served as a Japanese command post. Nimitz Hill, incidentally, takes its name from US Admiral Chester Nimitz, the first Commander of Naval Forces Marianas to take up residence on the hill.

War in the Pacific Park

War in the Pacific National Historical Park has its visitors centre and museum of WW II memorabilia in Asan, almost a mile south of Adelup Point on Route 1.

There are on going presentations in the centre's theatre, including a 12-minute slide show of WW II in the Pacific, which diplomatically presents both the Japanese and American perspectives, and a 30-minute footage film of the American invasion of Guam. You can also request to see anything in the centre's tape library, such as a short film on Guam's brown tree snakes, an hour-long film on Chamorro history and culture, or films on environmental issues, natural history and war battles around the Pacific.

The centre is open from 7.30 am to 3.30 pm Monday to Friday and from 8.30 am to 2 pm on weekends. Admission is free, as is a brochure that gives a chronology of the War in the Pacific and maps out the battle sites around Guam.

Seven separate parcels of land that were battlefield sites during WW II are part of the park's historical holdings, but only a couple are currently developed.

The park's Asan Beach Unit includes the visitors centre as well as Asan Point, which is a big grassy beach park a mile further down the road with guns, torpedoes and other war paraphernalia on the grounds. Asan Beach was the site of a major US invasion and just off the beach a couple of landing craft that never made it ashore can be seen at low tide.

Piti Bomb Holes

The Piti bomb holes, which are about 100 yards offshore and within the reef, are ideal for beginner divers as they bottom out at around 30 feet. Seen from Piti Beach they look like dark blue circles surrounded by the aqua shades of shallower water. It's just local lore that the holes are bomb craters – they're actually natural sinkholes.

Snorkellers might enjoy the hard yellow corals around the edges of the holes, but the water is deep enough in the centres to make it difficult to see the bottom. Closer to shore you'll see bright blue starfish, zebra damsels, pufferfish and other small tropicals. If you want to snorkel out to the holes rather than wade, the best time is high tide, as otherwise the nearshore waters can be quite shallow. Watch out for strong currents around the holes furthest out.

The parking area is on the right about one-quarter of a mile after Asan Point, across the street from a metal warehouse.

Piti Guns

On a hill behind the Catholic church in Piti are three Japanese coastal defence guns, now part of the War in the Pacific National Historical Park holdings.

To get there, turn left off Route 1 just past the Mobil Station in Piti and at the stop sign turn right onto Assumption St. Park under the big monkeypod tree to the left of the church social hall, the building with the white cross on the front, and walk up the concrete steps leading uphill. The path is fairly well defined, although slightly overgrown with hibiscus bushes. It's only a few minutes up to the first gun, which is amazingly well preserved.

Apra Harbor & Beaches

Apra Harbor, Guam's huge deepwater harbour, was called San Luis de Apra by the Spanish who developed it in the 1700s for the Manila galleon trade.

The US Naval Station encompasses all of the land surrounding Apra Harbor, including Orote Peninsula to the south. In addition to home-ported US Navy vessels, Apra Harbor has extensive commercial operations, a small boat harbour and space for cruise ships. The harbour also contains a number of sunken ships which makes it a popular diving spot.

There are good beaches and reefs out on the Glass Breakwater, which encloses the north side of Apra Harbor. This long and thin artificial extension of Cabras Island is named after Captain Glass who took Guam for the USA in 1898. To get there, turn right off Route 1 at the USO in Piti, go straight past the commercial port and take the upper road at the right, just past the oil tanks. From this point you can usually drive right out on the breakwater, although the road is sometimes so rutted that it takes a 4WD vehicle. Also, when US Navy ships come in to port this area is sometimes closed for security reasons.

About halfway out the breakwater, look for a grove of trees on the left side of the road, from where you can climb down to a nice

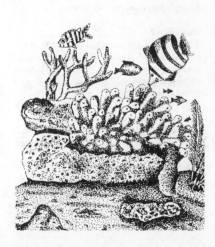

sandy harbourside beach called Family Beach.

Dogleg Reef, just to the right of Family Beach, is a good place for snorkellers to see both soft and hard corals as well as anemone colonies with clownfish. The waters are protected and the top of the reef, which starts just two to three feet underwater, is clearly visible from shore.

When the seas are calm, Luminao Reef, which stretches along the north side of the breakwater, can also be snorkelled. It has good coral and small fish in waters five to 15 feet deep and can be accessed in several places along the road by paths leading down to the water. Don't leave valuables in your car anywhere on the breakwater.

Back on Route 1, an artificial (we hope!) Polaris missile guards the entrance to Polaris Point, part of the naval station.

To continue south around the island, turn left at the traffic lights just past the US Army Reserve Center. This is not well marked and if you miss the turn you'll wind up at a guarded US Navy gate. South of the harbour, Route 1 becomes 2A, then 2 and later 4.

The bright yellow flowers growing tall along the roadside are *Cassia alata*, more commonly called golden candles, and the pink flowers winding amongst the trees are known as chain of love, as each tiny flower on the vine is shaped like a heart.

Gaan Point

The park at Gaan Point, on Route 2 in Agat, marks the site of the WW II invasion of southern Guam, where US marine and army combat divisions came ashore to battle with the Japanese infantry.

From their coastal caves and pillboxes the Japanese easily cut down the Americans in their landing crafts, until US tanks made it ashore and managed to knock the Japanese out from behind.

Known also as the War in the Pacific National Historical Park's Agat Unit, Gaan Point has a large 20 cm naval coastal defence gun, an anti-aircraft cannon and intact bunkers that can be explored. The park flies the flags of Guam, the US and Japan.

There's an American WW II amtrac underwater about 400 yards out and 50 feet down, popular with divers.

Much of the reef off the Agat area can be snorkelled or dived. Agat is also the site of a new small boat marina, Nimitz Beach Park and the Taleyfac Bridge.

Taleyfac Bridge

In the late 1700s the Spanish built a bullcart coastal road to link Agana with Umatac and other southern villages. The road, known as the Camino del Real, was connected by several stone bridges.

The best preserved bridge is in Agat at Taleyfac (Tailafak), just a little beyond Nimitz Beach Park, on the ocean side of the road. It's a few hundred feet back from Route 2 and easy to miss, as only a small roadside tourist sign marks the spot. Built in 1785, the bridge has twin stone arches that picturesquely span a small stream.

Southern Coastline Trail

Where the road rises and begins to wind away from the shore you enter the Territorial Seashore Park. The whole southern highway is being widened and reconstructed, so some of the directions that follow may be slightly affected.

Two miles from Taleyfac Bridge a sign reading 'Southern Coastline Trail' marks the start of a well-defined red clay path down to Sella Bay. The whole walk is wonderfully scenic but watch out for slippery mud and sword grasses that can cut. An old Spanish bridge crosses the Sella River close to the coast. Give yourself about 1½ hours to make the hike down and back.

Some people prefer to make a day of it, continuing south from Sella Bay along the shore to Cetti Bay and then up the Cetti River Valley. The valley dead-ends at Cetti Falls, but before that point there's a trail to the left that goes up to the main road.

Cetti Bay Vista Point

The best roadside vista on the south-west coast is at the Cetti Bay Vista Point. It's just a two-minute walk up the steps to the lookout, which offers a commanding view of the palm-lined Cetti River Valley and picturesque Cetti Bay. You can also see Cocos Island, the Merizo Barrier Reef which encloses Cocos Lagoon and the whole southwest coastline.

Mt Lamlam & Mt Jumullong Manglo

Inland from the Cetti Bay Vista Point and topped with large wooden crosses is Mt Jumullong Manglo, or Humuyung Manglu, the final destination of cross-bearers during the annual Good Friday procession.

The starting point for a trail that goes up the 1282-foot Mt Jumullong Manglo is across the road from the Cetti Bay Vista Point. You begin by heading up an eroded hill and continue along the mostly well-defined trail. At the divide, go to the right to get to the crosses. There are excellent views of both the coast and the interior forests on the way and the hike should take about an hour. A more difficult and more obscure trail continues left from the divide to the 1332-foot Mt Lamlam, Guam's highest point. Lamlam means 'lightning' and legends call it the source of the winds.

Memorial Vista

I Memorias Para I Lalahita Vista Point, a Vietnam War memorial about one mile north of Umatac, is marked by two garish blue and white cement latte pillars. Within the small park are two real latte stones as well as a good view of the surrounding mountains and valleys and of Umatac below.

Umatac

Umatac is an unspoiled, friendly village, steeped in history.

Magellan's 1521 landing in Umatac Bay is celebrated in the village each March with four days of activities, including a re-enactment of the event. There's a white concrete monument to Magellan in the village centre and a mural of Chamorros watching Magellan's ships sail into the bay painted on a stage behind the mayor's office.

The Spanish used Umatac Bay for more than 200 years as a major port of call for their

galleons, though little remains of the four forts that once protected the bay.

Opposite the Magellan monument are the ruins of the Saint Dionicio Church, which was originally built in the 1690s, reconstructed in 1862 and destroyed by an earthquake in 1902. Bougainvillea, the official flower of Guam, surrounds the carved stone pillars of the old church.

In Chamorro, bougainvillea is called *puti tai nobiu* which means 'it hurts not to have a sweetheart'.

The rusting skeleton of a Japanese midget submarine used to be visible offshore at the river mouth but it's now buried under the sand bar. There's a Japanese Zero in the bay about 150 yards from the beach and 50 feet underwater.

On your way out of town you'll see the new Umatac Bridge with its spiral staircase towers that are supposed to symbolise Guam's Chamorro-Spanish heritage.

Fort Soledad

Fort Nuestra Senora de la Soledad offers a spectacular hilltop view of Umatac village and bay as well as the coastline to the north. To get there take the ironwood-lined road on the right after crossing the Umatac Bridge.

The fort was built by Spain in the early 1800s to protect their treasure-laden Manila galleons from pirates roaming the western Pacific. Just about all that remains of the fort is a small hillside sentry post.

If you've got a keen eye you can see the remains of Fort Santo Angel which was built in 1742 on a rock jutting out on the northwest side of the bay.

Merizo

In the courtyard of San Dimas Church, in the village of Merizo, there's a monument to the 46 Chamorros who were executed by the Japanese in the Merizo hills in July 1944, one week before the US invasion.

The Merizo Conbento, next door, was built by the Spanish in 1856, soon after the smallpox epidemic which killed almost two-thirds of the population. The conbento (convent) was constructed of ifil wood and manposteria (burnt limestone mixed with coral rocks) and was still being used as a parish house until it was damaged by Typhoon Russ in December 1990.

Directly across the street is Kampanayun Malessu, the Merizo Bell Tower, built in 1910 under the direction of Father ristobal De Canals. It was restored in 1981.

Route 4 continues to follow the coast around the southern tip of Guam, offering nice coastal views.

Inarajan Pool

Along the roadside is Inarajan (Salugula) Pool, a natural saltwater pool with diving platforms and arched bridges. Jagged grey lava rocks separate the calm pool from the crashing ocean surf beyond making it an interesting place to take a dip.

There are freshwater showers, rest rooms and picnic shelters though unfortunately the site is rather rundown.

Inarajan Village

Inarajan, just down the road from the pool, is another sleepy village with a smattering of Spanish-era influence. Townspeople decorate their lawns with a remarkable assortment of plaster geese, elves and toadstools – à la '50s kitsch!

The body of Chamorro priest Jesus Baza Duenas is buried beneath the Saint Joseph Church. Duenas, his nephew and two other Chamorros were beheaded by the Japanese near the end of war for failing to reveal the whereabouts of US Navy radioman George Tweed who had survived the Japanese occupation in hiding.

Near the end of town is a crumbling concrete Baptist church, built in 1925. Next to it is a sculpture that depicts part of a story told about two powerful Chamorro chiefs, Malaguana of Tumon and Gadao of Inarajan.

It seems that one day Malaguana went by canoe to meet his rival, Gadao, and kill him. When Malaguana got to Inarajan a stranger invited him to dinner but unknown to him, that man was Gadao. When Gadao asked his guest to get a coconut for dinner, Malaguana

shook a coconut tree and the coconuts fell like rain. Gadao then took a coconut and pulverised it with one hand.

After a few more such contests Malaguana became worried – if this common Inarajan man was so strong, what would his chief be like? So Malaguana asked the man to take him back to Tumon by canoe. Both chiefs got in the canoe but paddled in opposite directions. The canoe broke in half but Malaguana, in his urgency to leave, was paddling so fast that he didn't even notice until he was back in Tumon.

The statue shows Gadao paddling his half of the canoe.

Gadao's Cave

From the statue you can see some caves in the cliffs across the bay, not far from the point. One of them is Gadao's Cave and has ancient pictographs said to be the canoe story drawn onto the wall by Gadao himself.

To get there, drive north out of town on Route 4. Just across the bridge take the road to the right, opposite the Papaniyoc Store, and park at the far end of the beach just before the road turns inland.

Walk along the beach and then take the trail across a meadow and up a cliff to the caves. The walk takes about 15 minutes. Some of this land may be private property, so if you see anyone along the way ask their permission to continue.

Talofofo Falls

Talofofo Falls is a two-tier cascade, with pools beneath each fall. There's a 30-foot drop on the top one, though it's usually gentle enough to stand beneath. The deeper and larger pool is at the base of the second fall, where the water flows gently over a very wide rockface. This is a popular swimming and picnicking spot.

To get there, take the marked turn-off to the left about 2½ miles past Inarajan. About 1½ miles down, just before the NASA Tracking Station, turn right onto a dirt road. The falls are about a mile further on.

Talofofo Falls is open from 9 am to 5 pm daily. Admission is $4. You can either park in the lot above the falls and walk from there or brave the steep winding one-lane road down to a lower parking area. If you walk, it will take less than 10 minutes to get down but probably double that to walk back.

Talofofo Beaches

Back on Route 4, Talofofo Bay Beach Park is just ahead. This is one of Guam's prime surfing spots. Guam's longest and widest river, the Talofofo, runs out into the bay and the sand is chocolate brown.

A couple of miles down the road is Ipan Beach Park, another popular swimming place with calmer water and ironwood shade trees.

Pago Bay Vista Point

A viewpoint just past the town of Yona looks over the Pago River as it empties into Pago Bay. The inhabitants of a Spanish village at the mouth of the river were wiped out by the 1856 smallpox epidemic.

The area between Pago Bay on the east coast and Agana Bay on the west is the narrowest part of the island.

According to legend a giant fish who wanted to divide Guam in half used to visit the island and nibble away at this neck of land. Guam was saved by the women of the island who cut off their long hair, wove a big net from their locks and scooped up the fish with the net.

COCOS ISLAND

Cocos Island is three miles offshore from Merizo, within the barrier reef. The left side of Cocos has been developed into a 100-acre resort hotel. The right side, formerly the site of a US Coast Guard station, is a public area and part of the territorial park system. Cocos Island has good beaches and the calm waters of Cocos Lagoon are good for most water sports.

Getting There & Away

The return ferry trip to the resort costs $20 for tourists and $5 for residents of Guam. As long as you're not getting off a tour bus, you should be able to slide by as a local. There's also a $3 landing fee.

Boats go at least once an hour between

5.30 am and 10.30 pm with the heaviest schedule between 9 am and 2 pm. The trip out takes 15 minutes. You can get an idea of where the resort's coming from by its 'No Outside Food or Beverages Allowed on Cocos Island' sign.

To get to the public side you have to hike over from the dock on Cocos or find a private boat from Merizo.

OFFSHORE ISLANDS

About four miles from Merizo, the offshore islands of As-Gadao, Fofos and Agrigan come into view. Although it's possible to wade out to the islands across the coral reef, much of the shoreline is posted 'private property'.

PLACES TO STAY
Camping

Camping information is available from the Department of Parks & Recreation (☎ 477-7825), 490 Chalan Palasyu in Agana Heights. The office is open 8 am to 5 pm weekdays. The staff will sell you a $2.50-per-day camping permit which they say is required; beyond this they seem completely at a loss as to why you might want to camp or which places are safer than others.

The truth is, camping is not that common on Guam. If you do camp it's advisable not to choose a roadside park as there's apt to be a few rowdy drinkers cruising the roads at night. Guam's crime rate is high enough for potential campers to think twice. Camping in a group or in the wilderness shouldn't pose problems.

Cocos Island is one of the 15 approved camping locations in the park system and is one of the more frequently recommended spots.

Hotels

The majority of Guam's 6000 hotel rooms are in the high-rises lining Tumon Bay. These resorts are geared for Japanese package tourists and are generally not a good value for independent travellers, who end up paying high rack rates.

It can be difficult booking a room in

Guam, particularly during Japanese vacation and honeymoon times from late-December to early March and from June to September. Generally the farther you go from Tumon Bay, the easier it gets to find a room.

The good news is that the last few years has seen the construction of a handful of less expensive locally owned hotels. These often bill themselves as business-oriented or family-style, and for the most part don't get as heavily booked during the holiday crunch times. Some of the best deals can be found on Route 8, just outside Agana centre.

Except where noted all rooms have aircon, private bathrooms and a 13% room tax.

Hotels – bottom end *Pagoda Hotel* (☎ 646-1882), Box 4285, Agana, Guam 96910, in Upper Tumon, opposite St John's School on Route 1, has 41 rooms that are tiny, but clean and sufficiently comfortable. They have TVs, refrigerators and phones and cost $45 for a single or double. There's free morning coffee. The Pagoda is quite popular and a good value for the Tumon area.

The new *Maite Garden Hotel* (☎ 477-0822), Box 2925, Agana, Guam 96910, is a modern, 48-room hotel, 1¼ miles up Route 8 from its intersection with Route 1. The rooms are tastefully furnished and have soft carpeting, phones, TVs and refrigerators. There's also a small swimming pool. It's a bit out of the way, across from the Naval Air Station, but rooms are half the price of what you'd pay for similar quality in Tumon. Singles/doubles cost $45/55.

The *Plumeria Garden Hotel* (☎ 472-8831), Box 7220, Tamuning, Guam 96911 is on Route 8 in Maite, one-quarter of a mile up from Route 1. The 78-room hotel is of modern, cinder-block construction, built motel style. Rooms are comfortable and have TVs and phones. There's a large swimming pool and free coffee and doughnuts in the morning. This is a popular place with repeat business travellers. Singles/doubles cost $45/50.

The *Kina Court Hotel/Motel* (☎ 477-1261), Box 804, Agana, Guam 96910 in Barrigada is a converted three-storey apart-ment building. The 31 units each have a full kitchen, dining area, phone and cable TV with HBO movies. There's free morning coffee and newspapers, a coin laundromat and a swimming pool. Rates are $45 for studios, $49 for one-bedroom units and $55 for two-bedroom units. This is a good value if you're tired of cramped hotel rooms or want to do some cooking but a major drawback is aeroplane noise as the hotel is directly above the airport. From Route 1, go 1½ miles up Route 8 to the second traffic light and turn right onto Route 33 (Toto-Canada Rd). Kina Court is on the first corner.

Guam Garden Villa (☎ 477-8166), Mrs Herta Laguana, Box 10167, Sinajana, Guam 96926, is a pleasant B&B in a family setting in Ordot, about three miles from Agana. The house is large, with a porch and garden, and has three guest rooms with a shared bathroom. The rate is $35/45 for singles/doubles, including a hearty breakfast. Mrs Laguana can provide airport transfers for $10 each way and the public bus stops infrequently nearby, but overall it could be inconvenient without a car.

The 18-room *Golden Motel* (☎ 646-9118), Box 10328, Tamuning, Guam 96911, in Tamuning promotes itself as a romantic hotel, which means, among other things, that you can pay by the hour. Overnight rates are $45 for rooms with one double bed or $55 for the VIP room with a round double bed, a jacuzzi and two drinks.

The *Mid-Town Hotel* (☎ 649-9882), Box 1263, Agana, Guam 96910, behind the Ben Franklin department store, has rooms with refrigerators, phones, TVs, orange satiny bedspreads, full-wall mirrors and old carpeting. It's overpriced at $45/55 for singles/doubles.

The *Hafa Adai Motel* (☎ 646-6542), on Route 1 in Tamuning, has boxy, cheerless rooms that cost $40 for singles or doubles.

The *International Marina Hotel* (☎ 477-7836), 470 West Soledad Ave, Agana, Guam 96910, formerly the Downtown Hotel, is an aging, overpriced business hotel near the centre of Agana. The 44 rooms have TVs, phones and refrigerators. Singles/doubles cost $48 for regular rooms, $55 for VIP rooms. Apparently the difference is that in the regular rooms the air-con is on low and in the VIP rooms it's really cold!

Hotels – middle The *Terraza Tumon Villa Hotel* (☎ 646-6904), Box 8588, Tamuning, Guam 96911 is an older three-storey hotel with just 20 rooms. Though it's none too spiffy it's adequate and is the cheapest place near the beach at Tumon Bay. Rooms have TVs and refrigerators and cost $60 for singles or doubles.

The new *Tamuning Plaza Hotel* (☎ 649-8646), Box 2925, Agana, Guam 96910, near the Ben Franklin department store in Tamuning, has 40 very large rooms, each with refrigerator, TV and two full beds. It's operated by the same people who own the Maite Garden Hotel and, like the Maite, has friendly management. Rates are $65 for singles or doubles.

The 26-room *Cliff Hotel* (☎ 477-7675), 178 Francisco Javier Drive, Agana Heights, Guam 96910, built in 1975, is one of Guam's oldest hotels and caters to businesspeople. It's on a cliffside location, with views of Agana below. Rooms have tables, TVs, phones and small verandas. There's a swimming pool, tennis and racquetball courts and a health club. Rooms start at $70/75 for singles/doubles.

The *Cliff Condo Guest House* (☎ 477-7276), 178 Francisco Javier Drive, Agana Heights, Guam 96910, has 31 privately owned condo units in the same building as the Cliff Hotel. Rates start at $55/90 for singles/doubles for a room without kitchen and go up to $135 for a three-bedroom unit with kitchen.

The *Guam Horizon Hotel* (☎ 646-6851), Box 8349, Tamuning, Guam 96911, on Route 1 above Tumon Bay, has 104 two-bedroom condo-like units with fully equipped kitchens for $96. They also have a row of older studios out back which rent on a first-come basis for $58. There are two swimming pools and standard amenities. This is a popular place with military families, who get a discounted rate.

The *Hotel Mai'Ana* (☎ 646-6961), Box 8957, Tamuning, Guam 96911, is on the airport road, three-quarters of a mile below the airport. Rates are $68 for a studio and $84 for two-bedroom units. All have kitchens, TVs and phones and there's a pool. They offer a free airport shuttle, though if you arrive in the middle of the night when there's only one clerk on duty, you'll probably have to walk or take a taxi.

The *ITC Hotel* (☎ 646-6825), Box 8676, Tamuning, Guam 96911, has 47 fairly standard rooms, with TV and phone and a view of the town. Rates are $75/90 for singles/doubles, $5 more to face the ocean. The location, on the 7th and 8th floors of the commercial ITC Building, seems rather odd. The lobby is on the 9th floor.

The *Fujita Tumon Beach Hotel* (☎ 646-1811), 153 Fujita Rd, Tumon, Guam 96911, was the first hotel built at Tumon Bay. This sprawling low-rise Spanish style complex has some nice touches, such as tile murals on the exterior walls depicting Guam's history and legends. There's a pool and tennis courts. Though the hotel is older, the rooms are as nice as you'll find in some of the newer high-rises and it's a relatively good deal at $86/90 for singles/doubles.

Cocos Island Resort (☎ 828-8691), Box 7174, Tamuning, Guam 96911, has 140 bungalow-style rooms on Cocos Island, off the southern tip of Guam. Rates start at $90/100 for singles/doubles. The resort has a tennis court and swimming pool and specialises in water sports, catering mainly to the younger Japanese set.

Hotels – top end The *Guam Hilton* (☎ 646-1835), Box 11199, Tamuning, Guam 96911, is at the quieter end of Tumon Bay, beside Ypao Beach. The Hilton has the most international clientele of all Guam's luxury hotels. The 476 rooms have verandas and there's a swimming pool and lighted tennis courts. Singles/doubles cost $130/155 for rooms with mountain views, $140/170 for ocean view rooms.

Guam Reef Hotel (☎ 646-6881), Box 8258, Tamuning, Guam 96911 is an 18-floor,

297-room complex, part of the Nikko Hotels chain. It's the swankiest of the highrises and all rooms have verandas with ocean views. Rates start at $150/175 for singles/doubles.

The 19-storey *Pacific Star Hotel* (☎ 649-7827), Box 6097, Tamuning, Guam 96911, built by the Republic of Nauru, has 436 rooms. Rates start at $155/170 for singles/doubles and go up to $1500 for the presidential suite.

In addition, Tumon Bay has the following high-priced high-rise hotels:

Guam Plaza Hotel, 1328 San Vitores Rd, Tumon, Guam 96911 (☎ 646-7803); 520 rooms, from $100.

Sotetsu Tropicana Hotel, 825 San Vitores Rd, Tumon, Guam 96911 (☎ 646-5851); 200 rooms for $110.

Guam Dai-Ichi Hotel, Box 3310, Agana, Guam 96910 (☎ 646-5880); 337 rooms, from $120.

Hotel Sun Route Guam, Box 10839, Tamuning, Guam 96911 (☎ 649-9670); 66 two-bedroom suites, $140 for up to four people.

Guam Hotel Okura, 185 Gun Beach Rd, Tumon, Guam 96911 (☎ 646-6811); 225 rooms, from $150.

Pacific Islands Club, Box 9370, Tamuning, Guam 96911 (☎ 646-9172); $185 per person, including meals and recreation.

PLACES TO EAT
Types of Food
Chamorro food is a rich mix of Spanish, Filipino and Pacific dishes.

Ahu is grated coconut boiled in sugar water.

Bonelos Aga is bananas dipped in a sweet flour batter and deep fried.

Cadon Guihan is fish cooked in coconut milk with onions and sweet peppers.

Escabeche is fresh fish marinated in vinegar and soy sauce.

Kelaguen is minced chicken, fish, shrimp or Spam mixed with lemon, onions, pepper and shredded coconut.

Lumpia is similar to an egg roll, but dipped in garlic sauce or vinegar.

Pancit is a mix of shrimp, vegetables and garlic over noodles.

Poto is a ricecake of tuba, sugar and ricemeal.

Other local delicacies include whole roast pig, tropical fruits, coconut crabs, fruit bat soup, red rice made with *achiote* (annatto)

seeds and anything barbecued. To turn ordinary dishes into a Chamorro meal ask for *finadene*, a hot sauce made from fiery red peppers.

You'll find the best Chamorro food at village fiestas and private feasts. Otherwise, one of the few places where Chamorro food is served is the *Public Market* on Marine Drive, beside the Agana Marina. A line of food stalls sells fixed plate lunches of local favourites such as spicy chicken kelaguen or barbecued spareribs with red rice for $3 to $4. This is a popular place for Agana office workers to get a quick take-away meal. The market is open from 9 am to 5.30 pm daily and there's also a produce section where you can buy fruits, vegetables, betel nut and tuba.

Guam's tap water is treated and safe to drink.

Restaurants
Guam's multi-ethnic population and thousands of tourists support more than a hundred restaurants in the greater Agana area. There are a lot of cuisines to check out including Japanese, Chinese, Korean, Italian, French, Vietnamese, Filipino and Thai.

The *Adventist Book & Food Center*, in the church across the street and up the hill from Government House, is a fully stocked health-food store. It's open from 9 am to 5 pm Monday to Thursday, and to 3 pm on Fridays. The vegetarian lunch counter, open from 11 am to 2 pm on weekdays, has soups, salads, baked potatoes with toppings, sandwiches and baked goods. Try the 'Hard to Handle' soybean burger for $3.15 and a fruit smoothie for $1.75.

Sizzler Steak House in the Agana Shopping Center has a great all-you-can-eat salad bar which includes not only green salad with all the fixings, but also pasta salads, soups, a taco bar, spaghetti and meatballs, spareribs, fries, a dessert bar with cobbler and soft ice cream, and best of all, a good variety of fresh fruit such as watermelon, pineapple and kiwi. It costs $7 at lunch, $9 at dinner, and is recommended for salad lovers. Sizzler also has standard steak and seafood meals. It's open from 11 am to 9.30 pm daily.

The buffet at *Shakey's Pizza* in Tamuning includes pizza, spaghetti, fried chicken, a taco bar, soups, salad and fruit. It's not on par with the one at Sizzler's, but it's cheaper and will fill you up. It costs $6 from 11 am to 5 pm, $7 from 5 to 8.30 pm.

You can get good Thai food at *Marianas Trench*, a hole in the wall that's basically a quiet bar with a couple of pool tables, a jukebox and a few tables off to the side for diners. Try the hot and sour beef salad with rice or the Pad Thai with shrimp, each $7. It's opposite Gibson's shopping centre in Tamuning.

Somjai Restaurant, a family-style Thai and Chinese restaurant on Route 1, one-quarter of a mile north of its intersection with Route 8, has lunch specials for $3.50 from 11 am to 3 pm. Otherwise most dishes from the menu average $6 to $9.

Caravelle Vietnamese Restaurant on Route 1 in Tamuning, a couple of buildings south of Ben Franklin, offers up *pho*, a beef soup with bean sprouts, noodles, mint and lettuce for $5. Most dishes cost $6 to $8, with specials for $4.50 from 11 am to 2 pm.

Another Vietnamese restaurant is *Lien's* in the Hafa Adai Exchange in Tamuning. It's a popular place for fried lumpia which is served with lettuce, bean sprouts, noodles and a vinegar dipping sauce. The lumpia costs $7 for six pieces, or you can get fish or beef dishes for the same price.

The *Mini Cafe*, near the police station in the centre of Agana, serves a full range of standard Chinese dishes, most around $7. The food's good and the best deal is the special at lunch when $5 will buy you fried rice and a couple of entrees. It's open from 10 am to midnight.

Marty's Mexican Restaurant, in the Royal Lanes bowling alley opposite the ITC Building, serves acceptable formula Mexican dishes in a dark, bar-like setting. Prices are moderate. If you just want a cheap burrito try *Taco Bell* across the street.

The *Micronesia Mall* on Route 1, a mile north of Tumon, has a small food court with stalls that serve Chamorro, Hawaiian, Filipino, Chinese, Japanese and American food. Most have plate lunches with combos chosen from steamer trays for $4 to $5.

Fast food enthusiasts can choose from *McDonald's, Kentucky Fried Chicken, Wendy's, Burger King, Pizza Hut, Winchell's* and a host of others. *Sub Station II*, on Camp Watkins Rd near Marine Drive, serves submarine sandwiches from $3 and is open 24 hours a day.

ENTERTAINMENT

The large Tumon Bay hotels have live music nightly, ranging from classical to jazz and hard rock. The Guam Hilton, Pacific Star and Guam Reef hotels have discos, though the island's hot spot is Lights Disco, on Camp Watkins Rd near Marine Drive in Tamuning. A rock 'n' roll group with local flavour that's worth catching is the band Chamorro.

The Beach House is an open-air bar right on the beach at Tumon Bay, just below the Fujita hotel. It's popular with windsurfers and beach bums and there's occasionally live music.

There's a good sunset view from the wrap-around windows at the Salon del Mar in the Hotel Okura. Beer costs $1.75 and tropical drinks cost $3.25 during happy hour from 4 to 7 pm.

A bellwether for Tumon Bay's future may well be the new, extravagant SandCastle Theatre, a big, glitzy Las Vegas-style entertainment complex on San Vitores Rd. It has $100 dinner shows, cabarets, a disco and several bars.

Many of the hotels have expensive 'Polynesian' dance shows that are geared for package tourists.

There are also several shooting galleries that round up Japanese tourists. In part because of strict gun controls back in Japan, this has become one of Guam's most popular side attractions, with visitors dishing out $75 to shoot off a round of shells. Many shops add a Wild West facade to it all, and tourists can don cowboy costumes and Indian headdresses to videotape their own shoot-outs.

For more local flavour, Guam has a greyhound racing track, raceway park, bowling alleys, legalised cockfights, golf courses, movie theatres, tennis courts and windjammer cruises.

THINGS TO BUY

With all its shopping centres and gift shops, you'd think Guam would have a better selection of handicrafts than it does. Instead you'll mostly find tacky slapped-together wood carvings, shell art and weavings made in the Philippines and then tagged with 'souvenir of Guam' labels. Occasionally you'll run across some crafts made on other Micronesian islands, though quality ones are hard to find, and all carry a heavy mark-up.

However Guam is the best place in Micronesia to buy supplies you may need on other islands, as the supermarkets and shopping complexes are fully modern. Micronesia Mall, on Route 1 in Dededo, is Guam's largest shopping centre. It has a Safeway grocery store, Sterling Department Store and nearly a hundred smaller shops, boutiques and eateries. Other big shopping centres are Gibson's in Tamuning and the Agana Shopping Center in Agana centre.

Though more expensive than in the USA, film is cheaper in Guam than elsewhere in Micronesia. Check the expiry dates carefully. It's not advisable to purchase film from the stands set up in the market places or around tourist attractions.

US citizens returning to the States from Guam are allowed a higher than usual duty-free exemption on articles acquired abroad. They are permitted $800 worth of duty-free items ($400 is usual), 1000 cigarettes and four litres of alcohol. No more than $400 worth of these purchases are supposed to have been acquired outside Guam.

GETTING THERE & AWAY

Guam is serviced by a variety of airlines with direct flights from the USA, Australia, Japan, Indonesia, the Philippines, Korea, Taiwan and Papua New Guinea.

For complete information on getting to Guam refer to the Getting There & Away chapter at the start of this book.

Airport

The Guam International Airport in Tamuning has a foreign exchange booth, restrooms, pay phones, hotel courtesy phones, car rental booths, a duty-free shop and an overpriced snack shop. There are no lockers and if you have a layover of more than six hours you have to go through customs.

GETTING AROUND

It's challenging getting around Guam without a car, especially if you want to tour the whole island, and hitchhiking is not a common practice.

To/From Airport

A couple of the hotels in Tumon, including the Hilton, provide airport transfers but most do not. You might see the ANA trolley bus cruising between the airport, central Agana and the hotels – it's strictly for passengers of All Nippon Airways.

Bus

A fledgling public bus system operates routes around the island, with buses going to virtually every village. As a means of exploring Guam, however, it's not terribly practical as buses are infrequent and you'll often have long waits, even around Agana. The service may get better in the future, as there are plans to beef up the schedule.

The fare is 75 cents for adults and 25 cents for children upon boarding, plus 25 cents more for a transfer. For schedule information call ☎ 649-9846.

Taxi

Taxi fares, which start at $1.80 at flagdown, are $3 for the first mile and 60 cents for each quarter-mile after that. It costs about $10 (plus $1 per piece of luggage) to get from the airport to Tumon Bay. Outside the airport, you'll probably have to phone for a taxi. Some of the companies are Hafa Adai Taxi Service (☎ 477-9629), City Taxi (☎ 646-4170) and Guam Taxi (☎ 649-6842).

Car

Avis, Hertz, Islander and Toyota have rental

booths at the airport, though you can get a better deal from Thrifty which is just a mile outside the airport and has a free shuttle.

Thrifty's office (☎ 646-5555), at the Exxon petrol station at the intersection of the airport road and Route 1, is open from 5 am to 8 pm. Rates start at $22 for small older cars without air-con, $30 for cars with air-con.

Elsewhere, daily rates for compact cars with manual transmission start at $30 at Toyota (☎ 646-1876) and National (☎ 649-0110), $32 at Avis (☎ 646-1801), $37 at Islander (☎ 646-8156) and Dollar (☎ 646-7000), and $40 at Hertz (☎ 649-6283). All have free unlimited mileage.

Many companies have a variety of discounted and business rates, but you have to ask for them when you book as they won't always volunteer the information. The collision damage waiver option costs about $10 per day.

It's a good idea to book in advance (the international companies can be booked from overseas), especially if you want the cheapest class of car. Otherwise the cheaper cars aren't always available and during the busiest times many companies book out completely. You won't lose anything by making a reservation, as there are generally no deposits or cancellation fees.

The speed limit is 35 miles an hour unless otherwise posted. US and foreign driver's licences are valid for 30 days after arrival on Guam.

Commonwealth of the Northern Marianas

The Northern Marianas, which has opted for closer political ties with the United States of America than other Micronesian island groups, is now a US Commonwealth, similar in status to Puerto Rico.

Saipan, Rota and Tinian are the main islands of the Northern Marianas. Saipan, the largest island, is the centre of commonwealth activities. It has 87% of the population, dominates in economic development and political strength and gets most of the tourist trade. Rota and Tinian are thus far unspoiled, quiet and friendly. All three islands have good beaches.

The Northern Marianas, the scene of some of the Pacific War's most devastating battles, woos the Japanese these days by turning war ruins into sightseeing spots, erecting peace monuments and encouraging the development of resort hotels.

With new US passports in hand, the people of the Northern Marianas are hurtling head-long after the American dream and in the rush to look, eat and act American, much of their cultural heritage is being lost. Yet the traveller who chances upon a village fiesta or christening festivities can still get a glimpse of the more traditional Chamorro life.

History
Pre-European Contact Prior to European contact, the Northern Marianas were populated by the Chamorros whose culture and origins were the same as the people of Guam. (Information on early Chamorro culture is given in the Guam section.)

Spanish Period First named the 'Islands of Thieves' by Magellan in 1521, the Mariana Islands were renamed 'Las Marianas' in 1668 by the Spanish priest Sanvitores, in honour of the Spanish queen Maria Ana of Austria.

Spanish galleons, on their annual routes between Acapulco and Manila, passed between Guam and Rota each year in early June. So that they would not have to pass by in darkness, the Spanish ordered that fires be lit nightly on Rota's (and Guam's) highest points. The Rotanese would sail out in hundreds of canoes to meet the ships, hoping to trade food for iron nails and tools.

Around 1700 the Spanish swept down through the Marianas and took all the Chamorros they found to Guam in order to control them better. Several hundred Rotanese hid in the hills and avoided capture. Consequently some of the purest Chamorro blood in the Marianas today is in Rota.

The other Northern Marianas were left uninhabited. Explorers that landed on the abandoned islands (including the British captain Samuel Wallis in 1768, soon after 'discovering' Tahiti) sometimes took advantage of the wild cattle and chickens found there, but most went instead to Guam to stock up on provisions.

Around 1820 the Spanish allowed islanders from the western Carolines to move to the larger Mariana islands. The Carolinians managed Spanish cattle herds and maintained a presence on the islands at a time when Spain was skittish over German intentions in the area.

After the pope declared Spain's sovereignty over the Marianas in 1885, the subdued 'Spanified' Chamorros were encouraged to move back to the Northern Marianas from Guam. They were given land for farming, though the Carolinians had already settled some of the best coastal land.

German Period Germany bought the Northern Marianas from Spain in 1899, as part of its Micronesia package deal. Germany's primary interest was in copra production.

The Northern Marianas were never heavily staffed with foreign administrators during either the Spanish or German years, although a handful of teachers and priests did

Farallon de Pajaros
(Mariana Is)

Maug Islands
(Mariana Is)

Asuncion Island
(Mariana Is)

Agrihan
(Mariana Is)

Pagan
(Mariana Is)

**Commonwealth
of the
Northern
Marianas**

Alamagan
(Mariana Is)

Guguan
(Mariana Is)

Sarigan
(Mariana Is)

Anatahan
(Mariana Is)

Farallon de Medinilla
(Mariana Is)

Saipan
(Mariana Is)

Tinian
(Mariana Is)

Aguijan
(Mariana Is)

Rota
(Mariana Is)

Guam
(United States)

MARIANA TRENCH

| 0 | 50 | 100 km |
| 0 | 50 | 100 m |

live on the islands. At any rate, there weren't many islanders to administer.

Japanese Period When the Japanese took the Northern Marianas from Germany at the beginning of WW I there were fewer than 4000 Chamorros and Carolinians on the islands.

The Japanese had little interest in copra but had great expectations for sugar cane. They chopped down groves of coconut trees and cleared tropical forests and jungles to create level farmland. When latte stones from ancient villages got in the way, they were cast aside.

In the mid-1920s, after Saipan's sugar industry was determined a success, plantations were set up on Tinian and Rota. On all three islands sugar cane was loaded from the fields onto bullcarts and hauled to little narrow-gauge railroads where steam-powered trains carried the cane to mills for processing. Both sugar and alcohol made from the cane were major export items.

By the mid-1930s sugar operations in the Marianas were providing the Japanese with more than 60% of all revenues generated in Micronesia.

Many of the people who worked the cane fields came from Okinawa, where poor tenant farmers were recruited to work for low wages. The high influx of foreigners and the tendency of the colonisers to turn villages into miniature Japanese-style towns overwhelmed the indigenous culture.

At the outbreak of WW II there were more than 45,000 Japanese and immigrant workers in the Northern Marianas – more than 10 times the number of Micronesians.

WW II One of the largest military operations in all of WW II was 'Operation Forager' which captured the Mariana Islands for the USA. Beginning in Saipan and attacking Guam just days later, an American invasion force of 127,000 soldiers, 600 ships and 2000 planes took part. US pre-invasion bombing attacks included the first-ever wartime use of napalm.

On 15 June 1944 two US Marine divisions

landed on Saipan's south-west coast. The Japanese had 31,000 soldiers waiting. Resistance was fierce but by evening the USA had 20,000 men ashore.

That same night the Japanese First Mobile Fleet was detected in the Philippine Sea heading toward the Marianas. When squadrons of Zeros took off from those ships on 19 June, the US forces were ready. In the battle that became known as the 'Marianas Turkey Shoot' both sides took part in a wild all-out air fight west of the Marianas. In two days the Japanese lost 402 planes and three aircraft carriers. The Americans lost only 50 planes in the dogfights, but on the return 80 more crashed into the sea when they ran out of fuel.

With the defeat of their fleet, Japanese forces in the Marianas lost any chance of rescue or support. On Saipan the Americans advanced northward and into the island's mountainous interior.

Garapan, the Japanese administrative centre, fell on 3 July. When the battle for Saipan was declared over on 9 July, 3500 Americans, 30,000 Japanese defenders and 400 Saipanese were dead. After the fall of Saipan, the Japanese had no hope of holding onto Tinian. Still, the 9000 Japanese soldiers on Tinian chose to fight to the death rather than surrender.

The Americans made their first beach landing on Tinian's north-west shore on 24 July 1944. They secured the island after nine days of heavy combat and the loss of 390 American and more than 5000 Japanese lives. US troops immediately began extending the Japanese airbase, using it to stage air raids on Japan, including the atomic bomb drops on Hiroshima and Nagasaki.

American invasion forces bypassed Rota. The US bombed the northern airstrips, but the Japanese held the island until the war's end and Rota came through the conflict relatively unscathed.

Postwar Period The fierce fighting had reduced whole towns to rubble and in the years following the war there were no attempts to rebuild the sugar industry. The USA administered the islands by giving hand-outs rather than by supporting economic development.

In 1948 the CIA closed off half of Saipan to islanders and outsiders alike, using the island for secret military activities. When the CIA moved out in 1962, the Northern Marianas was finally opened to visitors. The UN Trust Territory administration then moved its headquarters to Saipan, taking over the CIA offices.

In 1961 Saipan and Rota petitioned the US government, asking to become integrated with Guam. The requests were made nearly every year until 1969 when Guam voters were allowed to vote on the issue and rejected the idea. One reason cited for the rejection was that many Guamanians still harboured ill feelings toward the Saipanese who had acted as interpreters during Guam's occupation by Japan.

In June 1975 the people of the Northern Marianas voted to become a US Commonwealth, and in doing so became the first district to withdraw from the Trust Territory. The commonwealth agreement went into effect in January 1978 and in November 1986 the new commonwealth covenant became fully effective and the islanders became US citizens.

The Northern Marianas, situated between Japan and the Philippines, the politically sensitive sites of some of America's largest overseas military bases, is considered by the US Defense Department to be a potential back-up site in the event the Americans are booted out elsewhere. In an attempt to win the islanders over, the USA has long provided the Northern Marianas with more federal funding per capita than any of the 50 states. Exercising a land-use option built into the commonwealth agreement, the US has leased two-thirds of Tinian for $33 million. The 50-year lease allows use of the land for weapons storage and military training.

Although the majority of Tinian residents voted for the commonwealth package, complete with military lease options, not all Tinian landowners are happy with the current arrangement. A lawsuit trying to stop military exercises on Tinian, by claiming that the training violates federal environmental protection laws, has been brought before US courts.

Geography

The Mariana Islands rise more than seven miles from the floor of the ocean, marking the dividing line between the Pacific Ocean and the Philippine Sea.

The highest point in Micronesia is in the Marianas, on the remote island of Agrihan. Though Agrihan is only 3166 feet above sea level, the Mariana Islands are but the emerged tips of what would constitute the world's highest mountains if measured from their bases deep in the Mariana Trench. The trench, a canyon which extends 1835 miles along the floor of the Pacific, east of the Mariana Islands, contains the world's greatest known ocean depth of 38,635 feet.

Guam is the southernmost island in the Marianas chain, but has a separate political identity. The Commonwealth of the Northern Marianas is made up of the other 14 islands in the archipelago which stretch 400 miles northward from Guam in an almost straight line.

All the islands are high types of either volcanic or limestone formation and the total land mass is 184 sq miles. Saipan is 47 sq miles, Tinian is 39 and Rota is 32.

Northern (Outer) Islands Except for Aguijan which is just south of Tinian, the smaller Mariana islands run north of Saipan. From south to north they are Farallon de Medinilla, Anatahan, Sarigan, Guguan, Alamagan, Pagan, Agrihan, Asuncion, Maug and Farallon de Pajaros. All are rugged volcanic islands and most are uninhabited.

Pagan, which is 18½ sq miles, is the largest of these outer islands, and one of the most beautiful. Maug and Sarigan are protected nature preserves. Farallon de Medinilla is used on occasion as a bombing and gunnery target by the US Navy and Air Force.

Micronesia's only active volcanoes are among these islands. Following weeks of earthquakes, Pagan's volcano erupted in May 1981, shooting up flames, rocks and clouds of ash as high as 60,000 feet. Almost half of all the arable land was covered with lava flows. All 54 residents were evacuated to Saipan and the island remains restricted.

In April 1990, all 21 residents of the island of Anatahan were evacuated to Saipan following an earthquake that measured 7.4 on the Richter scale and signs that a volcanic eruption was imminent. They too have not been allowed to return.

The 1000-foot peak on Farallon de Pajaros and Asuncion's 3000-foot mountain sometimes send up smoke and steam as well.

Climate

Saipan, which is listed in the *Guinness Book of World Records* as having the world's most equable temperature, averages 81°F (27°C) year-round. The rainy season is July to October, when rainfall averages about 12 inches a month, while from December to May the monthly rainfall averages only about four inches.

The climate of the Northern Marianas is very similar to Guam's and, also like Guam, the islands lie directly in the typhoon track. The most common months for typhoons are August to December.

Government

The Northern Marianas elects its own governor, lieutenant governor and a legislature with nine senators and 14 representatives. Each main island has its own mayor. Although the people of the Northern Marianas are now US citizens they have no vote in US elections and the representative they send to Washington DC is merely an observer and lobbyist.

Economy

During the first six years of the new covenant agreement, the USA is providing $228 million in funds for capital development, government operations and other programmes in the Northern Marianas. The government is the largest employer, providing about 2200 jobs.

The Northern Marianas imports a large number of low-paid Asian labourers, the majority from the Philippines and China. A number of Korean bars bring in Filipinas to entertain, often keeping their passports to make sure they can't leave. The women clean the bars during the day, entertain in the evenings and are only let out if they're escorted. Filipinas are also commonly brought in as low-paid house maids.

To take advantage of Saipan's duty-free access to the USA, several foreign-owned garment factories set up shop on the island in the 1980s. Some employ as many as 500 people, mostly from mainland China. On paper, workers are paid the minimum wage of $2.15 per hour, though because they live in factory dorms their rent, food and other expenses are taken out of their pay, leaving them only a fraction of that. For hosting the factories, Saipan receives about $2 million annually in taxes.

Tourism is the largest industry in the Northern Marianas. There are about 500,000 visitors annually, with more than 80% coming from Japan.

The majority of Saipan's resort hotel rooms are pre-booked, with all expenses pre-paid in yen back in Japan. Most people travel in tour packs, stay an average of four nights and use vouchers to eat in hotel restaurants. With most hotels owned and run by Japan-ese, only a small percentage of these tourist dollars see their way into the Saipanese economy.

People
The Northern Marianas is the fastest growing area in Micronesia. There were 9640 residents in 1970, 16,780 in 1980 and 43,555 in 1990.

The 1990 census counted 39,090 people on Saipan, 2118 on Tinian, 2311 on Rota and 36 people in the northern islands. Almost half are resident aliens, with the majority from the Philippines. Of the indigenous population, roughly 75% is Chamorro, while the remainder are Carolinian. Most islanders are Roman Catholic.

Language
English is the official language, Chamorro and Carolinian are the local tongues and Japanese is spoken in most hotels and some shops. *Hafa adai* is the standard greeting, as it is in Guam.

Holidays & Festivals Public holidays in the Northern Marianas include:

New Year's Day
  1 January
Commonwealth Day
  9 January
President's Day
  3rd Monday in February
Memorial Day
  Last Monday in May
US Independence Day
  4 July
Labor Day
  1st Monday in September
Columbus Day
  2nd Monday in October
Citizenship Day
  4 November
Veterans Day
  11 November
Thanksgiving
  4th Thursday in November
Constitution Day
  8 December
Christmas Day
  25 December

Most villages have an annual fiesta in honour of their patron saint, which is the big village bash of the year. Rota and Tinian have one fiesta each, Saipan has seven.

Saipan

Saipan has only Guam as a rival in the crush of Japanese tourists that flock to its shores. In the past few years Saipan has become the fastest growing, most haphazardly developed island in Micronesia, with new golf courses and resorts popping up all around the island. Tourists and alien workers now outnumber the Saipanese and the island has lost much of its Micronesian character.

Saipan has gentle beaches on its west and south coasts, a rugged and rocky east coast, a hilly interior and dramatic north coast cliffs. The island is about 14 miles long and five miles wide.

Orientation is simple. The airport is at the southern end of the island and most of the major hotels and services are on Beach Rd which runs along the west coast.

The main tourist sights are in the west coast town of Garapan and in the Marpi area at the northern end of the island. By car, most sights can be touched on in just a few hours, though a more leisurely exploration would take a full day.

Information
Tourist Office The Marianas Visitors Bureau (☎ 234-8325) is just outside the airport in one of the fortified concrete buildings that once served as a Japanese communications station. The office is open from 8 am to 5 pm, Monday to Saturday. There are plans to open a branch office at Sugar King Park in Garapan.

For 24-hour recorded weather information call ☎ 234-5724.

Money The Bank of Guam has offices in Garapan and Susupe, and the Bank of Hawaii is in the Nauru Building in Susupe. Banking

hours are from 10 am to 3 pm Monday to Thursday, to 6 pm on Fridays. Credit cards are widely accepted in Saipan.

Post Saipan's main post office, which is in Chalan Kanoa, is open from 9 am to 4 pm Monday to Friday and from 9 am to noon on Saturdays. It's a busy office and if you want to beat the lines, go to the branch post office on Capitol Hill (CHRB, used in some addresses following the box number, designates this branch, though all mail to Saipan uses the zip code 96950).

Telephone Long-distance calls can be made from phone booths and most hotels, as well as from the MTC telecommunications office in Susupe between 8.30 am and 7 pm weekdays and from 8.30 am to 2 pm on Saturdays. Per-minute rates for direct-dialled calls are 80 cents to Guam, $2.25 to the USA and $2.60 to Japan. Calls to Palau, the FSM or the Marshalls are $8.25 for three minutes.

Consulates Japan has a consulate office (☎ 234-7201) in the Nauru Building in Susupe and the Philippines has a consulate (☎ 234-1848) off Beach Rd in San Jose. The US Immigration Office is on the 4th floor of the Nauru building.

Bookshops & Newspapers Saipan's only bookstore, Faith Book Store on Beach Rd in Susupe, has a good selection of books on Micronesia. The college has a small library. The island's first full-service public library is under construction near the police station in Susupe.

There are two newspapers published on Saipan, the *Marianas Variety* and the *Saipan Tribune*. Guam's *Pacific Daily News*, flown in daily, has a weekly supplement on the Northern Marianas. You can pick up papers at many stores and the larger hotels.

Airlines The Air Mike office (☎ 234-6492), in the JoeTen Building in Susupe, is open from 9 am to 5 pm Monday to Friday and from 8 am to 4 pm on weekends.

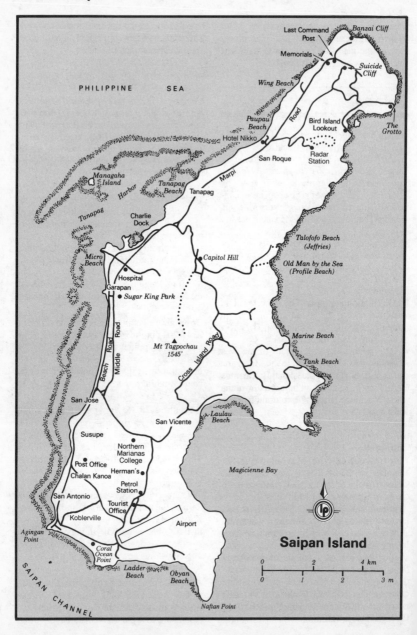

PHILIPPINE   SEA

Last Command
Post

Banzai Cliff

Memorials

Suicide
Cliff

Wing Beach

Paupau
Beach

Hotel Nikko

San Roque

Bird Island
Lookout

The
Grotto

Marpi
Road

Radar
Station

Managaha
Island

Tanapag
Harbor

Tanapag
Beach

Tanapag

Charlie
Dock

Talofofo Beach
(Jeffries)

Tanapag

Capitol Hill

Old Man by the Sea
(Profile Beach)

Micro
Beach

Hospital

Garapan

Sugar King Park

Mt Tagpochau
1545'

Beach Road

Middle Road

Cross Island Road

Marine Beach

Tank Beach

San Jose

San Vicente

Laulau
Beach

Susupe

Northern
Marianas
College

Magicienne Bay

Post Office

Chalan Kanoa

Herman's

Petrol
Station

San Antonio

Koblerville

Tourist
Office

Airport

Agingan
Point

Coral
Ocean
Point

Ladder
Beach

Obyan
Beach

Saipan Island

0   2   4 km

0   1   2   3 m

SAIPAN CHANNEL

Naftan Point

Emergency For the police call ☎ 911. Saipan's modern hospital, the Commonwealth Health Center (☎ 234-6115), is on Middle Rd in Garapan.

Holidays & Festivals

Village fiestas are held at Our Lady of Lourdes Shrine in early February, in San Jose in early May, at the Mt Carmel Cathedral in Chalan Kanoa in mid-July, in San Roque in mid-August, in Tanapag in early October and in Garapan in late November.

The San Isidro Fiesta in mid-May honours the patron saint of Saipan's Carolinians and includes traditional Carolinian dances.

The Flame Tree Festival is a two-week celebration at the end of June, when the brilliant orange-red blossoms of the royal poinciana trees are at their peak. The festival celebrates the American liberation of the islands and ends on 4 July, US Independence Day. Festivities includes a parade, a queen contest, nightly entertainment, games and food booths.

There's an arts festival in May, an agricultural fair in June and a fishing derby in July.

Activities

Diving & Snorkelling

Saipan's most unusual dive is the Grotto, a natural cavern with waters 50 feet deep and tunnels to the open sea. Though it's a popular spot for locals to swim and for divers with a guide, the tricky currents can be dangerous for the uninitiated.

Other popular dives are war wrecks in Tanapag Harbor, caves and garden eels at Obyan Beach and a huge coral head offshore from the Saipan Grand Hotel.

Saipan's best snorkelling is at Managaha Island. Paupau and Wing beaches have reasonably good snorkelling, as does Bird Island though it requires a hike. You can also snorkel out around a couple of US Army tanks which rest in the shallow waters south of Garapan where US invasion forces first came ashore. It's best to stick to the tank nearest the beach, as jet skiers race around the tank further offshore.

Dive Shops Saipan has a score of dive operations, most of them Japanese operated.

Ben-Ki Water Sports (☎ 235-5063), Box 31 CHRB, Saipan, MP 96950, on the beach fronting the Dai-Ichi Hotel, is locally owned by Ben Concepcion. Two tank boat dives cost $80, including gear, lunch and hotel pick-up. Two beach dives, one of which is usually the Grotto, costs $70. Ben also does a $45 introductory dive and rents snorkel sets for $10 a day.

Windsurfing Saipan, inside the old WW II bunker in front of the Hyatt hotel, does a single beach dive for $45, a boat dive for $55 and night dives for $65. They also rent snorkel masks for $5.

Other Water Sports Windsurfing is popular on Saipan, which is the only island in the Northern Marianas with a large lagoon. *Windsurfing Saipan* at the Hyatt rents windsurfing equipment for $10 an hour or $30 for a half day. Windsurfing lessons are $20 an hour and snorkel sets rent for $5 a day.

The annual Micronesian Open Boardsailing Regatta and the Saipan Laguna Regatta are international windsurfing and Hobie Cat competitions held concurrently in front of the Hyatt in mid-February. Another Hobie Cat regatta is held in front of the Dai-Ichi Hotel in mid-November.

The four beach stands in front of the Dai-Ichi rent various water sports equipment, including kayaks and catamarans, and can make arrangements for water skiing, parasailing and trolling.

Submarine The 45-passenger recreational submarine *Mariea-I* (☎ 322-9600) makes four dives a day, except Thursdays, in the lagoon between Saipan and Managaha islands. Because the lagoon is fairly shallow, the sub descends only to about 45 feet. Sights include the ruins of a Japanese freighter, a Zero fighter and an American B 29. It costs $66 for adults, $44 for children.

Organised Tours A number of tour companies with offices at the larger hotels offer land tours, sunset cruises, fishing excursions and trips to Rota and Tinian.

Land tours of Saipan are predominately geared for Japanese package tourists and they don't take you anyplace you can't easily explore on your own. Five-hour sightseeing tours of Saipan cost about $35. Some companies that offer tours in English are Tasi Tours (☎ 234-7148), PDI (☎ 234-6210) and MMC (☎ 234-6976). Macaw Helicopters (☎ 234-7000) does flightseeing tours of Saipan, operating out of Coral Ocean Point in Koblerville. A 20-minute spin costs $65 and a 30-minute ride costs $90.

Freedom Air (☎ 234-8328) has Piper Cherokee six-seater planes that can be chartered for sightseeing at $280 an hour.

GARAPAN

The Japanese developed Garapan, their administrative centre in the Marianas, into one of the most bustling towns in Micronesia. Its streets were lined with neat rows of houses for the town's 15,000 residents and its central area looked like a little Tokyo, with bathhouses, sake shops, Shinto shrines, Japanese schools and office buildings.

Garapan was bombed to smithereens by the Americans during WW II and it wasn't until the 1960s that Saipanese began to resettle the area.

These days Garapan is booming, thanks again to the presence of the Japanese – this time as tourists. The streets are lined with signs in Japanese announcing sushi shops, souvenir stores, karaoke clubs and the like. Walking around the Micro Beach area it'd be easy to imagine you were in Okinawa.

Micro Beach

Micro Beach, Saipan's most attractive white sand beach, is travel poster material. In fact, it's not that uncommon to find Japanese film crews out shooting TV commercials on the shore. The broad beach has brilliant turquoise waters, a good view of Managaha Island and a fine angle for catching the sunset.

Although it's a long walk out through Micro Beach's shallows to get to water deep enough for swimming, it's pleasant enough to wade across as the bottom is sandy. The only obstacles are the sea cucumbers that dot the bottom.

American Memorial Park, the large grassy park backing Micro Beach north of the Hyatt, is under the auspices of the US National Park Service. Recreational facilities include a good jogging/cycling path that's nicely shaded by ironwood trees and continues from the beach 1½ miles up the coast.

Saipan's museum is at the edge of the park. Two tanks, three guns and a torpedo sit rusting in the parking lot, while the museum itself has been closed and neglected for years.

Sugar King Park

Sugar King Park is a hodgepodge of historical and memorial sights on the east side of Middle Rd. The bright red railroad engine on the grassy knoll makes the park easy to spot.

The steam-powered engine was once used to haul sugar cane from fields in the Marpi area to a factory in Chalan Kanoa where the Mt Carmel Cathedral now stands. The route was along the current Middle Rd, although none of the train tracks remain.

The bronze statue in the centre of the park is of Haruji Matsue, head of the Nanyo Kohatsu Kaisha (South Seas Development Company), responsible for developing the sugar industry in the Marianas. The statue was erected in 1934 and survived the war bombings.

Another survivor is a concrete building in the south-west corner of the park, which was a teacher's cottage before the war and has been renovated into a Marianas Visitors Bureau office. The park has some nice old trees and flowering bushes and is pleasant enough to stroll around, though the sights are less than inspiring.

At the far end of the park a red, riverless bridge leads to a Japanese shrine called the Katori Jinja. Originally built in 1911, it was destroyed in 1944 and rebuilt in concrete in

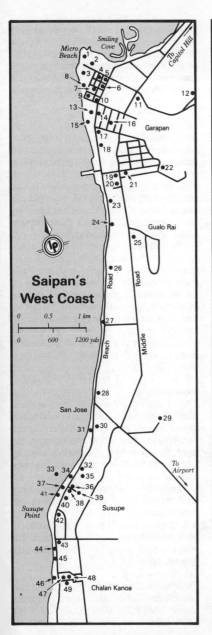

1   American Memorial Park
2   Museum
3   Hyatt Regency Saipan
4   Coconut-Tei
5   Fire Station
6   Islander Inn
7   Chamorro House Motel/Restaurant
8   Dai-Ichi Hotel
9   Remington Club
10 Winchell's
11 Commonwealth Hospital
12 The Light House
13 Hafa Adai Shopping Center
14 Poon's Restaurant
15 Hafadai Beach Hotel
16 Garapan Plaza Hotel
17 Bank of Guam
18 Saipan Ocean View Hotel
19 Old Japanese Hospital
20 Old Japanese Jail
21 Sugar King Park
22 Sugar King Hotel
23 Marianas Trench Motel
24 Hong Kong Restaurant
25 Maharani Indian Restaurant
26 China House Restaurant
27 Japanese Tank
28 Bowling Alley
29 Saipan Country Club
30 JV's Mart
31 Rudolpho's
32 Philippine Consulate
33 American Tanks (offshore)
34 Civic Center Park
35 Sun Inn Motel
36 Police Station/Courthouse
37 Saipan Diamond Hotel
38 JoeTen Shopping Center
39 Nauru Building
40 Air Micronesia
41 Saipan Grand Hotel
42 Faith Book Store
43 Mt Carmel Cathedral
44 Town House Shopping Center
45 Kentucky Fried Chicken
46 Pacific Gardenia Hotel
47 Movie Theatre
48 Post Office
49 Farmer's Market

1985. Behind the shrine, steps lead up to a 10-minute loop trail that climbs the hill in back and takes in a new hexagonal prayer temple dedicated to WW II Japanese soldiers.

Japanese Hospital

The ruins of the old Japanese hospital are directly across Middle Rd from Sugar King Park. The hospital entrance is at the back of the building, but beware of the two temperamental watchdogs in the yard next door.

The school bus stop in front of the hospital depicts the banners of the two major foreign powers which have dominated Saipan in the 20th century. The US flag is on the outside, the pre-war Japanese rising sun emblem is inside and the commonwealth flag has been painted on the back.

Old Japanese Jail

Rumours persist that aviator Amelia Earhart was held in the Garapan jail after being shot down over the Marshalls in 1937 by the Japanese, though most scholars assume she simply ran out of gas, crashed into the Pacific and died at sea. Still there are a few Saipanese who insist they saw Amelia on the island and the mystery of her demise adds a bit of intrigue as you look around the jail.

Tall grasses and weeds are attempting a takeover of the buildings, but you can still walk down the corridor past the damp concrete cells, some of which still have their barred steel doors attached. The main cell block row was for male civilian prisoners, while geishas who stole from their customers' pockets and women who didn't complete their employment contracts were held in a smaller building.

To get there take the first dirt road to the right off Middle Rd south of the old Japanese hospital. The jail is just a 100 yards down on the right.

NORTH OF GARAPAN

North of Garapan are Tanapag and San Roque, small villages that are being invaded by a slew of new resort developments.

The northern tip of the island, called Marpi, has most of Saipan's WW II tourist attractions and some of the island's prettiest scenery. Much of the roadside is lined with papaya trees and *tangan-tangan* bushes.

The defoliation of Saipan during WW II was so complete that the quick-growing tangan-tangan was aerially seeded to keep parts of the island from washing into the sea. Today this pervasive shrub is the most prevalent plant on Saipan. Although it has prevented major erosion, it is choking out native flora and has upset the natural prewar ecosystem.

Tanapag

The quiet village of Tanapag was the site of what was perhaps the most fanatical attack during all of WW II. On the night of 6 July 1944, 4000 Japanese soldiers, many emboldened by *sake*, hurled themselves in a *banzai* attack into the lines of US forces on Tanapag Beach. Some of the Japanese had guns, but most were armed just with clubs, bayonet sticks, bamboo spears and grenades.

The Japanese, honour-bound to die one way or another in the face of defeat, were intent on taking as many Americans with them as possible. As wave after wave of Japanese soldiers rushed down in the surprise attack, the Americans were pushed out into the water, across Tanapag Harbor and all the way back onto the reef – firing all the while at the unrelenting enemy. By the next morning it was all over and 5000 men were dead.

Paupau Beach

The splashiest hotel on Saipan is *Hotel Nikko*, at the south end of Paupau Beach. You can get an excellent view of Saipan Lagoon by taking the glass elevator to the top of the hotel. The foreground view is dominated by an elaborate water slide and swimming pool, which gives the hotel an amusement park air.

Paupau Beach has soft white sand, fairly shallow waters and good snorkelling and swimming during high tide.

Though you could park at the Nikko, to get to a quieter section of Paupau take the dirt road just north of the Nikko and drive right down to the beach.

PACBAR Radar Facility

In 1989, the US Air Force constructed a radar facility (called PACBAR) at the top of the 942-foot Mt Petosukara in the Marpi Commonwealth Forest. The radar is used to spy on foreign satellites and keep track of other resident space objects.

A 2¼-mile paved road leads up to the facility. There are ocean views from a scenic viewpoint along the way and from the radar station parking lot, as well as a roadside WW II bunker half a mile from the summit.

The best reason to take this road, however, is to hike the Laderan Tangke Trail, which the US Air Force agreed to develop and maintain as a condition for building the radar facility. To get there, turn off Marpi Rd onto Matuis Rd, just past the Hotel Nikko. The trailhead is 1½ miles up, on the left.

Laderan Tangke Trail This 1.8-mile loop trail through the Marpi Commonwealth Forest is one of the nicest in Micronesia, as it's a well-maintained public trail through the sort of dense jungle that's generally not easily accessible to hikers.

The trail passes through a raised limestone forest of tall trees, tangan-tangan and lots of ferns. It continues along the Laderan Tangke Cliff, from where you get an ocean view. The last half mile, along an overgrown dirt road, brings you back to the start. As parts of the terrain are steep and rocky, sandals aren't recommended.

Fifteen interpretive markers identify flora, fauna and geological features. The first marker, which is beside a WW II foxhole, identifies pandanus, which traditionally has provided islanders with both food and fibre for weaving.

The forest is a habitat for numerous species of birds, including the easily spotted bright red cardinal honeyeater. There are also three endangered species: the Vanikoro swiftlet, the Micronesian megapode and the nightingale reed-warbler.

As you walk along the trail you'll probably notice the shells of giant African snails scampering around – they're occupied by hermit crabs which are born in the ocean and climb up to the forest!

Wing Beach

Wing Beach was named after the US Navy aircraft wing that lay half buried in the sand for decades before falling victim to an aluminium recycling programme.

The south end of the beach has a shoreline coral shelf, but the north end is sandy and has good snorkelling.

Wing Beach is a mile north of Paupau Beach. Turn left off Marpi Rd just beyond the country club swimming pool. The road changes from packed coral to dirt after one-third of a mile. You can pull off to the side at this point if the rest of the road isn't passable and walk to the sandy section in a few minutes. The area is thick with white and purple morning glory.

Memorials

A series of WW II memorial parks are lined up along the road starting about 7½ miles north of Garapan. The first is the Korean Peace Memorial, the second park is dedicated to Okinawans and the Last Command Post of the Japanese is straight ahead.

Banzai Cliff

Waves crash onto the jagged rocks below Banzai Cliff, one of the spots where hundreds of Japanese civilians jumped to their deaths as the Americans were taking over the island in 1944.

Whole families lined up in order of age. Each child was pushed over the edge by the next oldest brother or sister, until the mother pushed the oldest child and the father pushed his wife before running backwards over the cliff himself. Although US soldiers dropped leaflets and shouted through loudspeakers that those who surrendered would not be harmed, the mass suicides were deemed preferable to the shame of capture and to the torturings the Japanese had been convinced the Americans would inflict upon them.

Over the years the Japanese have put up a number of plaques and memorials to commemorate the spot, including a large statue of Heiwa Kannon, the 'Peaceful Goddess of Mercy'.

The turn-off to Banzai Cliff is off Marpi Rd opposite the Okinawan memorial.

Last Command Post

It was at the spot now known as the Last Command Post that troops of the Japanese Imperial Army readied themselves for their final desperate battle against American invasion forces.

Lieutenant General Yoshitsugo Saito, acknowledging defeat, asked his remaining soldiers to each take seven American lives for the emperor, triggering the suicide banzai attack at Tanapag Harbor. Saito then committed hara-kiri by thrusting his sword into his stomach while his aide shot him in the head.

Guns, torpedoes and tanks have been placed on the lawn below the concrete bunker which served as the command post. The bunker was built into the rock face and is cleverly concealed. You can climb up inside and scramble around.

Banadero Trail The Banadero Trail runs from behind the Last Command Post bunker up to the top of Suicide Cliff, coming out near the rest rooms. It takes about 45 minutes to reach the summit, but you might want to consider hitching back as the trail is very steep in places and you have to climb over some rocks and roots, which makes it safer going up. There's also a fair amount of sword grass, so knee socks or long pants are a good idea. The trail, which is marked with orange ribbons, leads through a thick forest with large trees and lots of birds. Two of the native birds you're apt to spot are the golden white-eye, a small bright yellow bird, and the rufous fantail, which is brown with a russet belly and brow and has a tail that spreads like a fan.

Suicide Cliff

Half a mile beyond the Last Command Post, you'll come to a fork where you should bear right. At a second fork, which is a mile farther, bear left to get to the Grotto and Bird Island, or right to get to Suicide Cliff.

From there, it's two miles up to Suicide Cliff. Halfway along, at a T-intersection, bear right and continue on the coral road to the top.

The 820-foot sheer rock face of Suicide Cliff was another site for Japanese suicides, similar to those that took place on Banzai Cliff.

The cliff provides an excellent view of the northern tip of the island. Below the lookout you can see the remains of the North Field runway, an old Japanese fighter strip. White-tailed tropicbirds and fairy terns swoop and soar in the wind drafts along the cliffside.

A small monument at the lookout reads:

The purpose of the Peace Memorial is to console the spirits of those who died, irrespective of nationality in this historic area, as well as to remind our posterities the tragic futility of war, with our sincere hope that everlasting peace and friendship may prevail amongst all mankind.

The Grotto

The Grotto, Saipan's most unique dive spot, is a collapsed limestone cavern with a pool of cobalt blue seawater filled by three underwater passageways. Sometimes the Grotto is calm and at other times powerful surges of water come whooshing in and out. Once, locals who wanted to swim in the Grotto had to shimmy down a rope but there are now steep concrete stairs down to the water. Tiny stalactites drip from above and massive spider webs hanging overhead make interesting photographs if caught in the right light. The glowing blue light at the bottom of the rock wall comes from the tunnels which lead to the open sea. There's a viewpoint looking down into the Grotto at the top of the stairs to the left.

To get to the Grotto, turn left one-quarter of a mile past the Suicide Cliff turn-off and follow the road to the end.

Bird Island Lookout

Bird Island, a rocky limestone islet close to shore, is a wildlife sanctuary that provides habitat for brown noddies and other seabirds.

The windy lookout point affords a scenic view of Bird Island, whose east side is battered by open ocean while the inland side is protected by a calm reef. The purple beach morning glory which grows prolifically

AIR FORCE POLICY NOTICE

Three **ENDANGERED**

Bird Species live in the Marpi Commonwealth Forest that surrounds this Radar Station.

VANIKORO SWIFTLET
YAYAGUAK

Found only in the Mariana Islands. May be seen in Saipan's interior valleys. Sightings have been reported in the Radar Station area.

MICRONESIAN MEGAPODE
SASNGAT

A ground-dwelling bird found only in Micronesia and Palau. Several have been sighted in the vicinity of this Radar Station.

NIGHTINGALE REED-WARBLER
GA' GA' KARISU

Found only in Micronesia. Several hundred may be present in the Radar Station area.

It is against Federal Laws and the Laws of the Commonwealth of Northern Mariana Islands to disturb these Endangered Birds or their nests. Violations are punishable by up to one year in prison and up to a $100,000 fine (16 U.S.C. 1531 *et seq.*, 1540).

Fruit Bats, *Fanihi,* are a Protected Species (Candidate Endangered Species). They are limited to a small number in the Marianas Islands and may be present in the Radar Station area.

Please Help Protect these Endangered Birds and their Forest:

- Do Not Disturb or Harm them
- Prevent and Report Fires
- Keep Pets Out of the Area

SSD/DEV, June, 1989

around the lookout cliff is called *alalag tasi* in Chamorro.

Bird Island Trail You can hike down to Bird Island but not from the lookout. Instead, head back the way you came and look for the start of the trail three-quarters of a mile on the right, just before the turn-off to the Grotto.

The beginning of the dirt footpath looks like an eroded driveway and leads down the hill through tall grass and a canopy of tangan-tangan.

At the bottom there's a coral sand beach. The water is clear and coral formations provide good snorkelling between Bird Island and the beach. Currents are rough beyond the reef.

CROSS-ISLAND RD

The Cross-Island Rd heads north of Garapan, turns inland to Capitol Hill, circles around Mt Tagpochau, goes south through San Vicente and then heads back to the west coast, passing the Northern Marianas Community College on the left and ending up on Beach Rd in San Jose.

From various spots around Capitol Hill, and on the drive up from Garapan, there are excellent views of Tanapag Harbor, Managaha Island and the brilliant turquoise waters of the lagoon.

Capitol Hill

Capitol Hill is the site of most government offices for the Commonwealth of the Northern Mariana Islands, including those of the governor and the legislature.

The complex of houses and office buildings that make up Capitol Hill was built in 1948 by the CIA as a base camp for secretly training Nationalist Chinese guerrillas to fight against Mao Zedong. The soldiers were trained in the Marpi area.

After the CIA moved out in 1962, Capitol Hill became the headquarters for the Trust Territory government. In recent years, as the Trust Territory has been slowly dismantled, the buildings have been turned over to the emerging commonwealth government.

Mt Tagpochau

You can drive right to the top of Mt Tagpochau which, at 1545 feet, is Saipan's highest point. To get there take the crossroad opposite the convention centre on Capitol Hill, drive a short way up through the housing project and turn right up to the former Congress of Micronesia buildings, now marked as civil defence and energy agencies. Continue a few hundred yards beyond the buildings and take the dirt road heading down to the right. If it's been raining heavily you may need a 4WD vehicle from this point, but otherwise a sedan takes about 15 minutes to the top.

Mt Tagpochau is the destination each Easter for hundreds of Saipanese who hike up, carrying a heavy wooden cross to plant on the top. There are excellent views of most of the island from the summit.

East Coast Beaches

Heavy seas beat against a rugged shoreline along much of Saipan's east coast although there are some protected areas. Most of the east coast beaches are difficult to reach, and a 4WD vehicle may be required, particularly if the roads are muddy. All this may well change as a number of golf courses and resorts are being planned for the area, including developments at Profile and Laulau beaches.

Profile Beach is a small, isolated pocket beach with a limestone islet called Old Man by the Sea, which looks remarkably like the laughing head of an old man. To get there turn off the Cross-Island Rd at Escolastica Store (pick up homemade papaya turnovers or Chamorro cookies for the beach!) at the south end of Capitol Hill. Take a left at the Y-intersection and park about a hundred feet down. The trailhead is on the right side of the road and it's about a 20-minute hike to the beach.

Jeffries (Talofofo) Beach is a small beach in an area that has natural arches and blowholes. To get there go down past the Escolastica Store and follow the road to its end. You don't have to hike to get to this beach, though it requires a scramble down a rather steep cliff.

Tank, Marine and Laulau are other east coast beaches that can all be reached by dirt roads. Laulau Beach, on the north side of Magicienne Bay, is one of the more popular and protected beaches on the east coast and is good for beach dives.

SOUTH OF GARAPAN

San Jose, Susupe, Chalan Kanoa and San Antonio were once distinct villages on Saipan's south-west coast until a decade of development turned Beach Rd into a nearly continuous strip of nightclubs, porno shops, restaurants and shopping centres.

Susupe has the police station, courthouse and other government offices. Prior to the recent high-rise hotel boom, Susupe's multi-storyed Nauru Building was Saipan's tallest and most pronounced landmark.

Chalan Kanoa has the main post office, the island's only remaining movie theatre and the picturesque Mt Carmel Cathedral. San Antonio, though it's being developed, is still the quieter end of it all.

Southern Beaches

Ladder and Obyan are two nice south coast beaches that get a few local picnickers, but are well off the tourist track. To get to them, take the airport road, turn right after the petrol station near the airport entrance, go behind and past the large bunkers that were part of the Japanese communications station and continue around the tip of the runway. The first paved road to the right leads to Chalan Kanoa, the second (three-quarters of a mile from the first) to Koblerville and the third (one quarter of a mile more) to Ladder Beach.

Ladder Beach is a rounded cove backed with 30-foot limestone cliffs. Most of the beach is covered with chunky coral pebbles, though there are some white sand patches for sunbathing. There are large caves in the cliffs which are used as picnic shelters, complete with picnic tables. From the parking area, a 10-minute walk along a dirt road through a jungle of tangan-tangan leads to an ocean-

side plaque honouring the 15,000 Americans who served with the 73rd Bombardment Wing on Saipan.

Obyan Beach is a pretty white sand beach with calm waters protected by Naftan Point. The beach, which is much larger than Ladder's, is good for shelling and snorkelling. At the head of the parking area is a large WW II concrete bunker and about 75 yards east, just inland from a grove of coconut trees, is a latte stone that's been carbon dated to around 1500 BC. The turn-off down to Obyan Beach is 1½ miles beyond Ladder Beach.

Sunken Treasure In 1638 the Manila galleon *Nuestra Senora de la Concepcion* went down east of Agingan Point, scattering its treasure along the shallow reef that now borders the Coral Ocean Point golf course. In 1987, after searching through archives in Seville, Mexico City and Manila to research the location and cargo, an international crew of 30, including historians and archaeologists, began a two-year salvage operation. Some 10,000 dives later they had recovered scores of cannonballs and ballast stones, 1300 pieces of gold jewellery, many inlaid with precious gems, and 156 storage jars, some still filled with fragrant resins. Some of the pieces were recovered in as little as two feet of water. A Japanese company has purchased the collection for $5 million and many of the items are to be eventually displayed in Saipan.

MANAGAHA ISLAND

Managaha, the island 1½ miles northwest of Micro Beach, is an old patch reef which geological forces lifted above sea level some 10,000 years ago. It's now covered with a fringing white sand beach and has Saipan's best snorkelling. The clear waters surrounding the island have lots of colourful tropical fish and good coral close to shore.

The island has the rusting remains of a few war relics and a small monument marking the burial site of the Yapese chief Ahgrub who established a Carolinian settlement on Saipan during the Spanish era.

Managaha is popular with both picnicking Saipanese and tourists on day trips. It's a small island that takes only 15 minutes to walk around and it has no permanent residents. For visiting day-trippers there's a refreshment stand, picnic tables and toilets.

Getting There & Away

The main boat to Managaha is the *Jambalaya*, which leaves from Charlie Dock at 9.30 and 10.30 am and 12.30 pm. You can return at 1, 2.30 or 4 pm. The cost is $20 return for tourists, though islanders get to go for free.

Another way to get to Managaha is from the water sports concession stands at Micro Beach, which charge $20 to zip you over by speedboat.

PDI (☎ 234-6210) has a glass-bottom boat which passes over a Japanese Zero and some coral heads on the way to Managaha. The cost is $31 for adults, $22 for children.

PLACES TO STAY
Camping

Rip-offs and crime are issues on Saipan that need to be considered by campers. Generally the more isolated your campsite, the less likely you'll be to bump into drunks and vandals.

Managaha used to be a great camping spot, though the island is small and with hundreds of tourists now going over for day trips, you'll probably have far more company than you want. The island also has rats and if you do camp there you may be better off sleeping on the picnic tables than the ground.

Saipan's largely undeveloped east coast also has some good spots. Profile Beach, which requires a 20-minute hike, is a nice place to camp as it's isolated and you don't have to worry much about unwanted visitors. Though less isolated, nearby Jeffries Beach would also be a good spot for camping and you can reach it from the road without having to hike.

None of these spots has water.

Hotels

Saipan has more than 2100 hotel rooms, with another 6000 on the drawing boards. All hotel rooms in Saipan have air-con and private bathrooms. Top-end hotels have the usual resort amenities like swimming pools, tennis courts, restaurants, nightly entertainment and water sports equipment rentals. Saipan adds a 10% hotel tax to room rates. Most hotels, including all the bottom-end places listed here, accept credit cards.

During the Japanese holiday season, particularly Christmas through January and mid-July through August, it can be very difficult to find accommodation.

Hotels – bottom end The Japanese-run *Remington Club* (☎ 234-5449) Box 1719, Saipan, MP 96950, a 24-room pension-style hotel in Garapan, is popular with young Japanese divers and beach bums on a budget. The cheaper rooms are run down, with old stained carpet, mildewy bathrooms and scuffed-up walls, but you can't beat the price and still be just a block away from Micro Beach. Rates are $35 for singles or doubles. A handful of larger and spiffier rooms with a partial kitchen cost $60. Payment is required at check-in and there's a steep $30 key deposit.

The *Sun Inn Motel* (☎ 234-6639), Box 920, Saipan, MP 96950, behind the baseball field in Susupe, has 18 rooms that are rather spartan but have phones and refrigerators and cost $40/42 for singles/doubles.

The *Sugar King Hotel* (☎ 234-6164), in a quiet area above Sugar King Park, has 27 rooms in concrete duplex cottages. Rates are $44 for one or two people in a room with a platform-style double bed, refrigerator, kitchen sink and TV, but the rooms are rather cramped and you wouldn't want to spend a lot of time hanging around inside. Also, bed coverings are skimpy and you may need to ask for an extra blanket. One big plus is the large, uncrowded swimming pool with its distant ocean view. The hotel has a coin laundry and moped rentals for $25 a day. Advance reservations are not taken, you must pay in advance upon checking in and there's a 'No Refunds' sign in the window.

Rooms can also be rented by the month for $550.

The *Islander Inn* (☎ 234-6071), Box 1249, Saipan, MP 96950 is on the 2nd floor of an office building on Beach Rd in Garapan, a few blocks up from Micro Beach. The 27 rooms have TVs, refrigerators and phones and cost $45/55 for singles/doubles.

Hotels – middle The locally owned *Chamorro House Motel* (☎ 234-7361), Box 875, Saipan, MP 96950, above Chamorro House Restaurant in Garapan, is a couple of minutes walk from Micro Beach. The 14 rooms are large and pleasant with TVs, phones, refrigerators, bathtubs and soft carpeting. Rates are $55/60 for singles/doubles.

The new 26-room *Garapan Plaza Hotel* (☎ 234-7437), Box 1551, Saipan, MP 96950, a couple of blocks inland from Beach Rd in Garapan, is one of the better values in the middle price range. The rooms are modern and have nice furnishings, cable TV, phones, carpeting, refrigerators, and bathrooms with tubs and marble counters. Rates are $55/65 for singles/doubles, plus a 5% fee if you pay by credit card. The hotel is owned by a commonwealth congressman.

Saipan Ocean View Hotel (☎ 234-8900), Box 799, Saipan, MP 96950), a small two-storey hotel on Beach Rd in Garapan, has modern rooms with phones, safes, mini-refrigerators, cable TV and video movies, bathtubs and carpeting. Rates are $55/65 for singles/doubles and they offer free airport transfers.

Marianas Trench Motel (☎ 234-3146), Box 755, Saipan, MP 96950, a 12-room hotel on Beach Rd in Garapan, is basically OK, though expensive for what you get. Rooms have TVs and are slightly kitschy, with vinyl headboards and see-through plastic phones. Singles/doubles cost $55/65.

The locally owned *Pacific Gardenia Hotel* (☎ 234-3455), Box 144, Saipan, MP 96950 is on a busy section of Beach Rd at the north end of Chalan Kanoa. There are 14 rooms, all on the 2nd floor along an atrium-like hallway. Rooms are large and nicely furnished, with kitchens, TVs, phones and cable TV with video movies, and cost $78. There's a coin laundry and free airport transfers. The staff is helpful and can provide cribs, ironing boards and the like upon request.

Marine Sports Hotel (☎ 234-1462), Caller Box PPP158, Saipan, MP 96950 is a three-storey, 14-room hotel in San Antonio. Rooms have the usual amenities, as well as balconies which overlook the beach, and cost $80. Airport transfers are free.

Hotels – top end The larger hotels, thriving on the package tour trade, have less need to be receptive to independent travellers and room rates are typically high. With few exceptions, the atmosphere is more Tokyo than Micronesia.

Saipan's best hotel is the seven-storey *Hyatt Regency Saipan* (☎ 234-6811), Box 87 CHRB, Saipan, MP 96950 right on Micro Beach. All 183 rooms have balconies with sunset and ocean views. The rates start at $180 for rooms on the 2nd floor, with prices going up as the floors do. The Hyatt is the oldest of Saipan's resort hotels, though it's been completely refurbished. It has the most international clientele and the best beach location. If money is no object, this is the place to be.

Other first-class hotels in Saipan are:

Saipan Grand Hotel, Box 369, Saipan, MP 96950 in Susupe (☎ 234-6601); 146 rooms, from $100.
Pacific Islands Club, Box 2370, Saipan, MP 96950) in San Antonio (☎ 234-7976); 220 rooms, $120.
Chalan Kanoa Beach Club, Box 356, Saipan, MP 96950, in Chalan Kanoa (☎ 234-7829); 28 units, $120.
Coral Ocean Point Resort Club, Box 1160, Saipan, MP 96950, on a golf course south of San Antonio (☎ 234-7000); 82 rooms, $130.
Hafadai Beach Hotel, Box 338, Saipan, MP 96950, in Garapan; 280 rooms (☎ 234-6495); from $135.
Saipan Diamond Hotel, Box 66, Saipan, MP 96950, in Susupe (☎ 234-5900); 265 rooms, from $150.
Aqua Resort Club, Box 9, Saipan, MP 96950, in Tanapag (☎ 322-1234); 91 rooms, from $150.
Dai-Ichi Hotel, Box 1029, Saipan, MP 96950 in Garapan (☎ 234-6412); 175 rooms, from $150.
Marianas Resort Hotel, Box 527, Saipan, MP 96950, adjacent to the Marianas Country Club in San Roque (☎ 322-0770); 50 cottages, from $170.

Hotel Nikko Saipan, Box 152 CHRB, Saipan, MP 96950, in San Roque (☎ 322-3311); 313 rooms, from $180.

PLACES TO EAT

Chamorro food is basically the same in the Northern Marianas as it is on Guam, except it's harder to find. One exception is the *Chamorro House*, a popular restaurant in the Micro Beach area, which has been serving quality local food for years. Their lunch specials are the best deals, with Chamorro dishes from $5 to $8.50. Dinner prices are about double.

There are a slew of authentic Japanese restaurants in the Micro Beach area, though many are overpriced. The best value is *Coconut-Tei*, a hole in the wall on a back street, one block inland from the Hyatt. Set lunches, including yakiniku, fried fish or beef curry, cost $5. Coconut-Tei opens at noon.

The Hyatt's *Kili Terrace* has an excellent $9 lunch buffet from 11.30 am to 1.30 pm Monday to Saturday. You can sit out in the pleasant open-air terrace and eat your fill of such dishes as reef fish, beef curry, sushi, soba, spareribs, pizza, breads, luncheon meats and a variety of soups, salads and fresh tropical fruits. *Poon's* in Garapan has Indonesian food, such as gado-gado and beef or chicken satay, at reasonable prices. An Indonesian family runs the restaurant so the food is authentic, though portions are rather small.

China House Restaurant, on Beach Rd in Gualo Rai, has a following, though the food's on the expensive side. Almost as good, and quite a bit cheaper, is the nearby *Hong Kong Restaurant*, which has a full Chinese menu, including vegetarian food and hot & spicy dishes, most in the $5 to $7 range. Hong Kong Restaurant is one mile south of the Hafadai Beach Hotel.

Rudolpho's, in a flamingo-pink building right on the beach in San Jose, has good, reasonably priced Mexican and Italian food and a nice mix of local and expatriate regulars. There's an indoor bar and both indoor and outdoor tables. You can get a taco, burrito or enchilada plate with rice and beans for $5 or spaghetti with garlic bread for the same price. They also have seafood and steak meals from $6.50 to $22, as well as pizza and sandwiches. To find Rudolpho's, turn off Beach Rd at Kim's Tofu Factory & Auto Repair, one-quarter of a mile south of the road to the airport.

Herman's Modern Bakery, on the way to the airport, is a popular local eatery. Besides being a good place for coffee and doughnuts, the coffee shop serves inexpensive breakfasts, lunch specials for $3.75 and sandwiches for about $2. The bakery makes a good cracked wheat bread. Herman started his bakery in 1944 to bake bread for American GIs. By the time the GIs had moved out, Saipanese had developed a taste for bread and Herman's continues to supply most of Saipan's bread and pastries.

Maharani, on Middle Rd in Gualo Rai, features a full menu of Indian food, including chicken tandoori, biriyani, curries and nan. Prices are generally expensive, with dinner dishes ranging from $13 to $27. Lunch prices are about a third cheaper and there's a very simple lunch buffet for $8.50.

La Pergola, on the road climbing up to Capitol Hill, has good Italian food and distant ocean views. They make their own home-made pastas and both meat and vegetarian sauces. Pasta dishes with salad and garlic bread are $6.50 to $8.50 at lunch. At dinner they're $1 more, but don't include salad. Steak and seafood dishes are $16 to $22. It's open from 11.30 am to 1.30 pm Monday to Friday and from 6.30 to 10 pm nightly.

The old Japanese lighthouse on Navy Hill has been tastefully renovated and turned into *The Light House*, a fine dining restaurant that serves Italian and Mediterranean dishes. The food has a good reputation, though the cheapest dishes are pastas for about $15, while four-course dinners average $45. If you just want to catch the view, visit when they're not busy and they'll let you climb to the top of the lighthouse for a sweeping view of Garapan, the reef and Managaha Island. There are plans to add a bar & grill halfway up the lighthouse tower. The restaurant is open for lunch, dinner and mid-afternoon tea. To get there, turn off Middle Rd at the hospital and follow the signs.

Tipping has caught on in Saipan and a tip of at least 10% is expected at most restaurants.

With the exception of *Winchell's* doughnut shop in Garapan, the only fast-food franchise on the island is *Kentucky Fried Chicken* in the Town House Shopping Center in Susupe. Where else does the Colonel serve his chicken with red rice cooked with achiote seeds?!

Saipan Farmer's Market, the 'Co-op of the Hardworking People', is a fruit and vegetable market opposite the post office in Chalan Kanoa. It's open from 8 am to 6 pm on weekdays and Saturdays, and from 8 am to noon on Sundays.

You can get a big bottle of sweet tuba at JV's Mart on Beach Rd in San Jose (next to Mama's Nite Club) for $4.

Supermarkets sell almost everything you'd find in Western stores, except that prices tend to be substantially higher and much of the produce is tired.

ENTERTAINMENT
Rudolpho's, on the beach in San Jose, is one of the cheapest places to knock back a few beers, with a bottle of Bud or San Miguel only $2. The beachfront patio is a nice place to be at sunset.

In Garapan, Martin's Ocean Bar & Grill, just south of the Dai-Ichi Hotel, is another place with local atmosphere and reasonably priced drinks.

Most of the large hotels have discos, Polynesian' dance shows and other high-priced tourist entertainment.

There are lots of flashy nightclubs, dance spots and seedy massage parlours up from the hotels at Micro Beach. Most of the signs are in Japanese and have names like Club Passionate Love and Folk Pub Massage Services. The most flamboyant dance club in the Micro Beach area is Discoteque Gig, which has a large Sphinx out the front and charges 25 admission.

Saipan has three golf courses, with several more planned. Fees are $15 at the local nine-hole Saipan Country Club near San Jose and more than $100 at the 18-hole courses at the Marianas Country Club in Marpi and the Coral Ocean Point Resort Club at Agingan Point.

There's a movie theatre in Chalan Kanoa next to the post office, a 12-lane bowling alley on Beach Rd in San Jose and cockfights at the Saipan Cockfight in Garapan. For a different sort of entertainment, take the glass elevator to the top of the Hafadai hotel to catch the night view of Garapan.

THINGS TO BUY
Virtually none of the carvings, woven wall hangings or other handicrafts in Saipan's shops are made on the island. Most are imported from the Philippines and generally the prices are high and the quality low. Postcards, T-shirts and plastic knick-knacks bearing the island's name are just about the only souvenirs 'unique' to Saipan.

A fair amount of shopping goes on in Saipan nonetheless, largely by the Japanese who are obligated to take souvenirs home. Duty-free shops with high-priced designer products are a big hit, Saipan has stylish tropical print cotton clothing and film is available.

Saipan's main shopping centres are JoeTen in Susupe, Hafa Adai in Garapan and Town House in Chalan Kanoa. All three have modern grocery stores.

GETTING THERE & AWAY
Continental Airlines flies direct to Saipan from Manila and the Japanese cities of Fukuoka, Nagoya, Sapporo, Sendai and Tokyo, as well as from Guam via Air Mike.

Japan Air Lines flies direct to Saipan from Nagoya, Osaka and Tokyo; All Nippon Airways from several cities in Japan; Northwest Airlines from Tokyo; and Korean Air from Seoul.

All FSM and Palau connections to Saipan go through Guam, as do connections from Australia, Bali, Manila and Honolulu. For more details see the Getting There & Away chapter in the front of the book.

Though other airlines have flown the route in the past (and will probably do so again), Air Mike is currently the only carrier shuttling passengers between Guam and Saipan. From Guam, Air Mike's cheapest ticket to Saipan is $35 on the 5.20 am flight. All other flights cost $66 one way, though you can stop in Rota with this fare. Excursion tickets cost $98 with a Rota stopover, $73 without. If you're flying Air Mike to Guam from Koror or Honolulu, you can sometimes add Saipan on for about $20 more.

Airport

Saipan's modern airport, eight miles south of Garapan, has car rental booths, a small handicraft shop, a foreign exchange booth, a restaurant, a duty-free shop and a separate commuter air terminal.

GETTING AROUND
Bus

The public bus system, with the ambitious name of Saipan Rapid Transit (☎ 234-0567/5550), has a bus that runs up and down Beach Rd from 6.30 am to 10.30 pm daily. It stops at bus signs, major hotels or wherever it's flagged down. The minimum fare is $1, which will cover a ride anywhere in the greater Garapan area. The fare between Garapan and Chalan Kanoa is $2. Whether the service will stay up and running is rather an iffy affair, as it's dependent upon grant money which has come and gone over the years.

Taxi

Taxis are private with rates calculated on distance, regardless of the number of passengers. Typical charges are $14 from the airport to Micro Beach, $7 from Garapan to Susupe.

Car

The phone numbers and cheapest rentals of the car rental agencies at the airport are: Islander Rent-A-Car (☎ 234-8233; $30), Hertz (☎ 234-8336; $40) and Thrifty (☎ 234-8356; $26). Unlike the others which offer late-model cars, Thrifty rents old, beat-up cars for its lowest rate. Based on our most recent experience, we can't recommend these 'bargain' cars.

The first car Thrifty gave us never made it out of the parking lot and the replacement car overheated near Suicide Cliff on the remote north coast. We managed to get back to Garapan only to have the starter fail!

The best deal to be found is at ESPN Rent A Car (☎ 234-8249), opposite the Dai-Ichi Hotel in Garapan, where Suzuki Alto 'minicars' rent for $22 a day. ESPN has plans to open a booth at the airport.

Most companies charge about $10 a day for the optional collision damage waiver. You must be 25 years old to rent cars from Islander or Thrifty, while at ESPN or Hertz the minimum age is 21. None of these companies charges extra for mileage.

Expect to see bumper-to-bumper traffic on Saipan. The traffic between San Jose and Chalan Kanoa, in particular, can slow to a crawl at any time of the day, and at rush hours it's often traffic-jammed.

Bicycle

A souvenir shop in front of the Hyatt in Garapan rents bicycles for $15 a day.

Hitching

Saipan's main routes are reasonably good for hitching. Be wary of accepting one-way rides to secluded areas, both for the usual safety reasons and because it can be a very long time between vehicles when you want to get back.

Tinian

Tinian, a peaceful one-village island just three miles south of Saipan, has a notorious place in history as the take-off site for the aircraft that dropped the atomic bombs on Hiroshima and Nagasaki.

It's an attractive island with ancient latte stones, ranch land with grazing cattle,

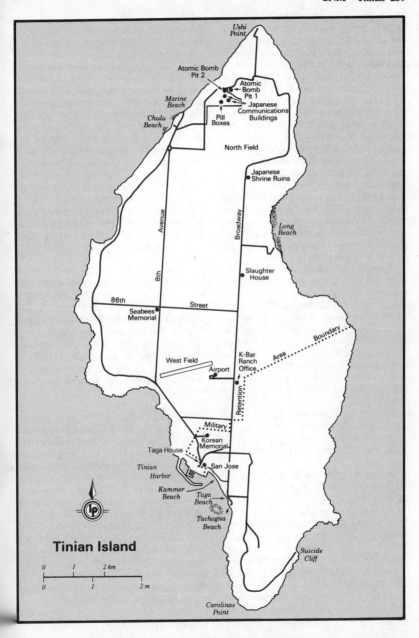

Tinian Island

Ushi
Point

Atomic Bomb
Pit 2

Atomic
Bomb
Pit 1

Japanese
Communications
Buildings

Marine
Beach

Chulu
Beach

Pill
Boxes

North Field

Japanese
Shrine Ruins

Long
Beach

8th

Avenue

Broadway

Slaughter
House

86th   Street

Seabees
Memorial

Boundary

Area

West Field

K-Bar
Ranch
Office

Airport

Retention

Military

Taga House

Korean
Memorial

Tinian
Harbor

San Jose

Kammer
Beach

Taga
Beach

Tachogna
Beach

Suicide
Cliff

Tinian Island

0   1   2 km

0   1   2 m

Carolinas
Point

secluded sandy beaches and scenic vistas. The sleeper of Marianas tourism promotions, Tinian's handful of small hotels and restaurants are insufficient to support package tourism which makes the island an ideal destination for individual travellers.

Tinian is the second largest island in the Northern Marianas, about 12 miles long and five miles wide, and is the least mountainous, with a top elevation of 690 feet.

The island's fertile soil was used to advantage by the Japanese who levelled the forests and turned the island into a chequerboard of sugar cane fields. Its level terrain was also ideal for the airfields which were built later. Only a few Chamorros lived on Tinian during the Japanese occupation and they were greatly outnumbered by the nearly 18,000 Japanese, Okinawans and Koreans, most of whom were farm labourers.

Homesick Americans who captured the island in 1944 and quickly developed it into a huge air base decided the shape of Tinian was not too different from New York's Manhattan Island. They named the roads they constructed Broadway, 42nd St and 8th Ave and called one section of the island Harlem and another Central Park. Some of the road names are still used today, though having an 86th St seems a bit out of place on an island that now has little traffic and only a few paved roads!

After the war Tinian reverted back to pastoral ways and ranching took hold. The island became known for its beef and dairy products which were exported to neighbouring islands.

Tinian may be destined to become the next US military base in the western Pacific. The northern third of the island has been leased to the US military for its sole control and use. The middle third is also leased to the military, though it includes some areas in joint use with the Tinian government (such as the airport and harbour) and other areas such as pastureland that are being leased backed by Tinian residents.

Though there aren't yet any permanent military facilities, Tinian is used sporadically for US Marine Corps training, and access to the northernmost part of the island is restricted during those times.

In a recent referendum, Tinian voters approved of gambling and the development of casinos on the island, a move that will be likely to create some radical changes. Though still in the planning stages, the government intends to initially license up to five casino developments. There are also plans to develop the first golf course resort on the island. Though many people feel that their rural lifestyle is at risk, the big bucks that overseas developers have been flashing have resulted in a number of islanders giving up their land to become instant millionaires.

Tinian's days as a tranquil getaway may be numbered, but in the meantime it retains an unhurried small-island charm long since lost on neighbouring Saipan.

Festivals

Tinian's fiesta is held on the first weekend in May in honour of San Jose, the island's patron saint. Everyone is welcome to the feasting and fun although finding accommodation at that time can be a problem.

A cliff fishing competition, open to anyone who wants to participate, is held each year in early November. Tuna weighing a good 60 pounds have been caught from Tinian cliffs.

Activities

Diving Tinian has clear waters, an ocean bottom that slopes rapidly from the shore and a number of good dive sites a short distance from San Jose. One of the most popular is Dump Coke, which was a huge dumping ground for WW II junk and where small Japanese tanks, jeeps, trucks, shell casings and other munitions can be easily spotted.

Suzuki Diving Micronesia (☎ 433-3274), Box 100, San Jose, Tinian, MP 96952, across from the Fleming Hotel, is Tinian's only dive shop. They offer one beach dive for $40 or one boat dive for $80. Introductory beach dives for beginners cost $60 and two-hour snorkelling tours by boat cost $40.

Organised Tours Many Saipan tour operators offer day-long sightseeing tours of Tinian for $95 to $110, including lunch and transportation to and from Saipan.

The M&F Corporation at Fleming Hotel (☎ 433-3232) offers a sightseeing tour of the island, with either an English or Japanese-speaking guide, for $19 without lunch, $27 with lunch.

SAN JOSE

The quiet village of San Jose, where most of Tinian's 2100 residents live, was once the site of an ancient village of 13,000 Chamorros. The current population is partly derived from a group of Chamorros who had been living on Yap since the German era and who were resettled in San Jose by the Americans after WW II.

San Jose is a small village and easy to walk around.

Information

The Bank of Guam and a grocery store are in the same building as the Fleming Hotel. There's a laundromat next door. Tinian's post office is down behind the mayor's office, next to the farmer's market.

Taga House

San Jose's most notable attraction is Taga House, an impressive collection of latte stones said to be the foundations of the home of Taga the Great, legendary king of the ancient Chamorros.

The grassy park contains a dozen or so pitted limestone shafts and capstones as large as five feet in diameter and 15 feet high, and is included on the US National Register of Historic Places. The only latte stone still standing upright has an ironwood sapling rooted atop its broken capstone.

There are some small Japanese memorials on both sides of Taga House.

Tinian Harbor

San Jose's huge harbour and Broadway, the divided highway that connects the village to the WW II airstrips at the north end of the island, were both built by the US Seabees to unload and transport the scores of bombs that

were dropped on Japan in the final year of the war.

Today, Tinian's deepwater harbour is a tuna transhipment centre. Purse seiners come in and out of the harbour, loading their catch onto mother ships which stay docked until full and then sail for home ports in the Orient. Fish other than tuna that get caught in the nets are given away, so people on Tinian get to eat a lot of free fish.

Kammer Beach

Kammer Beach, also called Jones Beach, is a nice sandy stretch east of the harbour and an easy walk from the centre of town. It has picnic facilities, rest rooms and a view of Aguijan Island to the south.

During WW II, Americans staged a fake diversionary landing at Kammer Beach just hours before the actual invasion on the north-west shore.

SOUTH OF SAN JOSE
Taga & Tachogna Beaches

Taga Beach Park is one mile south of town on Broadway. From the cliff above the beach there's a striking view of San Jose and some of the most brilliant turquoise waters you can ever expect to see. Stairs lead down the cliff to a small sandy beach. The water gets deep fairly quickly, which makes it good for swimming.

Tachogna Beach Park, immediately beyond, has a broad white sand beach and is another good swimming area. The water may be a bit choppy at high tide, but at low tide snorkellers can wade right out to the shallow coral patch visible just offshore.

Suicide Cliff

To get to Suicide Cliff, follow the road inland from Taga Beach another four miles, bearing right first at the crossroads and then at the fork. Along the way there are excellent views of the south-west side of the island looking back toward San Jose. The grassy road to Suicide Cliff is usually passable in a sedan.

In the hills above the cliffs are the natural and artificial caves that were the last defence position and hide-out for the Japanese army.

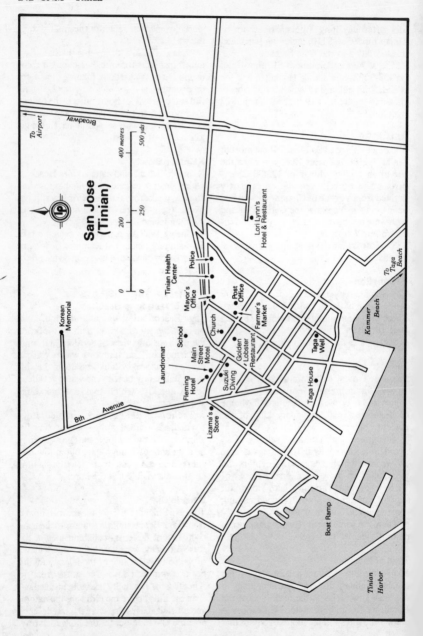

San Jose (Tinian)

Though Tinian was secured by the USA after nine days of combat, it took an additional three months to rout out the Japanese from the caves in these cliffs. Most of the 4000 Japanese defenders never accounted for are assumed to have committed suicide inside the caves.

A peace memorial at the site remembers the Japanese civilians who leapt from the cliffs in a smaller version of the suicidal jumps that took place on Saipan. The jump site along the cliff is now barricaded by a fence.

Cow patties (step lightly!) attest to the grazing done in the area, Polynesian rats hop across the road and on a clear day you can see Rota.

NORTH OF SAN JOSE

Heading north on Broadway from San Jose, the road passes through lots of green pasture land which makes for a nice country drive.

Ranches

Though Tinian has a number of small local ranches, the island's ranching is dominated by K-Bar Ranch, the largest cattle operation in Micronesia. K-Bar grazes about 4000 head of cattle on 7500 acres of leased land, mostly on the east side of the island. Supermarkets in Guam and Saipan still sell K-Bar beef, though the dairy is long gone. The K-Bar offices are opposite the airport turn-off.

Up ahead, the former Japanese communications building with its heavy metal window grates is now a slaughterhouse for Tinian cattle and, when needed, it also serves as a typhoon shelter.

Japanese Shrines

About four miles from the airport turn-off a large Shinto torii (gate) on the left, visible from the road, marks the entrance to the site of a former Japanese shrine.

Just ahead, the road circles a roundabout which has another old Japanese shrine in its centre. A little past this, Saipan comes into view. Along the rocky north-east coast waves crash against the cliffs, in places bursting up through blowholes.

North Field

The main road loops around North Field, a massive network of landing fields and crossroads that once comprised the largest military airbase in the world.

At the outbreak of the battle for the Marianas, the Japanese already had two 4700-foot runways completed and three other airstrips under construction. After Tinian was taken, the US Seabees immediately began building four airstrips, each 1½ miles long. These strips were take-off sites for fire-bomb raids on Japan's home islands and later for the planes that carried the atomic bombs.

Once inside the field, there's a confusing maze of roads, airstrips and overgrown crossroads that can all look the same. It's easy to get lost – more than 29 miles of airplane taxiways alone were built at North Field!

The abandoned runways that once held rows of planes now have only lazy monitor lizards basking in the sun.

Ushi Point

A road to the right, about eight miles past the airport turn-off, goes to Ushi Point, the northern tip of Tinian. At the point, a cross and memorial stand in remembrance of Tinian islanders who have died at sea. The cross is replaced every Easter.

Atomic Bomb Pits

Back on the main road circling North Field a dirt road leads to the loading pits for the atomic bombs that were dropped on Japan.

The road to the pits is on the left about three-quarters of a mile beyond the turn-off to Ushi Point and 4½ miles from the Japanese shrine roundabout. The pit sites are neat and sterile, marked with signs, plaques, plumeria and coconut trees. Some locals think the puny size of the coconuts indicates that radioactivity is present.

Little Boy & Fat Man

In the early evening of 5 August 1945 a uranium bomb code-named 'Little Boy' was loaded aboard the Enola Gay, an American B 29 aircraft. The four-ton bomb had been brought to Tinian from San Francisco aboard the heavy cruiser *Indianapolis*.

The Enola Gay and its 12-man crew took off from Tinian at 2.45 am on 6 August and headed for Hiroshima, 1700 miles away. The bomb was dropped at 9.15 am Tinian time. It exploded in the air above the city, forming a fireball which quickly mushroomed into a dark-grey cloud three miles wide and 35,000 feet high. More than 75,000 people were killed and the age of atomic warfare had begun.

The second atomic bomb loaded on Tinian was a 4½-ton plutonium bomb named 'Fat Man'. It was dropped on Nagasaki on 9 August 1945. ■

Japanese Buildings

There are some Japanese WW II installations nearby in the overgrown brush. Go south a few hundred yards from the loading pits until the road splits and turn to the left, then take the first right and first right again onto a runway. Continue on the runway until you notice a small overgrown road to the right which goes straight in to the complex.

The reinforced concrete building at the right is the easiest to spot but hidden, straight ahead, is a larger two-storey former communications building. It was once used in conjunction with an underwater cable system which connected Tinian to Saipan. Low concrete pillboxes with gun holes are concealed in the brush to the left as you face the main building.

Invasion Beaches

From the Japanese buildings turn right, back onto the runway, and at the end of the road turn left, then take the next right to get to Chulu Beach. A little to the north of Chulu Beach is Marine Beach. Both are attractive white sand beaches.

Chulu and Marine beaches, which were dubbed White Beach I and II by US forces, are the invasion beaches where more than 15,000 US troops landed in July 1944. The beaches are so narrow it makes you wonder where they found space to put them all.

A coastal road and the more direct 8th Avenue both lead back to San Jose.

Seabees Memorial

A memorial on the corner of 86th St and 8th Ave has a plaque and a map of wartime Tinian. The plaque reads:

To the men of the 107th United States Naval Construction Battalion and all the Seabees who in 1944-45 on Tinian, Mariana Islands, participated in the largest engineering feat of WW II. Seabees constructed four runways and created the world's largest air base enabling the US Armed Forces to end the war in the Pacific. We of the ex-107th Seabees consecrate this ground to our fallen comrades. May God help us to avoid WW III.

Korean Memorial

Seven miles south of Chulu Beach on 8th Avenue (just under half a mile north of Lizama's Store in San Jose), turn inland onto a grassy path lined with palm trees. Not far from the road is a memorial, built on the back of a carved stone turtle, honouring Koreans who died during WW II.

In the hills to the right are caves where the Japanese hid from invading US forces and through the grass, to the left of the turtle, is a brick oven which was a crematorium for Koreans who died before the war.

AGUIJAN ISLAND

Aguijan is an uninhabited island less than five miles south of Tinian. During the Spanish and Japanese administrations it was sporadically inhabited but now it's nicknamed 'Goat Island' after its current residents. Goat hunting takes place in season. Birds are abundant too.

Aguijan is part of Tinian's political district and it's necessary to get a permit from the mayor of Tinian before visiting the island. The boat ride takes 20 minutes, but there are no beaches and landings are usually made by jumping ship close to shore and wading in. Thorns can be a deterrent to exploring the interior.

PLACES TO STAY
Camping
Tinian is one of the better islands in Micronesia for camping, though the usual precautions apply. No permission is needed to camp on public beaches.

Kammer Beach, at the edge of town, has a sandy beach, running water, toilets, barbecue pits and picnic tables.

Taga and Tachogna beach parks, about a mile from town, are other possibilities. Both have picnic tables and town water.

If you want someplace more remote, try the white sands of Chulu Beach on the northwest coast, but take water with you.

Hotels
The new *Lori Lynn's Hotel* (☎ 433-0386), Box 50, San Jose, MP 96952, owned by a friendly local family, has 12 rooms with TVs and refrigerators that cost $35/45 for singles/doubles. Rooms on the 2nd floor are $5 more. Airport transfers are provided on request.

The *Fleming Hotel* (☎ 433-3232), Box 1268, Tinian, MP 96952 has 13 rather ordinary rooms that cost $50/60 for singles/doubles. Fleming's (officially the Meitetsu & Fleming Hotel) caters mostly to Japanese tourists. Airport transfers are $3.50 each way.

Main Street Motel, a few doors down from Fleming Hotel, has five rooms that are a bit cheaper than Fleming's.

All rooms on Tinian have private bathrooms and air-con and add a 10% tax to room rates.

PLACES TO EAT
Lori Lynn's Restaurant is a good place to eat, though the service can be quite slow. The $4.50 lunch specials which include an entree such as teriyaki chicken with soup, salad and rice are a good deal. At dinner, they serve Japanese, Chinese, Chamorro and American food in generous portions for under $10. Hours are from 6 am to 10 pm daily. To get to Lori Lynn's, head towards Broadway from town and take the third right past the police station.

The *Golden Lobster Restaurant*, in the centre of town, has an upscale international menu and good food. An extensive list of lunch specials includes such dishes as mahimahi sauteed in butter and wine, served with rice and cole slaw, for $6 or Chamorro-style shrimp kelaguen with tortillas for $6.50. Dinner dishes range from seafood spaghetti or Filipino pancit for $7 to steak and lobster for $23. It's open from 7 am to 2 pm and from 6 pm to 2 am.

Tap water is treated on Tinian and safe to drink.

GETTING THERE & AWAY
Air
Freedom Air (☎ 234-8328 in Saipan, 433-3288 in Tinian) flies six-seater Piper Cherokee planes between Saipan and Tinian. The first scheduled flight leaves Saipan at 8 am and the last returns from Tinian at 5 pm. Though the schedule shows only seven flights, they essentially shuttle back and forth as passengers show up, flying as many as 30 flights a day. The flight takes just 10 minutes. The fare is $25 one way, $50 return.

Surprisingly, Tinian has a modern terminal building with airline and car rental counters, restrooms and a snack bar.

Sea
Private speedboats and cargo boats sometimes make runs between Saipan and Tinian. The best way to find out about them is to go down to Charlie Dock on Saipan and ask around. The channel between the islands is generally rough and the ride can take a couple of hours.

GETTING AROUND
Car
Freedom Air can arrange for a car rental, as can any of the hotels, or you can make arrangements directly with Islander Rent-A-Car (☎ 433-3025 on Tinian, 234-8233 on

Saipan). Rates are from about $35 a day. The main island roads are paved and in good condition.

Hitching

It's possible to hitch the 2½ miles from the airport to San Jose or you could just ask the airline staff if they know of anyone going to town. San Jose itself is OK for lifts, but outside the village there isn't enough traffic to count on hitching. To get to Suicide Cliff or the sights to the north you really need a vehicle.

Rota

Rota, about halfway between Guam and Saipan, is just beginning to get an overflow of tourists from those larger islands. Rota's a sleepy island and though it's beginning to awaken, the pace remains slow. The main village of Songsong still gets by without a single shopping centre or traffic light.

Rota is roughly oblong, measuring three miles by 10. It has small farms, good spring water, enough deer to have a hunting season and fiery orange sunsets that light the evening skies. Locals call the island Luta.

Rota is a very picturesque island. The main sightseeing spots and beach parks are neatly landscaped and well maintained, and most of the road from the airport to town is lined with flowering plumeria trees.

It's surprising that Rota has never been nicknamed 'The Friendly Island'. Without fail, Rota drivers wave to each other in passing, a tradition so strongly entrenched that those who don't wave are immediately recognised as off-islanders.

Throughout the 1980s, Rota was spared the kind of resort development that flourished on Saipan and Guam, leaving the character of the island pleasantly local, low-keyed and friendly. In late 1990 Rota changed course and approved of plans for three large resorts with 18-hole golf courses, all on leased government land.

The first of the developments to break

ground is just north of the airport and encompasses 1½ miles of shoreline, including the natural swimming hole at Agusan. A second north shore development will be at Mochong Beach. The third and smallest development will be inland, on the road to Mt Sabana.

The scale of construction will require hundreds of workers to be brought in from off-island and it may not be long before the Rotanese find themselves a minority on their own island.

At least for now, Rota's laid-back character is still its leading attraction. Not only that, but where else can you swim right in town and still have the beach all to yourself?

Reader B M Bourke of Salisbury, Queensland sent this report:

This was our first holiday with our new baby. She was seven months old and naturally we were concerned with her well being. However she thrived in Guam and Rota and our biggest problem was the Chamorros' love of babies. Particularly in Rota, my wife was frantically trying to track our daughter's whereabouts as she was passed from hand to hand. At the end of our week in Rota I would estimate that half of the 1500 population were best of friends with our little girl.

Festivals

The largest and most popular fiesta in the Northern Marianas is held on Rota on the second weekend in October. It's a celebration in honour of San Francisco de Borja, the patron saint of Songsong Village. People flock from Saipan, Tinian and Guam for days of Chamorro food, drinks, religious processions, music and dancing. If you can secure accommodation, this is the island's finest hour.

Rota also annually hosts a 10-km fun run in mid-June, a cliff fishing derby in early September over the Labor Day weekend and a food fair in mid-September.

Activities

Diving & Snorkelling One of the highlights of diving Rota is the excellent visibility. One popular area is Coral Gardens, in Sasanhaya Bay, known for its huge platter corals. Rota also has interesting cave and tunnel dives.

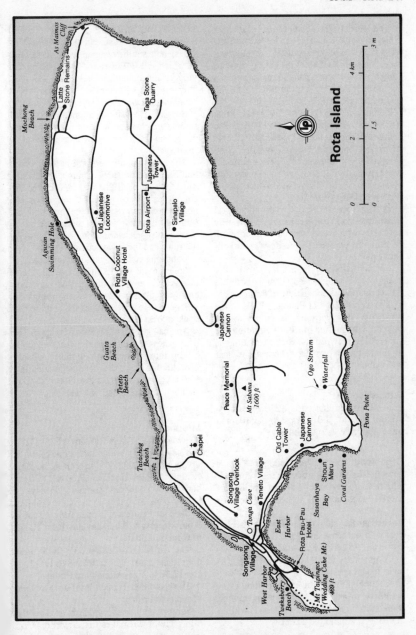

Rota Island

The wreck of the *Shoun Maru*, a Japanese freighter sunk by an aerial torpedo during WW II, lies offshore about 80 feet underwater in Sasanhaya Bay. The wreck contains trucks and assorted paraphernalia such as bathtubs, bicycles and motorcycles, all encrusted with coral.

Dive Rota (☎ 532-3377), Box 941, Rota, MP 96951, owned and operated by Mark and Lynne Michael, is a small, personalised dive operation. One dive costs $45, two dives cost $60 and night dives are $55. Dive Rota fill tanks, rents diving gear, and rents mask, fins and snorkel for $5. They can also take people out waterskiing or trolling.

A 1½-hour snorkel trip to the Coral Gardens is $25. We heard from one snorkeller who found herself swimming with 30 dolphins on one of Dive Rota's snorkelling trips!

For snorkelling from the shore, the entrance to Sasanhaya Bay boat harbour has soft corals and a good variety of tropical fish.

The small island at Pinatang Park, at the north end of Songsong, is by no means teeming with marine life, but swimming and snorkelling between the rock formations is an interesting experience. The water is clear and calm.

Submarine The Rota Pau-Pau Hotel has a mini-submarine that costs $220 for an 80-minute ride to 100 metres or $550 for a three-hour ride to 300 metres.

Organised Tours The Coconut Village hotel has full-day sightseeing tours for $45, which includes lunch, and a variety of shorter beach, boat and sightseeing tours for $20 to $35.

The Pau-Pau charges $52 for a sightseeing tour with barbecue lunch, $28 for a sunset cruise and $32 for a boat tour.

Commentary for all hotel tours is likely to be in Japanese.

A better option, if you're not renting a car, would be to ask around Songsong to find someone with a pick-up truck who is willing to take you around the island.

SONGSONG VILLAGE

Songsong village is spread along the neck of the island's south-west peninsula, at the end of which is Mt Taipingot. Overlooking the village, and rising to a height of 469 feet, Taipingot is nicknamed Wedding Cake Mountain because of its layered appearance.

Songsong boasts an abundance of latte stones, which stand in front of the mayor's office and the library, as well as in people's front yards.

The most notable building in town is the San Francisco de Borja Church, which still rings the same bell that was placed atop the church during the period of German occupation. Across the street from the church are the ruins of the first priest's house. A hand-carved outrigger canoe is on display between the ruins and the senior centre.

Songsong is easily explored on foot. The potholed roads of the village are miserable in a vehicle anyway, though that may soon change as plans call for the road through the village to be paved as far as the commercial dock at West Harbor.

You can get a good view of Songsong by taking the rough dirt road that leads up to the hilltop above Tonga Cave. It makes a hardy hike, though it could also be negotiated in a 4WD. The road begins behind Dean's Mobil station at the north end of Songsong.

Information

The Marianas Visitors Bureau (☎ 532-0327), in a new building with a latte stone motif, is up the hill a couple of blocks from the Blue Peninsula Hotel. Hours are 7.30 to 11.30 am and 12.30 to 4.30 pm Monday to Friday.

The Bank of Guam, in the same building as the Blue Peninsula, is open from 10 am to 3 pm Monday to Thursday and from 10 am to 6 pm on Fridays.

The Air Mike office (☎ 532-3893), next door to the bank, is open from 8 to 11.30 am and 12.30 to 5 pm Monday to Friday.

The post office is open from 9 am to 3 pm Monday to Friday.

Songsong's library, which is used by the high school as makeshift classrooms on weekday mornings, is open to the public from 2 to 4.30 pm Monday to Friday.

Rota Wash Land is across from Dean's Mobil station and there's another laundromat at B&M store at the north side of the playground. You can pick up *Pacific Daily News* at Lucky Store.

Tonga Cave

One of Rota's most impressive sights is Tonga Cave, a damp limestone cavern of stalagmites and dripping stalactites, some of them eight feet long. The cave, which sits above the village, begins at the back of a grassy park with orange-flowered flame trees. It's just a few minutes walk from the centre of town. Be careful on the stairs leading up to the cave, as they're quite slippery when wet.

Tonga Cave was used by the Japanese during the war as a hospital shelter and the Rotanese have used it as a refuge from typhoons. Go through the cave and follow the short path leading out to the left for a good view of Songsong and Mt Taipingot.

Sugar Mill & Train

Down near the harbour are the remains of a Japanese sugar mill, most of which was dismantled after the war.

Although Rota's soil was not as good for cane as the soil on Saipan or Tinian there was enough sugar to support two refineries, as well as distilleries for making whisky and port wine from molasses. In the mid-1930s Rota's sugar industry employed nearly 800 Chamorros and 5000 Japanese and Koreans.

A tiny locomotive, once used to haul sugar cane from the fields, has been painted bright red and is on display in front of the mill.

In-Town Beaches

The beaches along Songsong's west shore are sheltered and calm.

Pinatang Park, at the north end of town, has a footbridge leading to a small island with picnic tables and a couple of small, sandy beaches. The water is fairly good for snorkelling and the jagged offshore rock for-

mations make the area a picturesque place to catch the sunset.

Unain Man Amko Beach Park has a couple of large rusted boats right near the shore that attract small fish and make for interesting snorkelling when the tide is high.

Tweksberry Beach & Mt Taipingot

The dirt road that runs south of town past the commercial dock leads through orderly rows of coconut trees to Tweksberry Beach, an attractively landscaped beach park. The grassy park has picnic tables, restrooms and lots of red hibiscus bushes.

The white coral sand beach is lined with ironwood trees. Though the waters are protected, much of the narrow beach has a low rocky shelf that makes it less than ideal for swimming.

A trail made by the Youth Conservation Corps starts up Mt Taipingot about 100 yards before the beach parking lot, between the first two coconut trees on the inland driveway. The trail is well maintained and marked with orange ties. The climb is steep but not too difficult, takes about two hours up and back, and ends near the edge of a cliff at a grove of ironwood trees. The views encompass Mt Sabana, Songsong, Pona Point and Sasanhaya Bay.

CENTRAL & NORTHERN ROTA

The remains of a two-storey Japanese building, probably once an observation tower, are on the left side of the road a quarter of a mile east of the airport. Another half-mile along, a road to the right goes to the Taga Stone Quarry.

If you don't turn down to the quarry, the dirt road circles around the airport, past fenced-off farms, pastures and an old Japanese locomotive and continues on around to the main paved road.

Taga Stone Quarry

The Taga Stone Quarry has nine latte shafts and seven capstones still sitting in the trenches where they were being quarried

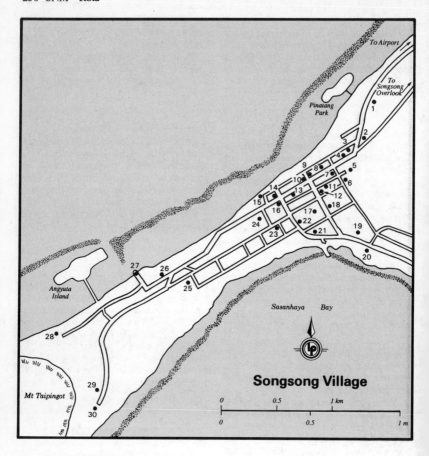

Songsong Village

before being inexplicably abandoned. Mosses, grasses and tiny ferns have grown up around them.

The early Chamorros were able to quarry the latte stones without the benefit of metal tools. It's believed they built fires in trenches around the stones and then used basalt stone adzes to cut into the softened limestone.

For anyone interested in Chamorro culture, this is an impressive sight and it's easy to get to. The road into the quarry is marked by a sign. The quarry itself, which is

half a mile from the turn-off, is in a grassy park alongside the road.

According to legend, the ancient Chamorro king, Taga the Great, jumped from Guam to Rota to establish a kingdom on Rota. He then put the islanders to work quarrying these latte stones as foundation pillars for his royal buildings.

Sinapalo

The village of Sinapalo, south of the airport,

1	Public Market
2	Petrol Station
3	Laundromat
4	Marianas Bistro
5	Tonga Cave
6	Immigration Office
7	Laundromat
8	Blue Peninsula Hotel, Bank of Guam
9	Leng's Pastry Shop
10	Village Mart
11	Tennis Court
12	Marianas Visitors Bureau
13	Playground
14	As Pari's
15	Unain Man Amko Beach Park
16	Municipal Library
17	Hospital
18	Office of Mayor, Police
19	Rota Elementary School
20	Petrol Station
21	Dive Rota
22	Post Office
23	Lucky Store
24	San Francisco de Borja Church
25	Rota High School
26	Japanese Sugar Mill & Train
27	Dock
28	Tweksberry Beach
29	Liyo Cafe
30	Rota Pau-Pau Hotel

was created a decade ago to provide homestead property for Rota's landless.

When the government failed to follow through with promises to extend power and water lines, many homesteaders who had already built houses hooked up their own water catchment tanks and generators and settled in. Utilities were finally brought in to Sinapalo in 1990 and the settlement began to boom. Plans now call for Sinapalo to be extended to the north side of the airport road, all of which will make it Rota's biggest village.

Sabana Peace Memorial
Japanese peace memorials abound in Micronesia. Rota's was erected in 1973 near the top of the 1600-foot Mt Sabana. The road up to the memorial, which is marked, starts about two miles west of the airport.

Though the coral road is in fairly good condition most of the way, this 5¼-mile drive can be rather disappointing as the memorial itself is nondescript and there's no real view of the island from the mountain plateau.

More interesting than the memorial is a camouflaged Japanese cannon that sits inside a cave in a park-like setting about two miles up from the paved road. The cannon site is also one of the most likely places to spot fruit bats, a species that has been hunted nearly to extinction on the other inhabited Mariana Islands. About 1000 fruit bats remain on Rota.

Tatachog
In the 1930s there was a resettlement of Rotanese in the Tatachog area and the ruins of some of the buildings can still be seen near the main road.

On the slopes above Tatachog is a tiny chapel built during the German era. To get there, take the coral road leading inland just south of Tatachog Beach Park and bear right when the road forks (the left fork goes to the dump). One mile up, turn left onto a grassy dirt drive. The chapel is in a clearing that looks deserted, but don't be surprised to find candles burning or fresh orchids at the altar.

West-Side Beaches
There are sandy coves and beach parks all along Rota's west shore, alternating with scenic outcrops of craggy rocks and tidal pools.

Tatachog Beach Park, 2½ miles north of Songsong, has shallow water and is lined with jagged rocks, a combination that makes it uninviting for water activities, but attractive for picnics, which is its main use.

Teteto Beach Park has a pretty white sand beach. The water is deep enough for swimming except when the tide is low. Waves crash just outside the reef but inside it's calm and protected and snorkellers will find a fair variety of fish. As the Japanese hotels shuttle their guests to Teteto Beach, it can get a bit busy at times, though if you catch it in between tours you'll probably have it to yourself.

The hut across the road from Teteto Beach, which opens when the shuttles drop off tourists, sells cold drinks (soda for $1.50, Bud for $2) and a few pricey snack items, and rents out snorkel gear for $8.

Guata Beach Park, midway between Teteto and the turn-off to the Coconut Village hotel, has picnic shelters and a beach which is a mix of white sand and rocks.

Natural Swimming Hole
When the road is in passable condition, a visit to the swimming hole at Agusan is well worth the drive. It's 2¼ miles in after turning off the main road toward Coconut Village.

This natural basin, a big scooped-out hollow in the rocks, is right on the shoreline. Unless the tide is high or the seas unusually rough this deep hole is almost as calm as a swimming pool, with incoming waves just trickling in over the top and outgoing water pulled out through small cracks in the rocks below. It's a good place to snorkel as the fish are captive.

Though the swimming hole is to be encompassed by one of the new resort developments, access will remain public.

Mochong Beach
Mochong Beach is an expansive, attractive white sand beach. Nearby is the site of an ancient Chamorro village, which has been carbon dated to 640 BC, and the remains of latte stones.

In the past, exploration for the stones often proved frustrating as the site was overgrown, access was across private property and the road leading in was not always passable. As the area is part of a new planned resort development, access should become easier in the future. The jungle around the latte stones has already been cleared out.

EAST OF SONGSONG
The packed coral road heading east of Songsong edges along Sasanhaya Bay. There are several scenic views across to Mt Taipingot, looking out across waters of intense turquoise and cobalt blues. In places

the road cuts along the coastal cliffs and in other places it goes through jungle, shaded with a canopy of tropical vegetation.

Beware of very steep drops along the edge of this road, which are often covered with foliage and not always obvious. If you were to go off the side, the drop could well do you in.

Old Cable Tower
On the east side of Sasanhaya Bay the Japanese once had a phosphate mill and ceramic factory. If you look up the hillside about two miles east of Songsong, you can still see the rusty remains of an old cable tramway tower that carried phosphate from the Sabana plateau down to ships in the harbour.

Japanese Cannon
A Japanese cannon points straight out to the harbour and Mt Taipingot from its concrete shelter on the road 2½ miles east of Songsong. The gun barrel can be moved from side to side but don't leave it sticking straight out or the next car going by could get whopped. Also don't park your rental car too close to the barrel as once it starts moving, it's hard to stop.

Pona Point & Ogo Stream
Just over a mile past the cannon, there's an open grassy field on the right side of the road which slopes down to Pona Point. Though it's usually possible to drive down to the point, it's also only a three-minute walk from the field.

Pona Point is atop a wind-whipped rocky outcrop and offers a good view of the area's rugged coastal cliffs. There is also excellent cliff fishing from the point.

Half a mile farther down, the main road passes above Ogo (also spelled Okgok) Stream, which features some small waterfalls. After this point the road deteriorates and is barely passable.

PLACES TO STAY
Camping
Rota has quite a few public beach parks

where camping shouldn't be a problem. The island at Pinatang Park looks like a tempting location, as it has picnic facilities and is just a few minutes walk from town, but it does have a noticeable rat population.

Hotels

Until the new resorts are built, Rota has just three hotels. A 10% tax is added to all room rates. Only the Rota Pau-Pau Hotel accepts credit cards.

The 20-room *Blue Peninsula Hotel* (☎ 532-3541), Box 539, Rota, MP 96951) has the cheapest rooms on the island and is the best value. As the only hotel in Songsong, it also has the most convenient location, especially if you're trying to avoid renting a car. Anywhere in town, including the beach, is an easy walk. Rooms are simple, but have been recently renovated and have mini-refrigerators, air-con and new tile bathrooms. Singles/doubles cost $50/55. The Blue Peninsula, which has no sign, is above Penny's Meitetsu store.

The modern *Rota Pau-Pau Hotel* (☎ 532-3561), Box 503, Rota, MP 96951 is overpriced and geared to packaged tourists. It has an expensive restaurant, an expensive gift shop, a swimming pool and diving facilities. The 50 rooms start at $120/140 for singles/doubles (government and military personnel get a 50% discount). Airport transfers are $24!

Rota Coconut Village (☎ 532-3448), Box 855, Rota, MP 96951, also caters to package tours from Japan, and has a swimming pool and restaurant, but it's cheaper and more relaxed than the Pau-Pau. The 10 duplex cottages are decorated in a sort of upgraded island style, with peaked roofs, wood trim, rattan furnishings and *ofuros* (individual hot tubs) in the bathrooms. Unfortunately, the place has become run down over the years. Singles/doubles cost $70/80. As the Coconut Village is out of the way, you'd probably need a car to get around. The hotel staff does ferry small groups to the swimming hole or Teteto Beach for $4 return and to the airport or Songsong for $10 return.

PLACES TO EAT

It's hard to get excited about restaurants on Rota. In most places the quality depends on the latest cook, usually someone with a work visa from the Philippines. Though this can add a nice accent to the food, there's not a lot of consistency as the cooks change frequently.

The restaurant and bar beneath the *Blue Peninsula* is open from 6 am to 2 am daily. Though you can get coffee and a danish for $1.50, full breakfasts cost about $5. Sandwiches or yakisoba are $2 to $5, and meat or fish dinners are $7 to $13. The food's OK, but service can be excruciatingly slow and the mealtime 'entertainment' is loud music and the whir of poker machines.

As Pari's restaurant and bar in Songsong is the best place to eat in Rota. It's clean and comfortable, with well-prepared food, reasonable prices and music at a lower decibel. A good cheese omelette with toast and coffee is $4 at breakfast (6.30 to 10.30 am). Hamburgers with fries are $3.75 at lunch (10 am to 2 pm) and chicken or fish dinners (6.30 to 10.30 pm) are $7 to $8. They also have pizza and noodles.

Leng's Pastry Shop & Restaurant is open from 6 am to 2 pm and from 6 pm to 2 am daily. They bake fancy pies and frosted cakes which are reasonably priced ($5 for lemon pie, $8.50 for strawberry cheesecake) when bought whole, but $3 per slice if served in the restaurant. Leng's serves full breakfasts for about $5 and hamburgers for $3. Fish or chicken meals are about $7 at lunch time and a few dollars more at dinner when they include salad and desert.

The *Liyo Cafe*, out near the Pau-Pau, opens at 7.30 am with Chamorro breakfast (fried rice, eggs and Spam) for $5. Lunch is simple, with sandwiches averaging $3; avoid the grilled cheese, which is a greasy, egg-dipped concoction. Most dinners are $6 to $9 and include rice and vegetables. An outdoor bar is under construction.

At the *Pau-Pau* hotel, a breakfast of eggs, bacon and coffee will set you back $8. Overpriced lunches, such as curry rice, begin around $10, and dinners start from $20.

The *Coconut Village* hotel serves dinner Japanese style, with very small entree portions starting at $8, rice or soup for $1 extra and service so slow you might want to take a good book. The full-course fish dinner is $20. Lunch is more reasonable, with spaghetti or curry rice for $5. Breakfast also starts around $5. Hours are 7.30 to 9.30 am, 11.30 am to 1.30 pm, and 6 to 8.30 pm.

North Wind Restaurant & Bar, an attractive new place in the village of Sinapalo, will probably be serving dinners only. To get there, turn left at the Sinapalo sign, three-quarters of a mile west of the airport.

The *Mayflower Restaurant* at the airport is open from 6 am to 6.30 pm daily, with breakfasts, burgers, sandwiches and soba for $4 to $5. It's adequate if you're waiting for a plane, but not worth going out of your way for.

Despite claims of Rota's prolific fruit, visitors may be hard pressed to find any. In fact, fruit can be so difficult to find that the Coconut Village and the Pau-Pau actually hold 'fruit-hunting tours', for $15 and $28 respectively!

Fortunately, with the opening of the new Public Market (Mitkaon Publiku), you shouldn't have to search so hard. The market has seasonal Rota-grown watermelons, limes, bananas, yams, taro and a few green vegetables. Watermelons on Rota are infested with the melon fly and therefore are not exportable, but as long as they're not soft they should be fine to eat. The market is open from 7.30 am to 5.30 pm Monday to Saturday, until noon on Sundays.

To save a few dollars, you might want to buy rolls and open cans of tuna for a meal or two. Finding provisions isn't too hard, as every fifth building in Songsong is a store of some sort, but freshness can be a problem, so check the expiry dates. Produce such as apples, carrots and lettuce are commonly imported from California via Guam on, by the looks of them, a very slow boat.

Rota's water comes from a natural water cave and may be the best in Micronesia. They've even considered bottling it for export to other islands.

ENTERTAINMENT
The biggest entertainment hit around Rota is the laser karaoke, which consists of video renditions of pop songs with the lyrics written in English across the screen and a live microphone for would-be stars to croon along. As Pari's, Leng's Pastry Shop and the Blue Peninsula restaurant all have laser karaoke that play night and day.

Marianas Bistro has karaoke from 7 to 10 pm and disco dancing from 10 pm to 2 am Monday to Saturday. There's no admission fee. The drinking age on Rota is 21.

Cockfights are held just north of the public market at 7 pm every Saturday.

GETTING THERE & AWAY
Air Mike is the only airline that flies to Rota. Fares to Rota from either Guam or Saipan cost $100 return, on a two to 14-day excursion ticket. One-way flights between Guam and Saipan, with a stop in Rota, are $60. It's $45 for accompanying spouse and children, if you ask for the family plan. It's best to get a return or through fare, as the one-way fare from Rota to either Guam or Saipan is $65!

The airport is nine miles from Songsong. Upstairs in the Mayflower Restaurant there are a few interesting old photos from the Japanese administration period. The airport has rest rooms and a pay phone.

GETTING AROUND
Rota is just beginning to get paved roads, with the stretch from the airport to Songsong by far the best. Depending on recent rains and how long it's been since the roads have been graded, you may not be able to manage some of Rota's more remote rutted dirt roads in a sedan without getting stuck, though getting to most of the main sights usually isn't a problem.

Car
Rota has three car rental agencies with booths at the airport. All take credit cards and offer optional collision damage waivers.

ESPN (☎ 532-0343), Box 569, Saipan, MP 96950, rents Suzuki Alto 'mini-cars' for $29 with standard transmission or $34 with automatic transmission. Mid-size cars rent for $47 and 4WD jeeps rent for $68 to $78. Collision coverage is $6 to $12 more.

Paseo Drive Car Rental (☎ 532-0406), Box 555, Rota, MP 96951, rents Toyotas for $43 and 4WD jeeps for $78. Collision coverage is $8 more. All cars have air-con and stereos.

Budget (☎ 532-3535) has automatic compact sedans with air-con for $35 to $40, mid-size cars for $45 to $50 and station wagons for $55. Collision coverage is $7.50 extra and a 5% service charge is added on to everything. Reservations can be made through the Budget office in Guam.

Bicycle
Bicycle rentals are available at the Pau-Pau Hotel for $10 a day.

Hitching
It's fairly easy to get lifts around the main parts of the island, such as between the airport and Songsong, though traffic is likely to be too infrequent in other areas to make hitching practical.

Glossary

Bai – a traditional men's meeting house in Palau.

Banzai attack – a mass attack by troops without concern for casualties, as practised by the Japanese during WW II.

Beche-de-mer – a type of sea cucumber (also called trepang) with an elongated body, leathery skin and a cluster of tentacles at the oral end. They burrow in sand or creep on the sea bed and were gathered by early traders and sold in China and South-East Asia as a delicacy and aphrodisiac.

Benjo – an outhouse.

Betel nut – the fruit of the Areca palm tree which is commonly split open, sprinkled with lime, wrapped in a pepper leaf and chewed as a digestive stimulant and mild narcotic.

Breadfruit – a tree of the Pacific Islands, the trunk of which is used for lumber and canoe building. The fruit is cooked and eaten and has a texture like bread.

Chamorro – the indigenous people of the Mariana Islands.

Copra – dried coconut kernel, used for making coconut oil.

Dapal – a women's meeting house in Yap.

Dugong – a seal-like, herbivorous mammal inhabiting shallow tropical waters around Palau.

Faluw – a Yapese meeting house for men.

Iroij – traditional Marshallese chief.

Jambos – Marshallese picnics or trips.

Kahlek – night fishing, using burning torches to attract flying fish into hand-held nets, practised in Pohnpei.

Korkor – a Marshallese dug-out fishing canoe made from a breadfruit log.

Latte stones – the stone foundation pillars used to support ancient Chamorro buildings in the Marianas. The shafts and capstones were carved from limestone quarries.

Lava-lava – a wide piece of cloth of woven hibiscus and banana fibres, worn as a skirt by women throughout Yap and in Chuuk's outer islands.

Lumpia – a fried food similar to an egg roll, which is usually dipped in garlic sauce or vinegar.

Manposteria – a building material, used in the Marianas, made from burnt limestone mixed with coral.

Modekngei – the traditional religion of Palau.

Mwaramwars – head wreaths of flowers and fragrant leaves worn throughout the FSM.

Nahnmwarki – a district chief in Pohnpei.

Noddy – a tropical tern, or aquatic bird, with black & white or dark plumage.

Omung – perfumed love potion used in Chuuk.

Oyako domburi – a Japanese dish of sweetened chicken and egg served over rice.

Pancit – a dish of shrimp or meat, vegetables and garlic served over noodles.

Pebai – a Yapese community meeting house.

Rai – Yapese stone money.

Sakau – a mildly narcotic Pohnpeian drink made from the roots of a pepper shrub.

Sake – Japanese rice wine.

Saudeleur – member of a tyrannical royal dynasty that ruled Pohnpei prior to Western contact with the islanders.

Seka – a narcotic, ceremonial drink (similar to sakau) of Kosrae.

Tangan-tangan – a shrub that was mass-planted in the Marianas to prevent erosion.

Thu – a loincloth worn by Yapese males and by outer island Chuukese.

Tridacna clam – the giant clam, *tridacna gigas*, is the largest known bivalve mollusc. It is collected and farmed in Palau for its edible flesh, and is poached throughout the Pacific for its valuable adductor muscle, considered a delicacy and aphrodisiac in the Orient.

Trochus – a shellfish commercially harvested for its shell and flesh.

Tuba – an alcoholic drink made from coconut sap.

Udoud – traditional Palauan money, either beads of glass or fired and coloured clay.

Wunbey – a Yapese meeting platform.

Index

ABBREVIATIONS

CNM - Commonwealth of the Northern Marianas

FSM - Federated States of Micronesia
G - Guam

Mar - Republic of the Marshall Islands
Pal - Republic of Palau

MAPS

Agana, Central (G) 201
Angaur Island (Pal) 186
Babeldaob Island (Pal) 180
Chuuk Lagoon (FSM) 134
Chuuk State (FSM) 122
Colonia (FSM) 150
Commonwealth of the Northern Marianas 219
D-U-D Municipality (Mar) 67
Dublon Island (FSM) 135
Federated States of Micronesia 84-85
Guam 191

Kolonia (FSM) 106
Koror (Pal) 168
Kosrae State (FSM) 86
Lelu Island (FSM) 93
Majuro Atoll (Mar) 64
Maloelap Atoll (Mar) 77
Marshall Islands (Mar) 57
Micronesia 12-13
Moen Island (FSM) 127
Moen Centre 131
Nan Madol (FSM) 113
Peleliu Island (Pal) 182
Pohnpei Island (FSM) 100

Republic of Palau & Palau Islands 162
Rota Island (CNM) 247
Saipan Island (CNM) 224
Saipan's West Coast (CNM) 227
San Jose (CNM) 242
Songsong Village (CNM) 250
Tamuning & Tumon (G) 204
Tinian (CNM) 239
Tofol (FSM) 91
Yap Proper (FSM) 148
Yap State (FSM) 141

TEXT

Map references are in **bold** type.

Adelup Point (G) 206
Agana (G) 201-203, **201**
Agat (G) 208
Aguijan Island (CNM) 244-245
Agusan (CNM) 252
Ailinglaplap Atoll (Mar) 81
Ailuk Atoll (Mar) 81
Airai State (Pal) 180
Airok (Mar) 78
Angaur (Pal) 186-189, **186**
Ant Atoll (FSM) 115
Apra Harbor (G) 207-208
Arakabesang Island (Pal) 171
Arno Atoll (Mar) 78
Arno Island (Mar) 78
Aur Atoll (Mar) 80-81
Awak Village (FSM) 111

Babeldaob (Pal) 179-181, **180**
Balabat (FSM) 150-151
Banadero Trail (CNM) 230
Banzai Cliff (CNM) 229
Bechiyal (FSM) 153-154
Bikar Atoll (Mar) 81
Bikini Atoll (Mar) 60-61
Bird Island (CNM) 230-232

Bkul Omruchel (Pal) 184
Black Coral Island (FSM) 114-115
Bloody Beach (Pal) 185
Bloody Nose Ridge (Pal) 184
Blue Corner (Pal) 176

California Beach (Mar) 79
Camp Beck Dock (Pal) 184
Capitol Hill (CNM) 232
Carp Island (Ngercheu Island) (Pal) 177-178
Cetti Bay (G) 208-209
Chalan Kanoa (CNM) 233
Chulu Beach (CNM) 244
Chuuk (Truk) (FSM) 121-140, **122**
Chuuk Lagoon (FSM) 122-123, 125, 133-138, **134**
Cocos Island (G) 211
Cocos Lagoon (G) 200
Colonia (FSM) 148-151, **150**

Darong (FSM) 113
Darritt (Rita) (Mar) 68
Delap (Mar) 66-68
Dogleg Reef (G) 207

Dublon Island (FSM) 133-136, **135**
D-U-D Municipality (Mar) 66-68, **67**
Dump Coke (CNM) 240

Eauripik Atoll (FSM) 159
Ebeye Island (Mar) 72-74
Eil Malk (Pal) 178
Elato Atoll (FSM) 159
Enewetok Atoll (Mar) 61
Enipein Marine Park (FSM) 105
Eten Island (FSM) 136

Faichuk Islands (FSM) 136-137
Fais Island (FSM) 158
Falos Island (FSM) 137
Fanif (FSM) 152
Faraulep Atoll (FSM) 159
Federated States of Micronesia 83-160, **84-85**
Fefan Island (FSM) 136

Gaan Point (G) 208
Gaferut Atoll (FSM) 159
Garapan (CNM) 226-228
German Channel (Pal) 176
Gilman (FSM) 152

Grotto, The (CNM) 230
Guam 191-217, **191**
Gun Beach (G) 204

Hall Islands (FSM) 139

Idehd (FSM) 112
Ifalik Atoll (FSM) 159
Inarajan Village (G) 210
Ipan Beach (G) 211

Jabwor (Mar) 80
Jaluit Atoll (Mar) 80
Jeffries (Talofofo) Beach (CNM) 232
Jellyfish Lake (Pal) 176, 178
Jemo Island (Mar) 81
Joy Island (FSM) 114

Kammer Beach (CNM) 241
Kapingamarangi Atoll (FSM) 116
Kapingamarangi Village (FSM) 108
Kariahn (FSM) 112
Kayangel (Pal) 189
Kepirohi Waterfall (FSM) 111
Kili Island (Mar) 80
Klouklubed (Pal) 184
Kolonia (FSM) 105-108, **106**
Koror (Pal) 167-176, **168**
Kosrae (FSM) 86-99, **86**
Kwajalein Atoll (Mar) 72-75
Kwajalein Island (Mar) 72

Ladder Beach (CNM) 233
Laderan Tangke Trail (CNM) 229
Lamotrek Atoll (FSM) 158-159
Langer Island (FSM) 114
Laulau Beach (CNM) 233
Laura (Mar) 68
Lelu Island (FSM) 92-94, **93**
Liduduhniap Waterfall (FSM) 110
Likiep Atoll (Mar) 78-79
Longar (Mar) 78
Longar Point (Mar) 78
Luminao Reef (G) 207

Majuro (Mar) 64-71
Malaay Village (FSM) 152
Malakal Hill (Pal) 171
Malakal Island (Pal) 170-171
Malem (FSM) 91, 95
Maloelap Atoll (Mar) 77-78, **77**
Managaha Island (CNM) 233-234
Marine Beach (CNM) 244

Marine Lakes (Pal) 178
Marpi (CNM) 228
Marshall Islands, Republic of the 57-82, **57**
Mejato Island (Mar) 74
Mejit Island (Mar) 79-80
Merizo (G) 200, 209-210
Metukercheuas Uet (Pal) 178
Micro Beach (CNM) 226
Mili Atoll (Mar) 76-77
Mochong Beach (CNM) 252
Moen (Weno) Island (FSM) 126-133, **127**, **131**
Mokil Atoll (FSM) 115
Mortlock Islands (FSM) 138-139
Mt Jumullong Manglo (G) 209
Mt Lamlam (G) 209
Mt Petosukara (CNM) 228
Mt Tagpochau (CNM) 232
Mt Taipingot (CNM) 249
Mt Tonaachaw (FSM) 127-128
Mt Tumuital (FSM) 136

Namishi (FSM) 111
Nan Madol (FSM) 112-114, **113**
Neco Island (Pal) 178
Nett Municipality (FSM) 110
Nett Point (FSM) 110
Ngaraard State (Pal) 181
Ngemelis Wall (Pal) 176
Ngerukuid (70 Islands) (Pal) 178
Ngoof (Pal) 152
Ngulu Atoll (FSM) 159
Northern Marianas, Commonwealth of the 218-255, **219**
Nukuoro Atoll (FSM) 116-117

Obyan Beach (CNM) 233
Ogo Stream (CNM) 252
Okau Village (FSM) 152
Olimarao Atoll (FSM) 159
Orange Beach (Pal) 184
Oroluk Atoll (FSM) 115
Orote Peninsula (G) 199
Outer Islands (Chuuk) (FSM) 138-140
Outer Islands (Marshalls) (Mar) 75-82
Outer Islands (Yap) (FSM) 157-160

Pago Bay (G) 211
Pahn Kadira (FSM) 112
Pakin Atoll (FSM) 115
Palau, Republic of 161-190, **162**
Palikir (FSM) 109-110
Paupau Beach (CNM) 228
Peleliu (Pal) 181-186, **182**
Peleliu Wall (Pal) 183

Picnic Islands (FSM) 137
Pikelot Atoll (FSM) 159
Pinatang Park (CNM) 248, (CNM) 249
Pingelap Atoll (FSM) 115
Piti (G) 207
Pohnpei (FSM) 99-121, **100**
Pona Point (CNM) 252
Profile Beach (CNM) 232
Pwusehn Malek (FSM) 110

Red Beach (Pal) 188
Rita (Mar) 68
Rock Islands (Pal) 176-179
Roi-Namur Island (Mar) 74
Rongelap Atoll (Mar) 61
Rota (CNM) 246-255, **247**
Rumung Island (FSM) 153

Saipan (CNM) 223-238, **224**, **227**
San Jose (CNM) 241, **242**
Sando Island (Mar) 74
Sapou (FSM) 133
Sapwuafik Atoll (Ngatik) (FSM) 116
Sasanhaya Bay (CNM) 246
Satawal Island (FSM) 158
Satawan Atoll (FSM) 138
Sella Bay (G) 208
Sinapalo (CNM) 250-251
Sipyen Waterfall (FSM) 95
Sokehs Island (FSM) 108-109
Sokehs Ridge (FSM) 109
Sokehs Rock (FSM) 109
Songsong Village (CNM) 248-249, **250**
Sorol Atoll (FSM) 159
South Field (FSM) 128
South-West Islands (Pal) 190
Spooky Lake (Pal) 178
Suicide Cliff (Saipan) (CNM) 230
Suicide Cliff (Tinian) (CNM) 241-243
Susupe (CNM) 233

Tachogna Beach (CNM) 241
Tafunsak (FSM) 95-97
Tafunsak Gorge (FSM) 96
Taga Beach (CNM) 241
Taka Atoll (Mar) 81
Talofofo Bay Beach (G) 211
Talofofo Falls (G) 210-211
Tanapag (CNM) 228
Tanguisson Beach (G) 205
Taongi Atoll (Mar) 81
Tarague Beach (G) 205
Taroa (Tarawa) Island (Mar) 77

Tatachog (CNM) 251
Tatachog Beach (CNM) 251
Temwen Island (FSM) 112
Tinian (CNM) 238-246, **239**
Tinian Harbor (CNM) 241
Tofol (FSM) 91-92, **91**
Tol Island (FSM) 136
Tomil-Gagil Island (FSM) 152-153
Tonga Cave (CNM) 249
Tumon Bay (G) 200, **204**
Turtle Cove (Pal) 176
Tweksberry Beach (CNM) 249
Two Lovers Point (G) 204-205

Uliga (Mar) 68
Ulithi Atoll (FSM) 157-158
Umatac (G) 209
Unain Man Amko Beach (CNM) 249
Uruno Beach (G) 205
Ushi Point (CNM) 243
Utrik Atoll (Mar) 61
Utwe (FSM) 90, 95

Walung (FSM) 90, 96-97
Wanyan (FSM) 153
Wanyan Beach (FSM) 153
West Fayu Atoll (FSM) 159
Western Islands (FSM) 139

Wichon Falls (FSM) 129
Wing Beach (CNM) 229
Woja Island (Mar) 81
Woleai Atoll (FSM) 158
Wotho Atoll (Mar) 81
Wotje Atoll (Mar) 79
Wotje Island (Mar) 79

Yap (FSM) 140-160, **141**
Yap Proper (FSM) 147-157, **148**
Yekula Waterfall (FSM) 96
Yenasr Islet (FSM) 91
Ypao (Ipao) Beach (G) 203

70 Islands (see Ngerukuid)

Keep in touch!

We love hearing from you and think you'd like to hear from us.

The Lonely Planet Newsletter covers the when, where, how and what of travel. (AND it's free!)

When...is the right time to see reindeer in Finland?
Where...can you hear the best palm-wine music in Ghana?
How...do you get from Asunción to Areguá by steam train?
What...should you leave behind to avoid hassles with customs in Iran?

To join our mailing list just contact us at any of our offices. (details below)

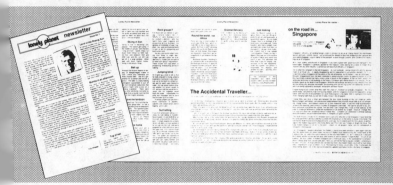

Every issue includes:

* *a letter from Lonely Planet founders Tony and Maureen Wheeler*
* *travel diary from a Lonely Planet author - find out what it's really like out on the road*
* *feature article on an important and topical travel issue*
* *a selection of recent letters from our readers*
* *the latest travel news from all over the world*
* *details on Lonely Planet's new and forthcoming releases*

Also available Lonely Planet T-shirts. 100% heavy weight cotton (S, M, L, XL)

LONELY PLANET PUBLICATIONS
Australia: PO Box 617, Hawthorn, 3122, Victoria (tel: 03-819 1877)
USA: Embarcadero West, 155 Filbert Street, Suite 251, Oakland, CA 94607 (tel: 510-893 8555)
UK: Devonshire House, 12 Barley Mow Passage, Chiswick, London W4 4PH (tel: 081-742 3161)

Lonely Planet Guidebooks

Lonely Planet guidebooks cover every accessible part of Asia as well as Australia, the Pacific, South America, Africa, the Middle East, Europe and parts of North America. There are five series: *travel survival kits*, covering a country for a range of budgets; *shoestring guides* with compact information for low-budget travel in a major region; *walking guides*; *city guides* and *phrasebooks*.

Australia & the Pacific
Australia
Bushwalking in Australia
Islands of Australia's Great Barrier Reef
Fiji
Melbourne city guide
Micronesia
New Caledonia
New Zealand
Tramping in New Zealand
Papua New Guinea
Papua New Guinea phrasebook
Rarotonga & the Cook Islands
Samoa
Solomon Islands
Sydney city guide
Tahiti & French Polynesia
Tonga
Vanuatu

South-East Asia
Bali & Lombok
Bangkok city guide
Myanmar (Burma)
Burmese phrasebook
Cambodia
Indonesia
Indonesia phrasebook
Malaysia, Singapore & Brunei
Philippines
Pilipino phrasebook
Singapore city guide
South-East Asia on a shoestring
Thailand
Thai phrasebook
Vietnam, Laos & Cambodia
Vietnamese phrasebook

North-East Asia
China
Mandarin Chinese phrasebook
Hong Kong, Macau & Canton
Japan
Japanese phrasebook
Korea
Korean phrasebook
Mongolia
North-East Asia on a shoestring
Taiwan
Tibet
Tibet phrasebook
Tokyo city guide

West Asia
Trekking in Turkey
Turkey
Turkish phrasebook
West Asia on a shoestring

Middle East
Arab Gulf States
Egypt & the Sudan
Egyptian Arabic phrasebook
Iran
Israel
Jordan & Syria
Yemen

Indian Ocean
Madagascar & Comoros
Maldives & Islands of the East Indian Ocean
Mauritius, Réunion & Seychelles

Mail Order

Lonely Planet guidebooks are distributed worldwide. They are also available by mail order from Lonely Planet, so if you have difficulty finding a title please write to us. US and Canadian residents should write to Embarcadero West, 155 Filbert St, Suite 251, Oakland CA 94607, USA ; European residents should write to Devonshire House, 12 Barley Mow Passage, Chiswick, London W4 4PH; and residents of other countries to PO Box 617, Hawthorn, Victoria 3122, Australia.

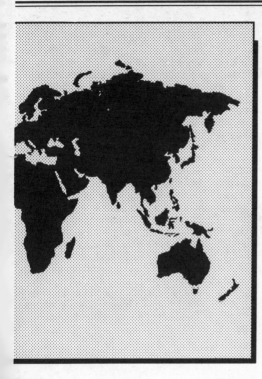

Indian Subcontinent
Bangladesh
India
Hindi/Urdu phrasebook
Trekking in the Indian Himalaya
Karakoram Highway
Kashmir, Ladakh & Zanskar
Nepal
Trekking in the Nepal Himalaya
Nepal phrasebook
Pakistan
Sri Lanka
Sri Lanka phrasebook

Africa
Africa on a shoestring
Central Africa
East Africa
Kenya
Swahili phrasebook
Morocco, Algeria & Tunisia
Moroccan Arabic phrasebook
South Africa, Lesotho & Swaziland
Zimbabwe, Botswana & Namibia
West Africa
Mexico
Baja California
Mexico

Central America
Central America on a shoestring
Costa Rica
La Ruta Maya

North America
Alaska
Canada
Hawaii

South America
Argentina, Uruguay & Paraguay
Bolivia
Brazil
Brazilian phrasebook
Chile & Easter Island
Colombia
Ecuador & the Galápagos Islands
Latin American Spanish phrasebook
Peru
Quechua phrasebook
South America on a shoestring
Trekking in the Patagonian Andes

Europe
Eastern Europe on a shoestring
Eastern Europe phrasebook
Finland
Iceland, Greenland & the Faroe Islands
Mediterranean Europe on a shoestring
Mediterranean Europe phrasebook
Poland
Scandinavian & Baltic Europe on a shoestring
Scandinavian Europe phrasebook
Trekking in Spain
Trekking in Greece
USSR
Russian phrasebook
Western Europe on a shoestring
Western Europe phrasebook

The Lonely Planet Story

Lonely Planet published its first book in 1973 in response to the numerous 'How did you do it?' questions Maureen and Tony Wheeler were asked after driving, bussing, hitching, sailing and railing their way from England to Australia.

Written at a kitchen table and hand collated, trimmed and stapled, *Across Asia on the Cheap* became an instant local bestseller, inspiring thoughts of another book.

Eighteen months in South-East Asia resulted in their second guide, *South-East Asia on a shoestring*, which they put together in a backstreet Chinese hotel in Singapore in 1975. The 'yellow bible' as it quickly became known to backpackers around the world, soon became *the* guide to the region. It has sold well over half a million copies and is now in its 7th edition, still retaining its familiar yellow cover.

Today there are over 100 Lonely Planet titles – books that have that same adventurous approach to travel as those early guides; books that 'assume you know how to get your luggage off the carousel' as one reviewer put it.

Although Lonely Planet initially specialised in guides to Asia, they now cover most regions of the world, including the Pacific, South America, Africa, the Middle East and Europe. The list of *walking guides* and *phrasebooks* (for 'unusual' languages such as Quechua, Swahili, Nepalese and Egyptian Arabic) is also growing rapidly.

The emphasis continues to be on travel for independent travellers. Tony and Maureen still travel for several months of each year and play an active part in the writing, updating and quality control of Lonely Planet's guides.

They have been joined by over 50 authors, 48 staff – mainly editors, cartographers, & designers – at our office in Melbourne, Australia and another 10 at our US office in Oakland, California. In 1991 Lonely Planet opened a London office to handle sales for Britain, Europe and Africa. Travellers themselves also make a valuable contribution to the guides through the feedback we receive in thousands of letters each year.

The people at Lonely Planet strongly believe that travellers can make a positive contribution to the countries they visit, both through their appreciation of the countries' culture, wildlife and natural features, and through the money they spend. In addition, the company makes a direct contribution to the countries and regions it covers. Since 1986 a percentage of the income from each book has been donated to ventures such as famine relief in Africa; aid projects in India; agricultural projects in Central America; Greenpeace's efforts to halt French nuclear testing in the Pacific and Amnesty International. In 1992 $45,000 was donated to these causes.

Lonely Planet's basic travel philosophy is summed up in Tony Wheeler's comment, 'Don't worry about whether your trip will work out. Just go!'